The Boundaries of Liberty and Tolerance

The Boundaries
of Liberty
and Tolerance

*The Struggle Against
Kahanism in Israel*

Raphael Cohen-Almagor

With a Foreword by Geoffrey Marshall

University Press of Florida

Gainesville / Tallahassee / Tampa
Boca Raton / Pensacola / Orlando
Miami / Jacksonville

Library of Congress Cataloging-in-Publication Data

Cohen-Almagor, Raphael.
    The boundaries of liberty and tolerance: the struggle against
Kahanism in Israel / Raphael Cohen-Almagor.
       p.   cm.
    Revision of the author's thesis.
    Includes bibliographical references and index.
    ISBN 0-8130-1258-9 (alk. paper)
    1. Freedom of speech. 2. Freedom of speech—Israel. 3. Lib-
erty. 4. Toleration. 5. Kahane, Meir. 6. Israel—Politics and
government. I. Title.
JC591.C64 1994   93-33425
323.44'3—dc20   CIP

The University Press of Florida is the scholarly publishing agency
for the State University System of Florida, comprised of Florida
A & M University, Florida Atlantic University, Florida International
University, Florida State University, University of Central Florida,
University of Florida, University of North Florida, University of
South Florida, and University of West Florida.

University Press of Florida
15 Northwest 15th Street
Gainesville, FL 32611

To Zaavit, Sara, and Izhar

Contents

Foreword

"There is a limit to legislative interference of collective opinion with individual independence," wrote John Stuart Mill in the essay *On Liberty*. But, he added, "though this proposition is not likely to be contested in general terms, the practical question where to place the limit is a subject on which nearly everything remains to be done."

More than a century later Mill's words remain true. The theory of toleration on which modern liberal societies take their stand contains some unresolved dilemmas. Insofar as it proclaims a principle of toleration (or liberty; either word is apt) for the expression and communication of opinion—even (as Mr. Justice Holmes once put it) for opinions that we loathe and believe to be fraught with death—it rests upon a complex and hazardous presumption. We know that the expression of opinion through the written and spoken word and by collective manifestation of what are often strongly held views may damage the esteem and even the physical well-being of others. But our theory of toleration requires us to presume that the impact of one person's opinion on another cannot do damage that can legitimately be penalized by law. Restraints, it has been supposed, may be placed upon the time, manner, and place of speech and expression, but no content-based censorship is to be permitted.

Many modern liberals, while supporting these views when contemplating the toleration of violent attacks on religious, philosophical, or political positions with which they do not in any event feel a close sympathy, have become uncomfortable when faced with what seem extremist views that express hatred or contempt for values, interests, or groups in society with whom they do feel sympathy, or when attacks are made upon the democratic or constitutional bases of liberal society itself. Should those who are intolerant of our tolerant principles themselves be tolerated? And may bans be placed on membership of, or on the expressive activities of, groups that profess belief in revolutionary or anti-constitutional doctrines? The Basic Law of Germany proscribes anti-constitutional parties. In the United States the limits of First Amendment freedom were tested by the Nazi marches in Skokie. Israel has faced the problem of extremist political grouping represented by the followers of Rabbi Meir Kahane.

Raphael Cohen-Almagor in this book maps the course of this struggle in the Israeli courts and legislature. But he places it firmly in the context of the traditional controversy over the limits of toleration, providing us with a rigorous examination of the damage principle as it applies to speech and expressive activities. He forces us to face the question why, if we refuse to tolerate the damage done by thefts, assault, fraud, or murder, we should tolerate the potential damage that can be brought about by aggressive or violent speech. His work blends together political philosophy, contemporary history, and constitutional theory. It deserves the close attention of students of all three disciplines. But it should fascinate and provoke also all those who wish to confront what is probably the principal dilemma of the modern democratic practice.

GEOFFREY MARSHALL
THE QUEEN'S COLLEGE, OXFORD

Preface

In August 1985 I participated in a demonstration against Rabbi Meir Kahane, a religious, quasi-fascist propagandist who was elected to the Israeli Knesset (parliament) in 1984. Kahane had come to advocate his ideas to the citizens of the city of Givatayim, and in the gathering place he was met by thousands of people, led by the mayor of the city. The small public square was crowded with those who stood against Kahane, screaming, shouting, and whistling in order to prevent him from speaking. I had just returned from summer school at Georgetown University, and this was not what I had expected. I had no idea that the confrontation would take this form, and thus I stood there with an increasing sense of uneasiness. I had come to protest, but in a different way. The demonstrators were using the same means against Kahane the man himself would use—if he had had the power—against any opposition. This person who raised his voice against democracy was now demanding in the name of democracy the right to be heard, while advocates of democracy were standing against him, determined to deny him this same right. The paradox, so brightly illuminated in this incident, of denying in the name of democracy one of its basic tenets—freedom of speech—was the preliminary force that drove me to concentrate my research on this subject and to focus on the tensions that evolve from the very foundations of democracy.

Indeed, one of the problems of any political system is that its underlying and characteristic principles may also, through their application, endanger it and bring about its destruction. Democracy, in its liberal form, is no exception. Moreover, because democracy is a relatively young phenomenon, it lacks experience in dealing with the pitfalls engendered in the working of the system. This is what I call the *catch* of democracy.

The primary aims of this research are to formulate precepts and mechanisms designed to prescribe boundaries for liberty and tolerance conducive to safeguarding democracy and, in light of the theory, to analyze a case of a democratic self-defense. Hence, I employ the formulated philosophical principles to the study of Israeli democracy, evaluating the political and legal measures to which it resorted in its struggle against Kahanism.

In the first part of my study I examine two of the main arguments commonly offered as answers to the question Why tolerate? The first is the Respect for Others Argument, and the second is the Argument from Truth. I introduce some qualifications to these arguments, asserting that our primary obligation should be given to the first and that, in case of conflict between the two principles, the former should take precedence over the latter.

Through the review of the Millian theory and some more recent theories I try to prescribe boundaries for liberty. With regard to freedom of expression I state two arguments, the first under the Harm Principle, and the second under the Offense Principle. Under the Harm Principle, I argue that restrictions on liberty may be prescribed when there are sheer threats of immediate violence against some individuals or groups. Under the Offense Principle, I explicate that expressions that intend to inflict psychological offense are morally on a par with physical harm and therefore there are grounds for abridging them. In this connection, I review the Illinois Supreme Court's decision that permitted members of the National Socialist Party of America, a Nazi organization, to hold a demonstration in Skokie.

In part 2, moving from theory to practice, I apply the theory and the conclusions reached to Israeli democracy, observing its struggle against the Kahanist phenomenon as it developed through the last two decades, especially following the election of Meir Kahane to the Knesset in 1984. I examine the mechanisms applied in this anti-Kach (Kahane's party) campaign, the justifications given for the limitations that were set, and how justified they were according to the formulated philosophical and legal guidelines.

This book is a revised version of my doctoral thesis at Oxford University. Its completion never could have been accomplished without the assistance of teachers, colleagues, and friends at Oxford and in Israel. It is a pleasant duty to acknowledge their help and to express my gratitude to them.

I owe a special debt to my supervisors, Wilfrid Knapp and Geoffrey Marshall, for their kindness. Their advice and constant support helped me through the different stages of the project. We had many vital discussions during which they provided help, criticism, and encouragement.

I have benefited a great deal from talks, debates, and exchanges of ideas with Ronald Dworkin and Avner De-Shalit. I am indebted to them for their wise counsel and for the intellectual inspiration they offered me. Several others have kindly agreed to read the manuscript or some of its chapters. I wish to thank Hillel Steiner, John Gardner, David Heyd, Chris McCrudden, Eric Barendt, Eli Salzberger, Izhar Tal, and Tziporah Kasachkoff for their fruitful comments. My thanks also go to Joel Feinberg, Will Kymlicka, Sir Zelman Cowen, Saul Smilansky, Zeev Utitz, and Brendon MacLaughlin for their valuable suggestions.

Also, during the early stages of the project I had stimulating discussions with Michael Freeden, G. A. Cohen, and Joseph Raz. I thank them for their incisive criticism.

Chapters 7 and 8 contain material that was published in "Harm Principle, Offence Principle, and the Skokie Affair," *Political Studies* 41, no. 3 (September 1993). Chapter 9 contains material published under the title "Vigilant Jewish Fundamentalism: From the JDL to Kach (or 'Shalom Jews, Shalom Dogs')," in *Terrorism and Political Violence* 4, no. 1 (Spring 1992). Chapter 12 contains material that is due to be published in "The Fighting against Kahanism in Israel: A Legal Perspective," *The Anglo-American Law Review* (1994). I am grateful for permissions to use these articles.

My doctoral and postdoctoral studies were financed by several grants and foundations. In particular I thank the AVI fellowship and Professor Sir Isaiah Berlin; St. Catherine's College, Oxford; the Van Leer Jerusalem Institute; and Bar-Ilan University for their generosity. I also acknowledge the support of the Israel Association of Graduates in the Social Sciences, the David and Florence Mellows Memorial Fund, the Anglo-Jewish Association (AJA), and the Roy Lee Memorial Fund.

Finally, my greatest debt is to my wife and parents. I thank them for their love, understanding, and unfailing support. This work is dedicated to them.

Part One

Theory
*Boundaries of Liberty
and Tolerance*

What is toleration? It is a necessary consequence of our
being human. We all are products of frailty: fallible, and
prone to error. This is the first principle of the law of
nature, the first principle of all human rights.
—Voltaire

To be truly free is to have power to do. When I can do
what I want to do, there is my liberty for me.
—Voltaire

The issue of what should be the boundaries of liberty and tolerance has not been addressed adequately in the past. Liberals prefer to speak of liberty and tolerance but show reluctance to prescribe boundaries for them, being afraid of the "slippery slope syndrome." This study addresses specifically the delicate issue of what mechanisms democracy should employ in self-defense, suggesting ways of dealing with threats to its existence. It focuses on the ethical question of the constraints on liberty. Thus, following John Stuart Mill's philosophy, theoretical and legal principles are proposed to overcome what I call "the catch of democracy." The argument is that these principles are compatible with just liberal principles and therefore may be acceptable to liberal societies.

Some explanation is required to clarify the meaning of "the catch of democracy." Any political system—theocratic, liberal, Marxist, Leninist, Maoist, or other—is based on a given set of principles. The working of these principles is designed to promote values that those systems hold dear. However, these same principles might endanger the very foundations of the political systems. The case is clear when authoritarian systems are pondered. People want to free themselves and break the coercive bonds. But the same risk is also involved in the working of liberal-democratic principles.

This research concentrates on two of the concepts that underlie liberal democracies: tolerance and liberty. My primary aims are to outline boundaries of tolerance and liberty through the formulation of principles conducive to safeguarding democracy and, in the light of the theory, to analyze a case of a democratic self-defense. Thus, the research combines theory with application, viewing how a democracy dealt with a specific problem that was conceived as a danger to some of its basic principles as a democratic state. I employ the theoretical discussion of the concept of tolerance and the formulated philosophical principles to a detailed study of the Israeli democracy in its struggle against Kahanism.

The analysis is primarily conceptual. It is not a historical study of how democracy as a system of government has evolved over the course of years, nor is it an investigation of how it accommodated itself to changing circumstances. The theoretical part will open with a discussion of the general concepts of tolerance and liberty. I shall deal with these two concepts simultaneously. When reading the literature I noticed that many appear to think there is a theory (or theories) of tolerance and a theory (or theories) of freedom. However, an overlap occurs between tolerance and liberty; in fact, a theory of tolerance *is* a theory of liberty. Any instance of tolerance is an extension of liberty.[1] By prescribing the confines of tolerance we set constraints on liberty. By arguing that we cannot tolerate everything, we hold that some limitations on freedom have to be introduced: everything and anything cannot be allowed in the name of freedom. Through toleration we restrict our own freedom in not exercising our disapproval, and consequently we do not restrict the liberties of others of whose conduct we may disapprove.

I explore the scope of tolerance in chapter 2. I first consider the *paradox of tolerance* and then offer useful distinctions regarding tolerance and compromise. I provide a perspective according to which acts of tolerance, carried out solely on prudential grounds, are not to be considered as tolerance in the genuine sense of the word as understood here. Only those people who tolerate others out of respect are conceived of as tolerant beings. I distinguish between two forms of tolerance, manifest and latent, and make a further distinction concerning the concept of compromise between principled and tactical compromise. The principled kind is said to be compromise that is motivated by respect for the other party; tactical compromise is made up of partisan interests without a real intention of respecting the agreement.

In chapter 3, I analyze the deontological arguments that are commonly suggested as an answer to the question Why tolerate? In this context I analyze the Respect for Others Argument and consider the ideas of neutrality and impartiality that are forwarded by liberal thinkers to explain why we should tolerate different conceptions of the good. Then, in chapter 4, I examine the importance of cultural norms and what part they play in requiring us to tolerate others out of respect. I insist that the key qualification to be made here is *mutual* respect for others.

Insertion of this qualification allows the Respect for Others Argument to provide grounds for and set limits on tolerance and liberty. With regard to liberty I lay emphasis on the distinction between liberty of *action* and of *expression*. Following John Stuart Mill and Thomas Emerson, I argue that although this distinction between expression and action

is problematic, it is crucial, for we should allow expression greater latitude than we allow action. In borderline cases the determination of
whether a certain conduct is to be treated as expression or action rests
upon whether the harm it causes is immediate, whether it is irremediable,
and whether regulation of the conduct is administratively consistent with
maintaining a system of freedom of expression.[2]

In chapters 5 through 7, I address the subject of freedom of expression.
In the first two chapters I postulate the arguments for freedom of expression, then, in chapter 7, provide necessary restrictions to expression. I
begin the discussion by considering the grounds that lend special status to
freedom of expression. Arguments for these grounds will be subdivided
under the considerations of autonomy, democracy, infallibility, and truth.
I proceed with a detailed examination of the Millian Truth Principle.
Here I note that while the Respect for Others Argument refers both to
action and expression, this Millian, utilitarian argument gives grounds
for toleration of speech alone. I will specifically reflect on Mill's essay *On
Liberty* and also on his earlier article "Law of Libel and Liberty of the
Press," which has not received the adequate attention of scholars. I show
that to reconcile the arguments expressed by Mill in this article with what
he wrote later in *On Liberty* is difficult. I argue that in a case of conflict
between the Respect for Others Argument and the Truth Principle, our
first obligation should be given to the first principle, which should take
preference over the second. Viewing truth as superior to all other social
values may endanger the very element the Truth Principle is intended to
safeguard; that is, tolerance. The holding of truth as the most important
value may result in harming individuals and in generating an atmosphere
of intolerance.

In chapter 7, I elaborate on the ethical question of constraints on
speech. In this context I state two arguments: the first under the Harm
Principle, the second under the Offense Principle, both derived from the
Millian theory. Under the Harm Principle I argue that restrictions on
liberty may be prescribed when there are clear threats of immediate violence against some individuals or groups. Under the Offense Principle
I explicate that expressions that intend to inflict psychological offense are
morally on a par with those that intend to inflict physical harm, and
therefore we have grounds for abridging them. Thus, I suggest that some
speech-acts that either harm individuals directly or offend unwilling listeners who cannot avoid being exposed to them can properly be consid-

ered as actions, because the harm they cause to these individuals is direct and irremediable by attempts at regulation.

Many works on liberty and tolerance are theoretical and refrain from applying the suggested philosophical principles to case studies. I see as imperative the need to apply the theory and the conclusions that are reached to specific cases. We may note two major advantages in resorting to this methodology. The first is to provide some fresh insights into two intriguing affairs that exemplify the difficulties we face when trying to prescribe boundaries for liberty and tolerance. The second is to examine the practicability of the theory when applied to real-life situations and to given circumstances. Although each of these two test cases—the Skokie affair and the struggle against Kahanism in Israel—has its specific characteristics, reference to other cases in which fundamental rights of individuals and groups were infringed on by antidemocratic movements seems to be a plausible task.

Thus, building on the framework of analysis offered by J. S. Mill, Ronald Dworkin, and John Rawls, my aim is to sharpen the general concern for the enduring issues of democratic politics. In chapter 8, the discussion shifts from theory to practice, employing the formulated principles to review the Skokie affair, a legal case that arouses much controversy. I argue that the Illinois Supreme Court's ruling which allowed American Nazis to hold a demonstration in Skokie was flawed, because it did not pay adequate attention to the seriousness of psychological offenses that are morally on a par with physical harms.

The discussion on Skokie takes us to part 2 of the study in which I apply the theory and the conclusions reached to Israeli democracy, analyzing its reaction to political parties that were conceived to be a threat to its system of ruling. I examine how this democracy tried to cope with internal dangers and what safeguards it developed as an answer to the threats it encountered. Here I consider the cases of Kach (Kahane's List) and the Progressive List for Peace (PLP) in the 1984 elections and of Kach in the 1988 elections. Specifically I observe the reaction of the Israeli political system to the Kahanist racist phenomenon as it developed through the 1970s and 1980s and increasingly following the election of Meir Kahane to the Knesset in 1984. The fight against Kahanism was one of the most significant struggles of Israeli society, a young democracy committed to liberal ideas on the one hand and to its Jewish identity on the other.

In evaluating the Israeli reaction to the Kahanist phenomenon, I follow two different though complementary roots of analysis. The first reflects on the reaction of the Israeli society—its political system, voluntary groups, the media, the educational and cultural systems—to Kahane, while the second canvasses the juristic aspects that are interwoven in this matter. I begin by discussing the Kahanist phenomenon. Thus in chapter 9, I consider Kahane the man, his ideology and political program. In this context I also examine the mechanisms employed in the anti-Kach campaign.

In chapter 10 I will supply the necessary legal background for evaluating the legal restrictions that were enacted against Kahane. I examine the major legal criteria that were applied, such as the probable danger test, bad tendency, the clear and present danger test, and the balancing approach. Then, based upon the legal guidelines, I review the factors put forward in legislation and court decisions when requests to withhold Kahane's fundamental freedoms were submitted. In chapter 11, I discuss the *Neiman* decision of 1984, which allowed Kahane to participate in the elections that brought him to the Knesset, and show how the decision was flawed. I present an ethical perspective explaining why we should withhold tolerance when proponents of movements such as Kach wish to be elected to parliament. On this issue my view differs significantly from those of John Rawls, Thomas Scanlon, and Frederick Schauer, among other philosophers. While they prefer to concentrate their discussions on the practical consideration of the magnitude of the threat, I address the ethical question of the constraints of tolerance. I hold that the fundamental question is ethical rather than practical. Thus, I argue that as a matter of moral principle, violent parties that act to destroy democracy or the state should not be allowed to run for parliament.

In turn, in chapter 12, I consider the attempts to restrict Kahane's freedom of expression and movement. I review the justifications given for the limitations that were set and how justified they were according to the formulated philosophical and legal guidelines. I argue that the broadcasting authority had acted *ultra vires* in banning Kahane and that, therefore, the court was right in ruling in Kahane's favor. I maintain that the act of restricting Kahane's freedom of movement was proper because there was no other way to stop him from making his provocative visits to Arab-Israeli villages, where he intended to preach his Orwellian idea of "emigration for peace." However, I differentiate between restricting Kahane from holding rallies in Arab places and withholding his freedom of demonstration *as such*. While the act of prohibiting those rallies was necessary, the act of denying his freedom of demonstration abridges a fundamental right without a sufficient reason.

Finally, in chapter 13, I discuss the *Neiman II* decision and some implications of the Kahanist phenomenon for Israeli society. I argue that although Kahane was killed twice, first politically and two years later physically, Kahanism is still very much alive in Israel. It would take a long educational process as well as a political solution regarding the Palestinians to uproot the deep feelings of hostility toward Arabs that prevail in Israel today.

Before starting the analysis, a note on terminology is in order. The terms *toleration* and *tolerance* are employed interchangeably throughout the study,[3] and so are the terms *liberty* and *freedom*.

Chapter 1

Liberty and Tolerance: General Insight

The Duty to Be Tolerant, the Right to Be Tolerated

The root of the terms *tolerance* and *toleration* is found in the Latin word *tolerabilis,* meaning "that which can be endured." In its earlier history, the expression implied the general notion of enduring beliefs (say religious beliefs) as well as forms of behavior. Tolerance arose, to a great extent, because it was viewed as the suitable alternative to endless religious rivalry. The notion was not enunciated as an ideal one but more as a necessary evil. It became a necessity in Europe once Europeans saw that neither side in a religious controversy was going to gain the upper hand decisively. The notion was that law ought to be obeyed because it was right; hence, a common moral authority that would determine what was right had to be established. In general, it was assumed that tolerance had to prevail to make living together possible.

Many in the liberal tradition have argued that no right to be intolerant exists but that a right to be tolerated does exist. According to this view we have to be tolerant not because we cannot really avoid it, but because we think it is right and desirable. Rather than being driven to toleration, it is a claim of our conscience, a part of our conception of justice, a virtue acknowledged to be the distinction of the best people and the best societies. Tolerance has been conceived as a good in itself and not as a mere pragmatic device or prudential expedient.[1] This view has made every discussion on the confines of tolerance problematic.

At first glance, toleration involves self-restraint. Tolerators, by definition, are free to put into effect their disapproval of some group, idea, or conduct; and when they decide not to exercise their power against the unfavorable object, they relinquish a freedom they once enjoyed. However, by suppressing their intended behavior, tolerators may have increased their autonomy. The notion of autonomy (to be discussed in the following section and explored further in chapter 3) involves the ability to reflect upon beliefs and actions and the ability to form an idea regarding them in order to decide which way to lead one's life. For by deciding between their own conflicting tendencies, agents consolidate their opinions more fully and review the ranking of values for themselves with a clear frame of mind. The importance of the moral ideal of toleration is that it is rational for an individual to freely consent to being tolerant; that tolerance should be something the person actively wishes to exercise even though it curtails his or her freedom.

Thus, imposing restrictions on ourselves is a necessary part of being tolerant and, therefore, a constituent part of our freedom. By restricting our own liberty, we agents grant liberty to another. By tolerating we introduce some overriding principles that bring us to interfere with our liberty. Those who are tolerated gain freedom from interference by an agent or agents. Exercising liberty in order to restrict another's liberty means that we agents do not find overriding considerations to justify the restriction of our own liberty. In this connection liberty can exist without any corresponding toleration, but toleration cannot exist without a corresponding liberty.[2] We can exercise our liberty without being said to be tolerated or without acting as tolerators.

People want to be free to decide their priorities and to achieve what they conceive to be desirable; hence, objects of freedom are to be defined in terms of the wishes of the agent involved. However, the essence of the value of freedom is that to be free of something is to be that much less impeded in the attempt to achieve a good life. Thus, Isaiah Berlin writes, "I am normally said to be free to the degree to which no human being interferes with my activity. Political liberty in this sense is simply the area within which a man can act unobstructed by others."[3] Berlin further argues that to be free is to be able to make an unforced choice, and that degrees of freedom are constituted by the absence of obstacles to the exercise of choice. The more avenues people can enter, the broader those avenues, the more avenues that each opens into, the freer they are. The better persons know what avenues lie before them and how open they are, the freer they will know themselves to be.[4] Berlin's assertions could be interpreted to mean that the given alternatives should be significantly distinct from one another and entail different consequences. At least some of them should be regarded by the agent as valuable. If we are to choose an option from a set of similar options (say a copy of this book from a shelf containing a dozen copies of this same book), or, worse, we are confronted by a your-money-or-your-life dilemma, then such choices hardly can be said to make us freer. The alternatives open to an individual must not be coercive ones, and the situation of choice itself must facilitate our volition and ability to choose.

Furthermore, in order to choose, a person must be capable of understanding how and to what extent various choices may affect his or her life. Consideration is given not only to our rationality but also to our awareness regarding the options open to us. Essentially we must be able to recognize an alternative for it to be considered as an option. A person, for example, may have physical strength, height, and coordination similar to Michael Jordan's, but he never saw his future in sports. When a scout from the New York Knicks comes to his college, he is indifferent to the scout's visit; therefore, that visit cannot be said to constitute an option for him. Choice has any positive bearing on the doer's freedom if at least one of the alternatives is valuable, or desirable, to the doer.

The underlying presupposition of the concept of freedom is that those who enjoy freedom may assert themselves, make critical reflections, and lead their lives independently. A person who does not enjoy autonomy is said to be unfree. Thus, it has been argued that whatever we think ought to be included in what passes for a liberal view, the affirmation of a picture of individual political autonomy, and institutionalized tolerance for that autonomy cannot be left out.[5] This brings me to the relationships between liberty and autonomy.

Liberty and Autonomy

Liberty is a necessary condition for individuals to exercise their capabilities independently. It is required to enable people to discover, through the open confrontation of the ideas that are cherished by their society, their own stances, their beliefs, and their future life plans. The central idea of autonomy is self-rule, or self-direction. Accordingly, individuals should be left to govern their business without being overwhelmingly subject to external forces. We are said to be free when our acts are not dominated by external impediments, thus enabling us to form judgments, to decide between alternatives, and to act in accordance with the action-commitments implied by our beliefs.

In this context three notes are relevant. First, we may decide not to do a thing; and as long as we reach that decision without any constraints, then autonomy is exercised. To determine not to act also constitutes a decision; indeed, it is also an action. In other words, autonomy implies the making of decisions. It does not necessarily imply the taking of an active action. Second, not all external forces are regarded by the individual as impediments. Some are taken to be facts of reality, as part of our existence. Otherwise the entire notion of impediments would become absurd. Walls, for example, would be viewed as hostile barriers not only in the case of a jail, but also when free citizens recognize the necessity for their need for shelter and privacy. The third note is concerned with the notions of self-realization and autonomy. Joseph Raz asserts that these are different though related notions. He makes two hypotheses: the first holds that self-realization consists in the development *to their full extent* of *all* the valuable capabilities a person possesses. He contemplates that autonomy may be exercised in the decision to abstain from developing one's capabilities. Raz's second hypothesis maintains that we can stumble into a life of self-realization or be manipulated into it or reach it in some other way that is inconsistent with autonomy.[6]

Reservations are required in the consideration of both accounts. Why Raz insists that self-realization necessarily consists in *full* development of *all* valuable capabilities is unclear. True, we may have capabilities we may not wish to develop (the capability, say, for self-sacrifice). Yet we may decide not to cultivate that faculty precisely because we wish to cultivate another inherent faculty of ours (such as showing love and affection to our dear ones) through which we attain self-realization. We may choose one path that is regarded as valuable to the extent that it outweighs other capabilities with which we are blessed. We may think we could achieve self-realization by preferring one option to the others and pursuing that path alone. Can it be said that because we decided to concentrate our efforts on developing one faculty rather than another, precisely in order to realize ourselves, we really did not realize ourselves because we neglected one (or more) of our other valuable capabilities? In this example, we deliberately made this decision, thinking that if we would try to develop both capabilities simultaneously, we may not be able to realize ourselves through any of them, because each necessitates considerable effort. Thus we acknowledge that we could best realize ourselves through the cultivation of one ability that we appreciate most. Alternatively, we may decide to cultivate various valuable capabilities but not to the fullest extent. Either way, if we satisfy our aims in life, we may feel we have realized ourselves.

As for the second hypothesis, Raz explains that the ability of people to choose the course of their lives can be developed by stimulation and deceit, by misleading them to believe that they control their destiny. This may be true. Yet unclear is how people can "stumble" into a life of self-realization. Do they recognize that they have stumbled? For if they do not, then in what sense can we speak of *self*-realization? And if they do, can we assume that they did nothing to realize themselves and just stumbled? In any case, we can postulate that the notion of self-realization is intelligible only if we make a decision independently; that is, if we exercise our autonomy. Prior recognition of how they want to live their lives must occur by the doers for the notion of *self*-realization to be meaningful.

Raz maintains that autonomy is exercised only if an adequate range of choice is available. To be autonomous we need a variety of options to choose from, some of which may be of significance to the agent, and some the agent may find useful to dismiss. Having options enables the doer to sustain activities he or she regards as worth pursuing, and the reaching of such a conclusion—what is worthwhile and what is not—is often arrived at by reflecting on diverse, often conflicting, alternatives. Persons are autonomous if they have a variety of acceptable options available to them and lead their lives through their choices of some of these options. As Raz notes, a person who has never had any significant choice or was not aware of it or never exercised choice in significant matters but simply drifted through life is not an autonomous person.[7]

An autonomous choice does not have to be the best one available. It presupposes that the agent exercises some extent of rationality but not perfect rationality. A person may not choose the best decision and still be considered autonomous. Moreover, objective limitations stand in the way of making the best decision. We hardly ever make a fully informed choice or have all the existing data about a given case. Limits constrain our efforts, and instead of looking for all the existing information, we speak of the *required* data. Then it is our decision to determine what is *relevant* and what is not and when to stop searching for more information. In addition, we have the questions of availability of data and of access to information.

The distinguishing feature of autonomy is, therefore, the forming of our discretion in a way that is supported by our reason, though our rationality may be impaired. We may disregard some relevant data required for making a decision either because we do not acknowledge its relevance or because its meaning is incomprehensible. Sometimes we may find it preferable to ignore some facts because they conflict with beliefs we are not willing to yield. Nevertheless, the agent is still said to be autonomous.[8] The agent is not coerced to choose one alternative over another. Our ability (or lack of it) as agents may restrain us from taking the best alternative available. Yet from our point of view, we are taking the best one that we can possibly conceive of, given our inherent deficiencies. Choosing the best option or thinking correctly is not a requirement for autonomy so long as the doer exercises deliberation in assessing the alternatives. The emphasis is not on deciding the "best" options nor on holding the "true" opinions, but on the way in which we come to make the decisions and to hold our opinions.

Some words of explanation are in order regarding the term *deliberation*. Deliberation presupposes a process of examining alternatives in an effort to determine which course of conduct to pursue. This process may include habitual actions. In such instances the reasons for action enter automatically into the process of deliberation. The agents have made their calculations, considered the alternatives, and have decided which option is preferable to others. We intentionally reduce the number of options in order to avoid spending time again and again deciding which data are relevant for assessing different courses of conduct in familiar circumstances. In a similar vein, persons often categorize actions, people, facts, objects, etc., to save time when encountering familiar data. We put labels on things, for instance: *library, bedroom, theater, summer, liberalism, ethnicity*. These categories contain information that facilitates discussion and spares the need for tedious explanations.

When agents think new factors have emerged that deserve consideration, which—on balance—seem important enough, they may decide to reevaluate the previous decision and reshape their behavior. Thus, as

Martin Hollis asserts, habit is quite consistent with deliberation, provided the agents are also in the habit of monitoring their habits to check for internal as well as external changes, which may convince them to modify or to break their habit.[9]

I have stated that deliberation assumes some degree of rationality on the part of the doer. To deliberate may involve considerations that spectators may conceive to be irrational but that, from the doer's point of view, may be perfectly rational. Agents may act in a way that would make others perceive them as irrational persons, while irrationality may be precisely the notion the agents wish to convey to further their position. Sometimes a course of action others see as irrational can award agents more gain than they could possibly have achieved had they acted in an expected, "rational" way. In international relations, brinkmanship often has proved to be a sensible policy, bringing more gains than would have been the case had a conventional, "rational" policy been pursued instead. Some leaders have decided to cultivate an irrational image precisely in order to improve their positions. Furthermore, deliberation does not necessarily involve only rational considerations. A person who deliberates autonomously will not necessarily choose in a rational manner. Emotions may have a bearing on the course of conduct the doer decides to take. Autonomous persons may act impulsively or emotionally, and, therefore, we may distinguish between autonomous *persons* and autonomous *actions*. Not every self-propelled act of an autonomous person may be regarded as autonomous. As Thomas Scanlon postulates, persons are autonomous when they see themselves as sovereign in deciding what to believe in and in weighing competing reasons for action, which may not necessarily be rational reasons.[10]

The requirements of autonomy are weak in Scanlon's view because, for him, we are autonomous if we independently apply canons of rationality when considering the judgment of others as to what we should believe or do. It does not matter to Scanlon that these canons of rationality may be substantially lacking. Consequently, it does not matter that a person may make decisions in an uncreative or weak-minded manner, revealing ignorance, emotions, lack of self-reflection, or any combination of these. For instance, John may decide that his love and affection for Jane outweigh the fact, which he recognizes to be relevant, that they share nothing in common but their love. We may say that John is not rational, and John himself may agree, but it is still more important for him to live (in spite of quarrels) with the woman he loves than act rationally and give up his relationship with her. Although we may say that John's emotions prevented him from having maximum control over the situation when making his decision, we cannot say that John did not act autonomously, for no external limitations were involved. As a rational person, John will be able to reconsider his decision in the future, to criticize and evaluate it in the light of his and Jane's experience as a couple. We may add that this example assumes a degree of independence and rationality on John's part. However, if a person is completely emotionally dependent on another, to the extent that he or she entirely lacks self-respect, independence, and self-confidence, then we may say that that person is not autonomous and, therefore, is unfree.

Hence, when speaking of autonomous conduct we should emphasize the way in which a decision is made rather than its result. We choose autonomously when we identify and evaluate the relevant factors pertaining to the choice, not all of which may be reconciled in a rational manner. This is not to say that autonomy does not require taking advice from others; on the contrary, it benefits the agent to hear different opinions and to consult others who may have more experience or information about the matter at hand, as long as these advisers do not resort to manipulation, that is, to elucidating their views by any possible means, while blocking the agent's exposure to opposing views. Agents may rely on another's judgment, but they must be able to hear contrary opinions and exercise their discretion. Exploring another's opinion is a step to help *us* to form *our* reasoning through critical thinking. Autonomy requires that the final judgment be the doer's after having gathered what he or she regarded as relevant and then assessing it.

This argument suggests that inherent restrictions do not make a person less autonomous. An autonomous person is one who has the ability to deliberate and to make decisions on the basis of reasons (rational and emotional) and without external limitations. Internal limitations inhibit rationality, make a person less comprehending, less capable of choosing the best alternative available; but it does not follow that such a person is less autonomous. Only external limitations make a person less autonomous and, therefore, less free. Now we face the task of explaining the meaning of external limitations. Do they include all societal limitations or only a part of them? Do they include, for example, norms, cultural beliefs, rules, traditional codes, and the like?

From our earlier discussion of habit the reader may infer that norms and tradition are not to be included among these limitations. We cannot divorce individual judgments from the social and cultural context in which they are made and, more specifically, from an individual's social background. For internalization of socially received concepts, beliefs, and norms is a necessary precondition for critical reflection on any specific project or practice. We accept some points according to which we are able to make judgments, review opinions, and form our views. As William Connolly explains, we always must accept some concepts and beliefs in order to isolate others for critical examination. We therefore must follow some practices unreflectively so that the source and rationale of others can be considered reflectively.[11] Thus, external constraints, when they are conceived by persons not as alien or in some way threatening to them but as necessary and even as conducive to their individuality, become self-imposed and cannot be seen to be contradictory to their autonomy. Individuals internalize norms that help them to define their convictions and to understand themselves and others as well as their surroundings. We accept norms because they help us to perceive the world in which we live and define our place in society. Accordingly, we adopt, say, the norm of commitment as part of our concept of friendship and of family, which places some restrictions on our autonomy. But these restrictions are not commonly viewed by us as impediments to our freedom or our autonomy. We willingly accept such norms as ways of expressing ourselves, and our sense of giving, of sharing, of love and any other affective notion that is valuable for defining our world as autonomous creatures living among others. We may have an interest in giving to others because the act of giving and the recognition that we make others happy contribute to our satisfaction, making us feel more humane and with a personality that has been bettered. Restricting ourselves in such cases does not go against our interests; instead, it is conducive to promoting our position through the effort of contributing to others. We all have an interest in promoting egoistic motives, but for similar reasons we also have an interest in furthering altruistic notions. Thus we are willing to take on sacrifices and restraints.

Although norms prescribe ways of conduct and consequently limit our autonomy to an extent, they do not ultimately coerce us. There is still room for nonconformism, still the possibility of rebellion, of changing the norm. A notable example in the context of democracy is the well-accepted norm of one person, one vote. This idea, which was considered ridiculous or even dangerous only a century ago, is fully established today. Societies and circumstances change and bring people to adjust to the new developments. People recognize the need for molding or replacing old norms with more acceptable ones. They accept a norm when it provides sufficient reasons for them to adhere to it and to act accordingly. The prevailing view is that citizens can, upon reflection, criticize norms and try to change them when they believe, for example, that new circumstances and new times require some form of accommodation. Norms may be changed because—assuming that people are autonomous and capable of forming judgments upon evidence—a continuous interchange occurs between the people and those who maintain norms and ascribe to them their institutional backing. As Connolly contends, it is not that autonomous persons take nothing for granted, but that they are able and willing to question any project or practice and to adjust their conduct on the basis of such reconsideration. Such persons may well accept upon examination most of the prevailing practices within their culture, but to the extent that they do so autonomously, reflective judgment and self-understanding enter significantly into their acceptance of these patterns.[12]

The internalization of socially received concepts, beliefs, and norms is a necessary precondition for critical reflection on any project or practice. The initial system of concepts and beliefs that helps us to define ourselves provides the materials out of which we define and comprehend our setting.[13] An autonomous personality develops against a background of social limitations, some of which exist as a part of life and that citizens do not regard as constraints at all. Others are regarded as limitations on liberty that citizens nevertheless accept willingly, recognizing their value in making living together possible. Therefore, it may be more suitable to treat impediments as limits on freedom only if they restrict options that may otherwise, under the given conditions and norms, be available and eligible. The major problem is to determine the restrictions that reconcile individual liberties and societal common interests. This is my prime concern here: What should these restrictions be and what are the grounds for introducing them? This is another way of asking What are the scope and confines of tolerance?

In the next chapter I begin to explore the scope of tolerance by examining the reasons for tolerance. I analyze two of the distinctions that were made regarding this issue. The first is Herbert Marcuse's distinction between passive and active tolerance. The second is Mary Warnock's distinction between the weak and the strong sense of tolerance. Then I will make two distinctions of my own: one between latent and manifest forms of tolerance, and one between principled and tactical compromise.

Chapter 2

The Scope and Characterizations of Tolerance

Reasons for Tolerance

In coming to evaluate tolerance, we have to examine the reasoning for the act of tolerance. Tolerance is conceived of as a policy that is adopted when consideration of others as bearers of rights is of significance in conducting our affairs. The ability to tolerate seems to rely upon the recognition that all people share some basic features. We tolerate others because we believe in the right of others to hold their beliefs and to exercise their choices freely (so long as they do not harm others). This qualification of not harming others is crucial (see chapter 7). Here I am intrigued by the issue of the grounds for tolerance. Commonly it is assumed that the reason for tolerance is respect for people as human beings, that is, respecting their right to live as individuals who are capable of reason and of deciding their own course of life (the notion of respecting others is considered in detail in chapter 3). But this may not always be the reason for tolerance. Some may view tolerance wrongly to include any act of toleration, regardless of its grounds. In so doing they ignore the possibility that we may tolerate a conduct or group for expedient reasons because it may be to our advantage to do so. We may tolerate a minority because we need its voice to be elected, or because it could be of benefit to our business. Tolerance that is exercised for purely instrumental reasons, motivated not out of concern for others but directed at advancing some selfish interest, is not tolerance in the genuine sense of the word. It is not, therefore, considered to be the subject of this study. In other circumstances current tolerators may adopt the opposite policy were this to serve their interests better. Tolerance that is carried out for egotistic reasons does not respect the other's interests but the tolerator's interests. It is only a tactic, and the grounds for tolerance today may supply grounds for intolerance tomorrow.

A policy of tolerance may be embraced not because of concern for the others as human beings but to ensure stability and order or because the tolerated person or group is conceived to be harmless and therefore not worth disputing. Again, it is difficult to affirm that a disliked group is being tolerated in the genuine sense, according to how the concept is viewed here, for the reason in both instances is not the belief that each should be granted equal respect and consideration. In the first instance those who decide to tolerate the group in question simply assume that not tolerating it may result in disorder, which could be perilous for society. Prudence prescribes tolerance for keeping the peace. In a different circumstance, the opposite conviction may be adopted using the same reasoning, for the purpose of avoiding disorder. In the second instance of tolerating a person or group considered to be harmless, tolerance is advocated simply because the individual or group in question is conceived to be an insignificant pawn who would not be able to increase his, her, or its power substantially. If it was thought that a group may have a real chance of becoming a major force in society, then intolerance would have been prescribed. In chapter 9 we shall see that this consideration guided many of the decision makers in Israel with regard to Kahane. Until the early 1980s Kahane was seen by many as a marginal phenomenon who had no power to implement his ideas and therefore should be allowed to pursue his activities. But an agent's act of putting up with people or activities in itself does not necessarily mean that the agent is a tolerant person. People can perform acts of toleration on prudential grounds, but this does not necessarily make them tolerant beings. It is not suggested that we tolerate in order to maintain or ensure stability, but that we tolerate because we respect others as human beings who should enjoy the ability to exercise choice and lead their lives as free, autonomous persons, so long as they do not harm others. The consequence of each may as well be peace and order in society, but the basis and reasoning are totally different.

Having established what should not be counted as grounds of tolerance, the next step is to canvass notions involved in the study of the scope
of tolerance. For tolerance is not a well-defined, static concept but a
conceptual framework within which different notions and degrees of the
term may be discerned. For example, Marcuse seeks to draw a distinction
between the passive and active sense of tolerance. Passive toleration is
said to be of "entrenched and established attitudes and ideas," even if
their deleterious effect on people and nature is evident; whereas active
tolerance is an official tolerance toward political parties, which increases
with the level of dislike the government feels toward the political ideas
and acts of the party in question.[1]

That distinction is not clear-cut and presents several problems. To
start with, who holds and promulgates those "entrenched and established attitudes and ideas" is not clear. Tolerance of ideas and of parties
are often connected, for parties are propagators of ideas. Ideas are obviously the ideas of someone, and, if ideas continue to prevail in society,
then they must be supported by some group of people. In any event,
whether to allow the passive toleration of ideas is a dilemma that often
confronts officials: Should entrenched attitudes be allowed to prevail or
should they have no place in society? Uprooting these ideas may require
educational and propagandistic measures. Sometimes this endeavor may
necessitate the taking of a legal form, through legislation aimed at dispos-
ing of those undesired ideas. On the other hand, advocates of tolerating
undesired ideas may equally adopt the same measures to protect themselves from intolerant groups seeking to curb those ideas and ensure their
being heard. The question, then, is to what extent the harmfulness of the
ideas plays a role in characterizing toleration as passive or active.

A stronger argument can be raised against Marcuse's implied supposition that tolerance is, in the main, a conduct of governments. He says,
"[T]he society seemed to practice general tolerance," but this within "the
effective background limitations imposed by its class structure."[2] Marcuse is silent regarding the actual part that citizens play in the practice of
tolerance. He does not specify in the first instance of passive tolerance
who actually tolerates, but we may infer from the active sense that he
means passivity on the part of the establishment: the government tolerates the disliked views, which bear no relation to any established body,
and allows them to keep floating around and have their damaging effect
on people. It is implied that the tolerance is passive because the ideas are

not affiliated with any party. If they were, then tolerance would become active, probably because then the government would tolerate not only ideas but also parties. The questions remain how ideas, in the first instance, come to prevail in society, and what role (if any) the citizens have in exercising tolerance.

Another pertinent distinction is between the weak and strong senses of tolerance. Warnock suggests the following: "In the weak sense, I am tolerant if I put up with, do not forbid, things which it is within my power to forbid, although I *dislike them or feel that they are distasteful.* In the strong sense I am tolerant only if I put up with things which it is within my power to prevent, even though I hold them to be *immoral.*"[3]

By tolerance in the weak sense Warnock reflects on our attitude about things or actions we find to be merely annoying. If we simply dislike something, then this something cannot be considered as harmful in any significant way. In turn, tolerance in the strong sense is applied when we forbear things or actions we find deeply disturbing and of which we disapprove. Warnock recognizes that here she is confronted with the central issue of Mill's *On Liberty,* which is, "whether the law can put up with that which is morally wrong."[4] This is another way of postulating the question: Should we tolerate disapproved *harmful* actions? Warnock does not say whether we should allow disapproved things only so long as they do not harm others. Instead, she concludes the discussion by saying that the issue of defining the limits of toleration is not one of theory only, and its solution cannot be deduced from any text, "neither the Bible, the Koran, nor *On Liberty.* For the limits of toleration must be defined piecemeal, each difficult case a matter of judgment and good sense."[5]

In making the distinction between toleration in the weak sense and the strong sense, Warnock recognizes that people's attitudes are influenced by the moral codes that prevail in their society, and that their personality may determine the extent to which they internalize the norms or decide to act in a nonconformist manner. In turn, they may develop preferences and tastes that will make them tolerate nonconformism. Warnock illustrates the distinction by discussing tolerating the torture of a child as opposed to tolerating the wearing of sandals with a suit. Toleration of this combination of the clothing is an example of weak tolerance, whereas tolerating a torturer necessarily requires strong overriding reasoning. Warnock would probably agree with the assertions that cultural and societal norms largely determine our attitudes and priorities, and that they are significant in crystallizing sets of beliefs and ordaining types of behavior in different circumstances. Warnock acknowledges that cultural norms prescribe our sense of dislike. Later, in chapter 4, I elaborate on these issues.

Warnock nevertheless is careful to refrain from saying that unified notions, based on norms, could enable us to say that some acts are immoral while others are distasteful. She implicitly recognizes that we may consider an action to be immoral, while another person may not see it as wrong in any sensible way. Warnock understands that the examples of torturing a child and wearing sandals with a suit are clear-cut, while on other issues no sharp line may be drawn between what we dislike and what we disapprove of. The distinctions between these two senses can be quite blurred. Because it is difficult to find the criteria for applying the distinction, we probably would have to resort to her suggestion that "the limits of toleration must be defined piecemeal, each difficult case a matter of judgment and good sense."

Warnock examines the issue of homosexual conduct between consenting adults. This is an illustration of conduct upon which it is difficult, maybe impossible, to reach a universal agreement regarding what people morally disapprove of and what they merely dislike. This practice is approved of by some (whether or not they take an active part in it), while others are indifferent to it. That same practice is disliked by many other people, and it may bring some of them to demonstrate their strong disapproval of it. This group conceives homosexual conduct as immoral though it does not harm others. The conduct may harm the individuals involved in this practice, but a liberal-democratic society assumes that people, as rational human beings, should weigh risks for themselves when they decide to do things that do not harm others, such as smoking, drinking, and making love. Government can, and should, promote awareness and warn against activities involving only the self that are harmful, but it must not outlaw them altogether. If it did, then either we would find it difficult to call such a society a liberal-democratic society, or the laws would not be worth the paper on which they were written. The constitutional ban on alcohol in the United States early in this century reminds us that, on such matters, law enforcement may prove to be a two-edged sword. The law did not bring more order, the authorities were not able to foster the ban, and it induced law-abiding citizens to break the law.

In this context considerations of culture are of great relevance. The culture may conceive a conduct at one time to be morally wrong and thus would consider it illegitimate. That same culture may react to changes within society, trends, fashions, or "pressures of the time" in a way that legitimizes modes of behavior by modifying cultural moral codes. What may be considered today as "objectively" morally wrong may be regarded tomorrow as a subjective, feeling. Cultures may adopt different moral codes in different times, as some have with regard to homosexual conduct.[6]

Moreover, only a few moral codes may claim universality, purporting to represent the view of any rational agent (the prohibition against murder, for instance). Most of them, however, are culturally bound. I elaborate on this issue later on; here, I ponder "the paradox of tolerance."

Popper's Paradox of Tolerance and Its Modification

In relation to the distinction between the weak and strong senses of tolerance, Susan Mendus, in her recent book *Toleration and the Limits of Liberalism,* modifies what Karl Popper calls "The Paradox of Tolerance." Popper explains that because of the strong belief in toleration, on the one hand, and the fear of being intolerant, on the other, people are inclined to extend toleration to those who spread intolerant ideologies that aim to destroy the very foundations of toleration. Many see themselves as committed to treating every individual as a moral agent and to allowing any person the opportunity to practice freedom—even if this attitude may prove conducive to promoting intolerance. Afraid of being intolerant, people tend to tolerate even those who clearly oppose the idea of toleration. However, the moral ideal of toleration does not require that we put up with anything and everything. Popper asserts that to allow freedom of speech to those who would use it to eliminate the very principle upon which they rely is paradoxical. He does not imply that we always should suppress utterances of intolerant philosophies; as long as we counter them by rational argument and keep them in check by public opinion, "suppression would certainly be most unwise." But "we should claim the *right* to suppress them if necessary even by force"; for it may easily turn out that the intolerant people are not prepared to meet us on the level of rational argument but may begin by denouncing all argument. Popper maintains that "they may forbid their followers to listen to rational argument, because it is deceptive, and teach them to answer arguments by the use of their fists or pistols."[7]

Mendus supplements this line of argument with the distinction between strong tolerance and weak tolerance originally made by Warnock. She argues that, in the first instance, tolerance is based on moral disapproval, implying that the thing tolerated can be conceived to be wrong objectively and therefore ought not to exist. The question that arises is, why, given the claim to objectivity incorporated in the strong sense of toleration, it should be thought good to tolerate. Mendus maintains that by contrast, weak tolerance involves cases in which toleration is based merely on dislike, which does not raise the same claim to objectivity. In her opinion, weak tolerance does not claim that objectivity for my dislike of something is distinct from my belief that the thing is morally wrong in just this sense, that there is not necessarily a commitment to the idea that the world would be a better place if the thing did not exist.[8] Mendus believes that the debate over whether the scope of toleration covers both things we dislike and things of which we disapprove is not merely a verbal dispute. Instead, it is part of a general philosophical debate about the status of moral judgments and the nature of the distinction between such judgments and judgments of taste or preference. She contends that only in cases where toleration involves more than mere dislike and has a moral force does a paradox arise, which involves explaining how the tolerator may think it good to tolerate what is morally wrong. In other words, Mendus explains, we need to show how we can claim consistently both that toleration is a virtue, and that strong toleration necessarily and conceptually involves reference to things believed to be morally disreputable, or evil.[9]

The problem lies in the distinction among the terms *dislike, morally disreputable,* and *evil*: Does any common definition distinguish immoral things or conduct from disliked ones? Secondly, can moral judgments claim objectivity? In the previous section I argued that different cultures and different individuals may have different outlooks regarding the same phenomenon. Here I claim that sometimes not the phenomenon as such determines our attitude toward it, but the combination of circumstances and conduct influences our judgment. An action may appear to be legitimate and tolerable if done in private, where no outsider can share in the intimacy; but if there is a chance of its being observed by others, then it could be considered immoral.

People form opinions on things conceived to be crucial after careful examination of circumstances and other factors. Sometimes they are not able to crystallize an opinion, deciding not to decide. Sometimes they leave the decision to the moment when they actually encounter specific issues. This is because it is not easy to form an opinion regarding them as it is in Warnock's examples of torturing a child and wearing sandals with a suit. If we contemplate the example of homosexual conduct, we may argue that some people may think it is not an immoral act per se but would still see it as repugnant. Therefore they would tolerate such a conduct only when it takes place in private. These people may be tolerant of public heterosexual conduct (because they appreciate variety, think it may stimulate and refresh relationships between consenting adults, etc.); whereas homosexual intercourse may be viewed as corrupting innocent young people who may witness it. We could then press the question, What if the same conduct were to take place in a private bedroom, with the curtains open? You could argue that it may then corrupt innocent neighbors.

Furthermore, people who may be indifferent to or tolerant of homosexual intercourse when it is performed between consenting adults may not tolerate it if one of the couple were an adult and the other, say, a fourteen-year-old, even if the youngster were willingly taking part in the activity. Different considerations are involved, and we can stretch the example into absurdity, discussing the extent to which curtains are open or the exact ages of the consenting participants. Moreover, one person may be inclined to agree with those who say that a conduct is objectively wrong, that no value will be lost if it is prohibited and, therefore, it ought not to exist. The same person at another stage of life (together with other persons) may only *wish* that the same conduct did not exist. The boundaries between what we morally disapprove of and what we merely dislike are not easily defined. Hence, when moral issues of this kind are concerned they necessarily involve subjective judgments. That moral judgments claim objectivity, while nonmoral judgments express purely subjective preferences, as Mendus suggests, is unclear. The line between preferences and moral evaluations is a fuzzy one.

The following section offers an alternative to Marcuse's distinction between passive and active tolerance and to Warnock-Mendus's distinction between a weak and strong sense of tolerance. Unlike Marcuse's distinction, my distinction conceives tolerance as a matter of personal attitude, as well as of institutions and laws. Like the Warnock-Mendus distinction, mine discerns different levels of tolerance not according to the criterion of moral objectivity but in accordance with the efforts the tolerator invests in doing acts of toleration. I distinguish between latent and manifest tolerance. This distinction is concerned with different ways in which tolerance exhibits itself, and, I think, it is better equipped than Warnock's to explain the scope of tolerance. Before I begin the analysis, a note on terminology is in order. While in the field of sociology the term *latent,* as coined and employed by Merton, implies neither intended nor recognized notions,[10] here the term is used to convey only the notion of something hidden, as opposed to open and expressed. Both forms of tolerance, the manifest as well as the latent, are understood to be intentionally exercised by conscious agents. I argue that degrees of manifest tolerance can be distinguished, and that the latent form of tolerance is significant, although it is not expressed openly. Latent tolerance is significant to the tolerator and to the overall notion of toleration that is upheld in society.

Latent and Manifest Tolerance

I have contended that tolerance is composed of a disapproving attitude and one or more principles that override that disapproval. The disapproval may be latent or manifest. If it is manifest, it can take several forms, ranging from a lenient attitude to manifest strong disapproval. The lenient attitude urges that every idea should be heard as long as it does not coerce other people, and hence that every manifest form of disapproval should not abridge the right to free speech in any way. The manifest strong disapproval shows objections to an opinion but nevertheless believes in its right to be heard.

A very lenient point of view argues that respect for others requires respect for everyone, whoever he or she may be, as well as respect for any opinion a person may wish to hold, however distasteful it may be. Every opinion has the right to compete in a free market of ideas, alongside our disapproval (see chapter 6). A less lenient attitude may convey counter-arguments or deeds designed to fight the disapproved and persuade the public to take sides against the disliked views. Disapproval also may take the form of manifest protest against these views, usually after hope of trying to influence the agent to moderate his or her conduct has been lost.

Yet the overriding principles restrict the freedom of the tolerator to exercise disapproval, with the result that the tolerated are allowed to continue carrying out their actions or conveying their beliefs. Let us examine this range of attitudes in detail.

In the first instance, during a debate we may think there is a point in trying to change the other's mind by exchanging views. As tolerators we are willing to face the other person, whose ideas or behavior we strongly resent; nevertheless, we respect the other's right to hold and preach them. We even may come to a debate determined to convince the other and simultaneously not be averse to changing our views. Attitudes of this sort afford tolerance of opponents in the belief that they are free to speak their opinions and that they may be right. Condescension is not at work in such instances, nor is opportunism nor indifference. This sort of tolerance is distinguished from indifference because the tolerator (who may or may not be a government official) does care about the other's conduct and preferences. Indeed, this is the real essence and meaning of the idea of tolerance and it may be called *strong manifest tolerance*.

A less strong manifest tolerance occurs when we are willing to confront the other but come with a different purpose in mind. Sometimes we may be willing to take part in a public debate not so much to influence the other participants (the gap between the views may be too wide and unbridgeable) as to influence those who attend the debate or are in some way exposed to it in the hope of scoring more points than our opponent.

A still weaker form of manifest tolerance is when we tolerate the conduct of others but are not willing to negotiate with them or do anything that might help them convey their views. Thus, on some occasions, we may tolerate an opinion but not be willing to share the same platform with the other, or put ourselves in any other way in what may be regarded as an equal position to the other for fear that so doing may legitimize the other's views. Another means of seeking to withhold another's views of legitimization is by walking out of the room whenever unpopular views are being expressed.

Whether these forms of action still can be considered as acts of tolerance may be reasonably questioned. You might argue that they may not, since such a practice is incompatible with the activity of rational debate or discussion, and that a way of life in which people normally refrain from listening to opposite views could not be considered an open society or one in which freedom of speech flourishes. However, these arguments ignore the concomitant effect of legitimization when an opinion is allowed a free hearing. Walking out on opposed views rather than rebutting them does not necessarily demonstrate little feeling for freedom of speech. It may imply that we don't want any part of what is said, that the gap between the views cannot be narrowed, and that we see no point in intellectual discussion because the entire fabric of presuppositions and values is different or even contradictory. Therefore, anything that may imply legitimization should be rejected.

Moreover, such a policy may be employed because democracy seems to be in danger; thus, it may be adopted as an appropriate measure of self-defense. The tolerators respect the right of their opponent to exercise choice and to lead his or her life as a free, autonomous person. At the same time they realize that the policy adopted may result in enabling the tolerated to harm others. When we speak of a democratic culture we speak of trade-offs between basic liberal principles and particular principles that may require ample consideration and that sometimes limit the extent to which we can apply the liberal principles. If we take the Israeli political culture as an example, this culture was shaped, and it is significantly still shaped, by the Holocaust. When the quasi-fascist Kahane was elected to the Knesset and continued to preach his ideas about the expulsion of the Arabs, most members of the Knesset adopted the habit of walking out of the plenum whenever Kahane rose to speak (the Israeli measures of self-defense against Kahanism are discussed in part 2.) This action was designed to show that nothing that might imply legitimization of Kahane's views should be allowed. It implied the gap between Kahane's views and theirs was too wide to be bridged, so that there was no point in exchanging views and debating. They respected the voters' decision to elect Kahane, and therefore they respected his right to speak and to represent the voters' views, but they did not want to be in any way associated with those views. Some of these members of the Knesset thought Kahane was entitled to advocate his views; nevertheless, they thought that such views simply had no place in Israeli society. The message they wished to convey was "Kahanism won't pass!"

Therefore, we may fight for the other's right to be heard and at the same time fight to curtail the influence of his or her distasteful views in order not to do anything that could be interpreted as giving those views equal status. Plausibly a tolerator may respect the other's right to voice opinions yet think that some defensive measures should be taken to

diminish their influence. These measures can include warnings and pre-
vention of legitimization.

Finally, in an even weaker type of manifest tolerance a person tolerates
speech and argues for the right of distasteful views to be heard but
opposes the right of the propagators of these views to stand for elections.
The argument that may be advocated here is that a liberal society should
allow the pursuit of every concept and value, whatever they may be
(provided that they do not inflict harm upon others), but no requirement
says that every view be allowed to gain institutional legitimization. That
is, we have to distinguish between freedom of expression and freedom to
compete in elections. Society can endure any opinion, but no obligation
exists that a parliament should represent each and every view. Harmful
and discriminatory opinions could be allowed to be pronounced (with
qualifications; see chapters 7 and 8), but they may have no place in the
house of representatives; they deserve no legitimization by democracy to
help them develop and attract more people. The underlying assumption
of this argument is that when opinions are denied the institutional mechanisms of legitimization, the propagators of these opinions will not be
able to transform them into an endangering power. This attitude shows a
qualified tolerance, for it denies the right to equal respect. Some ways of
exercising freedom and autonomy are denied because the overriding principle includes considerations of safety, either of the entire democratic
framework or of some parts of the community. It still allows for the
exercise of a wide range of freedoms, other than standing for elections.

Thus far I have considered manifest ways of expressing disapproval.
But a different sort of disapproval is latent, that is, not expressed *publicly*. Tolerance takes place when a person disapproves of conduct and
still decides to adopt some overriding principles. Accordingly, the clash
between the negative attitude toward a type of conduct and an overriding
principle of, say, the belief in mutual respect does not necessarily have to
be manifested. You do not have to act out your disapproval while safeguarding another's right to exercise basic liberties of free expression, free
association, free speech, etc. A person (a government official or any other
member of the community) may disapprove of a view and do nothing to
show this disapproval. This is still a form of tolerance, for it contains the
ability to understand those who differ from oneself or of respecting their
rights and liberties despite the fact that their opinions or conduct rouse
the tolerator against them. The tolerator still thinks that the others are

entitled to speak or act according to their beliefs and to exercise free choice in leading their lives. We may feel contempt for an opinion yet decide that out of respect for the person who expresses it, whom we appreciate, we had better remain silent. We may even assist such a person in spreading his or her views. Alternatively, we may feel that a disliked view should be tolerated, but we do not have enough reason to express our views. Perhaps we have no incentive to show our attitude, or we may feel reluctant to let our opinion be known because of the risk of raising extreme opponents of the disliked view in question against ourselves.

Furthermore, similarly to those who would not wish to converse with the other so as not to help that person gain legitimacy, we could think that any comment made regarding the disliked view may give it resonance and help spread it among the public. We may think that others we disfavor have the right to exercise their liberties, but we are not willing to help them in any conceivable way. We tolerate the conduct of the other, but we are not willing to do anything that may assist him or her gain support for carrying out the disliked conduct. This *latent* form of tolerance is a matter of conscience, as is the *manifest* tolerance, though it does not become public knowledge.

This latent position is a form of tolerance because a definite attitude opposes a conduct, and some overriding principles are held that make us refrain from exercising liberty to restrain that conduct. The only difference between this and manifest tolerance is that, for one or another reason, we decide to keep our position to ourselves. Latent tolerance does not differ from the manifest variety in the sense that manifest tolerance safeguards or extends the liberties of the tolerated, while the latent does not. Being tolerated in any form—latent or manifest—does not *necessarily* entail the extension of political or other rights. If the government publicly advocates tolerance of a group or secures the rights of the said group in legislation, then these acts would have positive effect in safeguarding the status of this group in society. But sometimes the taking of a manifest stance is no more than lip service, while the situation de facto is different. The official granting of rights does not necessarily entail that the minority group in question actually possesses full citizenship. For instance, the Israeli Arabs complain that although they are formally said to enjoy equal rights, in practice they are discriminated against by the Jewish community.[11]

In the context of latent tolerance, we also may speak of different senses of tolerance, though to speak of stronger and weaker forms of latent tolerance is more difficult. We may argue that when you disapprove of a group or a conduct but still assist this group in conveying its disapproved views (say, by providing the group with public forums) or help a group or an individual in carrying out a distasteful deed (say, a mother who helps her daughter to get a punk haircut), you exhibit a strong sense of latent tolerance. With regard to weaker forms of latent tolerance, we may note the difference in motivation between situations in which, for example, you hold this form of tolerance because you are afraid of risking your position in society, or because you think that any reference to the disliked or disapproved phenomenon may contribute to its legitimization.

A question arises whether the latent form of tolerance can be counted as significant. The argument can be subjected to the same criticism of practicability that previously was directed against Mendus's distinction between what is disapproved and what is disliked. What is the meaning of this tolerance when the tolerator resents a conduct but does nothing to manifest resentment? Although we recognize that latent tolerance cannot be regarded as indifference, we still could argue that when tolerance is latent, then silence prevails, and consequently we cannot distinguish it from indifference. However, when citizens adopt a tolerant attitude, the latent form included, they do have an opinion. The issue at hand does matter to them, and this attitude may have an impact on society, on the people's norms and general attitude toward a disliked group. A tolerated group may gain something from the lack of interference on the part of the tolerator. Ethnic minorities, for example, that are out of favor with the government may yet live in a tolerant atmosphere. Polls may detect the prevalent notions under the surface and give an indication of future policies regarding the tolerated, sometimes with regard to related concerns as well.

This point takes us to the further argument that explains why latent tolerance is significant. This is a meaningful form of tolerance because latent tolerance does not necessarily stay latent. A trigger may transform it into a manifest form of tolerance. And even if such a transformation does not take place, latent tolerance is valuable because it is significant to the *tolerator*. It indicates to tolerators the relationship of their priorities to those of the society in which they live. It is vital to any conception of self, society, or value. Latent tolerance, therefore, counts because of its contribution to shaping a frame of mind, a conception of the good and the right (this terminology is explained in chapter 3), and the establishment of priorities: Which principles are significant enough to override disapproval? When should disapproval be manifested? And at which point does the disgust, or revulsion, override the principles appreciated so as to limit the extent of toleration of the disapproved action? This contribution, I suggest, cannot easily be ignored.

Another valuable distinction that deserves mention concerns the principles that may lead a person to take a position, whether tolerant or intolerant. The conflicting principles may reflect a tension between citizens and their society, between their conceptions and ideas and those promulgated by the government. We may override cultural norms and hold tolerant views that are scarce in society. We can be said to be tolerant when we override our disapproval, and also when we override disapproving norms of society; for example, when showing consideration for others whose culture, nationality, or religion is disapproved of by vast sectors of our society. The focus here is on prevailing norms that we acknowledge and may even assume to have a firm basis. Still, agents adopt a more tolerant attitude than society, and thus we are willing to override negative feelings toward the phenomenon in question. Although we can argue that the norms a person internalizes are also the norms of society, the overriding norms internalized are not necessarily the norms that prevail in society. Someone may, for example, live a considerable period of life in a different culture, internalize its norms, and then return to his or her native country and apply the internalized standards to the immediate, close surrounding. Then the person may feel that the society should tolerate some norms or groups that currently it does not, and vice versa. Thus, in a democracy with no separation between state and religion and where all weddings are required to be religious ceremonies, some may feel that people should be able to get married in a secular ceremony. In such cases, when we adopt principles that clash with norms prevalent in society, we may prefer the latent type of tolerance so as not to arouse antagonism. Certainly, we would confront enormous difficulties in openly manifesting our overriding principles in favor of groups or forms of conduct that are unpopular in our society. To take another example, a pro-choice position concerning abortion in a society whose prevalent position concerning the fetus is pro life may portray the tolerator of abortions as one who is an enemy of life, an enemy of those who are yet to be born. Some tolerators may prefer to keep their opinion to themselves. I reiterate that in neither case—when we override our disapproval or when we override a societal disapproving norm—does it directly follow that the rights of the tolerated have been extended or even safeguarded. However, when tolerant views are shared by many, a cumulative influence affects society that makes it more open and pluralistic in its character. In such a case, the resultant contribution is one of noninterference, so that those tolerated are granted freedom from interference by the tolerator. In order for the rights of a disliked group to be safeguarded and extended, that group should enjoy some form of public support.

I must make one final comment regarding this connection. Earlier I argued that tolerance may evolve from two main sources: expediency, in terms of self-interest, and respect for others as human beings. I have excluded the first from being considered as a tolerant act, arguing that tolerance is concerned mainly with consideration for others. When persons adopt overriding principles that support positions in favor of granting equal rights to groups that are discriminated against in society, they may be inclined to adopt latent tolerance and make marginal improvements on behalf of that discriminated group, rather than trying to rebel against society. This is merely a sociological observation. Tolerant people living in a coercive and intolerant society may feel there is not much point in risking their position in society by rising to fight for the rights of that group. Although it is, in a way, a case of self-interest, this reason for tolerance differs from the "pure" cases of self-interest because the main reason in tolerating the other, or in tolerating a conduct, is still respect for the other's rights. This rather diluted form of tolerance stems from the view that not much point exists in taking an overt stand against society, knowing that the forces of intolerance are powerful enough to exclude the tolerator, in some way or another, from the society. People under such circumstances may argue that nothing comes of fighting windmills.[12]

A notable yardstick to measure the extent of tolerance that prevails in a given society is the amount of freedom enjoyed by its minorities. A great need for tolerance occurs when a multitude of deep cleavages exist within society. These may be created by differences in religion, ethnicity, race, culture, ideology, or language. A society that accepts the pluralistic idea is likely to acknowledge the need for the expression of every group interest within a society and to be willing to grant some autonomy to minority groups.[13] The motto of such a society can be phrased in the language of English civil law: "So use your own that you do not harm another." It may be true that amid the roots of acceptance may be a tacit tension between different groups and organizations that possess some power, but the guiding principle is that every group recognizes the demands of the others, and even if it does not accept the others' ideas, it does accept the others' right to express and to pursue them. The aim then is seen not as to secure complete agreement on every question, though democracy certainly welcomes crystallization of consensus, but to administer an exchange of views between different groups with different interests. This process involves free debate and open, mutual criticism; for when discussion is engaged in between the majority and minorities, or among the minorities themselves, the range of opinions is further broadened by the inclusion of new elements or by the modification of old ones. Free discussion is essential for reaching some form of understanding. The commonly accepted method in this process is compromise—a principle whereby that which divides is rejected in favor of that which unites the people.

Principled and Tactical Compromise

Compromise, according to the *Oxford English Dictionary,* is a "settlement of a dispute by which each side gives up something it has asked for and neither side gets all it has asked for."[14] The settlement may be achieved by consent reached by mutual concessions. It can be reached without any external interference or assistance or by arbitration. In other words, we may distinguish between two types of compromise: the directly negotiated one and the third-party compromise. In any event, when compromise takes place between two or more parties, the emphasis is on reciprocity; that is, the concessions are mutual. Compromise is made possible when each side values more the things that can be achieved than the things they are required to give up.

Compromise has preconditions. The discussion presupposes that some forms of communication and cooperation take place between the involved parties (notice that compromise requires some kind of cooperation, but not all forms of cooperation require compromise); and that the parties speak the same language, in the sense that they share some basic norms that form the grounds for potential understanding. When divergences become so fundamental that they can no longer be compounded, then no compromise can be reached. There is simply nothing to talk about. Thus, to reach an agreement or some form of understanding, an appeal to common norms has to be made. Sometimes the appeal also must include norms known to be of value to only one of the sides (say A). This can be done if these norms are not repugnant to the other side (B). B may regard some norms as inconvenient yet may view them as practical and acceptable, necessary to make communal life possible (for example, norms which demand that secular people not drive during the Sabbath in Jewish religious neighborhoods). Then B may recognize the force or sincerity of his or her opponent's view and—while not agreeing with A's position—accept A's right to hold it.

Another favorable condition for compromise is mutual respect. In compromise, interests are accommodated rather than regulated, and this accommodation should be inspired by the respect we feel for the autonomy of the other. When we are sensitive to the rights of the other, then we shall prefer settlement to coercion, and we shall be more willing to acknowledge the need for concessions in order to reach an agreement. I shall consider this principle of mutual respect more closely in the next chapter. Here, two further contentions are pertinent.

First, compromise is not only a matter of two or more parties dealing with a common subject of concern or resources. Sometimes a compromise is made by one side with regard to its aims, in deciding how to allocate the available means and in determining priorities. Compromise, then, often is required between the different demands, needs, and ideas that are to be pursued and satisfied, and between what is believed in and the circumstances. In short, people compromise between what *ought* to be and what *is*; between what they aspire to and what is given in reality. In this connection the given circumstances, conflicting goals, scarcity of resources, uncertainty, complexity of the subject involved, availability of means, and pressure induced by time may induce a party to compromise in making a decision.

A relevant distinction is between *principled compromise* and *tactical compromise*. A principled compromise is a mutual recognition by each side of the other's rights, which leads them to make concessions to enable them to meet on a middle ground. It is made in good faith and both sides reconcile themselves to the results. However, because political disputes frequently involve conflicts of personality, of character, and of distinct sectional interests, a settlement may turn out to be no more than a temporary arrangement reached as a result of constraints related to time. This type of compromise is not the result of an effort to bridge the gap between rival groups. Instead it is a compromise that at least one side is forced to accept under given circumstances. That side would have no qualms about violating the common understanding and trying to gain a further advantage at the expense of its opponent should a proper opportunity occur. This is what I call tactical compromise, to which agents resort without giving up any of their aims. It is reached not in good faith but rather only because one party realizes that the end could not be achieved by one decisive move and thus it should be reached realistically in stages. Here is no genuine willingness to give up part of the interests involved but only to postpone the deadlines for their achievement. If any compromise occurs here, it is *within* one party, and not between different parties. The essential component of compromise, namely mutuality, is lacking. This is not the sort of compromise being examined here, nor the one that is encouraged by democracy.

Second, compromise is not an end in itself. Compromise should not be made for its own sake, just because a need exists to take into account the preferences of others, no matter what these preferences might be. To extol the virtues of compromise simply because it resolves conflicts peacefully and satisfies the interests of some is to exalt means over ends and to judge the merits of the method used in settling a problem rather than its core. Nothing in the arguments for compromise suggests that compromise is a self-sufficient principle that can be divorced from moral or other considerations. Some claims are not permissible either to press or to accommodate, because there are limits on what may be decided democratically. Here we may speak of instances where compromise is being achieved between two or more parties regarding their common stance toward a third party. Situations can be envisaged where two parties come to sit together, and then, out of respect for each other, make concessions that are reached at the expense of a third party. A fundamental question of moral legitimacy precedes the act of compromise. The issue is whether compromise is compatible or incompatible with integrity and with justice in some sense. Compromise should be considered and reached according to the content of the demands, with regard to their substance and meaning. If the values at stake contradict human rights, inflicting harm on society or part of it, then tolerance prescribes a need to refrain from making concessions just to satisfy the wills of the exploitive parties. Here I refer to acts of appeasement, when one party may be willing to cooperate with another to exploit a third party. The fact that a combined power—joined through the making of compromises with the intent of exploiting a minority—is stronger than that minority does not imply that might makes right. A majority can hold destructive views, but the mere fact that a considerable number of people are involved does not make their beliefs just. It only makes the situation more terrible.

At this stage I begin the task of prescribing boundaries for liberty and tolerance according to the two basic principles conceived to be fundamental in a liberal society. These are to grant others equal consideration and respect and not to harm others. My analysis starts by considering in detail the Respect for Others Argument and the related antiperfectionist argument which professes neutrality on the part of the government or the state. This argument is advanced in order to maintain pluralism, with the result of enabling each citizen to pursue his or her conception of the good. I propose that this argument gives grounds and sets limits on tolerance. In subsequent chapters I explore the Millian theory and specifically the Harm Principle. The main question that will be addressed is What is to count as a justified restriction on choice, which amounts to the restriction of a person's liberty? In another phrasing, the question is What constraints should be placed on tolerance?

Chapter 3

Why Tolerate? The Respect for Others Argument

Preliminaries

The aims of this and of the following chapters are to analyze the grounds for toleration and prescribe restrictions on liberty. The arguments that I shall use are derived from the liberalisms of Kant and Mill, which are among the more celebrated creeds prominent in the literature.

THE RESPECT FOR OTHERS ARGUMENT

The Respect for Others Argument is based on the Kantian, deontological arguments as well as on the liberal tradition. The defense of personal liberties that advocates tolerance is founded on the assertions that we ought to respect others as autonomous human beings who exercise self-determination to live according to their life plans; and we respect people as self-developing beings who are able to develop their inherent faculties as they choose, that is, to develop the capability they wish to develop, not every capability they are blessed with. A person, for instance, may have the faculties to become someone like Florence Nightingale, but it is against her interest to develop them.

In turn we respect people in order to help them realize what they want to be. Each individual is conceived as a source of claims against other persons, just because the resolution of the others is theirs, made by them as free agents. If we pursue the idea of tolerance to its logical extreme, then to regard others with respect is to respect their decisions, because they are *their* decisions, regardless of our opinions of them. We simply assume that each of us holds that our own course of life has intrinsic value, at least for the individual, and we respect the individual's reasoning.

A related argument advocates tolerance on the part of citizens and government to enable citizens to live their lives according to their moral tenets and the values which they hold most dear. It urges that every person should be able to pursue his or her conception of the good, and that the government should adopt a neutral stance regarding these conceptions.[1] The first part of the argument needs to be qualified; otherwise it does not make sense, for it may bring about the negation of respecting others. I will express my reservations in a minute. The additional advocacy of neutrality on the part of the government, or the state, is part of the more general doctrine of antiperfectionism. This doctrine conceives state perfectionism as a policy that would distort free consideration of different ways of life; harden the dominant ones, whatever their intrinsic values may be; and exclude unfairly the values and aspirations of marginalized and disadvantaged groups within the community. It further argues that state perfectionism raises the prospects of a dictatorship of the articulate and would unavoidably penalize those who are inarticulate.[2]

In formulating the Respect for Others Argument, I insist on the need for presenting qualifications that constrain toleration without defeating its very idea. I argue that if we refrain from introducing qualifications, then we face the danger of transforming tolerance into a self-defeating concept and, in turn, we may undermine democracy (the democratic catch). We should give equal consideration to the interests of others and should grant equal respect to the others' life projects so long as these do not deliberately undermine their interests by interfering in a disrespectful manner. The focus here is on the rationale of *mutuality,* on all participants keeping the principles of the game.

THE HARM PRINCIPLE

Through the review of the Millian theory I formulate relevant criteria that should be taken into account when dealing with boundaries on liberty.[3] I briefly consider what restrictions were introduced by Mill on liberty of action and then discuss the constraints on liberty of expression.

Mill argued that as human beings should be free to form opinions and to voice them without reserve, so freedom of action is a precondition for the development of individuality. Without liberty of action we are not able to choose between different paths of action, nor can we experiment with different plans of life: "As it is useful that while mankind are imperfect there should be different opinions, so it is that there should be different experiments of living."4

However, these arguments are not tantamount to an assertion that acts should be as free as opinions. Mill contended, "[N]o one pretends that actions should be as free as opinions."5 He saw freedom of speech as a special case of other-regarding acts that should enjoy almost complete immunity from the state's interference or control. Mill warned against humankind's inclination toward intolerance and suppression, asserting that humans have a propensity for curbing unwanted criticism and imposing opinions as a rule of conduct on others.6 He did not deny that expressions may cause harm. In what he regarded as extreme circumstances, Mill explicitly admitted the importance of restricting them. I will discuss Mill's theory after the analysis of the Respect for Others Argument. Following his reasoning, I formulate two principles: the Harm Principle and the Offense Principle, asserting that these render speech liable to restriction when it is or is most likely to be harmful. I maintain that consideration has to be given not only to physical harm, but also to psychological offense, which is morally on a par with harm. If not, then freedom of expression might be abused in a way that contradicts, to use Ronald Dworkin's phraseology, fundamental background rights to human dignity and to equality of concern and respect, which underlie a free democratic society.7 Let me first discuss the Respect for Others Argument.

The Respect for Others Argument

Toleration has been viewed in positively charged terms: as a right, as a virtue, and also as an ideal.8 As a result, the idea of tolerance is closely associated with the idea of caring for and respecting persons as human -beings. John Dewey, for example, suggests that an anti-humanist attitude is the essence of every form of intolerance. Movements that begin by stirring up hostility against a group of people often end by denying them all human qualities.9 Similarly, Herbert Marcuse points out that tolerance is an end in itself by explaining that the elimination of violence and the reduction of suppression to the extent required for protecting people and animals from cruelty and aggression are preconditions for the creation of a human society. He includes the capitalist system as such within his conception of violence.

Marcuse concedes that tolerance is an end in itself only when it is truly universal.[10] In turn, John Rawls asserts, "[T]he public culture of a democratic society" is committed to seeking forms of social cooperation that can be pursued on a basis of mutual respect between free and equal persons.[11] We may recall that Dworkin regards not only tolerance but the entire political morality as resting on the single fundamental background right of everyone to human dignity and to equal concern and respect.[12] By *background* rights, Dworkin means rights that provide a justification for political decisions by society in the abstract without connecting them to any specific political institution. Let us consider this argument for a moment.

Dworkin implies that his claim is some rights are better viewed as universal, as applicable to every political framework, because they are essentially derived from the conception of people as human beings. Such is the right for equal concern and respect.[13] This right may be morally applicable to any political system, but Dworkin would agree that this right may not necessarily be morally convincing. That is, it may not necessarily be one that every society would wish to adopt. Indeed, the Respect for Others Argument can be said to underlie a liberal-democratic society and not just any society.[14] In a society of sadists, people may not see any contradiction in conceiving fellow people as human beings and doing their best to cause them to suffer. In such a society a person (A) who sees a fellow person (B) drowning in a river may not be indifferent to the scene. But instead of giving B a hand, A may smile and cheer on the drowning person to depart from the world as slowly as possible. A does not consider the possibility of saving B for what we regard to be humanistic reasons. Instead, A may save B's life if A thinks further pain can be inflicted on B for A's own enjoyment. Only then may A bother to calculate the risks involved in such a deed. A knows that if the situation were different, and A were in B's position, then A would have received the same treatment from B. In this sense, people in this society are accorded what we understand to be equal (dis)respect and (ill)concern. Furthermore, they may encourage the occurrence of such "happy" occasions. In a society of sadists, no one has a moral obligation to give a hand to one's fellows; no one has a moral right to be rescued by fellow members of the community. And if members of the community happened to be humanists, then they either would have to find a way to leave their community or to accommodate their views. Furthermore, if they would ask liberals from outside communities to help in changing the set of values of the sadistic community, then some could argue that for them to impose their values on that community would be wrong.[15] Thus, for practical purposes, instead of discussing *universal* background rights, I shall speak of the Respect for Others Argument in the context of a liberal society. We may note that sometimes Dworkin writes about the right of each person to respect and concern as an individual only in the context of liberal democracies.[16]

Treating people with concern means to treat them as human beings who may be furious and frustrated, who are capable of smiling and crying; while to treat them with respect is to treat them as human beings who are capable of forming and acting on intelligent conceptions of how their lives should be lived.[17] That is, respect for human beings involves the presupposition that others should be allowed to make their own decisions, based on their conception of what is good and just. Respecting a person results when you give credit to the other's ability for self-direction, acknowledging his or her competence to exercise discretion when deciding between available options. Accordingly, each person is viewed as speaking from his or her point of view, having perceived interests in his or her own way. We may be asked to give our opinion or decide to express our view anyway; nevertheless, we recognize the other's right to make choices. We recognize that the final decision rests with the agent, so long as persons operate within the area of tolerance, and so long as they do not harm others. We accept the idea that every person should be respected and treated as a moral agent whose views can be discussed and disputed, as a person who is capable of changing opinions if rational grounds are provided.[18] Respect for a person means conceiving of the other as an end, rather than as a means to something. As Kant explains, rational beings are designated "persons" (to be distinguished from "things") because their nature indicates that they are ends in themselves. Such beings are thus objects of respect and, so far, restrict all arbitrary choice. Such beings are not merely subjective ends whose existence as a result of our action has a worth for us but are objective ends, that is, beings whose existence in itself is an end. No other end can be substituted for such an end.[19]

Thus, tolerance is concerned primarily with the consideration of others. To invade another's way of making a decision for himself or herself by enforcing directions is to fail to recognize something private and valuable to that person. Respecting others is a matter of degree. We do not assume that every person grants every other person exactly the same respect. Some people are more to our liking than others, as some opinions are more appealing to us than others. Many factors influence our decision as to how we treat another and in what ways we should show respect toward our fellows. Here, however, I refer to the most fundamental level of respecting the right of others to hold beliefs and to put their interpretation on their life, to exercise their discretion, and to deliberate as autonomous human beings. The underlying ground is, to use Hillel's famous dictum, "What is hateful to you do not do unto your fellows."[20] As you expect others to appreciate the fact that your beliefs are of significance to you, so you must accept that their beliefs do matter to them.

I construe the Respect for Others Argument as grounded on Kantian and liberal ethics. The Kantian ethics is based upon reflexive self-consciousness. It speaks of respecting people as rational beings, and of autonomy in terms of self-legislation. Kant calls the ability to be motivated by reason alone the autonomy of the will, to be contrasted with the "heteronomy" of the action whose will is subject to external causes. An autonomous agent is someone who is able to overcome the promptings of all heteronomous counsels, such as those of self-interest, emotion, and desire, should they be in conflict with reason. Only an autonomous being perceives genuine ends of action (as opposed to mere objects of desire), and only such a being deserves our esteem, as the embodiment of rational choice. The autonomy of the will, Kant argues, "is the sole principle of all moral laws, and of all duties which conform to them; on the other hand, heteronomy of the will not only cannot be the basis of any obligation, but is, on the contrary, opposed to the principle thereof, and to the morality of will."[21]

The notion of obligation instructs us how to behave. According to Kant, an action has moral worth only if it is performed from a sense of duty.[22] Duty rather than purpose is the fundamental concept of ethics. It is the practical unconditional necessity of action and, therefore, it holds for all rational beings. For that reason it can be a law for all human wills. Duty commands us to accept moral codes because they are just, regardless of the other's attitude toward them. This deontological ethics proscribes a set of actions with the effect of constraining our range of options, not because the results will be useful, but because this set of actions is incompatible with the concept of justice. Transgression of the rights of others intends to make use of them merely as means, without considering that, as rational beings, they must always be esteemed at the same time as ends.[23]

Following this reasoning, the Respect for Others Argument urges us to give equal consideration to the interests of others and to grant equal respect (within limits) to their way of life. This kind of egalitarianism does not require that we perceive all interests of others in a similar fashion, nor does it command us to sacrifice our interests in the course of respecting others. The pursuit of the Kantian directive does not require us to grant toleration to another out of respect when that person may take advantage of it to curtail our liberties. Such an action may resemble a boxing match during which one boxer eagerly seeks to shake the opposing fighter's hand at the beginning of the fight and refuses to open the match before doing so, while the opponent ignores the referee and takes advantage of every such attempt (in which our fair fighter opens a defense) to punch as hard as possible and finish the fight before the other has started it. In such a case, insisting on respecting the other clearly and necessarily may be self-defeating.

This example is different from the case in which we extend our hand to another and are left with our hand in the air because the other decides to ignore it altogether. Both are examples of nonmutuality (a deontological idea), but the example involving the boxers also makes a point about self-defeating activities (a consequentialist concern). The lack of respect on the part of the unfair boxer harms the fair boxer and brings the fight to a halt before the fair boxer and the spectators think that the rules of the game apply. Consider another example where someone decides to become a Stalinist. In such a case we respect a minority's decision to follow Stalinist ideas. We democrats grant the minority respect as regards the democratic right to become a majority. We end up violating interests of various sections of the population or with no respect for human beings at all. Should we, then, tolerate the other whose ideas respect neither us nor the rules of the game (assuming that the idea of the dictatorship of the proletariat cannot be reconciled with liberal democratic norms)? In such a case, whatever policy we adopt, we are bound to violate someone's interests, either ours, or someone else's.

This scenario opens the issue of the boundaries of liberty and tolerance for debate. In this context I insist on the rationale of *mutuality*, that all participants abide by the rules of the game, otherwise they may exclude themselves from the class of participants. The argument is that we ought to show respect for those who respect others. This mutuality principle applies to individuals as well as to institutions. Democratic governments have to allow pluralism to prevail and respect each and every group in their societies, as long as these groups respect the institutions and accept the principles that enable the existence of liberal-democratic societies. When individuals decide not to abide by the given liberal principles, then the issue of limits of liberty and tolerance is open to question. That is, M regards N as a bearer of rights and would expect N to respect M in the same manner when reaching decisions. The argument is formulated in positive terms. It prescribes that people respect those who respect them, but we cannot derive from it that, under all circumstances, people should disrespect those who disrespect them. The boundaries of tolerance are determined by the qualification of not harming others that is added to the Respect for Others Argument. Since not all cases of disrespect are cases of harm (disobeying your parents need not be harmful), and apparently not all cases of harm are cases of disrespect (deserved punishment is in some sense required by respect for autonomy), the formulation would be logically inconsistent were it to hold that one must "respect those who do not harm others." This would be a rather mixed or unbalanced mutuality principle. Therefore, I insist that the mutuality principle speaks only of respect and that it supplements the requirement of not harming others, but it does not and cannot stand by itself.

The Harm Principle that qualifies the Respect for Others Argument holds that every person should be able to pursue that person's conception of the good as long as the person does not harm others.[24] Liberals often accept this principle and see it as necessary for prescribing limitations on tolerance. Here they follow J. S. Mill's theory as formulated in his *On Liberty*. Some neglect to acknowledge this qualification. We may recall that according to Bruce Ackerman's view, every person should be able to pursue his or her conception of the good, whatever this conception may be.[25] Ackerman asserts that any form of social life that makes sense to any significant group will find a place in the liberal state. He implies that people lead their lives in accordance with their ideals or conceptions of the good.[26] Ackerman maintains that any form of social life will survive so long as it continues to *convince* a fragment of the next generation that the ideal it puts forward deserves the respect of a free and autonomous person.[27] However, this argument would allow a Stalinist movement to go from strength to strength in the way that I have just described. The argument has to be rephrased with reservations; otherwise it may bring the negation of liberalism and the values that Ackerman so vigorously cherishes, namely, individuality and neutrality.

A counterargument that Ackerman may formulate in response is that he spoke of "any form of social life," while I took an extreme example of an all-encompassing ideology, which reshapes society. But then we have to explain the meaning of "any form of social life." In any event, sadism or bigamy or association with cults (like worshipping Satan) are surely forms of social life, so it may be better for Ackerman not to speak of *any* form of social life. The issue is not whether we speak of ideology, isms, forms of life, or specific activities. Not only may ideology or "any form of social life" change the character of society, but some conduct may even bring the same result; thus it is necessary to add the qualification of not harming others. Let us consider the following scenario to clarify my assertion.

A significant group in the liberal state of Nemgal decides to start performing experiments on, say, short people. For the sake of argument let us assume that no snowballing effect will apply to other spheres of life, and that in all other respects Nemgal is similar to any liberal state. The group sincerely believes that this is the best way to derive medical conclusions that would benefit humanity. It convinces the next generation of the value of this conduct, and it also may "convince" other people who believe that performing experiments on people, whether they be short, blond, old, twins, etc., is an appalling policy, to adopt this conduct. Ackerman does not explain which forms of "convincing" others are legitimate or whether some forms should be excluded from a liberal state. The result may be that all will be convinced or "convinced" to adopt the performance of experiments on short people as the best way to improve their lives. The question is whether we can call such a state a liberal state.

Until now I have not written much about neutrality and the idea of "the conception of the good." I shall clarify meaning in the next section. Before that, two notes are in order. It has been said that tolerance should prevail to enable each and every person to pursue his or her conception of the good. The first note is concerned with the term *pursue;* the other with the limits of state interference in the ways people decide to lead their lives.

I use different terms regarding what we may do with ideas. I frequently mention the terms *pursue, promote, preach, advocate, further,* and *advance.* They all convey the similar notion of making an effort to convince others about the "rightness," "truthfulness," or "goodness" of our conception of the good. These terms convey the notion that a person tries to gain support, vindicate, or recommend a set of values that he or she holds dear, a conception of the good the person sees to be meaningful. The terms do not necessarily involve the taking of action besides verbal reasoning. The reasoning may, at some point, lead to the taking of action. But saying that you advocate or advance a conception of the good does not imply that words are directly linked with action. I see a difference between presenting a view and convincing others to take steps to bring something about; between abstract preaching and urging others to take action. The government can give much more latitude to "furthering" of a conception of the good than to taking of measures to implement it and bring it about. As the United States Supreme Court held, a difference exists between advocating a mere abstract doctrine of the forcible overthrow of a government and an action to that end "by the use of language reasonably and ordinarily calculated to incite persons to such action."[28] I elaborate on this issue in chapter 7, when addressing the question What should be the confines of freedom of expression?

As for the second issue concerning the limits of state interference, I have stated that enabling each and every person to pursue his or her conception of the good does not mean that the role of government is to secure equal opportunity for individuals to promote *any* conception of the good they may decide to hold, whatever that may be. Some people may adopt a conception that they see as a conception of good, but that we regard as one of evil. If its consequences are harm to others, then we should not tolerate that conception. The question now arises, What should be the limits of interference? In other words, we may think of subcultures within a liberal society that would like to have the autonomy to exercise their values according to their traditions. Some of these values may not be compatible with liberalism. Should we interfere, or should we tolerate them? We may pose further the question of whether some shared ideas and values that characterize a liberal society constitute a basic conception of the good. That is, does a general conception of the good provide the basis for a liberal society? Let us now consider these questions.

Between Neutrality and Perfectionism

WHY LIBERALS ADVOCATE NEUTRALITY

It has been argued that the difference between liberal states and theocratic, communist, or fascist states is not that the liberal states promote different ideals of the good, but that they promote none. Unlike illiberal states, which consider it a primary function of the state to prescribe the moral character of society, liberal states shun such attempts and allow citizens the freedom to develop their conceptions.[29] Many defenders of liberalism argue that liberalism is in some sense neutral with respect to competing conceptions of the good;[30] that instead of adopting an interventionist policy, liberal states should adhere to neutrality. Liberals postulate that governments cannot use as their justification for any action the fact that one person's plan of life is more or less worthy than another's. In order to ensure that every person will be able to pursue his or her conception of the good, neutrality does not endorse any disposition that defines human good and human perfection to the exclusion of any other. It refrains from identifying essential interests with a particular conception of the good life and shrinks from the possibility that the government, which could be associated with one or more segments of society, may impose its values and ideals on others, either by propagation or by force. In sum, the assumption is that should governments not be neutral regarding the plurality of convictions that prevail in society, then their bias could generate intolerance.

Liberals often add separate, though related, arguments that in a democracy irreconcilable and incommensurable conceptions of the good often occur, and that having diverse ideals, in light of which people lead different ways of life, is the normal condition.[31] Furthermore, this variety is conceived to be a good thing; to quote Rawls, it is rational for members of a well-ordered society to want their plans to be different.[32] For, as Rawls explains, human beings have talents and abilities the totality of which is unrealizable by any one person or group of persons. We not only benefit from the complementary nature of our developed inclinations, but we take pleasure in one another's activities.[33] Hence, liberals urge that citizens be allowed to follow their conceptions of the good as far as it is socially possible, rather than being obliged to live with convictions they do not uphold. Neutrality is prescribed to ensure standoff from support for what, prima facie, is conceived to be valuable and moral conceptions of the good. The qualification *so far as it is socially possible* implies a place for some restrictions on citizens and organizations to maintain the framework of society, but when introduced they require some justification.

Two significant notions are central to our analysis. The first is the *conception of the good,* and the second is *neutrality.* My purpose here is to clarify the meaning of these notions. The notion of neutrality will be examined in the context of the more general concept of antiperfectionism. Focusing attention on the first notion, Raz contends that the easiest explanation of what conceptions of the good are is to say that they consist of all aspects of morality other than the principle of neutrality.[34] Although this explanation may indeed be the easiest, the question remains as to whether it makes any contribution beyond making a mere generalization. Moreover, Marxists and feminists contend that liberal conceptions are class based and sex based.[35] Thus, further explanation is in order.

Persons, as moral agents, have their conceptions of the moral life and accordingly determine what they deem to be the most valuable or best form of life worth leading. You may suggest that a conception of the good involves a mixture of moral, philosophical, ideological, and religious notions, together with personal values that contain some picture of a worthy life. But our conception of the good does not have to be compatible with moral excellence. It does not mean a conception of justice. Our conception of the good does not have to be dominated by moral considerations. Leading a valuable life does not entail leading a moral life. The moral life may guide a valuable life, when you develop your conception of the good, but it is equally plausible to think that the moral life may be subordinated to the valuable life. In that case morality is secondary to the desire of leading a valuable life, and the conception of the good is dominated by that desire. The assumption is that a conception of the good comprises a basic part of our overall moral scheme and that it is public in that it is something we advance as good for others as well as ourselves. Consequently we would want others to hold a conception for their sake. But when that desire is based on coercion, it cannot be said to be moral because people are no longer autonomous to decide on their way of life. They are then forced to follow a scheme which *they* do not consider to be a conception of the good life.

The way the Israeli establishment treated the Middle Eastern immigrants during the 1950s is a case in point. I claim at the outset that the behavior of the Israeli establishment was not unique. We can think of other democracies that treated their immigrants in similar ways, but wrongdoing in one place does not justify wrongdoing in other places. People arrived at Israel from different countries and cultures; but instead of encouraging cultural pluralism, the establishment did not hesitate to promote some ideals of the good to the exclusion of others. It funneled the freedom of individuals and groups to develop themselves in accordance with some preferred ideals and conceptions, demanding they forego other conceptions conceived to be backward and primitive. All were required to follow a given set of norms dictated from above, which was envisaged as valuable. The Middle Eastern immigrants were compelled by the establishment to accept some cultural norms and to waive others conceived to be incompatible with the desired framework of the newly established state. This was done under a slogan that endorsed a common heritage, creating "One People and One Language." The effort was to absorb the immigrants through modernization. By definition, this effort was anything but neutral or impartial in its attitude to cultural pluralism. It was claimed that in due course "they" (the Middle Easterners) will thank "us" (the establishment) for "showing them the light." The result was discrimination against everything that was connected with traditionalism. The immigrants were required to cast away their folk stories and popular legends and beliefs. They were expected to exchange their predominantly traditional attitudes and behavior for a modern, Western approach, and, ipso facto, to change their self-definition, identity, and culture. Contrary to the prevailing liberal outlook, Israeli democracy intentionally endorsed (especially in its first decade) dispositions that aimed to define human good and human perfection to the exclusion of other dispositions. One culture was looked upon as more worthy than other cultures.[36] The Middle Easterners were not able to enjoy the freedom to arrive at their own ranking, their own conception of the good, because this could have meant that Israel might become just another Arab country.[37] To avoid this consequence, the establishment identified itself with a particular conception of the good life and strove to impose its values and ideals on society.[38]

Thus, the phrase *conception of the good* means a more or less determinate scheme of ends that the doer aspires to carry out for their own sake, as well as a scheme of attachments to other individuals and loyalties to groups and associations. This aspiration is legitimate in a liberal society as long as it is not based on coercion. A person molds a way of life by bringing reasons for acting or reacting in one manner, for making decisions, and for reaching some practical conclusions in different situations. A person is free to revise his or her conception of the good if he or she so wishes when deciding to change his or her way of life (say, upon joining Hare Krishna) or in the face of new circumstances. A person's conception of the good is based on rational calculations and judgments about his or her self, his or her short- and long-term goals, immediate surroundings, and society as a whole. These judgments may be subject to revision time and time again. A person's conception of the good also involves some normative assumptions with regard to these subjects. Consequently, it is internally complex and plural, encompassing both personal values and societal circumstances that may influence these values in one way or another. A pluralism of values presents us with a choice concerning the values we incorporate into our conception of the good, and this, in turn, means that some value ranking is required. Everyone can make his or her combination of what is regarded as the most valuable.

It has been argued that people do not suppose that one uniquely correct objective ranking of values exists, one optimal mix that prescribes how trade-offs among values should be made. Whatever partial rankings of values are objectively correct occurs within some range.[39] Likewise, people do not suppose there is a single way to resolve conflicts between moral or other values. Ergo, if no one objectively "correct" set of values exists to guide us, then everyone should be free to arrive at his or her ranking and conception of the good. Tolerance has to prevail so as to enable individuals to pursue their convictions as they see fit and proper, provided they do not harm others. Tolerance is advocated on the part of both citizens and governments in order to enable citizens to live according to their moral considerations and the values they hold most dear. On the part of the government, or the state, an additional policy of neutrality is called for.

PRINCIPLES OF NEUTRALITY: FOUR TYPES

Liberals who endorse neutrality argue that governments should employ neutral considerations between conceptions of the good. But disagreement occurs among liberals with regard to the specific sense and form of neutrality. What does neutrality mean in practical terms? The following approaches have been suggested.

Procedural neutrality

This is the Rawlsian approach that holds that social and political institutions should be regulated in accordance with considerations any reasonable person would accept as the basis of moral claims regardless of his or her conception of the good.[40]

Concrete neutrality

This postulates that the state is not to do anything intended to favor or promote any one comprehensive doctrine over another, to give greater assistance to those who pursue it, or to limit individual liberty in ways that advance one conception of the good.[41] This conception of neutrality is advocated by Dworkin in his essay "Liberalism."

Neutrality of aim

This holds that the role of government is to secure equal opportunity for citizens to further any conception of the good they freely affirm.[42]

Qualified neutrality of aim

This holds that government's role is to secure equal opportunity for citizens to pursue any *permissible* conceptions of the good. By permissible is meant conceptions that appreciate the accepted principles of justice.

Conceptually, the four types of neutrality share an emphasis on plurality. Pluralism is commonly conceived to be an essential element of democracy, an indispensable feature of having the potential for a good life. Methodologically, the idea of neutrality is placed within the broader concept of antiperfectionism. The implementation and promotion of conceptions of the good, though worthy in themselves, are not regarded as a legitimate reason for governmental action.[43] The fear of exploitation, of some form of coercion, leads to the advocacy of plurality and diversity. Therefore, government is not to act so as to affect some idea in a way that differs from its attitude toward other ideas. It ought to acknowledge that every person's interest is in acting according to his or her convictions; that everyone should enjoy the possibility of considering alternative conceptions. No single belief about moral issues and values should guide all; therefore, each has to enjoy autonomy and have the freedom to hold his or her ideals.

Raz sheds further light on antiperfectionism, saying that it comprises the "political neutrality principle" and the "exclusion of ideals" doctrine. Raz views the "political neutrality principle" as holding that government policies should seek to be neutral regarding ideals of the good. It commands the government to make sure that its actions do not help acceptable ideals more than unacceptable ones, and to see to it that its actions will not hinder the cause of false ideals more than they do that of true ones. As for the "exclusion of ideals" doctrine, it does not tell governments what to do; instead, it forbids them to act for designated reasons. The doctrine holds that the fact that some conceptions of the good are true or valid should never serve as justification for any political action. Neither should the fact that a conception of the good is false, invalid, unreasonable, or unsound be accepted as a reason for a political action.[44] The doctrine prescribes that governments refrain from using one conception of the good as a reason for state action. They are not to hold partisan (or nonpartisan) considerations about human perfection to foster social conditions.

Raz's distinction generates some confusion. None of the four types of neutrality is in accordance with the "political neutrality principle." Instead, they endorse the "exclusion of ideals doctrine." The confusion is not only one of terminology. Raz argues that Rawls endorses the "political neutrality principle," but Rawls does not aim his theory to be neutral in its effects. In "The Priority of Right," Rawls writes that even if political liberalism can be seen as neutral in procedure and in aim, it may still affirm the superiority of some forms of moral character and encourage some moral virtues.[45] Similarly, the "qualified neutrality of aim" and "concrete neutrality" do not deny that not all conceptions of the good will fare equally under liberal institutions. Liberal thinkers see the aim of a just governmental system as furthering liberty and egalitarian values.[46] They differ over the ways by which the common good may be promoted permissibly. If we take Rawls's and Dworkin's theories as examples, both hold that persons should be free to choose any conception of the good that does not violate the principles of justice, no matter how different it may be from the prevailing conceptions widely held by their community. Rawls endorses procedural neutrality in order to warrant rights to basic liberties. Dworkin's aim in advocating concrete neutrality is identical, but his theory provides a wider range of individual liberties than that of Rawls. Dworkin sees neutrality as derived from every person's right to equal concern and respect and insists on moral neutrality to the degree that equality requires it. As a result, Dworkin argues that the government should ensure citizens an initially equal distribution and that it should assist them to increase their welfare.47

Dworkin also advocates subsidies for the arts and for liberal education. This is because art and education make a general contribution to the community as a whole. Dworkin sees art as a mixed public good. He justifies some state subsidy on the grounds that we are all trustees for protecting the richness of our culture for future generations, and we have the duty, "out of simple justice," to leave that structure at least as rich as we found it.48 This argument regarding obligations we have to future generations is driven by a premise of official neutrality. It is a rather weak argument because if we are to leave *everything* that is existing today to our children and children's children, and we are not allowed to apply a value judgment in deciding *what* they should inherit, then we should leave them—among other things—famine, homelessness, and ecological disasters, as well as parks, elephants, and art. The claim that we should leave some objects for future generations must rest on the assumption that these objects are good. Let me consider Dworkin's view in more detail.

DWORKIN'S CONCRETE NEUTRALITY

In Dworkin's theory, individuals are conceived of as being entitled to the respect that enables them to determine the course of their lives as reasoning beings who are capable of deliberation and of taking responsibility for their conduct as well as for the kind of life they wish to lead. That is, respecting others entails viewing others as people who are realizing themselves as autonomous choosers. Such choosers examine their goals and, when needed, revise not only their ideas regarding their goals but also their views about the ways to seek them.49

Dworkin believes governments that take a stance and regard one conception as better, truer, or more valid than others may detract from other conceptions of the good by the very taking of a position and thus deny pluralism. While citizens can follow their conceptions and debate with others so as to add more weight to their own conception, governments must grant citizens equal concern and respect and should secure possibilities for them to pursue their chosen plans of life. The role of government is not to assign citizens one path over another, but it should help citizens to promote their welfare; as Dworkin postulates, "Politics should aim that people have better lives, on the whole, and to aim at this in some way that treats that highest-order interest as equally important for each person."[50]

Dworkin makes two valuable clarifications. He explains that our highest-order interest lies in having as good a life as possible, a life that has in it as much of what a life should have. Then he maintains that the saying that people's highest-order interest lies in having a good life is quite different from the claim that any particular person's life is *in fact* good or that the conception of the good life is worthy. So the highest-order interest in having a good life could not provide an argument that people's lives are equally good or equally valuable lives or anything of that sort. It claims that, for any particular person, that person's life is, at least for him or her, a *subject* of value rather than an object of value.[51] Thus to respect people as free human beings, so that each and every person could have a good life, entails that governments must not influence individuals (by propaganda, not to mention more radical measures) to choose one course of action over another. Governments must not exclude any idea but must allow for meaningful individual choice so that every person, whether considered alone or within a group, is able to adhere to the conception of the good and to the values that person appreciates most. To that effect Dworkin, among others, holds that neutrality is the policy to be adopted because no one should be allowed to dictate to anyone else what the convictions and priorities in the life of the other should be.[52]

A key difference arises between the Dworkinian and the Rawlsian arguments for neutrality. Dworkin advocates neutrality in order to respect the faculties of persons as citizens free to choose their conceptions of the good for themselves. Whereas Rawls's view is minimalist, holding that it would be impossible to decide on what is good for everyone, and therefore we have to reach a consensus on the most fundamental matters so as to secure social cooperation and remain neutral in regards to all other matters.[53] Still Rawls's theory, as Dworkin's and other advocates of neutrality, has the following assumptions in mind.

First, a plurality of conceptions of the good is valuable, for people like to be exposed to different views, to enjoy a variety of possibilities. The argument is that it is better to have many conceptions and sets of values than one unified, dominant conception that may constrict life projects and prescribe one pattern for all, thereby excluding the values and aspirations of minority groups within society. Having the ability to choose between alternatives contributes to the development of personal tastes, creative imagination, and independent attitude. In making choices we define for ourselves the level of conformity with our society in general, and with prevailing specific fashions in different spheres. The making of choices may prove to ourselves how capable we are to face dilemmas and find solutions. In addition, the choosing between conceptions of the good contributes to the development of free, autonomous thinking. It fosters the intellectual and moral development of the individual. When we are faced with different options, we have to deliberate, to make calculations, and to reason what may be the best way of life to pursue.

Second, diversity entails openness and more opportunities for living a valuable and richer life. Thus, Dworkin argues that in the case of free political speech, we may concede that each person has a valuable interest in developing independent political convictions, because that is an essential part of personality and because those political convictions will be more authentically that person's, the product of that personality, the more varied the opinions of others encountered will become. Dworkin maintains that we also may concede political activity in a community is made more vigorous by variety, even by the entry of wholly despicable points of view.[54]

These arguments show that the advocates of neutrality, in their striving to convince us of the necessity of the doctrine, are conveying the assumption that the decision regarding the proper policy is crucial because its consequences are absolute: all (pluralism, diversity, freedom, public consensus, noninterference, vitality, etc.) or nothing (in terms of good outcomes). If we do not adhere to neutrality, then we will be left with none of these virtues, but with their opposites. This picture is misleading. A more appropriate one would involve less extreme implications. It would view the conduct of policies on a continuous scale between the two extremes of strict perfectionism and complete neutrality. The policy to be adopted does not have to be either the one or the other. It could well take the middle ground, allowing plurality and diversity without resorting to complete neutrality and involving some form of perfectionism without resorting to coercion. For perfectionism does not necessarily imply governmental exercise of force, it does not impose the values and ideals of one or more segments of society on others, nor does it strive to ensure uniformity, as neutralists fear. On this issue my view comes close to that of Joseph Raz. I call his view the *promotional approach*.

RAZ'S PROMOTIONAL APPROACH AND BEYOND

Against the assumption that moral pluralism necessitates neutral political concern, Raz argues that the introduction of some perfectionist elements is unavoidable in order to achieve this aim. He observes that many of the arguments in favor of any one of the antiperfectionist doctrines can be used to support the other. Thus, neutrality implies that governments must stay silent with respect to any individual's or party's endeavor to promote their or anyone else's ideals of the good (as long as those ideals do not entail harm to others). Expressing his disagreement, Raz explains that a liberal state is obligated to create and secure the conditions of autonomy as well as to promote pluralism of many forms of the good. However, these two obligations may come into a conflict, for pluralism has an inherent tendency to generate intolerance.[55] Raz sees the right of the state and its duty as fighting against worthless and demeaning conceptions of the good. He asserts, "Perfectionist goals need not be pursued by the use of coercion. A government which subsidizes certain activities, rewards their pursuit, and advertises their availability encourages those activities without using coercion."[56]

By perfectionism, Raz means that government should support valuable ways of life, arguing that perfectionist ideals require public action for their viability. He offers a pluralistic account of perfectionism that aims to promote pluralism, liberty, and autonomy, connecting personal autonomy with the ideal of free and conscious self-creation. According to Raz, self-creation must proceed through choice among an adequate (to be distinguished from endless) range of options. It requires awareness on the part of the agent of his or her options and of the meaning of his or her choices as well as freedom from coercion and manipulation by others.

This pluralistic view of perfectionism ipso facto draws governments away from neutrality. They allocate funds in a way that is conducive to liberty and autonomy of citizens. Against Dworkin's and Rawls's position Raz holds that neutrality is an undesirable and a morally unattractive idea.

Some may try to downgrade the importance of the dispute by asserting that Raz's position can be said to be much broader than that of Rawls and Dworkin, since Raz suggests that government can properly use its powers to subsidize worthwhile pursuits for citizens, and also because the range of options allowed by Raz is narrower than the one advocated by Rawls and Dworkin. But Raz's version of perfectionism endeavors to ensure diversity and plurality, the same values appreciated by neutralists. Consequently, no real difference separates Dworkin and Rawls from Raz. All three philosophers aspire to promote the same values. They all regard pluralism and diversity as essential to the development of personal autonomy. Furthermore, Raz and Dworkin agree that a liberal state is committed to the idea of autonomy.[57]

On these points, no controversy exists between them. But this is not really the issue. The crux of the matter lies in Raz's assertion that in deciding how to promote the social conditions and, in turn, individual freedom, an appeal to perfectionist ideals is unavoidable. On the other side, Dworkin and Rawls object to the making of such an appeal. Moreover, Raz regards the autonomy principle itself as a perfectionist principle.[58] In this respect the dispute between Raz (and Haksar) on the one side, and Rawls and Dworkin on the other, revolves around the issue of whether it can be said that by endorsing autonomy we are taking a perfectionist stand or still remaining neutral. Raz thinks that the liberal adherence to autonomy is a perfectionist principle because it permits and even requires governments to create morally valuable opportunities and eliminate repugnant ones.

Raz's reasoning is valid. The basic characterization of liberalism lies in focusing on the individual, on viewing the individual as the core of attention. Communitarianism, fascism, and Leninism, among other perfectionist doctrines, consider groups as the center of attention. The three doctrines see the role of government as promoting designated conceptions of the good. They assume that these conceptions should be pursued because they are conducive to human excellence and perfection. In liberalism, too, is an underlying assumption regarding questions of the good that directs governmental activities. The liberal perspective is that citizens can realize their conceptions of the good only when possibilities are supplied for advancing their autonomy. Rawls, for example, views the parties in the original position as people who are concerned with protecting their autonomy. But we can plausibly suggest that people in the original position can prefer to choose nonautonomous lives.[59] Rawls, however, thinks of the normative ideal of personhood as one which is "implicitly affirmed" by our living tradition of modern liberal democratic judgments and practices.[60] At any rate, adding autonomy to the original position implies that a government *can* use some kinds of reasons to justify political action. It may (and it does) promote a set of conceptions of the good rather than others. Consider, for instance, the educational systems of most (if not all) liberal democracies. Governments do cultivate values and symbols and endeavor to make them part of their civic cultures. In order to foster people's personal autonomy, liberal democracies provide information for different ways of life (not necessarily for *and* against) and also strive to secure some conceptions, such as respect for others and not harming others. This perfectionism is not only about the *reasons* for policies, but also about the *content* of beliefs.

Hence, we can find no sense in any suggestion of total or absolute neutrality with respect to every possible conception or to each and any option that may ever be exercised by any citizen in society. Rawls and Dworkin agree with this statement. Other liberal neutralists (like Ackerman) remain unclear concerning this issue. Moreover, many liberals (Rawls and Dworkin included) neglected addressing the connections between the concepts of neutrality, perfectionism, and autonomy in an adequate manner. It seems that questions about these concepts are more complex than the structure liberals have suggested.

Dworkin has recently changed his views regarding these matters. In comments to me on this chapter he wrote that he now thinks neutrality should be regarded as a theorem rather than an axiom of liberalism. That means that the character of liberal neutrality should be fixed not a priori, but as the result of a variety of arguments and considerations about equality, distributive justice, and the conditions of philosophical autonomy. By taking this view, Dworkin adds nuances to what he had said in the past. For my part I think that the introduction of some element of perfectionism is unavoidable. Here we may recall that Rawls, while saying that perfectionism would be rejected for not defining a feasible basis of social justice, maintains in the same breath, "Eventually of course we would have to check whether the consequences of doing without a standard of perfection are acceptable."[61] We may also note that the fundamental liberal concept of tolerance in itself is incompatible with neutrality, at least insofar as the process of establishing a position is concerned. True, the underlying reason for tolerance, that is, respect for others, may be neutral; nevertheless tolerance in itself *cannot* be neutral in value, for it assumes the taking of a disapproving stand against the conduct or phenomenon in question. Tolerance is thus bound to be biased in favor of some opinions and beliefs that are of significance to the tolerator. If we reflect on the implicit assumption that neutrality alone is conducive to pluralism, we may argue that no *inherent* contradiction arises between nonneutral policies and pluralism. Conductors of policies may reject perfectionism and still regard refraining from taking *any* position as being no less harmful than perfectionism. The middle ground I advocate combines perfectionism with the Respect for Others Argument without distorting or vilifying ways of life that some people hold to be valuable. It acknowledges the importance of cultural considerations and justifies granting of subsidies for public commodities that are valuable to us. This middle ground allows governments to take a stance on practices so long as the decision is based on justifiable grounds. Now I have to explain what constitutes justifiable grounds.

My midground position is influenced, even dictated, by two arguments. I suggest that any liberal society is based on the idea of respect for others, in the sense of treating people as equals, and on the idea of not harming others in the sense that government should interfere against attempts made to harm others, either physically or psychologically. Accordingly, restrictions on liberty may be prescribed when clear threats of immediate violence are made against some individuals or groups and also when the expression in question is intended to inflict psychological offense, morally on a par with physical harm. I shall develop this argument fully in chapters 7 and 8. Dworkin (among others) may argue that this midground position is not significantly different from the position he now takes, but then clarity necessitates resorting to different terminology. I suggest that governments should adhere to *impartiality* rather than to neutrality. Here Alan Montefiore's example of a referee in a football game is relevant. According to Montefiore there is only one class of conflicts in which the referee can intervene qua referee, "namely the class of game-conflicts, the very possibility of which is created by and dependent on the constitutive rules of the game." Montefiore maintains that the role of the referee "is a neutral one in that its duties are so defined that any influence that the referee may exercise on any footballing conflict is to be determined solely by factors for which provision is made within the rules of the institution and which could, in principle, count for or against any conflicting party."[62]

If we follow this example, when a referee allows a penalty kick against side A, the referee is obviously in one sense helping B. Yet we cannot accuse him or her of lack of neutrality, for the referee is applying the rules impartially, meaning that he or she is awarding penalty kicks only where appropriate fouls are committed, whether by side A or side B. Impartiality requires that referees not show more concern for one side (for which they may feel some affection, whether genuine or the result of antipathy for the other side) than for another. The impartial agent is a person whose judgment and reasoning are not prejudiced by selfish, partisan interests or by personal feelings. If we take a Rawlsian position we may say that an impartial judgment is rendered in accordance with the principles chosen in the original position. An impartial agent forms judgments according to these principles without bias or prejudice. The agent's impartial exposition will aim not to distort any of the rival views, insofar as they permit clear exposition.

Accordingly, a government has to play the role of umpire both in the sense of applying just considerations when reviewing different conceptions and also in trying to reconcile conflicting interests, trends, and claims. This is a delicate task that demands integrity as well as impartiality: to refrain from identifying with one group rather than with the other,[63] not to exploit its role for self-advantage, bearing in mind when making decisions the relevant considerations and demands which concern society as a whole and not only one or some fractions of it.

Governments should not reject out of hand considerations deemed to be relevant and cling to neutrality when this policy is thought to contradict basic values and rules. There must be rules, for otherwise there can be no game. This reasoning, which insists on the need for keeping the rules, can be applied to a football game as much as to democracy:[64] fundamental values and rules should bind everyone. These are not to harm others and to respect others. If we accept the validity of this assertion, then we *cannot* be neutral with regard to conduct that falls within

the parameter of harming others; when the dangers to democracy, to our
fellow citizens, to the moral basis of society, to values we hold dear, may
be too grave. I develop this argument in the following chapters. Here I
wish to reflect on a different set of arguments that are sometimes mentioned (not necessarily by antiperfectionists) in favor of noninterference.
These arguments evolve from the school of moral relativism. They are
held to be relevant because they are mentioned occasionally in support of
neutrality on the part of the government (or state), and in support of
tolerance on the part of the government and the citizens, so as to enable
individuals to pursue their conceptions of the good.

TWO VARIANTS OF RELATIVISM

The first variant of relativism, which may be called *cultural relativism,*
adopts the argument that a plurality of conceptions of the good is valuable, conceiving this argument within a cultural context. This variant of
relativism emphasizes pluralism and diversity, while postulating that moral
principles are relative to cultures. It urges that cultural differences differentiate one conception of the good from another, and a liberal democratic state has to tolerate these differences. It should not impose the
dominant values and culture on those who differ from that culture. This
argument presupposes that a liberal democratic society (or any society)
does not necessarily consist of one homogeneous culture. It assumes that
the decision about how to lead our lives may ultimately be left to ourselves; nevertheless, this decision is always a matter of selecting from
available options determined by the cultural context. Different cultural
contexts dictate different norms and values according to a particular
vision of morality. One section of society (A) may have codes of morality
that the other sections (not A) may regard as immoral but, this notwithstanding, not-A sections should not try to cause A to adopt their own
moral codes, compelling A to give up its convictions. For example, the
Eskimo tradition of abandoning the elderly in the snow is a cultural norm
that is part of their conception of the good. Moral relativists contend that
we may hold a different view of that norm, but we cannot say that our
conception of the good is better or more valid than the Eskimo's, nor
should we force the Eskimos to adopt our conception. Each person has to
be able to choose and pursue his or her conception of the good in the
light of his or her cultural experience, to decide what that person con-

siders to be the valuable options according to the cultural norms and values he or she appreciates.

Unclear, however, is whether cultural pluralism entails moral relativism, that is, whether recognition of the importance of cultural association implies that we should allow any cultural norm, whatever it may be. We may accept that a plurality of cultures can exist within a liberal democratic society; but what, then, characterizes the society as liberal? Common basis establishes a forum within which members of cultural communities are able to exercise their specific norms. Some moral codes constitute a public culture shared by all members of society, despite their cultural differences. What if some cultural norms challenge the fundamental moral codes that underlie liberalism? Relativism disregards this possible tension as it assumes that each culture is to be judged according to its criteria, and we cannot interfere in the business of the other because we cannot really insist that our norms should be adopted by members of other cultures. We can be a judge with regard to our culture, but not where other cultures are concerned. Noninterference in cultural norms is prescribed regardless of the possible need for reconciliation between norms, because no one is capable of being in a position to carry out such a project. Relativism considers this issue as lying beyond the confines of ethics.

The second variant of relativism, which is stronger than the first, urges that *no one is in a position to know* that one conception is as good as the other. According to this variant, it is impossible to show that one conception is more worthwhile or precious than any other, that one conception is intrinsically more valuable than others or even is as valuable as the others. No given set of values or terms exists to enable us to determine that one conception is better or more valuable than the rest. Consequently, every individual may hold a set of values in the order he or she wishes and act accordingly. The further assumption is that it is impossible to rank conceptions in some form or another, since any attempt at their elucidation involves the making of normative judgments. Any criteria that we may use to evaluate normative judgments are bound to be influenced by our conception of the good, which itself involves normative judgments. Therefore, how can we say that one set of normative judgments is better than the other? Likewise, it is impossible to say that the morality of one is more or less true than the other. In a similar fashion to the Truth Principle (to be discussed in chapter 6), it is argued that no moral values can be logically ordered without bias. We can never know which values are true, or whether some values are better or truer than others, because no moral grounds are shared by all.

This variant of moral relativism inevitably leads us to conclude that any moral debate is pointless. We should accept the fact that we cannot judge between moral codes and, therefore, each of the moral codes is equally valid and has to be allowed. Relativism defeats itself by claiming that it is true, because relativism is in no position to claim truth. Moreover, it is impossible to reconcile between values because this task necessarily involves the ranking of conceptions to decide how this process is to be effected. In addition, relativism rejects the introduction of constraints, and so it runs the risk of defeating moral principles with immoral norms that others hold dear. Consequently relativism could defeat morality. If we are not in a position to know whether or not, for instance, Pol Potism is as good as liberalism, then we should never interfere with the dissemination and implementation of either idea because we are not able to determine that one is more valuable or more just than the other. The implications of moral relativism for our context may make the introduction of confines for tolerance an impossible task, while at the same time it implies that tolerance has to make way when intolerant norms prevail because nothing allows us to say that it is more moral than intolerance. Hence the prescribed policy is impotence. Relativism leads to apathy when claiming that the discussion about conceptions and beliefs should be excluded from ethical debates. If we believe that democracy should allow each person to follow his or her inclinations and beliefs without interference, then we should permit every behavior. The first variant of relativism qualifies the argument by emphasizing the value of cultural justifications and norms. This could imply that although a conduct may be outlawed in society, members of a minority may be required by their culture to follow this conduct. Then culture may be said to supply enough reason to override law.

We should examine these variants of relativism in order to divorce them from the concept of antiperfectionism. All the neutralists mentioned do not claim that neutral political concern has to be employed because we do not know whether all conceptions of the good are as good as the others. It is acknowledged that establishing a position with regard to different beliefs is a matter of degree, and clearly some conceptions may appear more appealing, moral, or valuable than others. The egalitarian argument of Rawls and Dworkin assumes that each and every conception does matter (at least to its holders), and that it matters equally. But it does not assert that we are in no position to say that one is better than another. Moreover, as Dworkin exemplifies,[65] neutrality does not imply impotence. A liberal government should regulate conditions and distribute resources in a fair manner to enable citizens to pursue their different conceptions. It should also promote welfarism and enrich the citizens' lives.

At this point we are confronted with the inevitable question of whether neutralists assume—in the name of liberty, tolerance, and pluralism— that *all* conceptions of the good should be open as options to be pursued in a liberal democratic society. Bearing in mind that neutrality proscribes any attempts on behalf of governments to force others to lead lives in which they do not believe, should it prescribe that governments remain silent in the face of such phenomena as female circumcision, or preventing abortions even when there is a danger to the mother's life? The following discussion is concerned with the neglected issue of cultural pluralism. My focus is on the question of whether every norm, which any culture appreciates or considers to be of value, should exist within the framework of a liberal society.

Chapter 4

The Respect for Others Argument and Cultural Norms

The Dilemma

Reflecting on the dilemma of whether all conceptions may have a place in liberal democracies, Rawls concedes that no society can include within itself all forms of life. He argues that in a democratic culture a workable conception of political justice must allow for a diversity of doctrines and the plurality of conflicting, indeed, incommensurable, conceptions of the meaning, value, and purpose of human life affirmed by members of existing democratic societies.[1] But given the profound differences in beliefs and conceptions of the good, we must recognize that, just as on questions of religious and moral doctrine, public agreement on the basic questions of philosophy cannot be obtained without the state's infringement on basic liberties.[2] Rawls explains that conceptions that directly conflict with the principles of justice or that wish to control the machinery of state and practices so as to coerce the citizenry by employing effective intolerance should be excluded. The assumption is that these principles of justice underlie any conception of the good. Rawls further asserts that if a conception of the good is unable to endure and gain adherents under institutions of equal freedom and mutual toleration, we must question whether it is a viable conception of the good and whether its passing is to be regretted.[3] He writes there is no social world that does

not exclude some ways of life that realize in special ways some fundamental values: "By virtue of its culture and institutions, any society will
prove uncongenial to some ways of life. But these social necessities are
not to be mistaken for arbitrary bias or for injustice."[4]

To argue that some conceptions of the good may have no place requires a recognition that *there are* some values that underlie a liberal
society, which bring members of society to view some other conceptions
as uncongenial. Rawls (and also Berlin) implies some norms and moral
codes must be shared by members of the community despite their cultural differences. This is not to say that one dominant culture, or one
dominant conception of the good exists; but that some basic norms
should be safeguarded in order to make the working of a liberal democratic system possible and to ensure its survival. These accepted norms,
by virtue of their existence, enable each individual and group to pursue
their conceptions of the good, as long as convictions are not contradictory to them. These norms set limitations on the range of values that
society can respect. The most basic norms democracy has to secure are,
in my opinion, respecting others as human beings (under the Respect for
Others Argument) and not inflicting harm upon others, as will be formulated in chapter 7 under the Harm and the Offense Principles. Upholding
these two principles safeguards the rights of those who might find themselves in a disadvantageous position in society, such as women; ethnic,
religious, national, and cultural minorities; and homosexuals.

Rawls believes that the public culture of democracy is obligated to
pursue forms of social cooperation that can be achieved on a basis of
mutual respect. This cooperation involves the acceptance of common
procedures to regulate political conduct. Citizens should be accorded
equal respect in their pursuit of their idea of the good. Rawls's concept of
justice is independent from and prior to the concept of goodness in that
its principles limit the conceptions of the good that are permissible. His
ideal polity would not be congenial toward those who believe that their
personal conception of the good involves enforcing others to abide by it.
It would exclude some beliefs, such as those which entail coercion of
others, causing harm to others, or deriving profit at the expense of others.
The justification for excluding controversial beliefs from the original
position lies in the social role of justice, which is to enable individuals to
make mutually acceptable to one another their shared institutions and
basic arrangements. This justification is accompanied by an agreement

on ways of reasoning and rules for weighing evidence that govern the applications of the claims of justice. Mutual respect would enable social cooperation between individuals who affirm fundamentally different conceptions of the good. Thus, for instance, Rawls does not exclude religious groups with strong beliefs who may demand strict conformity and allegiance from their members, but he could not endorse the formation of a theocratic state, for some people lack such intensity of religious belief.[5]

Rawls's theory of justice as fairness is a moral conception that provides us with an account of the cooperative virtues suitable for a political doctrine in view of the conditions and requirements of a constitutional regime. It is a theory, in his view, of an "overlapping consensus" between different groups and individuals with divergent and even conflicting doctrines and life-styles as to the fair procedures for making political demands in a democratic society, where mutual toleration and fairness must be the norm. By an "overlapping consensus" Rawls means a consensus that is affirmed by the opposing religious, philosophical, and moral doctrines likely to thrive over generations in a more or less just constitutional democracy, where the criterion of justice is that political conception itself. Such a consensus, Rawls alleges, is moral both in its object and grounds and so is distinct from a consensus founded solely on self- or group interest. He acknowledges that such a consensus is not always possible. Indeed, we have little empirical reason to believe that all of the diverse conceptions of the good embraced by people provide the overlapping consensus of which Rawls speaks.[6] Nevertheless, Rawls thinks that through this idea we may be able to show how, despite a diversity of doctrines, convergence on a political conception of justice may be achieved and social unity sustained in a long-term equilibrium, that is, over time from one generation to the next. We may add that the consolidation of any long-lasting consensus inevitably necessitates some form of coercion.

Thus, an acceptance of a concept of justice can be achieved in spite of differences, but some conceptions may have no place within a well-ordered society. Notwithstanding Rawls's recognition that culture and institutions may cause people to reject some convictions, and that the cultural context of choice is important in deciding ways of life, Rawls does not explicitly state that culture is a primary good.[7] He does not single out culture as a necessary social condition to enable people to pursue their determinate conceptions of the good life and to develop and exercise their moral power. However, a close analysis of Rawls's argument for liberty as a primary good could imply that it is also an argument for cultural membership as a primary good. Rawls does not make this argument clear because his model of the nation-state is quite simplified, with the political community characterized as culturally homogenous. Dworkin and Raz seem to have the same simplified view.

A more realistic picture of the state as we know it consists of a plurality of cultures whose freedoms ought to be secured by the liberal state. Cultural membership is significant in pursuing our essential interest in leading a good life; therefore, taking account of that membership is an important part of assuring equal consideration for the interests of each member of the community.[8] If we place this line of argument within the context of the Rawlsian original position, we may say that behind a veil of ignorance, among the facts of which people are aware, is cultural membership. People in the original position know that they are representatives of cultural communities, but they do not know to which culture they belong. Neither do they know whether the contingencies of culture are to their advantage or to their disadvantage. Hence they would accept that tolerance should prevail so as to enable each and every one to be part of their cultural association. They would reject any sort of political and religious fundamentalism that urged that the best community is one in which only some preferred practices are allowed. Granting cultural membership the status of primary good will not provide fundamentalists with claims to further their aims, for, as Will Kymlicka explains, so long as every person has a share of the resources and the freedom to lead a chosen life within that person's cultural community, then the primary good of cultural membership is properly recognized: "Promotion of fundamentalist politics in these circumstances, far from appealing to the primary good of cultural membership, conflicts with it, since it undermines the very reason we had for being concerned with cultural membership—that it allows for meaningful individual choice."[9]

Kymlicka's object is to identify a defensible liberal conception of minority rights. He thinks that any theory that does not accord substantial civil rights to the members of minority cultures is seriously deficient from a liberal point of view. Kymlicka also believes that loss of cultural membership is a profound harm that reduces one's very ability to make meaningful choices. Our capacity to form and revise a conception of the good is intimately tied to our cultural membership, since the context of individual choice is the range of options passed on to us by our language and culture. Deciding how to lead our lives is, in the first instance, a matter of exploring the possibilities made available by our culture. Kymlicka maintains that some minority cultures need protection from the economic or political decisions of the majority culture if they are to provide this context for their members.[10]

Consider, then, the example of Orthodox Jewish sects that do not allow the study of biology in their schools. They do not welcome Darwin's theory of the genealogy of humanity. As long as they keep the restriction of this study to their schools we may say, by implication, that an outsider has no right to interfere. But when they try to force their truth on people outside their community, then we have a case for interference by the state. The reason for respecting the other's beliefs, as well as minority rights, is to enable "meaningful individual choice" so that every person, whether considered alone or within a group, can exercise liberties in the way he or she wishes. Thus, allowing religious coercion may be considered as giving the coercer "meaningful individual choice," but it comes at the expense of the right of the coerced to seek "meaningful individual choice." Therefore, the requirement of reciprocity in according due weight and respect to the other's choice making must be safeguarded as necessary. This is a derivative from our Respect for Others Argument, which recognizes that people have different conceptions of what constitutes a worthwhile life and at the same time guides us to contemplate restriction on toleration at the point where respect ceases.

So we may distinguish between intragroup relationships (a group imposing its views on its own members) and intergroup relationships (one group imposing its views on another group).[11] In the instance cited above I have tried to establish that a minority group has no claim to coerce the entire society into following its conception of the good and abiding by its cultural norms. In the event that a cultural minority makes such an attempt, the majority has to open further channels of communication and resolve the situation by peaceful means. And when these means fail, then it should resort to authoritative means to draw the boundaries and fight against coercion.

Now we face another difficult, related question that concerns intergroup relationships. The question is whether the dominant culture has any right to interfere with the business of the cultural minority, if one or more of their practices or norms cause some harm to members of that minority culture.

Kymlicka objects to the interference of one culture in the business of the other, arguing that people are bound to their cultural community, and that cultural structure is crucial not just to the pursuit of our chosen ends and convictions, but also to our capability of pursuing them efficiently. He supports his arguments with historical evidence that shows members of one culture reluctantly relinquish their cultural associations, even in the face of negative costs of membership. The affront minority groups feel when attempts are made to force them into another culture is grounded in the perception of real harm.[12] This argument objects to forcefully taking members of one culture and transferring them to another, or of assimilating one culture by forcing its members to accept another. I have no disagreement with either of these objections. Individual judgments cannot be divorced from the social context in which they are made, especially from their cultural background (see chapter 1). This, however, is not the issue I am addressing here. Instead, the question is whether liberal democracy should tolerate every norm that members of a cultural community possess, even if this entails that rights of some members of that cultural community are being curtailed. Do cultural norms hold enough weight to allow things that are conceived as having no place in a liberal community? May culture supply reasons for the toleration of behavior that is regarded as unjust or unacceptable when evinced by other members of society who are not members of the considered culture?

These questions involve conflicting considerations. Respecting one culture could entail allowing members of that culture to show disrespect to some of its members.[13] Suppose, for instance, that a cultural minority exhibits illiberal consensus with regard to women's role in society. Thus it limits the right of women to study at universities and to hold public offices. With Kymlicka I argue that if women who dislike this restriction can easily leave the community and enter the larger society, and if the minority group has some historical claim to local self-government, then this may mean that it would be wrong for us to coercively interfere and prohibit that practice.[14] However, the fact that intervention would be wrong does not mean that the practice in question is morally legitimate. On the contrary, from a liberal perspective the practice is unjust. But we do not have legitimate grounds to enforce our moral upon the group.

Let me push the issue further. The example considers the introduction of limitations by one sector of a cultural minority on the autonomy of another sector within that same minority. But should a liberal society tolerate *all* practices and norms so as to allow all members of society to follow their inclinations and beliefs without interference? My concern is now with two specific matters in which autonomy is curtailed in a irreversible way by the infliction of bodily damage, and cultural norms justify the taking of a person's life. If we believe that there is never a case for majority interference in the business of minorities, then we should tolerate things such as suttee, female infanticide, or female circumcision. Do these norms have a place in a liberal society?

A person (Z) may say that cultural groups who practice the above norms do not think they are disrespectful of their women; they believe they are acting appropriately for the nature and condition of women. Furthermore, the women of those cultures accept those norms as part of their cultural structure; through those norms they define themselves and their place in the world, making sense of their lives. Another person (X) may say that notwithstanding people's willingness, even desire, to belong to their culture, some may be of the opinion that norms of the kind mentioned should be excluded; that those norms had lost their validity in a liberal society. Individuals want to belong to their culture, but they do not necessarily accept all norms as valid within the society in which they now live.

A third person (Y) may accept X's reasoning but only in part. Y may distinguish between two situations. The first situation is one in which individuals immigrate to a liberal country, in which case X's reasoning is conceived to be valid. Thus, for instance, immigrants from Asia and Africa who wish to lead their lives in England and France are required to forego the norm that obliges some of them to circumcise their women or to burn their widows. This is because they themselves decided to live within the liberal framework. The situation is different when a liberal state expands and colonializes other communities who find themselves under a liberal sovereignty. This is the case of the Eskimo community in Alaska and of the Indians in North America who found themselves under American colonial rule. This is also the case of the Bedouins who found themselves, not of their own free will, under Israeli rule. Y would say that in those cases the liberal state should not add the sin of paternalism to the evils of expansion and colonialism. Therefore, no justification exists to forbid cultural norms such as deserting elderly people in the icy wasteland or circumcising female Bedouin children. In other words, Y argues that the question is one of choice and time precedence. We should allow the prohibition of cultural norms when individuals voluntarily immigrate to a liberal state. But we should not bar cultural norms, however distasteful and harmful we may see them, in the case where cultural minorities lived their life peacefully and the liberal state expanded and forced itself upon them.

Yet Y's arguments avoid the fundamental question. For the issue is one of principle, not a contingent question dependent on time precedence or, as Z argues, on the preferences of some members of a culture with regard to their tradition. I agree that the argument from paternalism contains some force, but it is not powerful enough to override considerations that concern the very existence of human life. Fundamentally, the question is whether norms of the kind mentioned, which deny basic rights that everyone is supposed to respect, have a place in a liberal democratic society. It may be true that to forbid those cultural norms is certainly to interfere with the possibility of making, to use Kymlicka's terminology, "meaningful individual choice"; thus, for instance, burning a man's widow may be considered giving him "meaningful individual choice." But, by the same token, this act abridges the woman's right to seek meaningful choice for herself, and it contradicts the two basic liberal norms that we have underlined: it violates the requirement of not harming others and that of *mutual* respect for others as enunciated by the Respect for Others Argument. Likewise, female circumcision involves inflicting physical harm, denying women the ability of full enjoyment of clitoral stimulation and orgasm, generating frustration that influences not only their sex lives but also their entire well-being as autonomous, imaginative human beings. It is argued (not only by feminists) that female circumcision denies the individual the ability of being a woman, of being a person.[15]

Let us press this argument one step further. Nozick comprehends that we individually and collectively can illuminate our understanding of what is good and moral by allowing individuals to lead their lives as long as their way of life includes reflection on and discussion of their tentative notions of value and of the best life.[16] Nozick's underlying assumption is that common ground for discussion exists, but this may not always be the case. We can argue that with some cultural minorities not even enough common ground exists for liberals to conduct a discussion. No common ground is available because their conception of the good, their cultural and political norms, their moral codes, are different to such an extent that the gap between that culture and liberalism becomes unbridgeable. Any form of discussion is an impossible task. If we recall our discussion on weak forms of manifest tolerance, we may refuse to debate with our opponent because we do not think that any sort of agreement or compromise can be reached. The only possible outcome of such a debate would be legitimization of the opponent, and this may conflict with our intentions (see chapter 2, "Latent and Manifest Tolerance"). Reflect, then, on the question whether a liberal democratic society should tolerate not only specific norms, but intolerant minority cultures as such. In considering this question I avail myself of Rawls's analysis of toleration of the intolerant, as presented in his *Theory of Justice*.

Not Tolerating the Intolerant: A Radical View

Toleration is conceived in the Rawlsian theory as part of justice. Accordingly, the principles of justice give reasons for tolerance. This, we may say, is the rule. The question is what should be society's attitude toward the intolerant. In his discussion on whether to tolerate the intolerant, Rawls argues that if an intolerant sect appears (Rawls does not say how) in a well-ordered society, the others should keep in mind the inherent stability of their institutions. The liberties of the intolerant may persuade them to a belief in freedom. Rawls explains that this persuasion works on the psychological principle that those whose liberties are protected by, and who benefit from, a just constitution will, other things being equal, acquire an allegiance to it over a period of time. He maintains, "So even if an intolerant sect should arise, provided that it is not so strong initially that it can impose its will straightaway, or does not grow so rapidly that the psychological principle has no time to take hold, it will tend to lose its intolerance and accept liberty of conscience."[17]

Rawls does not address the questions of who determines whether that group is "not so strong" and according to what criteria this decision is being made. Instead, he explains that the intolerant person loses intolerance because of the stability of just institutions, for stability means that when tendencies toward injustice arise, other forces will be called into play that work to preserve the justice of the whole arrangement. Thus, Rawls's underlying assumption is that society's benefit is to encounter such a phenomenon because it would strengthen the beliefs of its members in the face of the threat. But, Rawls warns, we should take into account that the extent of the threat not be too strong. Hence, tolerance should take place as long as it is safe for it to win over the threat and not in all events. If the threat seems serious, then justification for intolerance may be in order.

Rawls adds that the intolerant sect may be growing strong so fast that the forces seeking stability are unable to convert it into liberty. In such a situation, just institutions, or democracy, must be held prior to philosophy: "This situation presents a practical dilemma which philosophy alone cannot resolve."[18] In other words, then practical considerations of self-defense and survival take precedence, and these considerations may regard toleration as an inappropriate policy. Tolerance is derived from consideration for others, but it does not exclude consideration for ourselves. Adherence to a policy of tolerance does not imply that we have to give up our most fundamental interest of survival. Rawls postulates a second requirement, following the same line of reasoning, that circumstances too should be taken into account. He maintains that whether the liberty of the intolerant should be limited to preserve freedom under a just constitution depends on the circumstances. Change of circumstances may prescribe different attitudes to the same phenomenon: "Knowing the inherent stability of a just constitution, members of a well-ordered society have the confidence to limit the freedom of the intolerant only in the special cases when it is necessary for preserving equal liberty itself."[19]

Rawls concludes that the freedom of the intolerant should be restricted only when the tolerant sincerely and with reason believe that their security and that of the institutions of liberty are in danger. Someone who wishes to restrict tolerance should bring substantive overriding considerations to justify this action: the onus of justification is always placed on those who wish to exercise the restriction. The leading guideline must always be maintained, that is, to establish a just constitution with the liberties of equal citizenship.

Two salient criticisms may be suggested against these arguments. The first adheres to the Rawlsian line of practical reasoning that is contingent on the magnitude of the threat. Rawls fails to consider the intentions of the intolerant and whether these are strong enough to persuade the intolerant to manifest them in some way. Rawls does not acknowledge that it is not only a question of how strong the intolerant are and what are the circumstances, but also to what extent the intolerant are motivated to exercise some form of coercion. An intense, well-organized group, with strong motivation to exhibit intolerance, although it may not pose a threat to democracy, could nevertheless endanger their disliked target group. While the intolerant group may not be strong enough to impose its will, the conviction and determination of its members may plausibly be strong enough to resist the forces of liberty. Instead of convincing the intolerant to believe in freedom, the intolerant group may spread anti-democratic ideas and fight its way to gain further power through the democratic means that are open to its members.

The second criticism I wish to offer is that Rawls simply misses the point. Instead of discussing the ethical question of the constraints of tolerance, he shifts the discussion to the practical consideration of the magnitude of the threat. But this is a matter of moral principle, rather than an argument contingent on the level of the danger. The fundamental question is not practical, but ethical. Rawls pursues a line of argument that avoids the philosophical issue that is the essence of the question of what we may consider as constraints on tolerance and liberty. In a way similar to Scanlon's theory on freedom of expression,[20] he does not explain from an ethical perspective why we should withhold tolerance. Like Scanlon, Rawls prefers to concentrate on considerations of circum-stances and the extent of the threat. His contention is that tolerance has to prevail when no real danger arises that the consequences will be harmful: we should adhere to tolerance only if it is likely to win over the threat. For reasons of expedience, these considerations will be grouped under the heading *the Rawlsian Principle*. I will refer to this principle in part 2 as I explore this subject further, especially in discussing the clear and present danger test and its modifications as they find expression in the rulings of the Israeli High Court of Justice. Here, however, let us reflect on what we may call an extreme case, where the issue is not whether democracy is to tolerate an intolerant minority, nor interfere with its cultural norms, but more important, whether democracy should allow entry to a minority group, whose culture is known to conflict with liberalism. I assume that if we can establish that sufficient grounds exist in exceptional cases to deny entry to such a group, then democracy is not to tolerate similar extreme groups that are already present in society who strive to bring the end of democracy in its liberal form. Note that the discussion is not of tolerating the advocacy of opinions but of tolerating actions (or *incitement* to actions) aiming to bring about antidemocratic, illiberal consequences.

Consider then the question whether a liberal democratic society can exclude a minority culture whose members intend to immigrate to it on the grounds that its values are incompatible with the liberal values. In such a case, should all paths to pursuing life projects still be left open, or should some be closed to start with, even before entering a liberal society?

Suppose that a large group of Huns, who somehow survived, wishes to enter England. One person (Z) may argue that a liberal state cannot deny entrance merely on the basis of beliefs and that the Huns may establish their cultural community within the liberal society. If we deny them entry, we forgo the requirements of respecting others and respecting the ideas of others and we defeat cultural pluralism.[21] Another person (X) does not agree. X argues that the entire culture of the Huns is incompatible with and contradictory to the basic norms and moral codes that establish a state as a liberal democracy. X contends that we ought to limit immigration on the grounds of preserving human values and the rights of the community. X further maintains that the very nature of the Huns makes them resort to violence. The use of and incitement to violence has an integral role in what they may call "our Hunnish conception of the good," on which they base their culture and their entire way of life. The intolerant sect is so strong initially that the democratic forces making for stability cannot convert it to liberty. Consequently, the government may refuse them admission on the grounds that they are morally incapable of being tolerant, since their culture lacks a concept of tolerance and respect for others, and their ideas are hostile to the values of the liberal state, as well as because they are likely to have a negative impact on the values regarding the society's common good.[22] As Rawls argues, a limit exists to the extent that a liberal democracy can accommodate and allow all convictions and beliefs.

A counterargument can be made that the Huns may be willing to change their views and internalize the liberal norms through the socialization process. They may willingly relinquish their self-identification as Huns and characterize themselves instead as English. Even in such a case, X would regard this effort with suspicion, because X does not believe they are really capable of changing their entire moral view and adapting to a culture that is so different from theirs. At most they would be willing to make tactical compromises (the notion of tactical compromise was explained in chapter 2, "Principled and Tactical Compromise"), without changing their aims and priorities. Another person, Y, may take the middle ground and be less suspicious to the point of conceding that, in such a case, if they are sincerely willing to give up their Hunnish convictions, they may be admitted. Following Rawls, Y would say that the psychological effects of such an encounter would be of benefit for democracy, and that, given the Huns' willingness to give up their intolerant convictions and accept the prevailing norms, this is a risk worth taking. Even if the birth pangs were to be painful, the other members of the community would be helped to strengthen their beliefs. This combination of reasons makes, in Y's view, a strong case for tolerance. But if the Huns intend to keep their ideas, then democracy has no reason to allow them entry: a tolerant society ought not to supply conditions for Hunnish values to prosper, allowing them to undermine the liberal moral codes.

The example of the Huns is an extreme case, and its conclusions may be applied only to extremely radical groups. Democracy can deny entry to groups on the grounds of their holding a different set of basic beliefs only when their culture or their conception of the good is fundamentally different from the liberal culture (which may consist of subcultures, though all of its sects accept some basic liberal principles) to the extent where discussion and communication between the two cultures becomes impossible and the making of some common grounds implausible (cf. chapter 2). Toleration is not derived from practical necessities or reasons of state. Hence, whatever interest individuals may have in cultural membership, it is subordinated to their interest in securing what Rawls calls "the liberties of equal citizenship." The same applies to members of intolerant religious groups who may wish to coerce others to adopt their religion. Moral and religious freedoms follow from the principle of equal liberty, and, assuming the priority of this principle, the only grounds for denying equal liberties is to avoid an even greater injustice, an even greater loss of liberty.[23] Individual liberty is valuable to such an extent that in order to secure an extensive system of overall liberties for everyone, we may restrict a basic liberty of some sects. The principles of respect for others and not harming others provide grounds for and set limits to liberty and tolerance. Otherwise democracy may not be able to triumph over its own catch: the very principles that underlie democracy may bring about its end.

Taking a more realistic example, this could be the case if a considerable number of fascists or neo-Nazis were to organize elsewhere in Europe and then intend to take advantage of their status as European Community citizens and immigrate to England with the aim, known to the authorities, of leading the National Front to new prosperity. Here too we could argue that the nature of fascist movements makes them resort to violence. The use of and incitement to violence plays an integral role in their activities, on which they base their political platform and ideology.[24] Because of the size of their group, the power of the fascists would be strong enough to pose a real threat to democracy and to the minorities to which they object. United as a group under a fascist emblem, they would not be lacking in determination to fight for their convictions. England would be justified in denying entrance to that group on the grounds that the fascist convictions lack a concept of tolerance and respect for others; because fascist ideas stand in striking opposition to the liberal culture of this country; because fascism is hostile to human rights and to the fundamental values that underlie a liberal state. The business of government is to protect and foster the interests of the public, and allowing entry to this group does not coincide with these aims. Democracy ought to defend itself against threats, even if sometimes the measures include steps that exclude members of intolerant groups altogether from a democratic state.[25] As F. A. Hayek asserts, morals must be restraints on complete freedom, and the principle of tolerance does not require us to tolerate a wholly different system of morals within our community.[26] Thus, we have a strong case for exclusion where fascists are concerned because their ideas are incompatible with a commitment to human dignity and respect for others, and because they are likely to resort to violence to achieve their political aims.

The purpose of this discussion was to suggest that liberal democracy may be intolerant toward the intolerant; liberal democracy can interfere to curtail some cultural norms (like female circumcision) that undermine its basic principles; and democracy may prevent cultural groups from entering society not only because enough reason exists to believe that their strength is intimidating to the extent of confronting democracy with a substantial danger, but, more fundamentally, because the conception they regard as a conception of the good essentially conflicts with basic liberal democratic norms. In such circumstances the entire society may be regarded as the target group that is threatened. While every idea possesses a claim to equal validity within a democratic society, considerations of context and intentions must be taken into account, and they may require the introduction of constraints.

These arguments bring us to the question whether the intolerant has any right to complain. For when such far-reaching restrictions on freedom are introduced, then the groups in question may complain that something of value is denied them when they cannot exercise their liberties, their freedom of conscience is curtailed, something of value is denied society, and they are discriminated against. The claim of discrimination is raised by those who advocate unequal treatment of groups in their struggle to exercise their liberty so as to implement their discriminatory ideas. Let us now consider these complaints.

As to the first argument, something of value is lost whenever we prevent a person from pursuing convictions wherever that person may wish to do so and whatever these convictions may be. To a person who enjoys inflicting pain upon others, something of what *that* person considers valuable is denied when we restrict the person's acts. To sadists, torturing others is of value. Cruelty has a value for them and plays a part in *their* conception of the good. When we decide not to tolerate sadistic acts, sadists are unfree to do what they wish. Their liberty is diminished. We can say that a loss of value occurs whenever an agent's freedom is curtailed; at least, a loss occurs of what that person (wrongly) values. But is the diminishing of the sadist's liberty a bad thing? Fundamentally, the issue is whether acts of this sort should be allowed a place in a liberal society. If allowed, then torture and cruelty are to be included among the social values of a liberal society, among the liberal framework that encompasses conceptions of good.

Similarly, we may accept the argument that fascists are conscientious believers, in that they are true believers in their cause and ideas, who pursue their conception of the good according to the best of their knowledge. Yet equally evident is that their convictions may endanger democracy. Although fascists enjoy the right to freedom of expression, in some circumstances the utterance of these ideas may constitute a serious offense to some sections of the population. Then the issue of the proper boundaries of free expression becomes relevant (to be discussed in chapter 8). You may claim that we *always* ought to listen to their views, otherwise we cannot be certain that they are not well founded. But as Glenn Tinder postulates in relation to the anti-Semitic diatribes of American Nazis, being mortal we cannot waste our time with such remote possibilities.[27]

As to the third argument, it may be true that something of value is denied society when democracy defends itself against such phenomena; but this is not sufficient reason to imply that any conscientious conduct should have a place within a liberal society, especially when the conscientious believers may have the power to cause considerable harm to some disliked people. We should postulate as a matter of moral principle that the justification of tolerance also sets its confines, for what is implicit is the recognition that unrestrained toleration should not be accorded to those who would deny respect to others.

Lastly, in considering the fourth argument, whether fascists have a right to complain that they are discriminated against, we must explain first the meaning of *discrimination*. Discrimination is commonly defined as treating like cases differently. Here, however, like cases are not at issue, for it is difficult to consider conduct (acts as well as speeches) of discriminatory nature as any other conduct. Hence, sometimes the policy of equality of treatment has to clear the way for more crucial considerations, such as securing the dignity of individuals as human beings. In such instances an unequal policy is preferable to an equal one, simply because the cases differ significantly and cannot be viewed in the same light. As Rawls contends, intolerance of an intolerant person who wishes to coerce others does not supply grounds for that person to complain, because the intolerant person wanted to deny the principle of equal liberty. Rawls concludes, "Justice does not require that men must stand idly by while others destroy the basis of their existence."[28]

A different stand is postulated by Anthony Skillen. Like Rawls, he asserts that the intolerant cannot complain against illiberal treatment. Skillen nevertheless contends that we cannot derive from this that upholders of freedom cannot object to illiberal treatment of the illiberal, or that the illiberal have no political right to protest and ought not to be allowed to promote their illiberal views.[29] He explains that the illiberalism of a view no more justifies its suppression in the name of liberty than does the advocacy of torture merit torture in the name of humanity. Intolerance does not justify, a priori, retributive intolerance: "Suppression is, arguably, an evil in itself, simply qua restriction and frustration."[30] Skillen makes two further points: first, that as a general "tactic," illiberalism in relation to speech can be dangerous to its advocates. Movements that have called to "smash the fascists" have helped bring about a general increase of law-and-order legislation aimed not so much at suppressing fascists as at imposing tighter state control of public space. Secondly, Skillen claims that racism is the ideology of the excluded, a way of seeing the world as one in which you are defined as belonging through the exclusion of others. Skillen agrees that excluding the racist exhibits poetic justice but is more deeply characterized as playing the same game.[31]

The first point views the side effects of the defensive measures that liberal democracy takes as a main reason not to defend itself against those who wish to undermine democracy, hence tolerating everything.[32] The argument is founded on deep suspicion of the government, disregarding the effects that may result if we *do* allow every ideology, every conception of how we should lead our lives to be pursued. It advocates tolerance because of a speculative fear of possible further effects of restrictions. Thus, Skillen's argument may be interpreted to ascribe enough weight to these possible effects to outweigh no less significant considerations regarding the harmful effects that may result from fascist ideas. The argument suggests that a speech may dehumanize a category of people. No real attempt is being made to evaluate harm and to prescribe constraints on the grounds that the harm may be intolerable. No concrete endeavor is made to confront the ethical questions involved in the subject of freedom of speech. The consequentialist reasoning, be it of the speculative fear of a future underground movement or the fear of government's future attempts at exploitation[33] or the positive contribution that hateful speech may make to the shaping of a more tolerant society,[34] outweighs the significance of the actual pain. This reasoning does not concede, as Dworkin and Rawls postulate, fundamental basic principles that prescribe mutual respect and human dignity, principles that underlie a free democratic society.[35]

In response to Skillen's second point, I reiterate the Respect for Others Argument, which insists on *mutual* respect for others. This argument is similar to Rawls's emphasis on the requirement of *equal* liberty. When we exclude racists we are doing to them what they wish to do to others. In that sense the result is the same. But Skillen does not recognize that it is *not* the same game. It is not the same game because the rules of the game are different. Racists base their rules on *exclusion,* whereas liberals base their game on *mutual respect.* Racists wish to limit the respect granted to others from the start, according to a criterion that others cannot change or control, at least from the racist point of view. The liberal starting point is respect for every member of society, and restrictions may be introduced when the other is not willing to accept this primary rule; so we can say that when the racist is excluded, this is poetic justice. But the games of the racist and of the liberal are not the same.

Skillen further maintains, "[I]f I am told that I cannot present or discuss my core beliefs because they are disgusting or vile or dangerous or simply false, then I am, to that extent, placed outside the community, able to move normally within it only through adopting a hypocritical mask."[36]

But a significant distinction occurs between disgusting or vile or dangerous or simply false. Here the reference is only to the dangerous because of its striking incompatibility with the most fundamental liberal moral codes. We have two sides of the same coin, and each of them can be illuminated. We can say when considering the examples of the Huns and the fascists that they are excluded by the liberal society, and we may say with equal truth that the fascists exclude themselves by holding illiberal views that intend to transform democracy into an intolerant form of government through the implementation of coercive means. It is reiterated that fascists exclude themselves from liberal society not because they hold undesirable beliefs. Instead, the combination of holding illiberal, antidemocratic beliefs *and* acting in accordance with them affords grounds for exclusion.

The upshot of this discussion is that some constraints are substantive, as distinguished from contingent constraints. We may discern *substantial* or *irrevocable* constraints as distinct from *contingent* or *alterable* ones. The first category consists of constraints that are nonconsequentialist, prescribed by the most fundamental principles of liberalism: they present hard-and-fast restraints as a rule, urging that some things lie beyond the ability of society to tolerate. Democracy cannot endure norms that deny respect to people and that are designed to harm others, although they may be dictated by some cultures. Some norms are considered by liberal standards to be intrinsically wrong, wrong by their very nature. Such are norms prescribing discrimination on grounds that people are not able to change (sex, color, religion, race, ethnic affiliation, etc.). Such are practices like suttee, female infanticide, and female circumcision.

The second category consists of contingent constraints. Here the view is that some constraints may be removed when circumstances change; therefore, they are introduced conditionally: they are a matter of time, place, and manner. If the circumstances are altered, the constraints may be removed. This category includes familiar controversies on issues such as conscientious objection, alcoholism, drugs, capital punishment, sexual intercourse, abortion, euthanasia, and paternalism in matters of safety. This is not to say that a wide consensus may be reached with regard to every one of the above subjects. Some people will surely argue that some of these are matters of principle and should never be permitted (say, capital punishment) or prohibited (say, sexual intercourse between consenting men), regardless of the circumstances. But because prophecy is not guaranteed to philosophers, we cannot dismiss out of hand the notion of possible debate in future circumstances that are hard to envisage.

One final comment is relevant with regard to Skillen's arguments. In his defense of free expression Skillen emphasizes the distinction between speech and action. He postulates that an opinion does not necessarily entail action, and that we cannot treat speech in the same manner as we treat deeds because they cannot hurt in a similar manner. Skillen argues that when we silence opinions, we act as if words "could causally affect you in an almost physical way rather than through their according with your grasp of things and thus their being 'acceptable' to you."[37] Words, however, can have an effect in an almost physical way, and sometimes in a physical way. The maxim "Sticks and stones can break my bones but words will never hurt me" is plainly wrong. This is why I see it is essential to prescribe the confines of freedom of expression. This issue is the center of attention of the remaining discussion of the theoretical part of this book. Meanwhile I wish to make two brief comments, to be developed in full later: first, when words come near to being translated into action with harmful results, it is difficult, sometimes even impossible, to separate freedom of speech from freedom of action. The borderline between the two becomes blurred, and the speech cannot enjoy the special status usually reserved for expression. Then speech can be considered as part of an action.

Second, the United States Supreme Court has acknowledged that speech can hurt almost physically, and that some types of speech by their very utterance inflict injury.[38] It has been argued that some utterances cause psychological pain, which can be equated with physical pain. As Justice Powell asserted in Rosenfeld v. New Jersey, "[T]he shock and sense of affront, and sometimes the injury to mind and spirit, can be as great from words as from some physical attacks."[39] In such instances, those who suffer the injury will not find much use in the argument, shared by Skillen and Dorsen, among others,[40] that suggests fighting opinions with opinions, for psychological offense is not remediable by more speech.

The distinction between *expression* and *action* is designed to protect the whole general area of expression, regardless of whether that expression creates a danger of subsequent harm. In many situations the distinction is quite clear. However, in many other situations the line of demarcation between these two categories becomes obscure. In fact, expression frequently takes place in a context of action or is closely linked with it. Sometimes expression is equivalent to action in its impact. In these mixed cases we must decide, however artificial the distinction may appear to be, whether the conduct is to be classified as one or the other. This judgment must be guided by consideration of whether the conduct partakes of the essential qualities of expression or action. As Thomas Emerson argues, in the main this is a question of whether the harm attributable to the conduct is immediate and instantaneous, and whether it is irremediable except by punishing and thereby preventing the conduct.[41] This is the concern of the ensuing discussion.

Chapter 5

Freedom of Expression

Words: Keys of Thought and Triggers of Action

The extent of freedom of expression that democracies should tolerate is a subject of controversy among authorities in the field. While the defensive reaction of democracy toward those who violently aim to destroy it is commonly viewed by many scholars and theorists as the right and necessary step to be employed, the arguments are much more equivocal when the subject of freedom of speech without resorting to violent actions is discussed. Although it is widely recognized that words not only are keys of thought but also triggers of action, and that although free discussion often produces good, it often produces harm, freedom of expression still enjoys a distinct status. Some even argue that this status grants freedom of expression immunity, maintaining that speech has to be protected in principle, not only when it is considered harmless, but also despite the fact that it may generate momentous harm. These scholars prefer to concentrate on the good that speech may bring, and they overlook or underestimate the responses it may induce and the harm it may cause. However, even those "absolutists" who would wish to grant immunity to expression recognize as a rule that sometimes exceptions must be made. I elaborate on the "absolutist" view in the next section of this chapter. Others acrobatically develop arguments to accord freedom of expression special status, praising the need for this unique status while recognizing the harm that may result. Peter Nicholson's views are characteristic of such maneuvering.[1] He praises tolerance and, at the same time, recognizes the need for restrictions, saying that the crucial practical problem that remains is to identify the boundaries of tolerance, to draw the lines at when to tolerate and when to say stop. Nicholson concedes that we should tolerate the *advocacy* of intolerance, admitting that intolerant opinions can be spread and put into practice to challenge and undermine institutions and values we hold dear. But, Nicholson urges, "the mere possibility does not justify intolerance of the expression of opinions."[2] He asserts that toleration permits restrictions on itself when that is necessary to protect the moral values that justify it. Unclear, however, is what these moral values are. Nicholson neither postulates examples nor specifies when "mere possibility" occurs and when it is necessary to protect the moral values. It is unclear where advocacy stops and the acting out of opinions begins. There is little wonder why Nicholson is in trouble when he tries to draw the lines.

Witnessing these arguments, the pressing and inevitable question that comes to mind is What makes freedom of expression so special? Several arguments are commonly proffered to explain its significance and the need for securing special status for this freedom. These arguments can be subdivided under the headings of autonomy, democracy, infallibility, and truth. The basic arguments concerning autonomy already have been articulated. I will review them in brief and later reflect on them in the context of Scanlon's theory of freedom of speech. The discussion concentrates mainly on the arguments under the other three headings.

Grounds for Special Status

THE MAIN ARGUMENTS

The main arguments that explain the special status of freedom of expression and therefore insist on granting it broad protection can be summarized along the following lines.

The Arguments from Autonomy

The Arguments from Autonomy suggest that (1) freedom of expression is necessary to enable individuals to advance their faculties and to realize themselves by advocating ideas and beliefs.[3] To use a familiar phraseology, words are keys of thought and persuasion, and we need free communication to enable individuals to learn about the different options open to them.

(2) Emphasis is put on the contribution of free speech to rationality, asserting that freedom of expression is needed to make up one's mind, to decide what to believe, and to weigh reasons for action.4 It is maintained that although reliance on government acting as the arbiter of tastes and values (as in the case of pornography) provides no assurance that the decisions it makes for us will be the best ones, such reliance guarantees that whatever capability people have to make healthy choices for themselves will remain underdeveloped.5

(3) The argument holds that a need exists to convey beliefs, to vigorously contest the opinions of others, for otherwise opinions will degenerate into prejudices, with little comprehension of their rational grounds.6 Thus, freedom of expression is needed to ensure the development of individuals as autonomous, rational, and independent beings. It is required to protect the moral sovereignty of people and the self-determination of our moral powers of rationality and reasonableness in conceptions of a life well and humanely lived.7

A further argument has been made that (4) expressions have a validating function in promoting people's well-being. They give the relevant ways of life the stamp of public acceptability. Free speech helps people to identify with their way of life, their sense of its worth, and their sense that their way of life facilitates their integration into their society.

(5) Expressions also serve to reassure those whose ways of life are being portrayed that they are not alone, that their problems are common, their experiences known to others. This argument proceeds by saying that (6) public validation is an essential element in the process of cultural transmission, preservation, and renewal. Free speech facilitates the assertion of traditions and is employed in challenging traditions and experimenting with new forms of relationships, new attitudes and life-styles.8 Moreover, (7) free speech is protected not because it is instrumental to any societal good, but because it inheres in people solely by virtue of their being people.9

In addition, it has been proclaimed that (8) restrictions on free discussion and open exchange of opinions inhibit the intellectual and "spiritual progress" of individuals (see Justice Murphy in *Jones v. Opelika* 316 U.S. 584, 1942), and that (9) free speech is a precondition for social progress.10 Progress is valued in the sense of improvement in the moral and intellectual qualities of the individual, which will contribute to the development of society.11 This argument is closely related to the Infallibility

Argument and to the Arguments from Truth, which I shall elaborate on in chapter 6. Here they are introduced in short.

The Infallibility Argument

The Infallibility Argument is based on the assumptions that (1) all human beings are fallible and therefore should have the right to express their thoughts and to compete in the free market of ideas and that (2) any intolerance of opinions involves, ipso facto, a claim to infallible knowledge. Mill explained that this mischief, which involves the undertaking to decide questions for others, without allowing them to hear what can be said on the contrary side, assumes infallibility, and that these are exactly the occasions on which authority has been employed to root out the best persons and the noblest doctrines.[12]

The Arguments from Truth

In turn, the Arguments from Truth hold that (1) the principle of freedom of expression allows almost any opinion the right to be heard because no one is in a position to claim a monopoly on the truth. It is maintained that although an opinion may have been silenced because it was thought to be in error, it may have contained a portion of truth. This argument was also developed by Mill and at the beginning of this century was embraced by the United States Supreme Court. Thus, Justice Oliver Wendell Holmes, in a celebrated opinion, stated, "[T]he best test of truth is the power to get itself accepted in the competition of the market."[13] The underlying assumption is that truth will prevail in a free and open encounter with falsehood.[14]

(2) Freedom of expression is necessary for keeping the vitality of beliefs. The meaning of doctrines will be in danger of being lost "and deprived of its vital effect on the character and conduct" unless freedom exists to express any challenging opinion.[15]

(3) Toleration of any opinion, even one conceived to be in gross error, is vital because silencing such an error can lead to two negative consequences: it would open the gate for further constraints on free speech on the government's account; and it would intimidate discoverers of truth, discouraging them from investing in further efforts and leading to their silence.

The Arguments from Democracy

This argument brings us to the Arguments from Democracy. They assume that (1) an opinion does not necessarily entail action, and in most cases, opinions do not automatically translate into action. Thus enough time is available to stop ideas that aim to endanger democracy before they materialize. This argument is supported by the further assumption that (2) the public is rational enough to recognize evil expressions, and thus in a free discourse of opinions, the "good" are bound to triumph over the "bad": the open confrontation of ideas strengthens the self-correcting powers of society.[16] Also argued is that (3) even if speech may cause injury, it still should enjoy protection because the damage incurred from its restriction outweighs the harm that could result from exercising that speech.[17] Any restrictions on speech, once permitted, have a sinister and inevitable tendency to expand.[18]

(4) Moreover, freedom of expression should be protected because of the lessons that society is likely to learn from such experiences, and because these experiences contribute to the shaping of a wider culture of tolerance.[19] In addition, (5) freedom of expression has been argued to be a necessary component for securing participation in the democratic life.[20] It is the way in which relevant information is made available to the electorate who then can, on the basis of that information, decide their conduct. Furthermore, (6) acts of expression serve to familiarize the public at large with ways of life common to different segments of the public.[21]

Moreover, (7) given the fact that transitions are constantly in the making, freedom of speech is necessary for citizens to reflect upon their current situation and to suggest accommodations. Freedom of expression is needed to maintain a balance between stability and change in society.[22]

(8) Freedom of speech is a means for controlling the government and assuring its legitimacy, a means against the government's attempts at exploitation, a means against possible corruption of public officials, and a necessary requirement for securing the consent of the citizens.[23]

(9) Finally, freedom of expression is crucial to indicate causes of discontent, the presence of cleavages, and possible future conflicts.

These arguments make a strong position for freedom of speech. Thus scholars and judges who may be associated with what is commonly called the *absolutist* school assert that when free expression is considered, tolerance must prevail in any situation *as a principle*. Nevertheless "absolutists" do not hold that all restrictions on freedom of expression or assembly are automatically unconstitutional. They put their trust in the human being, believing us to be rational and clever. The "absolutist" school implies that people can recognize undemocratic notions and understand their destructive power, and that they would not help such notions to flourish. We have to tolerate every view in principle and appreciate others' rights to say whatever they wish and think right. This is one of the foundations of liberal democracy: to discover what we may call the will of the people through a process of constant discussion that reveals the range of opinions and allows for any idea to attract people and become the most influential one in society. Thus, it is argued that on the issue of group and individual libel, "one of the presumptions of citizenship in a democracy *must be* the ability of people to learn to restrain themselves in the face of symbolic provocations by others and to fight offensive speech with more and better speech rather than with fists and clubs."[24] Accordingly, so the argument goes, "children as well as adults *must develop* the ability to detect and reject dehumanizing values and false prophets, looking to the law to protect them only from those charlatans whose blandishments can lead directly and immediately to material loss or physical injury."[25] Let us look at the absolutist approach more closely.

THE ABSOLUTIST SCHOOL

The absolutists believe that once we limit the expression of opinions, the system will come under constant pressure to continue to do so. Thus, for the sake of democracy and its basic pillars, we must allow every political opinion to be heard; and should we choose to contest some ideas, this can only be done by posing contradictory opinions.[26]

Alexander Meiklejohn, one of the leading exponents of this school, takes the fifth Argument from Democracy (as postulated above) to be of such importance as to outweigh any restrictions on expression. He asserts that without freedom of expression, taking part in the democratic life is impossible. It is an essential means without which citizens cannot participate in the decision making. Meiklejohn argues that public political speech should be absolutely protected from all abridgment.[27] He claims that the principle that assigns equality of status to opinions springs from the necessities of the program of self-government, and that the First Amendment of the U.S. Constitution protects this commitment: when citizens govern themselves, it is they and they alone who must pass judgment upon unwisdom, unfairness, and danger.[28] Citizens may not be barred from speaking because their views are thought to be false or dangerous. The fact that speech can cause harm does not constitute in itself sufficient grounds to abridge that speech. The Free Speech Principle takes this possibility into account. Meiklejohn maintains that no suggestion of policy can be denied on the grounds that it is on one side of the issue rather than on another. Conflicting opinions, including the most absurd views, must be heard not because they are valid, but because they are relevant. He concludes by saying that to be afraid of ideas, any ideas, is to be unfit for self-government.[29] Speech cannot be restricted because of its content, but only if it interferes with "necessities of the community," such as when meetings are held in public places, and thus—for instance—causing traffic jams.[30]

The common criticism of Meiklejohn's arguments attacks the very core of his views. Although emphasizing self-government, Meiklejohn views the protection of speech as a restriction on the authority of government rather than as an individual right. He contends that free speech is required to make self-government work but avoids the question of what to do when citizens, in the self-governing process, decide to prohibit some types of speech. As Frederick Schauer remarks, "[T]he very notion of popular sovereignty supporting the argument from democracy argues against any limitation on that sovereignty"; it thereby argues against recognition of an independent principle of freedom of speech.[31] Not clear, therefore, is what Meiklejohn means by "self-governing" and why self-governing excludes putting restrictions on freedom of expression.

Moreover, I am disturbed by Meiklejohn's argument that in "emergency" situations, when something must be said and no other time, place, circumstances, or manner of speech will serve for the saying of it, a citizen may be justified in "taking the law into his own hands."[32] Meiklejohn does not clarify the meaning of "emergency" situations. He elucidates his contention only by bringing up Justice Holmes's trivial example that we cannot allow falsely shouting Fire! in a crowded theater,[33] arguing that if there is a real fire, one is duty bound to inform others of the danger. This is an obvious situation in which we are obliged to warn the others, but here we are not taking the law into our hands. We are simply exercising common sense without violating any law. A difference exists between the suggestion that in emergency situations we can take the law into our hands and this example. Meiklejohn's suggestion, in the strong phrasing that it is put, may open the way for challenging the law on quite vague and broad grounds.[34]

Whether Meiklejohn, according to his own standards, allows everything that is concerned with politics to be discussed in the open is another relevant question. Meiklejohn avoids addressing extreme cases in which such a debate may endanger life or in which political speech amounts to betraying one's country. In such cases he might have qualified his position. However, Meiklejohn refrains from testing the limits of absolutism. He has accorded political speech absolute freedom that is far broader than can ever realistically be accepted by any legal system.

Another scholar who can be associated with the absolutist school is Alf Ross. He defines freedom of speech as "the freedom to propose any political opinion whatsoever and agitate for it, irrespective of its substance, but on condition that the propaganda does not make use of inadmissible means, nor aim at using violence."[35] Not entirely clear is what "agitate" includes. Here Ross follows Justice Holmes's assertion that "every idea is an incitement."[36] The aim of ideas is to convey messages, to awaken people to action. Ross embraces the view that the public in democracies is rational enough to recognize evil expressions and to fight them to safeguard democracy (the second Argument from Democracy). Ross develops the argument further, explaining that when the ideas of liberty, justice, and humanity are rooted in society, they have the inner force to fight against conflicting ideas. He maintains that when democracy in Germany and elsewhere succumbed defenselessly, it was not because it recognized its opponents' right to speak, but because— among other reasons—the ideas of democracy had never seriously taken root in those newly democratic societies.

The first argument is peculiar. I find it hard to agree that every opinion that preaches violence is not considered as a part of free speech and therefore ought not to be heard. Let us contemplate, for instance, a mass or a minority struggle against a cruel and exploitive oppressor. Can we impose, in such a case, a taboo against agitation to counterviolence and condemn some groups to slavery? Is abstention from preaching violence, and the value of forbearance from violence, higher than the value of freedom? Is violence enacted by one group more terrible than violence enacted against the same group? If the answer to this triple dilemma is no, then the right of any enslaved group is to do anything it can to free itself from the condition of exploitation under which it lives.

The second argument emphasizes political culture. It implies that "ripe" democracies cannot be endangered by extremist threats for the simple reason that their democratic principles are well rooted in their societies, and the people are reasonable enough to acknowledge the risk involved so that they would never support threats that would result in the destruction of the system. Experience has shown that these assumptions are valid when states with long democratic traditions are considered, but what about those democracies which are not yet "ripe"? Ross's stand is unclear regarding young democracies, where "the strength and life of the people's love for and faith in ideas of liberty, justice and humanity" are lacking.[37] He does not believe that these ideas can be safeguarded by means of prohibitions.

We may concur with Ross that states with a long democratic tradition are less likely to face internal threats against democracy, and that even when fascist, antidemocratic groups arise (like Mosley's in England in the 1930s), they are less likely to gather considerable force than similar groups appearing in states with, say, authoritarian tradition. We also may agree that ideas of liberty, justice, and humanity cannot be safeguarded *only* by means of prohibitions. But I do not see why resorting to such prohibitions should be denied altogether from young, "unripe" democracies, which in the face of grave threat to their existence find it necessary to supplement the educational struggle with well-defined legal restrictions. This issue will be the concern of part 2 of this study. Should young democracies give their rivals the potential power to destroy them? Alternatively, maybe they should accept their destinies, adopting the fatalist view that they could do nothing since their future has already been determined by the lack of a democratic tradition. Ross overlooks these questions, and as to the "ripe" democracies, he advocates a simple rule: "[I]t is vital for democracy to adhere to the clear principle: Force may be used against force; opinions can be combatted only with opinions."[38]

This formula appears, at first glance, to be quite convincing. This may be because of its style of phrasing. But upon closer examination we can say that the formula is unrealistic and idealistic. We can understand the concern for open and free flow of opinions and entirely agree that to be able to talk freely, to be able to protest against injustice, to mold and be molded in open disputation with others are, indeed, essential components of self-realization. Therefore, the state should provide open channels for free discussion and exchange of opinions. We further may agree with the view that every opinion should be heard. Nevertheless, we may also think that the simple principle "Opinions can be combatted only with opinions" is too wide a generalization and should not be adopted as a guiding rule. Its implication is that freedom of expression should be extended to all groups, even those which seek to destroy it. What are we to do, for instance, if we try to combat discriminatory opinions by employing only opinions, and we fail at the end? Are we simply to surrender, even if we think that the opposing party is hazardous to the public good or to part of it?

Moreover, the statement "Force may be used against force" needs qualification. We must fight against force with any means we possess, but force should be the last resort after the peaceful options have been exhausted and failed. The *right* that the individual has to implement an act is not sufficient *reason* for the individual to perform it. Exactly the same applies when fighting opinions. Thus, for instance, the right to free speech does not supply sufficient reason for unjustifiably destroying the opponent's reputation; it does not imply that we can slander, disseminate false information, or make false charges against innocent individuals. This right does not include distributing unsubstantiated malicious publications that harm the reputation of individuals whose opinions are opposed.[39]

Ross states that delusion and fanaticism should not be repressed: if left alone they are as harmless as a germ that will be destroyed or purified in the fire of free criticism; therefore, "there must be freedom for evil as well as for good." In support, Ross cites Renan: "Freedom is the great means of destroying all fanatical opinions. When I demand freedom for my enemies, freedom for him who would like to oppress me had he the power, I actually present him with the smallest of gifts. Science can bear the virile force of freedom; fanaticism, superstition cannot bear it."[40]

Renan's assertion is quite a naïve one for three reasons: first, because the germ can spread and kill the body before the immunization device has a chance to react; second, that "smallest of gifts" may be viewed by the receiver as a springboard for curtailing further freedoms; and third, it is unclear who is to guarantee free criticism if the germ should grow to power.

A distinguished philosopher who does recognize the harmfulness of expression and thus refrains from granting it immunity is Thomas Scanlon. Scanlon attempts to construct a theory of freedom of speech that considers the extent to which defenders of freedom of speech must rest their case on the claim that the long-term benefits of free expression outweigh obvious and possibly severe short-run costs, and to what extent this calculation of long-term advantages depends upon placing a high value on autonomy and intellectual pursuits as opposed to other values. Scanlon's theory aims to limit the powers of a state to those which citizens could recognize while still regarding themselves as equal, autonomous, rational agents. Let us devote some space to his theory.

SCANLON'S THEORY

In "A Theory of Freedom of Expression," Scanlon aims at formulating a principle of freedom of expression that would provide a priori constraints on the authority of governments. Like Meiklejohn, Scanlon strives to accord this principle absoluteness or at least partial immunity from balancing against other interests. He, however, wants his theory to include all types of speech and not be limited to the political. Scanlon's starting points are Meiklejohn's self-governing argument and the Millian theory. He formulates his theory as constituting the protection of "individual autonomy," asserting that persons are autonomous if they conceive themselves as sovereign in weighing competing reasons for action. Scanlon examines several different ways in which speech-acts can bring about harm. A *speech-act* is defined in a broad manner as any act that is intended by its agent to communicate to one or more persons some proposition or attitude.[41] Scanlon emphasizes that the harms he mentions are not always sufficient justification for abridging speech, but that they can always be taken into account. He further asserts that the distinction between expression and other forms of action is less important than the distinction between expression that moves others to act by indicating what they see as good reasons for action, and expression that gives rise to action by others in other ways.

However, we can think of instances in which it is difficult to draw a line and determine when a justification for action superseded the agent's judgment.[42] Thus Scanlon's distinction may hold in clear-cut cases but not in borderline cases. Indeed, Scanlon admits that it is difficult to say exactly when legal liability arises in some cases. Then he formulates the principle of freedom of expression, which he entitles "the Millian Principle." According to this principle there are certain harms that, although they would not occur but for certain acts of expression, nonetheless cannot be taken as part of a justification for legal restrictions on these acts. "These harms are: (a) harms to certain individuals which consist in their coming to have false beliefs as a result of those acts of expression; (b) harmful consequences of acts performed as a result of those acts of expression, where the connection between the acts of expression and the subsequent harmful acts consists merely in the fact that the act of expression led the agents to believe (or increased their tendency to believe) these acts to be worth performing."[43]

Scanlon views the Millian Principle as the basic principle of freedom of expression and rejects any goal-based or consequentialist reasons that may interfere with this principle. Following the Millian defense of liberty of thought and discussion, Scanlon argues that speech may not be prohibited on the grounds that harms to individuals or society may result due to the individual's acceptance of the validity of the speech; individuals must be given the freedom to make judgments and decide for themselves. He assumes that autonomy, in his "weak" sense, is something all rational people conceive as extremely valuable (see chapter 1). Scanlon further argues that violations of the Millian Principle interfere with a person's autonomy and therefore ought not to take place. Citizens need to be exposed to all sorts of information to exercise their faculties and to make up their minds. Therefore, the harm of coming to have false beliefs is not one that autonomous persons would allow the state to protect them against through restrictions on expression. In other words, the authority of governments to restrict the liberty of citizens in order to prevent designated harms does not include the authority to prevent these harms by controlling the sources of information so as to ensure that they will maintain certain beliefs.[44] The legitimate powers of governments are limited to those which can be defended on grounds compatible with the autonomy of their citizens. This argument is similar to Meiklejohn's self-governing idea.

Ronald Dworkin's criticism of Scanlon's theory, which focuses on three points, is worth mentioning.[45] First, he says that Scanlon ignores the interests of the *speaker*. He asserts that Scanlon's conception of autonomy concentrates on the rights of those who wish to hear the speaker; yet some may feel that the right of free expression belongs, in the end, to the speaker and not to the potential audience. My view is that Scanlon and Dworkin are both right, that the right of free expression belongs to the speaker as well as to the listeners. Secondly, Dworkin notes that Scanlon suggests that the audience may consent not to hear opinions it detests and so warrant exceptions to the principle. Thirdly, we may infer from Scanlon's arguments that the government may be justified in restricting speech on the basis that it does not contribute any new ideas. Frequently speakers simply wish to repeat well-known arguments, and this type of speech does not fall within the Millian Principle.

Upon reflection, when canvassing his arguments in a recent article, Scanlon has arrived at the conclusion that his theory, in some respects, is inadequate. Bearing Dworkin's criticism in mind, Scanlon now distinguishes between interests of participants, interests of audiences, and interests of bystanders.[46] Yet again he speaks of the central interest of the audience in having a good environment for the formation of its beliefs and desires and ignores the fact that speakers have exactly the same interest. We all wish, as spectators and as speakers, to promote a framework within which we may pursue our ideas and beliefs. I find this point striking because Scanlon urges arguments from autonomy that are naturally concerned with the agents, but he reaches conclusions that characterize the arguments from democracy and from truth, conclusions that focus on the benefits for the wider range of society. However, Scanlon develops his theory of group interests as far as the category of bystanders is concerned and refrains from speaking of the overall societal interests in promoting a good environment. Scanlon continues to believe that speech-acts are fundamental human interests. He admits his mistake was that in the effort to generalize Meiklejohn's theory beyond the category of political speech, he took what were in effect features peculiar to this category and presented them, under the heading of autonomy, as a priori constraints on justifications of legitimate authority.[47] Scanlon further concedes that additional information is sometimes not worth the cost of getting it, and that we should not be willing to bear unlimited costs to allow expression to flourish under his principle. He also recognizes that speech not related to political issues may legitimately be restricted on paternalistic grounds. However, when political issues are concerned, Scanlon advocates a strong level of protection for expression: "[W]here political issues are involved governments are notoriously partisan and unreliable. Therefore, giving government the authority to make policy by balancing interests in such cases presents a serious threat to particularly important participant and audience interests."[48] I should note that Mill did not draw such a distinction between political and nonpolitical speech.

This argument concerning political speech serves Scanlon to affirm implicitly the Skokie decision, where it is quite difficult to think of any benefit for the audience witnessing the march, who clearly did not wish to communicate with the actors or be exposed to their ideas.[49] Here it is hard to see the rally as compatible with the "central audience interest" in having "a good environment." But Scanlon is not speaking of the *audience*'s interests at all. He recognizes that the racist expression is deeply offensive only to bystanders, without supplying any explanation for not considering the interests of the audience. And because the march is a political issue, this fact outweighs the offence imposed upon the audience. Scanlon's fear of interference by the government and his suspicion of municipal ordinances designed to prohibit expression bring Scanlon to allow speech-acts, however offensive they may be.[50]

Scanlon's theory is nevertheless valuable for several reasons. As does Meiklejohn, he sees the self-governing argument to be crucial in protecting freedom of expression, but unlike Meiklejohn he tries to construct a broader philosophical theory that does not resort to the United States Constitution. Scanlon prescribes the boundaries of government interference as derived from the respect that a legitimate government owes to personal autonomy. The state cannot enact laws to protect citizens against holding false beliefs, because in so doing, it would deprive citizens of the grounds for making independent judgments. Autonomy is valued because it promotes the effective pursuit of our opinions, and Scanlon ascribes primary value to this within his principle. He acknowledges the significance of the Millian Principle but recognizes that it is incapable of accounting for all the cases that strike us as infringements on free speech. Then, Scanlon appeals to our intuitive view of freedom of expression, which rests upon a balancing of competing goods, and he concedes the importance of circumstances. Scanlon explains that the Millian Principle allows us hazardous publication, which might inflict harm during a time of peace, while the same publication may be intolerable in wartime.[51] Scanlon maintains that several different justifications exist for the exercise of coercive authority. He concludes that it would take a situation of near catastrophe to justify coercion, but he does not elaborate what he means by catastrophe. The questions of whether harm to some part rather than to the whole of society would qualify as a catastrophe and what sorts of harms are not to be tolerated, are left unanswered.

Moreover, the essential question is, Why should we wait until the stage of catastrophe? Why should we wait until the last minute when we may clearly recognize that the speech in question is incompatible with the moral principles that characterize a liberal democratic society as such? Scanlon holds that we should tolerate political expressions as a matter of principle, but then he recognizes what I call the democratic catch, hence conceding the "near catastrophe" exception where it becomes legitimate for democracy to be on the defensive. Thus from Scanlon's standpoint, the issue of restricting tolerance is a practical rather than an ethical question. He prefers to ponder considerations of circumstances and the extent of the threat without explaining from an ethical perspective why we should withhold tolerance. Instead, Scanlon argues that tolerance has to prevail as long as no real danger occurs to democracy. As does Rawls, he avoids addressing the issue of whether we should have moral restrictions on tolerance, and, if any, what these should be.

Scanlon's hypothesis is designed to restrict government activities in matters of free speech. As such it supplies us with a general background theory of freedom of expression. The Harm Principle serves Scanlon to draw confines for state interference. I wish to go one step further and probe the subjects Scanlon discusses in brief at the end of his theory in order to expand upon his generalizations. My aim is to consider the Millian theory as a guideline for drawing boundaries for freedom of expression, which are conceived to be essential for the defense of democracy. My purpose is to confront the ethical question of the constraints of tolerance: What restrictions on tolerance may be prescribed by morality? The emphasis is set on the *harm:* Can we say that, sometimes, the harm caused as a result of speech constitutes such an injury that it cannot be tolerated? If it does, as Scanlon concedes, then we have to determine what harm is intolerable and whether circumstances are of significance. We should note that when speaking of restrictions on freedom of expression, these should be as clear and precise as possible. Too vague and overly broad a definition may lead to administrative abuse on the part of the government in its attempt to silence inconvenient views. An imprecise definition may have a snowballing effect, paving the way for a syndrome whereby freedom of speech may become the exception rather than the rule. Moreover, the restrictions cannot be occasional. We have to seek a criterion that could serve as an evaluative guideline and be suitable for a range of cases, covering different types of speech (racist, ethnic, religious, etc.).

In order to explore this issue, we must consider the Millian theory to see what Mill had to say when freedom of expression was under scrutiny. This is the concern of my next two chapters. I will first examine what *grounds* were supplied by Mill (and others who followed him) for tolerating expression. I emphasize the need for a free market of ideas to enable the discovery of truth. In the following chapter, I will probe the *confines* suggested by Mill of freedom of expression. Before doing that, however, in order to give a complete view of the Millian Harm Principle I wish to consider in brief how it was applied to *action*. The arguments are well versed in the literature and thus I do not wish to expand on them.[52] I will summarize them and then clarify how they are to be applied by an illustrative example.

The Harm Principle

Mill drew a distinction between self- and other-regarding actions. He prescribed interference in another's self-regarding conduct when doers are likely to harm themselves *and* sufficient grounds exist to believe that doers do not have an interest to do so *and* the circumstances are such that the time factor is pressing, and the opportunity to deliberate is denied doers. Whereas in other-regarding cases, when the doers' conduct inflicts harm upon others, interference in liberty of the doers is vindicated when (1) the conduct violates distinct and assignable obligations to another person. Mill clarified that a conduct can be seen to violate such an obligation when (a) the degree of harmfulness is weighty enough to outweigh the loss of freedom incurred as a result of the interference, *and* (b) the damage is definite.

In other words, with regard to other-regarding cases (a) + (b) are conducive to identifying (1). Nevertheless, the degree and the probability of the harm still do not explain Mill's intention when speaking of "assignable obligation." We may assume that by "assignable" Mill meant "undoubted": an obligation that we can clearly attribute to another.

But the entire distinction between self- and other-regarding activities is problematic. Mill was well aware of the inherent ambiguities and difficulties likely to be involved in trying to differentiate the two with regard to a conduct. Thus, in the *Logic* he admitted that all social phenomena are interrelated, and that no part of society could be described adequately in isolation from the effects of other phenomena.[53] In *On Liberty* Mill asked, "How . . . can any part of the conduct of a member of society be a matter of indifference to the other members? No person is an entirely isolated being; it is impossible for a person to do anything seriously or permanently hurtful to himself, without mischief reaching at least to his near connections, and often far beyond them."[54]

Mill concedes "that the mischief which a person does to himself may seriously affect, both through their sympathies and their interests, those nearly connected with him and, in a minor degree, society at large."[55] Nevertheless, Mill thought that from a methodological point of view we could gain further insight whose benefit may outweigh the potential vagueness of such a conceptualization. He assumed that in many spheres of life, with regard to a variety of actions, the implications of the self- and other-regarding principles may be clear enough to serve as guidelines. Let us reflect on the Millian formulation by considering the following example.

A gifted American athlete has failed for the second time to qualify for his country's Olympic team, and this is for him *the* dream of his life. The athlete thinks that only by participating in these games could he fully realize himself. He knows that given a chance to take part in the next Olympics he could represent his country well. He also recognizes that this would probably be his last chance. He decides to take the initiative and improve his chances of participating in the Olympics in any way that he can. Under the Harm Principle, as long as he does not harm others, he is free to take every option to realize his dream, including those which may require self-sacrifice. He may decide, after deliberation, to emigrate to another country and qualify there. Or else his national identity may be of more significance to him than his sexual identity. The athlete is free then to change his sex and gain the desired ticket as a woman. Further-more, he has the right to maim himself and so be eligible to participate in the disabled Olympics. Although it may be repellent, he does have this option and he can enjoy his liberty to harm himself without interference, so long as he is not coerced into taking either of these options. All three possibilities demand sacrifice, and all are permissible if he willingly de-cides to take them. Arguably, by taking either of these three alternatives our athlete deprives his compatriots of his achievements. Nevertheless, all three actions cannot be said to violate distinct and assignable obligations of other people. The athlete did not commit himself not to develop his career as he sees right only to satisfy enjoyments that others derive from watching him run. But if our athlete decides to take a different path and, say, exterminate those who are ranked above him in order to improve his chances, here his liberty has to be curtailed.

Thus far for liberty of action. In chapter 7 I will discuss the restrictions that were introduced by Mill to expression. Before taking this endeavor, it is in order to analyze the Truth Principle, which provides, in the sphere of expression, one of the most conspicuous answers to the question: Why tolerate?

Chapter 6

Why Tolerate? The
Millian Truth Principle

Preliminaries

One of the major arguments for tolerance of expression, frequently made
in order to grant immunity to expression that is not accorded to action, is
the Truth Principle. Incorporating the Infallibility Argument (see chapter
5, "Grounds for Special Status") it suggests that since a possibility exists
of being wrong, we must not rely only on what appears to us to be true.
That is, we have to remain somewhat uncertain even while being certain,
for toleration is connected with the willingness and the ability to acknowledge the presence of different approaches that are remote from
ours. We may discover in time that while grains of truth reside in our
view, it nevertheless remains partial and could be completed by joining
with other partial truths. Even if we believe that we know what the truth
is, we must not rest but should continuously submit our truth to trial-
and-error tests in order to prove to ourselves, as well as to others, that we
are not mistaken.

Further, we should guarantee each and every opinion the opportunity
to be heard, for otherwise we may put up barriers in the way of the
discovery of the truth. The assumption is that to admit the possibility
that the other's ideas may be true, though I do not believe in them myself,
is to acknowledge the possibility that my ideas may be false. The assumption is also that enough room occurs for groups and individuals
who may hold totally different opinions. Suspicion of views simply be-

cause they are held by a minority may hinder the discovery of new truths. After all, many new ideas, many innovations, start with a minority of one. And we have to bear in mind that even the most unpopular idea may contain some truth in it and may contribute to the advancement of knowledge.

The Truth Principle further commands us to contest those opinions which are believed to be true vigorously and earnestly to explore some further truth and to uncover their false aspects. This argument was utilized by the United States Supreme Court in several decisions.[1]

The argument that we should keep questioning what we hold to be true suggests that each of us may hold our truth and by seeking truth we develop our autonomy, our own faculties. Thus, if A offers B "the Truth," A's promised truth, without offering B some alternatives for searching for the truth through the exercise of B's power, then B's autonomy will be diminished. This is because one person's truth is not necessarily the other's truth, and everyone should be able to decide which avenues to pursue. No party enjoys a monopoly on the truth. No one has full possession of an exclusive truth. This argument may resemble an argument of skeptical spectators who contend that they believe the pictures they see are real and alive but question the objectivity of the photographer (or the director) who decides *where* to place the camera. Our spectators, therefore, wish to explore the same scene from every possible angle, not only from that of the photographer, so as to bring to light the whole picture. The underlying assumption is that the search for truth is infinite, and hence a free marketplace should exist for truths, in which every person is able to advance his or her partial truth while considering other truths.

In sum, we have to remain open to different views that may, on occasion, be contradictory to ours out of the respect that we feel for the other's freedom of thought and expression: because we realize that we are not infallible; because of the desire to advance the search for the truth; and because debates on different views help individuals become aware of the interests of others, which may be different from theirs, and thus contribute to a sense of community.

Let us consider the Millian Truth Principle in more detail. Mill was not the first (nor the last) to pronounce arguments from Truth.[2] Still, no other figure has emerged who is more closely associated with this argument than Mill. Under his influence this argument came to be a keystone of the plea for tolerance.

The Millian Truth Principle

According to Mill, the quest for truth is a vital as well as an expedient endeavor. He contended that every opinion should be checked against experience, without the fear of consequences, for when opinion is verified by experience and observation, then we have sufficient grounds for holding it to be true. This does not entail that it is true. We can never be sure that the truth in our possession is the truth, the whole truth, and nothing but the truth. We cannot expect to find more than beliefs that are provisionally regarded as true. The result of these views was Mill's avowed commitment to the idea that we can never be sure where the truth is to be found, hence all our answers must be tentative: a universal, single truth is not and cannot be found.

In formulating his Truth Principle, Mill regarded truth as an *ideal,* for absolute certainty can be a dream to which we should all aspire but one that never can be reached in reality. The search for truth is a search for beliefs that we may hold with more confidence, rather than for beliefs of which we could be absolutely certain. Mill put forth the familiar hypotheses: first, that we can never be sure the opinion we are endeavoring to stifle is a false one; and second, that even if we were to be sure, stifling it would be an evil.[3] He urged that false opinions be tolerated for the sake of the true, for it is impossible to draw any clear line that would distinguish between true and false views. Everyone who "has even crossed the threshold of political philosophy" knows that on many of its questions the false view is greatly the most plausible, and "a large portion of its truths are, and must always remain, to all but those who have specially studied them, paradoxes; as contrary, in appearance, to common sense, as the proposition that the earth moves round the sun."[4] Therefore, we should always question common beliefs that are held as "truths," for truth is an ideal that we can never reach but for which we should nevertheless continue to struggle.

Two crucial considerations in support of the Truth Principle were offered by Mill and his followers: the Infallibility and the Vitality arguments. The *Infallibility Argument* is based on the familiar assumptions that beliefs exist that claim truth in areas in which it is impossible to hold with certainty any belief to be true; and that any intolerance of opinions involves, ipso facto, a claim to infallible knowledge. Even those opinions of whose truthfulness we are confident, such as "Newtonian philosophy," must be exposed to scrutiny and doubts.5 Those who assume that they know what the truth is provide reasons against pursuing constant inquiry and debate, depriving humanity of exploring further truths and so block the wheels of progress. Silencing an opinion is likened to robbing the human race. Mill urged this argument in support of his demand for tolerance in the spheres of politics, morality, religion, and taste; spheres that frequently are invaded by intolerance.

The *Vitality Argument* suggests that without the free exchange of ideas, the common views would be rigid, lacking adaptability, and soon turn into dead dogma. However true an opinion may be, if it is not fully, frequently, and fearlessly discussed, it will cease to be held as a "living truth."6 While acknowledging the fact that "the dictum that truth always triumphs over persecution is one of those pleasant falsehoods which men repeat after one another till they pass into commonplaces, but which all experience refutes,"7 Mill reasoned that free and open discussion is bound to bring about truth. In a way similar to Adam Smith's belief in the function of the invisible hand in regulating the economic powers of the market, Mill believed in one such hand that regulates the marketplace of ideas, leading to the discovery of truth. He proclaimed that in the long run, truth never fails to prevail over error: it may be extinguished once, twice, or many times, but in the course of the ages people usually will be found to rediscover it.

Together Mill's arguments establish quite a powerful defense of tolerance in the name of truth. The question is whether it can be said that in the name of truth we should allow every opinion, whatever it may be, to be heard. We may press this question further, asking whether it follows that all paths to discovering the truth should be left open so as to enable each person to find his or her truth; and whether it is entailed that the Truth Principle is immune to qualification, that we should never lie. Surely this was not what Mill had in mind when formulating his principle, for he himself acknowledged that lying is wrong, depending on the circumstances. Despite his emphasis on truth, its value and its contribution to well-being, Mill was willing to allow exceptions to his professed principle. Look at the tentativeness of his remarks against lying, in support of the virtue of justice: "Yet that even this rule, sacred as it is, admits of possible exceptions, is acknowledged by all moralists; the chief of which is when the withholding of some fact (as of information from a malefactor, or of bad news from a person dangerously ill) would save an individual (especially an individual other than oneself) from great and unmerited evil, and when the withholding can only be effected by denial."[8]

If we bear this argument in mind, then we can envisage situations in which we may reach the paradoxical conclusion that lying may serve to safeguard the conditions for searching for truth. It is plausible to conceive of occasions on which we might resort to lying, believing that in so doing we could gain further knowledge. We might lie, for instance, in order to induce a friend to take a stand on an issue about which previously he or she had remained unclear, or to reveal information he or she decided to keep secret. We also might deny freedom of expression to others, claiming that they obstruct, with their "nonsense," the way to the discovery of truth. Thus, the Truth Principle might be stretched to absurdity, to a point at which it not only demands compromises but also allows for its refutation. In neglecting the task of prescribing well-defined boundaries for his principle, Mill opened the way for the negation of the principles in which he believed. Consequently, the Truth Principle might permit the defeat of liberty, tolerance, and the very Truth Principle itself.

Mill continued to say, in a similar fashion, that to break faith with anyone is confessedly unjust. Yet again, this obligation is not an absolute, but is "universally considered" as capable of being overruled by a stronger obligation of justice on the other side.[9] That is, if the withholding of some fact or information would save an individual, then the Truth Principle admits to possible exceptions. The direct derivative from this argument is, therefore, that restrictions on freedom of expression are legitimate if applied for the same reasons. In his early essay "Law of Libel and Liberty of the Press," Mill wrote, "There is one case, and only one, in which there might appear to be some doubt of the propriety of permitting the truth to be told without reserve. This is, when the truth, without being of any advantage to the public, is calculated to give annoyance to private individuals."[10]

Two points are in order: one concerns the place of this *Annoyance Principle* within the Millian theory, and the other touches on its practicality in relation to our discussion. First, this principle is quite puzzling, for Mill himself implied when formulating his theory that more than annoyance must be involved to justify interference in someone's liberty.[11] Second, the meaning of the term *annoyance* is unclear.[12] Mill preferred not to use the terms *harmful* or *offensive*, but this much more general term instead; one so vague that we may wonder if it could serve as a guideline at all. It is difficult enough to clarify the meaning of harm or of offense (chapter 7 analyzes the Millian Harm and Offense Principles), but annoyance may encompass so wide a range of possibilities that it resists any kind of systematic analysis. What annoys one may enchant another; and more fundamentally, what if truth may annoy some individuals?

Mill does not supply any answers to these questions. In any event, more than annoyance has to prevail to persuade us to restrict liberty. To take a common example, when someone decides to enter politics or to become a celebrity, a figure whose life is of public concern, then that person has to take into account the possibility of being criticized, laughed at, and discredited for things and behavior that he or she does or does not do. Some of the slurs may go well beyond mere annoyance, bordering on slander, and then sufficient reason would exist for appealing to the courts. Those who decide to live their life in the spotlight are well aware of the pros and cons involved, and they know that they may be the target of annoying jokes.[13] Therefore, to consider this Annoyance Principle seriously is difficult. Only when the level of annoyance is such as to bring about substantial harm to the point of ruining a person's name does a case exist for the courts to decide whether a reason is present for restraining the defamer's freedom.[14]

Incidentally, Mill spoke of another qualification concerning the publication of falsehoods. In distinguishing between the publication of opinions and of facts, Mill explained that although the publication of false opinions should be tolerated for the sake of the true, no corresponding reason exists for the publication of false statements of facts: "The truth or falsehood of an alleged fact, is matter, not of opinion, but of evidence; and may be safely left to be decided by those, on whom the business of deciding upon evidence in other cases devolves."[15]

Later in On Liberty, Mill modified his views, further compounding any attempt at reconciliation between these two qualifications and the general arguments as presented in this book. In On Liberty Mill contended that it is impossible to fix the bounds of fair discussion. He admitted that the manner of asserting an opinion may be quite objectionable and justly incur severe censure. However, the principal offenses of the kind are such that they are rarely brought to conviction. He maintained that the gravest are those which twist the facts: "to argue sophistically, to suppress facts or arguments, to misstate the elements of the case, or misrepresent the opposite opinion." Nevertheless, Mill urged, all this, "even to the most aggravated degree, is so continually done in perfect good faith" that it is rarely possible to stamp the misrepresentation as morally culpable, and still less could law presume to interfere with this kind of "controversial" misconduct.[16]

Another criticism of the Truth Principle concerns the Infallibility Argument. In formulating this argument Mill assumed that all suppression is based on the asserted falseness of the opinion to be suppressed. But this often is not the case; opinions are more commonly suppressed because their expression is thought to cause inconvenience or discomfort to powerful people. We can plausibly argue that the dissemination of some views, quite possibly true, ought to be banned under some circumstances because of their destructive impact on the public good. Putting restrictions on freedom of expression does not ultimately involve a claim of infallibility. As we have seen, Mill acknowledged this when he put qualifications on what otherwise would be regarded as an "absolute" principle.

Mill's arguments imply that the value of truth is superior to the value of other social interests. He believed that the inherent value of truth outweighs the values of those goods which are endangered through the discovery, or debating, process. His appeal was for "the fullest liberty of professing and discussing, as a matter of ethical conviction, any doctrine, however immoral it may be considered."[17] This assertion can hardly be reconciled with the annoyance qualification. In the name of intellectual development, Mill was willing to allow the expression of every opinion, however annoying these may be. Moreover, the endeavor of discovering the truth through the free expression of opinions may, as Mill thought, contribute to self-development and progress, but by the same token it may also endanger them by advancing, to use Mill's terminology, "false" views. Although he acknowledged that most of the people lack the degree of rationality he wished they would have, Mill allowed almost complete liberty of expression to convince them to believe in false views. This is because he believed that truth is bound to win out over the false *in the end.*[18] The problems are how to recognize that it is the end, and how significant are the developments that take place in the meantime. In addition, Mill ignored the possibility that an unscrupulous propagandist may cause a rationally grounded, true belief to be abandoned for a false one based on pure emotion, and that free speech can have a debilitating effect, weakening rather than strengthening human consciousness of truth.[19] For, as Rawls reflects, not all truths are established by ways of thought recognized by common sense, and to proclaim that everything is, in some definable sense, a logical construction of what can be observed or evidenced by rational scientific inquiry would be dubious.

Rawls has come some way since he offered us his constructivist model of justice, arguing unequivocally that justice is the first virtue of social institutions, as truth is of systems of thought, and that a theory must be rejected or revised if it is untrue,[20] to asserting nine years later in his third Dewey Lecture that "the idea of approximating to moral truth has no place in a constructivist doctrine."[21] Rawls explains that what justifies a conception of justice is not its being true to an antecedent order given to us, but its congruence with our deeper understanding of ourselves and our aspirations and our realization that, given our history and the traditions embedded in our public life, it is the most reasonable doctrine for us.[22] He implies that whenever the pursuit of truth comes into conflict with his doctrine, the doctrine must be held prior. This is in a similar line to his argument that in some situations liberty has to be limited in order to preserve just institutions.[23]

Mill probably would not agree with this assertion. He viewed truth as superior to all other social values without adequately considering the possibility that if we pursue this reasoning, the search for truth may come into conflict with our first argument for tolerance—the Respect for Others Argument.[24] This argument urges that, contrary to utilitarianism, each individual possesses inviolable rights that the benefit or welfare of everyone else cannot override. Consequently the loss of liberty for some is not made right by the greater sum of advantages to be enjoyed by the entire society as a result of discovering further truth. To grant toleration solely on the grounds that it advances truth is a proposition that may serve intolerance. The reason *for* tolerance could make tolerance a self-defeating idea, leading to discrimination and to the harm of others. We may ask the following: What if in order to achieve the desired end of "truth," a person (or people) would have to suffer? And, does the end of truth justify all costs? Let us first look at a case that involves infringement of individual privacy. Here the story of Oliver Sipple may serve as an example.

Sipple is the ex-marine who knocked a gun out of the hands of a would-be assassin of then President Gerald Ford. Shortly after the incident, it was revealed by the media that Sipple was active in San Francisco's gay community, a fact that had not been known to Sipple's family, who thereupon broke off relations with him. He then sued the newspaper for invasion of his privacy.

Sipple's homosexuality surely was not a fact relevant to the act of saving the president's life. The media would not have made a point of his being heterosexual if that had been the case; nevertheless, it did not distort the truth—it brought a true fact to public attention. Accordingly, a strict view may be offered that in the name of truth, every item that may be seen as relevant to the making of a story can be published, no matter what the consequences may be.

A less rigid view would qualify this, holding that the Truth Principle cannot be seen as a sufficient justification, and that attention should be paid also to the consequences of the publication. In this context some have argued that Sipple's sexual identity was relevant because members of the gay community found significance and value in this news report in that it publicized the idea that a homosexual could be a hero as anybody else could.[25] That is, in reflecting on this issue we should consider the benefit accruing to the entire gay community through the publicizing of Sipple's homosexuality. This argument, however, concentrates on hypothetical benefits for some while ignoring the actual damage inflicted upon Sipple. His act of bravery had shattered his family life. The crucial issue is, thus, whether the making of Sipple into a hero model for the gay community outweighs the harm that was caused to him and his family. The answer appears to be negative. The gay community would prefer to identify with someone who is proud of his sexual identity than with someone who tries to hide it. Moreover, we can assume that truth was not the main motivation of the journalist who revealed this fact about Sipple. The desire to sell more newspapers by generating gossip was the main drive, without paying enough consideration to the harmful results Sipple was likely to endure or appreciating Sipple's right to privacy. Hence, the consideration of privacy outweighs in such matters the consideration of profit (disguised as coming from consideration of truth) unless a public interest is at stake, such as when the issue involves a public figure whose trustworthiness is a matter of public concern.

Mill did not consider cases in which his Harm Principle clashes with the Truth Principle, and, therefore, it is not entirely clear what would have been his position regarding this matter. Bearing in mind Mill's Annoyance Principle, we nevertheless may assume that he might have argued for restricting freedom of expression in the said circumstances. We may expect that Mill would have favored respect for Sipple's privacy. This is provided that he would have thought the truth was of no contribution to the public. Now let us move from the particular to the general and consider two related though different issues in which the harm is inflicted on more than one individual. The one issue is concerned with commercial speech, the other with group libel.

Focusing on the first issue, liberals who generally favor a free market of opinions are reluctant to endorse this position when it comes to expressing views in the free market of goods. Justices Black and Douglas, probably the most vigorous proponents of free expression in the history of the United States Supreme Court, rejected protection of commercial speech. The common arguments are that given existing economic structures, commercial speech is not a manifestation of the liberty of the speaker, and that market determination breaks the connection between commercial speech and individual choice.[26] The inclination is to give precedence to the Harm Principle when it is proved that the good in question has harmful results, no matter whether the commercial speech promoting it is true or false. An example is the note incorporated into cigarette advertisements. An advertisement may claim that a brand of cigarettes is low in nicotine, excellent in taste, inexpensive, and made from tobacco of the highest quality, and all of these assertions may be true. Still, the advertisement is required (in the United States and Israel, as well as in other countries) to contain an additional statement that smoking is bad for your health.[27]

The matter of libel, particularly of group libel, presses the issue of weighing the end of truth against the costs involved. We can envisage situations in which the belief that we should tolerate anything that could assist the progress of truth may serve those wishing to curtail tolerance. Consider the case of the North American scientist who conducted research on the brain configuration of blacks and brought forward evidence to prove that they are intellectually inferior to whites. Let us assume for a moment that this scientific, or quasi-scientific, proof may contain a grain of truth. Moreover, let us say that this evidence is completely true. Should we allow the publication of this research?

One view answers this question positively, holding that we may allow the publication of the research. It may postulate that the reason for permitting the publication has nothing to do with whether its findings contain some truth, with the value or the "truth" of the research, or with its contribution to science. Instead, the underlying reasoning could be that through this research we may learn more about white-black relationships, the prejudices and feelings against blacks that pervade the white population of the United States and elsewhere. This knowledge could assist us in bridging the gap between races and in fighting these opinions. We may allow the publication not because consideration of the scientist and his followers is foremost in our eyes, but because consideration of the blacks and the whites who resent these findings as well as those who remain undecided is what really counts. The Truth Principle is still in place, but not the truth that the research explores. Instead, it is the truth with regard to race relations, the truth as emerged from the discussion of these findings.

Let us go one step further and add more factors to this example. Assume that we accept this view and allow the publication of these findings under the arguments of free inquiry and the search for truth; now, however, we give an account of the specific time, manner, and place in which this scenario takes place. Suppose that this scientist wishes to disseminate the results of his research in a vicious pamphlet in Atlanta, Georgia, during a time of severe riots against black people in the southern United States.[28] Should we remain faithful to our belief in the free exchange of opinions in the marketplace of ideas? Here it appears that the circumstances prescribe a restrictive attitude. This is not because the racist view has to be banned per se because of its repugnant content, but because of its harmful *consequences* and its probable inimical contribution to the current mood in the South. The general line that is plausible to pursue is that if truth is likely to lead to the persecution of some people, we ought better to leave knowledge in its present state without clinging to the desire of discovering a further truth. The mere possibility of contributing to the truth does not justify endangering groups in society by publishing unsubstantiated (or even substantiated) evidence that may be distorted by prejudices.[29] In this example the implications are that the possibility for the discovery of truth should be postponed. Sometimes, however, it may be argued that some possibilities in the pursuit of truth should be terminated altogether. Consider the following relevant issue.

Suppose a distinguished scientist, in opposition to all other experts in her field, and without relying on facts and scientific evidence, urges that the HIV virus can be passed to others by merely shaking hands with a homosexual. One person (X) may argue that publication of such an assertion, when it is not substantiated by facts, should be prohibited. AIDS is such a traumatic disease because a cure for it is yet to be found, and we could expect horrendous consequences for the homosexual community if this assertion were to be published. The search for the truth may be infinite, X would say, but the ways and means according to which the truth is advanced and pursued are finite.

Many liberals would dispute X's reasoning. Following Mill, they would allow the publication because this form of expression cannot be considered as an instigation. According to this view, grounds for restricting speech are provided when it is closely linked with action and thus may lead to causing harm to others.[30] To publish an unsubstantiated theory of this sort in a newspaper or journal is simply to advocate it, and the way to fight against it is by counterarguments, by more speech.

In response, X may then assert that although the scientist's theory may be denied by many other distinguished scientists who would show that what that scientist had said has no substance, still her theory is likely to get much publicity and to fall on prejudiced ears. X may maintain that nowadays experts explain time and again that the most common ways HIV can be transmitted to others are sexual intercourse, mothers infecting their unborn children, blood transfusions, or use of contaminated needles or syringes.[31] Still, many people do not want anything to do with people who are infected with HIV. Some doctors and nurses who are familiar with the scientific data nevertheless are reluctant to give medical assistance to persons with AIDS. So many prejudices occur with regard to AIDS that such a theory would create segregation between heterosexuals and homosexuals. It would vilify and condemn an entire group of people. Thus, X would agree that this is not a case of instigation, in the sense that the harmful results are immediate, but it is a damning of a group. This bogus argument, coming from a scientist, may even entail persecution of the entire homosexual community. It may condemn the homosexuals to live in isolation from the rest of society, bringing upon them the fate lepers suffered in the past. In such instances, after considering the reasonableness of the advocated truth, examining the grounds on which it is based, as well as the seriousness of the objections to it, if we come to believe that the "truth" is controversial, and that the consequences of preaching that "truth" may cause harm to others, then the Truth Principle does not possess sufficient force to demand toleration on our part.

Recalling Scanlon's argument, X may say that the interests of the homosexual community in particular and of society in general in having a "good environment" are more important than the interests of the scientist in publishing her beliefs.[32] X may argue in sum that the Truth Principle cannot justify cases where there are grounds to believe that the intention is to condemn a specific group.

If X is correct in the assumptions, we may have a new category of forbidden speech. This is the category of *group damning*. However, liberals would then argue that X is too pessimistic in the assumptions. They would further assert that not long ago three distinguished scientists had brought forward a somewhat similar theory, which might have condemned the homosexual community in the way that X describes. Nevertheless, reality shows that the homosexual community, although it may have suffered a drawback in its position in society, is not treated (not yet, anyway) in the way that lepers were treated in the past. We may recall that in 1988, Masters, Johnson, and Kolodny published a book claiming that it is possible to become infected with the HIV virus from skin contact with contaminated toilet seats and implying that people may contract HIV through mosquito bites.[33] Because AIDS is very much associated with homosexuals, their thesis might have had the potential for becoming group damning in the way described by X, leading to a proposal of segregation in order to prevent the spread of the disease. In reality this did not happen. The scientists' theory evoked much discussion and debate. It was not totally refuted nor substantiated by scientific research, but the scientific community did not adopt their theory.[34] As far as the homosexual community is concerned, it has not been persecuted nor segregated as a result of the publication of these hypotheses. Thus, the facts support the liberal viewpoint of affirming the publication. We have to be extra careful in considering prohibition on books and journals. For my part, I cannot think of cases in which prohibition on such publications should ever take place. Liberals would agree, however, that if we were to add considerations of time, manner, and place in a similar vein to our example of publishing a study about the inferiority of blacks in a malicious pamphlet during a period of riots, then the pursuit of truth should be held secondary so as to secure the safety of individuals and groups.

To summarize, if the two arguments for tolerance are to confront each other, then the Respect for Others Argument has to take precedence over the Truth Principle. This is not only for ethical reasons but also for methodological reasons; for we have seen that the Truth Principle cannot serve as a well-defined principle for prescribing tolerance and its confines within a well-organized framework, safe from the fallacies of the argument itself. Truth should not be held superior to other social values such as the liberty and autonomy of individuals.

Finally, I may add, truthfulness has not always been counted among the political virtues. Arendt carries the argument too far in her assertion that lies have always been regarded as necessary and justifiable tools not only of the politician's or the demagogue's but also of the statesman's trade.[35] Of course, not every issue that arises in political life is about discerning the truth; questions of public policy are not of a uniform character. In some, truth is at issue; in others it is not.

However, qualifying Arendt's observation we may say that on many occasions truth does not serve as a guiding principle. If we consider one of the basic principles underlying the working of democracies, then we may say the majoritarian principle is viewed as a more just procedure than minority rule not because it is thought the ideas of the majority are truer than those of the minority but despite the acknowledged possibility that the majority may be wrong. The liberal view is that it is not truth we ought to seek in politics, but a way in which we will be able to secure the rights and liberties of all citizens without supplying a basis for attempts at exploitation or allowing some to further their interests at the expense of others. The deontological arguments, as constructed above, qualified with the requirements of mutuality and not harming others, seem appropriate for this task by furnishing reasons for tolerating and prescribing boundaries for their working. The Truth Principle on the other hand defends tolerance, but its reasoning may open the way for the intolerant and, paradoxically, even for the negation of truth.

In the next chapter I examine the confines set by Mill on freedom of expression. I discuss two different principles—the Harm Principle and the Offense Principle. Before contemplating the Millian theory, two methodological notes have to be made: one with regard to the Offense Principle; the other with regard to the Harm Principle.

First, the common liberal interpretation of Mill is that any speech that falls under the category of *advocacy* is immune to restrictions. The examples of the prejudiced scientists discussed above are illustrations of how the distinction between *advocacy* and *instigation* brings liberals to assert that no advocacy is punishable. Only forms of instigation that bring about instant harm are punishable, and these cases constitute the exception to the free speech principle. My view is different. I argue that Mill introduced an exception to advocacy, holding that a category of cases of advocacy exists that has to be restricted. This category is concerned with offensive conduct done in public. I will show that some offensive expressions *may be* considered as advocacy that nevertheless should be prohibited. However, my view and the common liberal view differ only in terminology, not in essence. That is, some utterances do not induce anyone to take a harmful action but nonetheless should be excluded from the protection of the free speech principle because of their imminent offensive effects on those who are exposed to it. Some liberals probably would not agree with my vocabulary and would not consider what I call advocacy to be advocacy. They rather would put the case under the rubric of instigative speech. But I think they would agree with my conclusions.

The second methodological observation is that the Harm Principle, although grounded on utilitarian arguments, does not necessarily entail that its use amounts to accepting utilitarian ethics. We have seen that Scanlon views the Millian Principle as the "only plausible principle of freedom of expression" that applies to expression in general and makes no appeal to special rights or to the value to be attached to expression in some particular domain. Scanlon maintains that the Millian Principle specifies what is special about acts of expression as opposed to other acts, and it thereby constitutes the "usable residue of the distinction between speech and action."[36] Others who adopt a similar line of reasoning raise grave objections to grounding this principle on utilitarian argument. They maintain that it is not a corollary of utilitarian tenets, but the contrary. The basic desideratum of utilitarianism is to maximize the surplus of pleasure (or well-being) over pain (or deprivation). However, as D. A. J. Richards explains, in some circumstances utilitarianism would call for criminalization of conduct in violation of the principle. He gives an example of hatred of the nonconforming minority, which reinforces the majority's pleasurable feelings of social solidarity and self-worth in a way that toleration could not engender. Then the greater pleasure thus secured to the majority not only may outweigh the pain to the minority, but compared to the toleration required by the Harm Principle it results in a greater aggregate of pleasure. In order to avoid collapsing into a utilitarianism that is unable to capture either the force or the sense that

the Harm Principle intuitively carries with it, Richards concludes that we
should develop a background theory to explain why constitutional argument applies to some areas of conduct, and what the meaning of *harm*
is.[37] This is the aim of the ensuing discussion. I will first argue that in
some circumstances speech amounts to action. Then I suggest that grounds
for abridging expression exist not only when it is intended to bring about
physical harm, but also when it is designed to inflict psychological offense, which is morally on a par with physical harm, provided that the
circumstances are such that the target group cannot avoid being exposed
to it. The phrase *morally on a par with physical harm* comes to mean that
just as we view the infliction of physical pain as a wrongful deed, seeing it
as the right and the duty of the state to prohibit such an infliction, so we
should place boundaries on expressions designed to cause psychological
offense to some target group. I argue that in either case, when physical
harm *or* psychological offense is inflicted upon others, four considerations are pertinent: the content of the speech,[38] the manner in which the
speech is expressed, the intentions and the motives of the speaker, and
the circumstances in which the speech is made.

Chapter 7

Boundaries of
Freedom of Expression

The Millian Arguments

In formulating his Harm Principle, Mill did not say that any forms of expression ought to enjoy perfect immunity. Being aware of the fact that expressions are other regarding, and that as such they may inflict evil, Mill did not deny that they may cause harm. In chapter 2 of *On Liberty,* "Of Thought and Discussion," he recognized that in thinking, our activity is directed inward upon our consciousness and operates solely at the spiritual level, so that no reason exists for interference in our thought; whereas when people advocate ideas, their activity is directed outward and no longer exists only in their private domain, hence it may have a bearing on others. Mill did not argue that the liberty of expressing and publishing opinions is of the same importance as freedom of thought; he said it is *almost* as important. Nor did he say that the liberty of expressing and publishing opinions is identical or inseparable from the latter; he said that it is practically inseparable from freedom of thought.[1] Thus, freedom of expression does not enjoy absolute immunity as does freedom of thought. In Mill's methodological hierarchy we may say that Mill granted freedom of speech a midway immunity between freedom of thought and freedom of action: it does not enjoy absolutism, but we must be extremely careful when we consider interference with it.

Mill insisted as a general rule that the harmfulness of utterances was not sufficient to warrant their restriction. Nevertheless he did not argue that they ought *never* to be restricted. In what he regarded as extreme circumstances, Mill explicitly admitted the importance of restricting them. He proffered two main qualifications for the immunity freedom of expression should, as a general rule, enjoy, and in an earlier article concerning freedom of the press he formulated two other qualifications.[2] Mill did not introduce them in a systematic manner because he believed that the best way his ideas would receive the attention they deserve was by phrasing them in an unequivocal manner; were they to be qualified from the start, the exceptions might receive greater attention than the rules. Thus, for Mill, it was important to focus attention on the guiding rule that secured free speech and to allow for interference only in what he conceived to be extreme and special cases. The first qualification proposed in *On Liberty* was concerned with the case of instigative speech. The second qualification considered the case of indecent conduct that is performed in public. Let me first examine instigation.

As a consequentialist, Mill acknowledged that speech loses its immunity when it constitutes an instigation to some harmful action. However, he refrained from elaborating on this issue. Mill considered this subject of instigation in only two places in *On Liberty:* the first time not in the text itself but in a footnote at the beginning of chapter 2; the second time in chapter 3, when he briefly discussed the example of the corn dealer.

In the footnote Mill addressed the case of instigation to tyrannicide, asserting that in a specific case it may be a proper subject of punishment, "but only if an overt act has followed, and at least a probable connection can be established between the act and the instigation."[3] This definition of instigation is problematic. On one side it is too narrow, because it does not consider instigative speeches as such, irrespective of whether action follows. We may think of an instigation that does not lead to action because, for example, large police forces are present to stop the instigators or to stop the crowd they address before it starts to take action. Only if an overt act follows, only if actual consequences take place, will a speech be considered by Mill as instigation. On the other side this definition is too broad. Mill did not clarify the meaning of "an overt act" nor of "probable connection." As a result, an advocacy can be connected causally to action. Almost any form of speech may have a probable connection to "an overt act." Thus this definition cannot take us far in establishing what instigation is.

The picture becomes clearer when reflecting on Mill's example of the corn dealer. Mill asserted that opinions lose their immunity when the circumstances under which they are expressed constitute by their expression a positive *instigation* to some mischievous act. Thus, the opinion that corn dealers are starvers of the poor may be prevented from being delivered orally to "an excited mob assembled before the house of a corn-dealer, or when handed about among the same mob in the form of a placard."4 Nevertheless, that same opinion ought to go unmolested when simply circulated through the press. We may deduce that Mill considered as instigation a speech that intends to lead to some mischievous action, under circumstances conducive to the taking of that action. In instances such as that of the corn dealer, Mill would regard speech as instigation irrespective of whether overt harmful action follows. Although he did not explicitly say that, Mill implied that the intention to lead people to take a harmful action—in circumstances likely to mobilize people to take that action—constitutes an instigation.5 However, advocacy which does not induce someone to take an action, which is voiced as a matter of ethical conviction, is protected under Mill's theory. This is one of his major contributions to the free speech literature. Mill was the first to distinguish between speech (or discussion) as a matter of ethical conviction and instigation.

The essential distinction between *instigation* and *advocacy* or *teaching* is that those to whom the instigation is addressed must be urged to *do* something now or in the immediate future, rather than merely being urged to believe in something. Instigation is speech closely linked to action. With the corn dealer example, Mill implicitly opined that when an audience has no time for careful and rational reflection before it pursues the course of action urged upon it, this speech falls outside the protection of the free speech principle, since the people are too excited to be responsible for their acts. Similar reasoning, as far as shortage of time is concerned, guided Mill in supporting interference in the other's freedom in the case of the unsafe bridge. Mill did not restrict the advocating of opinions per se. Instead, the combination of the content of the opinion, its manner, the intentions of the speaker, and the circumstances necessitates the restriction. In the example of the corn dealer, the harmful results of a breach of the peace, disorder, and harm to others were imminent and likely; therefore, they outweigh the significance of free expression.

In parentheses, two clarifications have to be made. One relates to the

factor of *intention*, the other to *manner*. First we may question the relevance of intention to Mill's argument about instigation. We may argue
that the relevant consideration is whether circumstances are such that a
speech will cause a riot; that there appears to be sufficient reason for
intervention even when the speaker had not intended to cause a riot. I am
not convinced. The very use of the word *instigation* implies that the
intention exists to provoke a riot. I agree that unintended riots may
occur. But it is odd to use the term *instigation* in that context.

Second, *manner* characterizes the way expressions are made, be it an
oral or a symbolic speech. We can think of situations in which the manner is not so significant, yet the three other factors are sufficient to
constitute an instigation. Consider a leader of a fundamentalist religious
sect who urges his or her followers to some mischievous act in a cool and
quiet tone. In this case Mill would have had no qualms classifying such a
speech as instigation. I discuss this issue further in chapter 8.

The implications of the reasoning concerning instigation are that we
will not be correct in saying that all opinions bring the same results.
Justice Holmes's assertion that "every idea is an incitement" is too hasty.[6]
Instead, we may concede that words that express an opinion in one
context can become incendiary when addressed to an inflammable audience. The peculiarity of cases of instigation is that the likelihood of
an immediate danger is high, and we have little or no opportunity to
conduct a discussion in the open and to submit conflicting considerations
into play, which may reduce the effects of the speech. Justice Holmes
agreed that in some circumstances, when speech is closely related to
action and may induce harmful consequences, it should be curtailed. In a
way similar to Mill's example regarding the corn dealer, Holmes asserted
in a renowned opinion that we cannot allow falsely shouting Fire! in a
crowded theater.[7] Here, too, a restriction on speech is justified on the
grounds that the content of the speech (that is, its effects, not its intrinsic
value), the manner of the speech, and the intentions of the agent are
aimed to bring about harm, while the audience dwells under conditions
that diminish its ability to deliberate in a rational manner. Therefore such
a shout may lead it to act in a harmful manner (harmful to themselves as
well as to others).[8] Hence, to the extent that speech entails an immediate
effect, the arguments that assign special status to freedom of speech
are less compelling. Boundaries have to be introduced in accordance with
the context of the speech, otherwise the results could be too risky. As

Zechariah Chafee stated, "Smoking is all right, but not in a powder magazine."[9]

Thus incorporating the four conditions of content, manner, intention, and circumstances in Mill's and Holmes's examples, the following argument may be deduced.

Argument number one. Any speech that *instigates* (in the sense of meeting the four criteria of content, manner, intention, and circumstances) to cause physical harm to individuals or groups ought to be curtailed.

This argument is a much more decisive version of the Millian Harm Principle. This principle holds that something is *eligible* for restriction only if it causes harm to others. Whether it ought to be restricted remains to be calculated. This argument provides conditions in which a harm *ought* to be restricted.

Let us now examine Mill's second exception, which qualifies, in my opinion, the immunity Mill generally granted to advocacy. This exception considers the case of an indecent conduct that is performed in public. Although Mill spoke of "conduct" and did not explicitly mention speech, we may plausibly argue that he included utterances as well as acts when he displayed this qualification. Mill implied that some cases fall within the scope of social regulation where people not only have the right but the duty to put a stop to the activities of individuals. In a brief paragraph he discussed a category of actions that being directly injurious only to the agents themselves, ought not to be legally interdicted, but that, "if done publicly, are a violation of good manners, and coming thus within the category of offenses against others, may rightly be prohibited."[10] This argument is in accordance with Mill's position on the worth and significance of autonomy. Some intimate matters do not concern anyone but the individual, so long as they are done in private; but when they are done publicly, then they may cause offense to others, and the state may legitimately control them.[11] Of this kind, Mill said, are offenses against decency.

Hence, in some situations we are culpable not because of the act that we have performed, though this act may be morally wrong, but because of its *circumstances* and its *consequences*. Mill assumed that we can evaluate the rightness and wrongness of an action by considering its consequences, believing that the morality of an action depends on the consequences it is likely to produce.[12] Since we are to judge before acting, then we must weigh the probable results of our doing, given the conditions of the situation.

From these arguments we may infer that usually it is not the act itself that is crucial to taking a stand on this subject, but the forum in which it is done. A conduct in itself does not necessarily provide sufficient grounds for interference. But if that same conduct is being done in public, then it may be counted as morally wrong and thereby constitutes an offense; hence, to curtail it is legitimate. Enforcement of sanctions may be justified when a conduct causes offense to others.[13]

To sum up: the two exceptions brought forward by Mill touch upon the time factor that distinguishes speech from action. Thus, action—if it endangers the public, or part of it—may have immediate consequences; whereas speech, if it has any endangering effect, would have it in most cases sometime in the future, whether near or remote, thus allowing us a much wider range of maneuvers (as postulated above in chapter 5, argument number 1 from Democracy). Even if a specific view may cause harm or risk of harm to others, but the danger is not immediate, then free speech has to be allowed. However, in some circumstances the time factor may lose its distinctiveness, with the result that the effects of the expression in question are *immediate*. Both in the case of instigation as well as in cases of moral offense (say when you vulgarly praise in public the sexual attributes of your next-door neighbor, knowing the anguish that the neighbor could suffer as a result), the effects of the expression are instantaneous; thus they may bring about hurtful consequences *now*, rather than at a remote point in the future. When we discuss the issue of obscene speech or defamation,[14] the line between conduct and speech, according to the criterion of time, becomes blurred; consequently these utterances are not protected under the principle of freedom of speech.

The preliminary argument (*number one*) included the term *physical*. I have formulated the argument using this term to avoid at that stage the question of whether the formula ought to include other sorts of harm. I have now argued that in both the cases of instigation and cases of indecent conduct done in public, the effects of the communication are immediate. Yet, such conduct does not necessarily fall under the first argument, for offenses against decency may not be physical. Mill articulated other notions of injury when he introduced this qualification. The expression in question may fall under the heading *advocacy,* in that it does not induce anyone to take a harmful action. Nevertheless, the expression still may be excluded from the protection of the free speech principle because of its offensive effects on those who are exposed to it. This is the only exception implied in Mill's theory with regard to advocacy. The combination of the content of the advocacy, its manner, the intentions of the speaker, and the fact that it is done publicly offers grounds for restriction. Some types of advocacy constitute a violation of good manners, thus coming within the category of offenses, and consequently may rightly be prohibited. In order to understand what notions of injury may be included under this qualification, which may be put under the heading of the Offense Principle, let us devote some place to explain the distinction between *harm* and *offense.* Here Joel Feinberg supplies useful guidelines.

The Offense Principle

Feinberg explains that like the word *harm,* the word *offense* has both a general and a specifically normative sense. The general usage of harm includes in its reference any or all of a miscellany of disliked mental states (disgust, shame, hurt, anxiety, etc.), while offense refers to those states only when caused by the wrongful (right-violating) conduct of others. He postulates that offense takes place when three criteria are present: persons are offended when they suffer a disliked state, they attribute that state to the wrongful conduct of another, and they resent the other for his or her role in bringing them to that state.[15] Feinberg maintains that the seriousness of the offensiveness would be determined by three standards: "the extent of offensive standard"—which means the intensity and durability of the repugnance produced, and the extent to which repugnance could be anticipated to be the general reaction of strangers to the conduct displayed; "the reasonable avoidability standard"—which refers to the ease with which unwilling witnesses can avoid the offensive displays; and "the *Volenti* standard"—which considers whether the witnesses have willingly assumed the risk of being offended either through curiosity or the anticipation of pleasure.[16] The second and third standards are of relevance when we examine the circumstances in which an offensive speech is expressed.

Feinberg categorically asserts that offense is a less serious thing than harm, so he ignores the possibility that psychological offenses may amount to physical harm with the same serious implications. In chapter 8, I shall reflect on this subject through consideration of Feinberg's standards. Here, however, if we return to Mill's second qualification, we may say that morally wrong actions that concern others cause us to suffer a disliked state, which we attribute to the doer's conduct. Consequently we resent the doer for his or her acts. Nevertheless, offenses against decency are problematic because what is offensive to one party may not be regarded as offensive at all by another. If we want to make the Offense Principle an intelligible principle, the offense has to be explicit, and it has to be more than emotional distress, inconvenience, embarrassment, or annoyance. We cannot outlaw *anything* that causes some sort of offense to others. If the Offense Principle is broadened to include annoyance, then it would become too weak to serve as a guideline in political theory, for almost every action can be said to cause a nuisance for others. Cultural norms and prejudices, for instance, may irritate some people. Liberal views may cause discomfort to conservatives, while conservative opinions may distress liberals. Some people, for instance, may be offended when hearing a woman shouting commands or just by the sight of black and white people holding hands. This is not to say that these sorts of behavior should be curbed simply because some people are oversensitive to gender roles or interracial relations. Similarly, if some people are easily offended by pornographic material, they can easily avoid the pain by refraining from buying magazines marked with the warning The Content May Be Offensive to Some. Under Feinberg's reasonable avoidability and *Volenti* standards, the offense cannot be considered to be serious. To be restricted under the Offense Principle, injuries must involve *serious offense* to be infringed. Serious offense means that consideration has to be given to the reasonable avoidability, the *Volenti*, as well as the extent of offensive standard. The repugnance produced has to be severe so as to cause an irremediable offense that may affect the ability of the listeners to function in their lives.

Let me consider in more detail Feinberg's reasonable avoidability standard. Under this standard and Mill's argument regarding public immoral actions, the offense has to be committed in such circumstances that those offended by it cannot possibly avoid it in order for grounds for restriction to exist. Hence, for example, if a person takes a stool to Hyde Park corner and advocates getting rid of Parliament, throwing all Indians out of England, expressing the desire to become the new Stalin of tomorrow, and claiming that yesterday he or she was Napoleon, the offense at that point cannot be considered as more than annoying or as causing more than an inconvenience to the listeners, for they can simply leave the place and free themselves of the speaker's presence as well as of the speech. We are not able to say that the audience's interest in "having a good environment" is more prominent than the speaker's interest in conveying his or her thoughts.[17] Also, the argument that this communication does not carry substantive content cannot serve as sufficient reason for abridging it, for then we may supply grounds for curtailing many other speeches that just repeat familiar stands. In addition, the extent of offense standard, determined by the content and manner of the speech and the *Volenti* standard do not provide reasons for restriction.

The situation is different when the avoidance of offensive conduct in itself constitutes a weighty pain. Then we may say that the matter is open to dispute. That is, if those who are offended by a speech feel an obligation to stay because they think that they would suffer more were they to avoid the speech by going away, then grounds exist for putting restrictions on speech, provided that the extent of the offense is considerable. In any event, the combination of the content and manner of the speech, the evil intention of the speaker, *and* unavoidable circumstances warrants the introduction of sanctions.

I discuss in chapter 8 the decision of the neo-Nazis to march in Skokie, Illinois, as an illustration of this argument. This discussion is in order because principles are much more powerful when applied to life situations, making more sense when placed in the context of specific instances. In this case the conflict over freedom of expression involves the issue of freedom of assembly. I will assess the preliminary court decisions to ban the march, as well as the Illinois Supreme Court's ruling that allowed the demonstration. I proceed by exploring whether the Offense Principle supplies us with grounds for supporting one over the other. Before embarking on this endeavor, a clarification is needed. In applying the Offense Principle to Skokie, I do not claim that racist speech should be considered a distinct case, as some philosophers and commentators urge, thereby excluding it from the protection usually accorded to expression.[18] It may be suggested that if we are to speak on matters of principle, then racist speech is incompatible with liberal democracy and hence should be outlawed. My reluctance to accept this line of reasoning evolves from two basic considerations. First, I do not see why verbal attacks on race, color, religion, etc., should be regarded as a unique type of speech that does not deserve protection. I find it difficult to see why racist expressions should be thought different from verbal attacks on the most fundamental ethical and moral convictions—as, for instance, in the case of abortion.[19] I do not see why dignity or equal respect and concern is more at stake in the one case than in the other.

Second, agreement is lacking on the meaning of the term *racism*. Different countries and forums put different types of speech under the heading of racism. Thus, by excluding racist expressions we may open the way to curtailing expressions we may want to defend. For instance, Zionism was condemned as a racist ideology, so accordingly anyone who expresses the desire to live in Zion (Israel) may be considered by some as a racist. This claim is less strong than the first one, for we can define exactly what sorts of speech should be considered racist. However, this argument is in place because in applying common terms from one place to another, definition may be lost on the way.

Consequently, my intention is to formulate general criteria to be applied consistently not only to cases of racial hatred, but also to other categories of offensive speech. Any speech, be it on religious, ethnic, cultural, national, social, or moral grounds, should be submitted to the confines of the Harm and the Offense principles.[20] Speech that instigates the causing of immediate harm to the target group and speech designed to offend the sensibilities of the target group in circumstances bound to expose the target group to a serious offense (an offense morally on a par with physical pain) should be restricted.

Chapter 8

Applying the Offense Principle: The Skokie Controversy

Background

What came to be known as the Skokie case began in April 1977, when Frank Collin, the leader of the National Socialist Party of America (NSPA) announced that a march would be held in Skokie, Illinois, a suburb on the outskirts of Chicago inhabited mostly by Jews, some hundreds of them survivors of Nazi concentration camps.[1] The citizens of Skokie obtained a court injunction that banned the march. Referring to the *Brandenburg* case, they contended that the display of the Nazi uniform and the swastika was the symbolic equivalent of a public call to kill all Jews, and consequently that it constituted a "direct incitement to immediate mass murder."[2] After a long legal struggle that lasted until January 1978, the Illinois Supreme Court, in a seven-to-one decision (Judge Clark dissented without submitting any explanation), ruled in favor of Collin. The main argument was the content neutrality rule, according to which political speech shall not be abridged because of its content, even if that content is verbally abusive. Speech can be restricted only when it interferes in a physical way with other legitimate activities; when it is thrust upon a captive audience, or when it directly incites immediate harmful conduct. Otherwise, no matter what the content of the speech, the intention of the speaker, and the impact of the speech on noncaptive listeners, the speech is protected under the First Amendment to the U.S. Constitution.[3]

The court dismissed the main arguments of the citizens of Skokie; it enunciated that the display of the swastika was symbolic political speech intended to convey the ideas of the NSPA, even if these ideas were offensive. Similarly it argued that the plaintiffs' wearing of uniforms need not meet standards of acceptability. The judges further concluded that anticipation of a hostile audience could not justify prior restraint or restrict speech when that audience was not captive. Freedom of speech cannot be abridged because the listeners are intolerant of its content.[4]

Two basic points concerning this case are plain and generally agreed upon. First, Skokie was not a case of a captive audience, because the Jews had advance notification of the Nazis' intentions. Second, the argument that the Nazi march or speech was designed to convince some members of the audience to embrace all or part of the Nazi ideology was not an issue. Obviously, Collin's aim was not to convince his audience but to offend the Jewish population of Skokie. Nevertheless, the Illinois Supreme Court ruled that it was not a case of *fighting words,*[5] because the display of the swastika did not fall within the confines of that doctrine, and because the prevailing thought was no longer that it was up to the court to assess the *value* of utterances. The court ruled that the wearing of Nazi uniforms and the display of the swastika constituted political speech that was protected under the Free Speech clause.

I agree with the court's reasoning that the "fighting words" doctrine is not applicable to Skokie. Although you may suggest, following *Chaplinsky,* a place for a fighting *symbols* doctrine, I disagree. The crux of the matter in the fighting words doctrine is that some utterances are seen as having no essential part of any exposition of ideas; they do not communicate any ideas. Therefore they are ruled out of the free speech clause of the Constitution. On the other hand, the very use of a symbol intends to convey an idea, otherwise it would not be considered a symbol. It may be intended to insult or intimidate, etc.; but you cannot employ the reasoning of *Chaplinsky* here: fighting words contain no idea; symbols, by their characterization as such, *do* contain ideas.

In his examination of the Skokie decision, Feinberg agrees that the Nazis did not come with the intention of advocating their beliefs in order to convince the others of their "truth." They did not come to offer their opinions in the free marketplace of ideas. Their message was close to pure insult. Because the Nazis deliberately decided to march in Skokie, we can assume that their purpose was malicious: they came to offend the sensibilities of the Jewish population of Skokie. Feinberg acknowledges that the Jews would be offended by the demonstration not because of their curiosity, and certainly not from the anticipation of pleasure. He concedes that they did not willingly assume the risk of being offended. Hence the *Volenti* standard was satisfied. Nevertheless, Feinberg does not think that the reasonable avoidability standard was satisfied. With reference to the opinions of the Illinois Supreme Court and the lower federal courts that the display of the swastika is symbolic speech,[6] Feinberg argues that it is almost as absurd as saying that giving the finger or shouting Death to the Niggers! are the expression of a political opinion. Assertions of that kind or such as Jews Are Scum are not political speech; they are close to pure menacing insult, no less and no more.[7]

Feinberg does not regard the swastika and assertions such as Jews Are Scum as political speech.[8] He maintains, "Despite the intense aversion felt by the offended parties, there was not an exceptionally weighty case for legal interference with the Nazis, given the relative ease by which their malicious and spiteful insults could be avoided."[9]

In other words, since the Nazis announced the demonstration well in advance, it could easily be avoided by all those who wished to do so in most cases with but minimal inconvenience. Feinberg thus reiterates the reasoning of the Illinois Supreme Court in favor of the NSPA, in accordance with his reasonable avoidability standard. He contends that "the scales would tip the other way" if their behavior were to become more frequent, for the constant need to avoid public places at certain times can quickly become a major nuisance.[10] Because the issue concerned only one demonstration, the solution was easy enough: those likely to be offended could have been elsewhere when it was held. These assertions are in accordance with Feinberg's emphasis on the intensity and the durability of the repugnance produced.[11]

The Reasonable Avoidability Standard

From Feinberg's analysis we can deduce that the crux of the matter lay in the reasonable avoidability standard: the Jews could have ignored the offense, as others ignore someone's giving the finger. The Illinois Supreme Court ruled that the arguments of Skokie's inhabitants did not contain enough power to restrict a fundamental freedom because the Jews did not *have* to attend the rally. However, for these Jews this was no solution at all, because it took them back to the days when they had to hide from the Nazis. The survivors of the Holocaust had learned not to keep silent, not to wait until another wave of hatred was over. Hiding and running away was their solution in Europe, when they could not do anything else. That solution, they thought, was over and done with when they came to live in the United States after the war. For them, as Jews, when the Nazi phenomenon is at issue, no other way exists but to stand against it with all their power, especially when the Nazis decide to come to their neighborhood with the intention of hurting them and awakening their fear. Therefore, the suggestion that the Nazis would march in their front yard without their being present was inconceivable. It is not a matter of the nuisance involved in avoiding public places as Feinberg suggests; it is not a matter of a nuisance, nor of a public place. If the Nazis were to march elsewhere in Chicago (say in the city center), then their right to be heard is granted protection under the free speech principle.[12] Then we can say that this march is equally offensive to the Jews of Chicago, New York, or Tel Aviv.[13] But this is not the case when Nazis come to a neighborhood with a large Jewish population, when the clear and deliberate intention is to offend and excite the inhabitants, especially knowing that many of them are survivors of the Holocaust. Intentions and motives do matter because not knowing them may lead us to make a wrong interpretation as to the real and true motives of the agent. True, the same conduct may be interpreted in different ways, according to the motives of the doer. Witness, for instance, a farmer who takes her old donkey to the veterinarian to be killed because she wishes that the donkey not be subjected to further pain. We would regard this act as a humanitarian act per se. But if the same farmer takes her old donkey to be killed in front of the gates of the White House, not because its time is due but in protest against the high interest the farmers in the South are required to pay, which brings many of them to bankruptcy, and stating that a similar end awaits the Democratic donkey (referring to the Democratic president), then this act is surely a political act, and many humanitarians are likely to raise their voice in protest.

There is no fear of such confusion in the Skokie case. At issue is not a case of interpretation at all, for the Nazis voiced their reasons for coming to Skokie. Their intentions and motives were manifested by

Collin himself, who said that he had decided to march in Skokie in order to spite and offend the Jews. Under such circumstances, refraining from attending the march was not a solution for the Jews, as Feinberg suggests, for it would not make them evade the injury. It might even have increased it.

Clearly Collin did not mean to persuade the Jews that he was right or that his ideas were justified. He chose Skokie not only because it had a large community whom he could offend, but also because he wanted to gain public attention. As Dworkin has suggested to me in comments on this chapter, it was the grotesqueness of the venue that gained attention. This is true. The choosing of a venue is cardinal to the success of the demonstration. Protests are made where their messages can be conveyed best. We, for example, will not seriously consider a demonstration against sending American and British troops to Saudi Arabia, say, at a zoo. We would expect such a demonstration to take place outside draft offices or opposite the White House and 10 Downing Street. By the same logic, we would expect Nazis to propagate their ideas in a Jewish neighborhood. The question is whether our understanding of Collin's motives in choosing Skokie to attract public attention and media coverage should convince us to allow the march. My conclusive answer is no. I repeat: when the offense is serious, the intentions of the offender are clear, and the target group is not in a position to avoid the offense, then democracy should draw the line and constrain freedom of expression.

These arguments should not suggest that only the demonstrations meant to persuade should be allowed, whereas those meant to protest or to offend should be prohibited. The intention of the demonstrators is only one of the considerations we should bear in mind when deciding on boundaries of freedom of expression. No less significant are the seriousness of the offense and the circumstance under which the protest is being made; that is, whether the target group can avoid the demonstration without being hurt by the act of going away. In this context, historical experience is of relevance.

To recapitulate, avoiding the march, particularly from the viewpoint of the survivors, was tantamount to hiding, and this they could not have accepted, not in their own village. For the Jews there was no solution but to stand up and declare that Nazism won't pass! For them any other policy would effectively be the same as conceding the opposite, that Nazism may pass. The situation as it developed put the Jews of Skokie in such a position that in either case they would have been offended: to attend the demonstration would have required them to see the swastika, the Nazi uniform, etc.; not to have attended would have been tantamount to allowing Nazism to pass—and pass in their own neighborhood. However, our acceptance of that conclusion is a criticism of the main argument of the Illinois Supreme Court, later to be adopted by Feinberg. The argument that the Jews could not have avoided a Nazi march in Skokie does not in itself constitute sufficient grounds to imply that Collin's right to freedom of expression had to be curtailed in that instance. What we have tried to establish so far is that the seriousness of the offense was severe according to the *Volenti* standard and the reasonable avoidability standard. We still have to clarify the scope of the extent of the offense standard and explain how serious the offense has to be so as to make it liable to restriction. First we have to examine whether the case falls under the argument regarding the Harm Principle.

Reflection on *argument number one* brings us to conclude that Skokie does not fall under the Harm Principle. Recall that the argument provides grounds for abridging speech if it instigates the causing of physical harm to individuals or groups. We may say that Collin's advocacy was designed to offend the Jews, and that the very reason for coming to Skokie was to inflict pain upon them. But this case was undoubtedly not a case of instigation, since the time factor necessary to translate hate speeches into practice did not play a role. On this point I endorse the Court's decision in *Brandenburg*: the Jews were not in imminent danger of physical pain as a result of the march, and arguably the expression was not directed at producing imminent lawless action. However, the courts ignored the possibility that expressions—although they do not produce imminent lawless action—still may cause, by their utterance, detrimental results as action may do.[14] Thus the *Brandenburg* test is too strict in its demands and, therefore, restrictive in its application. My view is that the fact that Skokie was not a case of instigation might have been a sufficient reason to protect the expression and allow the march, *unless* we can say that the expression in itself constitutes pain that can be considered morally on a par with physical harm. In other words, although Skokie was not a case of instigation and therefore cannot fall within the confines of the Harm Principle, nevertheless, if strong argument were provided that the very utterance of the Nazi expression constitutes *psychological* damage that can be equated with physical pain, then we can make a strong

case against tolerance under the Offense Principle and in accordance with
the extent of offense standard. Then we may say, contrary to Feinberg's
presupposition, that an offense may be as serious as harm.[15]

Psychological Offense, Morally on a Par with Physical Harm

The issue of psychological damage is problematic for two reasons. First,
a general claim is that the law is an inappropriate instrument for dealing
with expression that produces mental distress or whose targets are the
beliefs and values of an audience.[16] Second, speaking of psychological
damage necessarily involves drawing a distinction between annoyance or
some emotional distress and a significant offense to the mental framework of people.

As for the first claim, Franklin S. Haiman has argued that individuals
in a free society "are not objects which can be *triggered* into action by
symbolic stimuli but human beings who *decide* how they will respond to
the communication they see and hear."[17] People are appropriately thought
of as rational human beings who carefully weigh arguments and decide
according to them. But, as I submitted in chapter 1, people also have
feelings, drives, and emotions, which are sometimes so powerful as to
dominate their view regarding an object, a phenomenon, or other people.
A personal trauma, for example, may prevent an autonomous person
who is usually capable of reasoning and making choices from developing
a rational line of thought about the causes of the trauma. However,
Haiman's position is that the anguish experienced by those exposed to
scenes that remind people of their trauma is a price that must be paid for
freedom of speech. Haiman admits that it is difficult not to seem callous
in holding this position, but he "must take that risk and so argue."[18]
Otherwise, those who display Nazi symbols would have to be prohibited
from appearing not only in front of the Skokie Village Hall but in any
other public place where they may be expected to be seen by survivors of
the Holocaust. Even a television documentary examining and vividly
portraying Nazi activity may have to be censored because of its impact
on survivors of the Holocaust.[19] However, both arguments do not suf-
fice to explain why the law should not deal with expressions that produce mental distress, for the avoidability standard takes the sting out of
them. The Offense Principle, as postulated, does not supply grounds for

restricting either of Haiman's examples. You can intentionally avoid an encounter with an offensive phenomenon in the city center or switch your television off; either of these acts may be deemed necessary to keep your peace of mind. However, intentionally going away from facing an offensive phenomenon occurring in your own neighborhood entails more than mere avoidance. It may be thought of by some people in the neighborhood as surrender. Haiman, like the Illinois Supreme Court and others, fails to understand this.

With regard to the second issue, the distinction between annoyance or some emotional distress and a severe offense to someone's psyche is not clear-cut, and it is bound to awaken controversy, for the task obviously requires professional judgments, which further complicates this issue. These reasons have influenced the literature so that it lacks sufficient consideration of the potential psychological injury that some speech-acts may cause. But these difficulties should not make us overlook the issue. Instead, because we are aware of the complexities that are involved, we must make the qualifications as conclusive as possible and the requirements equally stringent in order not to open avenues to further suppression of freedom of expression. We must insist that restrictions on freedom of expression be as clear as possible, for otherwise they may become counterproductive by denying our liberties instead of protecting them. Hence, when we speak of a psychological offense we refer to an offense well beyond inconvenience, irritation, or some other marginal form of emotional distress. Only a considerable pain, one that is not speculative or hypothetic and that is preferably backed by material evidence, may provide us with a reason to restrict freedom of expression under the Offense Principle, assuming that the circumstances make the offense inescapable. With regard to Skokie our task, therefore, is to establish that the offense was such as to constitute an injury that outweighed the special status reserved for freedom of expression.

Psychologists gave testimony about the possible injuries many Jews would suffer as a result of the march. They argued that this speech-act could be regarded as the equivalent of a physical assault.[20] This entails that the speech-act was properly subject to regulation (if we recall Scanlon's theory) as was any physical attack.[21] Thus, in opposition to the *Brandenburg* and *Skokie* decisions, the argument I am advancing is that the content of speech *is* of significance. In emphasizing content, my focus is put not on the truth of the speech but on its *effects*. When the content and the purpose of expression are overlooked, freedom of speech may be exploited in a way that rebuts fundamental principles that underlie a democratic society. Indeed, the United States Supreme Court recognized in a series of cases several classes of speech as having "low" value, and thus deserving only limited constitutional protection.[22] The Court held that otherwise speech can be exercised willfully to inflict injury upon the target persons and groups, thus transforming freedom of speech into a means of curtailing the freedoms of others. We should bear in mind the content of speeches, for when they are designed to inflict psychological damage upon their target group, there is a basis to consider their constraint. The Illinois Appellate Court's ruling, later to be overruled by the Illinois Supreme Court, justified the restriction of the Nazi march because of the likelihood of such injury. The appellate court said "the tens of thousands of Skokie's Jewish residents must feel gross revulsion for the swastika and would immediately respond to the personally abusive epithets slung their way in the form of the defendant's chosen symbol, the swastika."[23]

The court maintained that the swastika was a personal affront to every member of the Jewish faith, especially to the survivors of the Holocaust. These beliefs were powerful enough to rule in favor of Skokie's residents and against Collin. However, this ruling supplies a weaker standard than the one that was just declared for restricting free speech. "Gross revulsion" and "personally abusive epithets" make a more general standard for constraining freedom of speech. As I remarked, some people may be offended simply at the sight of black and white people holding hands. Another may feel gross revulsion when watching a commercial featuring a woman in a bathing suit. We cannot extend the scope of the Offense Principle to include any potential reaction of disgust on the part of some people. Therefore, we ought to insist on the more stringent requirement that holds that a restriction on freedom of speech under the Offense Principle is permissible only if we can show that the speech in question causes psychological offense that may be equated with physical pain.

Now we face the problem of making intelligible this distinction between an offense that causes *emotional distress* or *personal affront* and an offense that causes *psychological injury* amounting to physical pain. Donald Vandeveer has argued that offensive acts in general cause unpleasant distressful psychological states to one degree or another. To be offended is, by definition, to suffer distress or anguish.[24] The Offense Principle allows infringement of freedom of speech only in specific cases when the damage is deemed to be irreversible. Skokie is a relevant case because racist utterances, as mentioned, have a damaging psychological impact on the target group that is difficult to overcome or to reverse. Consequently, the extent of offense standard is satisfied to an extent that Feinberg does not acknowledge when formulating his standards. In some instances the seriousness of the offense can be viewed as morally on a par with physical harm. A Nazi march in a Jewish neighborhood populated by survivors of the Holocaust is a case in point.

A further clarification is called for in order to make the argument under the Offense Principle more precise. The principle does not provide grounds to restrict racial hatred *as such*. It insists that we should take into consideration the circumstances under which the speech is made. In this respect my view is somewhat different from that of criminal codes of some European countries, such as Sweden or Britain.[25] Chapter 16, section 8, of the Swedish Criminal Code (amended in 1982) reads, "Anyone who publicly or otherwise in a declaration or other statement which is disseminated to the public threatens or expresses contempt for an ethnic group or some similar group of persons, with allusion to race, color, national or ethnic origin or religious creed, shall be sentenced for agitation against ethnic groups by imprisonment of up to two years or, if the crime is petty, to a fine." With regard to the British stance, sections 5 and 18 of the Public Order Act of 1986 are relevant.[26] Section 5 prohibits threatening, abusive, or insulting speech likely to cause harassment, alarm, or distress.[27] There need be no intention to insult; sufficient is that an ordinary person may feel so insulted.[28] In turn, section 18 of the 1986 act reads, "(1) A person who uses threatening, abusive or insulting words or behaviour, or displays any written material which is threatening, abusive or insulting, is guilty of an offense if (a) he intends thereby to stir up racial hatred, or (b) having regard to all the circumstances racial hatred is likely to be stirred up thereby."[29]

If we are to follow the British reasoning, then grounds may be established to prohibit a Hyde Park speaker from conveying racist opinions. This book postulates that such a speaker should not be denied expression because the listeners are free to leave the place at will, thereby avoiding the offense. Relying on the Millian formulation of the Offense Principle, which speaks of a combination of consequences *and* circumstances and

also on Feinberg's standards that determine the seriousness of the offensiveness, I insist that the fact that some types of speech (such as racial and
discriminatory advocacy) create great psychological distress is *not* in
itself a sufficiently compelling reason to override free speech. The Home
Affairs Committee of the House of Commons in 1979–80 recommended
not to create power to ban marches where there was a likelihood of racial
incitement. Eric Barendt, concurring, writes, "[H]owever distasteful the
views of these [racist] organizations may be, they are entitled to the same
freedom of speech as those with more orthodox opinions, and the suppression of such views may be the first slide down the 'slippery slope'
towards total government control of political discourse."[30]

Prescribing of boundaries to freedom of expression has to be a pains-
taking effort, involving careful consideration and lucid articulation so as
to avoid sliding down the slippery slope. I must, nevertheless, express
reservation in regard to the traditional British position that emphasizes
solely the fear of provoking a breach of the peace. This reasoning comes
close to *argument number one*. Indeed, looking at the way the British
authorities have dealt with fascist and racist demonstrations over the
years, we can assume that this reasoning would have been invoked in
order to ban a Skokie-like demonstration.[31] The British approach is at
variance with that adopted in the United States.

In Britain, unlike the United States, there is no guaranteed right to
demonstrate. The view is that public processions are prima facie lawful;
that is, *peaceful* demonstrations are lawful.[32] Accordingly, a procession
may be banned only on the ground that it is likely to cause "serious
public disorder."[33] Herein lies my disagreement with the British stance.
My view is that the apprehension of serious public disorder should not be
the sole ground for the prohibition of processions and assemblies.[34] Thus
I have offered the Offense Principle as another reasoning for abridging
expressions. The British authorities considered this line of reasoning in
the Green Paper of 1980 and the White Paper of 1985 and rejected it on
both occasions.

In 1980 the British Home Office considered the question whether it
would be right for marches to be banned where serious offense is likely to
be caused to sections of the community—"for example, on racial or
religious grounds"—even though serious disorder is not likely to ensue.
The Home Office's answer was negative.[35] The same issue was put on the
agenda in 1985, and again it was concluded that such a ban "would place

an impossible task upon the police and be an unacceptable infringement of freedom of speech."[36] The Home Office Committee reiterated that considerations of public order should continue to be the sole test for banning of processions. However, I do not see why in delicate or (resorting to familiar phraseology) hard cases—such as Skokie—the police have to be left to decide whether to allow the demonstration in question. And this reasoning underestimates the extent of harm that is inflicted upon the target group, which cannot avoid being exposed to the offensive utterances.

An additional comment has to be made before formulating our argument under the Offense Principle. Among the justifications voiced for the *Skokie* decision was the contention that if the Nazis were denied free expression, this would jeopardize the entire structure of the right to freedom of speech that has been erected. According to this argument, to permit Skokie to ban this speech because of its offensiveness would mean that southern whites could ban civil rights marches, especially those that are held by blacks.[37] Let us assume as plausible the argument that the degree of the irritation resulted in this case amounted to psychological offense. Then the southern whites could claim that these demonstrators act in a manner they found to be seriously offensive; that the marchers maliciously, recklessly, or negligently disregarded the southern whites' interest in not being harmed by seriously offensive actions, such as marching in *their* territory; that the corollary of these marches was severe injury, conducive to further impairment of those whites who were offended, and difficult to reverse. However, the Offense Principle is intended to defend against the abuse of freedom by those who deny respect for others. It is not to assist those whose motivation is to cause harm to others, whose aim is either to intimidate or to discriminate and to deny rights to others.[38] A set of values underlies a liberal society, and we judge in accordance with it. The fact that some individuals are offended by a speech that advocates equal rights cannot supply sufficient reason for its restriction. The principle bears its effects on freedom of expression when the speech in question contradicts fundamental background rights to human dignity and to equality of concern and respect (see chapter 3). Otherwise, every speech that some may find psychologically offensive may be curtailed. Members of the civil rights movement who come to demonstrate in the southern United States do not deny the rights of any group of people. In contrast to the Nazis in Skokie, they are not deliberately setting out to upset southern whites. The intentions of the civil rights marchers are not to offend but rather to protect the rights of those who are discriminated against by those who now claim that they are being offended. The right to freedom of speech is here exercised out of respect for others, aiming to preach values that are in accordance with the moral codes of a liberal society, not values that deny these accepted moral codes. Those who are offended by the values adopted by the entire society implicitly argue when wishing to prevent the demonstration that their problem is not with the march as such. Instead, their problem is a matter of principle that concerns their place within a liberal society.

Hence, I suggest four major elements be taken into account when we come to restrict expression on the grounds of psychological offense: the content of the expression; the tenor and the manner of the expression; the intentions and the motive of the speaker; and the objective circumstances in which the advocacy is to take place. As noted, sometimes the manner of the expression is not important (see chapter 7, the example of a fundamentalist leader who calmly calls for a Jihad). On the other hand, sometimes the manner of expression also covers the requirement of content. When the manner of the expression (say symbolic speech) is explicit to the extent that it does not leave room for misinterpretation and can be regarded as pure speech carrying unmistakeable content, then the manner of expression also covers the requirement of content.[39] That is, when a group comes to a Jewish neighborhood, wearing Nazi uniforms with swastika armbands, they do not have to say anything. Their message is clear enough given their appearance.[40] Then the requirements for abridging the harmful expression are satisfied. Were the Nazis to decide to hold their demonstration elsewhere other than in a Jewish neighborhood, then no right would have existed to restrict their freedom, for we can say that the offense is equally shared by Jews wherever they are, without specifying a target group in a particular place. Alternatively, if the Nazis were to wear street clothes and not display the swastika, then again we may not have a case to withhold expression.[41] In both instances the conditions do not satisfy the standards, outlined by Feinberg, that constitute a serious offense.

In Skokie, however, the manner of the expression was intended to cause an offense, and the objective circumstances were such as to make the obvious target group exposed to that serious offense. Applying Scanlon's distinction between interests of participants, interests of audiences, and interests of bystanders,[42] we see that the interest of the audience in avoiding the demonstration outweighs the interest of the Nazis in practicing their right to freedom of expression in the heart of a Jewish neighborhood. It is quite difficult to think of the rally as compatible with the "central audience interest" in having "a good environment," for the audience that was to witness the planned march clearly did not wish to communicate with the actors or be exposed to their ideas.[43] It is also difficult to claim that the Nazis wanted to have a "good environment" for the formation of their beliefs and desires, specifically in the village of Skokie. Thus, the special circumstances of Skokie make a strong case against tolerance, and accordingly we can now lay down our second qualification of free speech. This restriction is made under the Offense Principle.

Argument number two. Under the Offense Principle, when the content or manner of a speech is designed to cause psychological offense against a target group, and the objective circumstances make that group inescapably exposed to that offense, then the speech in question has to be restricted.

This argument differs from my reconstruction of the Millian Harm Principle in two crucial respects: it covers damages that are not physical, and it restricts types of speeches that fall within the category of *advocacy,* as distinguished from *instigation.*

At this stage one last point has to be made. It could be argued that the Offense Principle as formulated here may be good for Skokie, but that the circumstances of Skokie make it a special case. Therefore, the applications of the principle are extremely limited. I agree that the applications of the Offense Principle are limited. I made every effort to prescribe it as precisely as I could. I think that any principle aiming to restrict freedom of expression has to be well defined so as not to open the way to further restrictions. The Offense Principle outlines specific conditions as grounds for abridging speech. Skokie satisfies these conditions, and thus my conclusion is that the Illinois Supreme Court's decision was flawed. But Skokie is not the only incident to which the Offense Principle may be applied. Skokie makes an interesting case, but it is not a unique case. We can think of other instances in which the same reasoning is applicable. I will show in part 2 that Kahane's visits to Arab villages is a case in point.

Here I wish to consider for a moment the Salman Rushdie affair as a further example.

I will not delve into the entire range of complexities of this story.[44] My intention is to suggest that it is one thing to allow the publication of *The Satanic Verses* and quite another to grant Rushdie permission, if he should wish to do so, to disseminate his ideas out of spite in a religious Pakistani neighborhood in England. Suppose that Rushdie would decide to hold a rally in promotion of his book outside the central mosque of Bradford. The point of coming to that neighborhood could be only to affront, insult, and lacerate the feelings of the Pakistani population. Even if Mr. Rushdie himself were willing to take the risk and bear the consequences of his act, the offense involved in such an act to the relevant neighborhood remains too great to be overridden by his right of free speech. Forms of freedom of expression should be compatible with a commitment to human dignity and respect for others. If they are not, then the given circumstances and the evaluation of the likely result should be taken into account. This example is clearly a case of disregard for the beliefs of people. Here we have reason to believe that the speech is psychologically offensive to an extent that is equivalent to physical harm. A specific target group exists, and the circumstances are such as to make the offense unavoidable. Hence, we have strong justification against tolerance. Similarly, a cross burning by the Ku Klux Klan may be more easily tolerated in a field outside a southern town than in Harlem.[45] Analogous considerations guide us when assessing Kahane's visits to Arab villages. In all three examples the interests of the audiences are more significant than the interests of the participants. In these instances Feinberg's standards are satisfied.

To sum up, we ought not to tolerate every speech, whatever it may be, for then we elevate the value of freedom of expression, and indeed, of tolerance, over other values deemed to be of no less importance such as human dignity and equality of concern and respect. Tolerance that conceives the right to freedom of expression as a carte blanche allowing any speech under any circumstance may prove to be counterproductive, assisting the infliction of pain upon individuals by intolerant movements and helping them to flourish.[46] Therefore, we have to be aware of the dangers of words and restrict forms of expression when designated as levers to harmful, discriminatory actions; for words, to a great extent, are prescriptions for actions. Moreover, when suggesting defensive principles of democracy, with the aim of putting liberty and tolerance within boundaries, I speak of restricting expression intended to inflict physical or psychological pain upon others, of opposing ideas and theories that dehumanize a category of people according to general criteria that clearly involve no criminal commitment, criteria of race, religion, color, sex, sexual preference, status, class, etc.

These concluding assertions take us to the second part of this study, in which I analyze the struggle of the Israeli democracy against Kahanism. I will examine the mechanisms applied in this anti-Kach (Kahane's party) campaign, the justifications given for the limitations that were set, and how justified they were according to the Respect for Others Argument and the Harm and the Offense Principles.

Part Two

Application
Democracy on the Defensive: Israel's Reaction to the Kahanist Phenomenon

What is hateful to you do not do unto your fellow people.
—Hillel (Babylonian Talmud. Sabbath 31a)

The aim of this part of the analysis is to apply the theoretical principles to a case study and to see how a democracy dealt with challenges that threatened to undermine its existence. I propose to look at the Israeli democracy and its fight against the Kahanist phenomenon. Doing so has two major merits. First, we should combine theory with application, for generalities and principles are much clearer when they are illustrated by instances. Hence, the following discussion will analyze the reaction of society to Kahane, reflecting on the inherent problems that were theoretically discussed: What should the limits of tolerance be? What constraints on freedom should be introduced? And in what circumstances?

Second, the subject of the Israeli struggle against Kahane has not been developed and explored to a satisfactory degree. I do not know of any study that analyzes how Israeli society dealt with the phenomenon or discusses whether its treatment of Kahane was in accordance with democratic principles.

I shed light, in chapter 9, on Kahane's character and his activities in the United States and Israel. In this chapter I also deliberate on the principal ideas that made Kahane the enemy of the establishment. The reading of his proposals will explain why extraordinary measures were taken against Kahane's movement (Kach) not only by the political system, but also by the media and the educational system. These measures included attempts to delegitimize Kach and to obstruct its activities. To this end, members of the Knesset (with the exception of some members of ultra-Orthodox parties) united to abandon the plenum whenever Kahane rose to speak. Organizations were established with the aim of fighting Kahanism. Parties, groups, and individuals refrained from meeting and debating with Kahane, thinking that any such act might help to legitimize him.

Since much of the struggle against Kahanism involves legal considerations, I provide in chapter 10 the necessary background for understanding the judicial decisions concerning Kahane. I probe the normative considerations and the doctrine of precedent that guided the Supreme Court in formulating its decisions. Attention will be given to the Declaration of

Independence and to three precedents that the court often cites when constitutional matters are at issue. These are *Kol Ha'am* (1953), *Jeryis* (1964), and *Yeredor* (1965). The discussion will address the issue of whether the justices acted in accordance with the law. That is, attention will be given to the written law and to the existing normative considerations that allow justices an exegetic latitude. Then we will be in a position to decide whether the justices were correct or incorrect in their judgments in the light of the law (written as well as unwritten). Further consideration will be given to the question of whether the existing legal arrangement is a desirable one or whether it should be replaced by something more suitable.

I probe, in chapter 11, the attempts that were made to restrict Kahane's freedom to compete in the elections. I will mainly discuss the *Neiman* decision of 1984, which allowed him this freedom, arguing that it was flawed. My basic contention is that the court was incorrect in ignoring the licensing effect of its decision, and that democracy does not have to allow an electoral list propounding the destruction of democracy to fulfill its aim. It is not morally obligatory nor morally coherent to expect democracy to place the means for its own destruction in the hands of those who wish to bring about the physical annihilation of the state or to undermine democracy. These two cases are the only ones in which democracy has to introduce self-defensive measures and to deny representation in parliament to lists that convey such ideas and that act to realize them. Therefore, when a political list such as Kach bases its political platform on discrimination and disrespect toward others, aiming to harm some people and to undermine democracy, it should be disqualified, as Kach indeed was in 1988. The basis for this disqualification was an amendment to the Basic Law: The Knesset (1958) that prohibits a party with a political platform that is antidemocratic or incites racism or negates the existence of Israel as the state of the Jewish people from standing for elections. This legislation was specifically aimed at banning Kach.

In chapter 12 I reflect on the attempts to restrict Kahane's freedom of expression and movement. Applying the Offense Principle, I argue that the decision to restrict Kahane's freedom of movement was justified. No other way existed to stop Kahane from conducting his provocative visits to Arab villages, where he intended to preach his Orwellian idea of emigration for peace. However, I differentiate between restricting Kahane from holding rallies in Arab places and withholding his freedom of demonstration *as such*. Although restricting rallies was necessary, the denial of free demonstration abridged Kahane's fundamental rights without a sufficient reason.

I also discuss, in chapter 12, Kahane's appeals to the supreme court, seeking its assistance in securing his rights. No less than five of these appeals were against the speaker of the Knesset, Shlomo Hillel, who stood at the forefront of the campaign against Kahane. The court upheld Kahane's right to raise motions of no confidence in the Knesset, to submit racist bills, and to express his opinions in the media. I will review those decisions, arguing that although the decision to allow him to submit racist bills was flawed, the other decisions were correct. Applying the Harm and the Offense Principles, I reiterate that freedom of expression may be abridged if the expression in question comes under one of these principles. But a difference exists between allowing the expression of racist diatribes and permitting a racist list to gain legitimacy through elections and to further its aim of discriminating against others through legislation. Bearing the *Neiman* ruling in mind, the court was consistent in allowing Kahane to introduce his bills. For my part, I contend that both decisions were flawed.

I close by discussing some of the developments since the disqualification of Kach, arguing that although Kahane is no longer present on the political scene, his ideas have gained deep roots in Israeli society. I am not arguing that antidemocratic, racist ideas have emerged only since Kahane's ideas became known to the public; instead, these ideas were discussed more in the open as a result of Kahane's activity on the political scene, and he helped establish them as part of the political agenda. A long process of education, accompanied by a significant political effort to solve the Israeli-Palestinian conflict, would be needed in order to change the current feelings toward the Arab minority and its status in Israeli society.

Chapter 9

The Kahanist Phenomenon

Background

Meir Martin Kahane was born in 1932 in Brooklyn, New York. In his youth he joined the United Zionist-Revisionist Movement of America, which was affiliated with the world organization of the Heirut party in Israel.[1] In June 1968 Kahane, together with Bertram Zweibon and Morton Dolinsky, founded the Jewish Defense League (JDL). The slogan they adopted was Never Again,[2] and their symbol was the Jewish Magen David (Star of David) with a clenched fist. At first the JDL's main aim was to fight against anti-Semitism and more specifically to defend the Jews of New York City from attacks by blacks. The emphasis was on a return to Jewish roots, combined with physical and quasi-military training involving the use of weapons. Later, the JDL became more and more involved in the struggle for Soviet Jewry. In December 1969 Kahane announced that henceforth the league's primary concern would be Soviet Jewry. The league opened a campaign against the Soviet Union: it suggested a boycott of American companies trading with the USSR, disrupted Russian cultural events, had members phone Soviet agencies and residences in the United States day and night, harassed Soviet diplomats, and generally made the lives of Soviet delegates in the United States difficult.[3]

At the peak of its success, in the year following the Skokie affair, the JDL organization had enrolled 19,000 members throughout the United States and in several other countries. However, Kahane and the JDL never gained the support of leading Jewish organizations. The Jewish leadership denounced JDL activities against the Soviet Union and what

seemed to be unnecessary violence by the JDL in the Jewish neighborhoods of New York City. Another factor that decreased Kahane's status
in the eyes of the Jewish leadership was his association with Joe Co-
lombo, the head of a Mafia family in New York City.

The early 1970s was a period of détente in East-West relations, and the
JDL's activity was anything but a contribution toward easing the tensions
between the two sides. According to confidential State Department documents, President Nixon became concerned that Kahane would wreck the
Strategic Arms Limitations Talks.4 For this reason, the FBI, whose attitude toward the JDL's violent acts had been quite lenient until then,
decided to adopt a new policy toward the league. Evidence was gathered
against Kahane connecting him with several illegal activities: holding
weapons without a license; planting bombs in several offices, including
those of the Palestinian Liberation Organization (PLO) and Soviet organizations;5 participation in violent rallies; attacking Russian buildings
and harassing Russian and Iraqi diplomats; and disturbing the peace.6 At
that time many JDL activists decided to leave the United States in order
to escape trial. Israel served their purpose as a state of refuge.

In July 1971 Kahane stood trial in the United States, charged with
conspiracy to violate provisions of the Federal Firearms Act of 1968. He
received a suspended prison sentence of five years together with a fine of
$5,000.7 He was warned not to deal any more, directly or indirectly,
verbally or actively, in any business involving violence and the use of
weapons.8 Kahane decided to immigrate to Israel and to make Jerusalem
his permanent base. In the summer of 1971 he announced the opening of
the JDL International Office in Jerusalem and the adoption of *aliya* ("immigration to Israel") as the core of league ideology.

For financial reasons, among others, Kahane had to keep in close
contact with the American organization; consequently, he made frequent
visits to the United States. In May 1972 an American court decided that
Kahane had violated his probation conditions by aiding the dissemination of information about weapons in Brooklyn.9 The stringency of Kahane's probation conditions was increased. A few years later, in January
1975, during a visit to New York City, Kahane created disturbances near
the Soviet Mission to the United Nations. Two shots were directed at the
mission. Kahane was brought before a judge and this time he was sentenced to one year's imprisonment. Kahane tried to appeal against the
decision but his motion was denied.10

From the time of his arrival in Israel in September 1971, Kahane was active on the political scene. At first he thought of continuing his terrorist acts. Thus, following the massacre of eleven Israeli athletes in the 1972 Olympic games in Munich, Germany, Kahane initiated an operation to sabotage the Libyan consulate in Rome. The security forces foiled that attempt at Ben-Gurion Airport. Kahane was not arrested in connection with the operation, but the failure certainly had an impact on him, convincing him of the need to be extra cautious in planning his future illegal activities. Nevertheless, he continued to propagate his extreme views, and from time to time he resorted to violent activities. Despite those views and actions, the attitude of the political and judicial systems toward Kahane (like that of the United States systems from 1968 through 1971) was quite lenient.[11]

The first step to limit Kahane's activity was taken in September 1972, when the military commanders of the West Bank and the Gaza Strip prohibited his entry into the territories. Seven months later, in April 1973, an indictment against Kahane was submitted by the attorney of the district of Jerusalem. It said that between December 1972 and January 1973 the Jewish Defense League of Israel (Kach) had launched a campaign among the Arabs of Israel, calling on them to emigrate from Israel in return for compensation. The charge against Kahane was sedition.[12]

The trial began in May 1973 but was never brought to a conclusion. Itzhak Zamir, who later became the attorney general,[13] explained that the sedition law was problematic because every newspaper daily published things that could be seen as a violation of this section. Therefore, this was not the appropriate instrument to deal with Kahane's statements.[14]

On 7 June 1973 Kahane was arrested for conspiring to commit acts of violence in the United States and for attempting to harm American-Israeli relations. This was after letters written by Kahane to friends in America were intercepted by the Israeli military censor. In these letters Kahane gave instructions for the blowing up of the Iraqi Embassy in Washington, D.C.; the assassination of Russian diplomats;[15] a shooting attack on the Soviet Embassy; and the placing of a bomb at the offices of Occidental Petroleum as a warning against deals with the Russians. Kahane was convicted and received a suspended sentence. Judge Bazak said he doubted the seriousness of Kahane's criminal intent because he had sent the letter "by regular mail, without using any form of code." He maintained, "It seems more likely this was an emotional and noisy presentation than it was an actual underground plan."[16]

The same year, two months after the outbreak of the Yom Kippur War, Kahane stood for elections for the first time and failed, although he came quite close to his goal. To be elected, a candidate had to gain the support of 1 percent of the electorate. Kahane received 0.81 percent (12,811 votes).

In 1974 Kahane started advocating the idea of Jewish terror against Arab terror. At that time the right-wing movement *Gush Emunim* ("the Block of the Faithful") was going from strength to strength, and Kahane had to find a strategy to distinguish himself, creating a rubric for Kach by crossing the Rubicon. He exacerbated the political atmosphere by initiating violent encounters with Arabs. His position of a strong Jewish stand inspired the first illegal bodies who held that *lex talionis* ("an eye for an eye") is the only answer to the rivalry with the Arabs. Three years later Kahane ran for election for the second time. His failure then was more dramatic. He received only 0.25 percent (4,396 votes) of the electoral vote.

These failures did not discourage him, nor did they induce him to change his opinions. On the contrary. The Camp David accords radicalized Kahane even further. He thought that the way to increase his popularity would be to resort to more extreme and violent activities. He adopted the same methods in Israel that had served him well in the United States. Kahane advocated militant solutions, used black-and-white slogans drawing a distinction between *us* and *them,* and manipulated the media by staging newsworthy events. Kahane always believed that it was not enough to speak; activities had to be undertaken to show *them* (in Israel the term *them* refers to the Arabs) that he was serious in his plans and to attract the attention of the media. Neither the political nor the judicial systems learned from the American experience in their dealings with Kahane. Thus Kach enjoyed great latitude in conducting its activities. Three major violent incidents are worth recalling.

On 18 October 1978 members of Kach, headed by Yossi Dayan, then general secretary of the movement, penetrated the Abraham Avinu Synagogue, situated in the heart of the city of Hebron. They ignored a military ordinance that declared the place a closed area and attacked soldiers who were instructed to get them out. The maximum penalty for such an act is five years in prison. Dayan was the only person who was convicted. He received a six-month conditional sentence and a fine of IL 1,000 (Israeli lire).

Dayan learned from this incident that he could continue his activities. On 20 January 1979, despite an ordinance that prohibited him from the Cave of Machpelah (the burial place of the patriarchs and their wives) in Hebron, Dayan entered the area and prevented a soldier from doing his job. He was prosecuted and this time his sentence was two weeks' imprisonment and a fine of IL 2,000. The defendant appealed for amnesty to the local military commander, who reduced the punishment.

At the end of March 1979 a violent incident in the Temple Mount involved Kach activists. The bill of indictment included threats, religious insults, terrorist attacks, and trespassing. The sentence was twenty-three days in prison, which later was reduced to a six-month conditional term.

If asked to explain this lenient attitude I would say that the tendency at that time was to repress the issue by not placing it on the public agenda. Many people within the establishment believed that if Kahane were ignored then his legitimacy would be curtailed. They thought that Kahane's opinions did not deserve to be discussed like any other idea in the marketplace of ideas, and that any open disputation with them would help Kahane generate a better atmosphere to spread his views. The widely held view was that democracy had to tolerate any idea, but that nothing required anyone to take part in debates on the same platform with Kahane, an action that could be interpreted as a suggestion that his ideas had a legitimate place in society (see my discussion on weak forms of tolerance, part 1, chapter 2, "Latent and Manifest Tolerance"). In fact, the outcome was that the problem was ignored.

This was typical of decision making in Israel, a country whose politicians like to postpone confronting problems as long as possible. The tendency is to fall back on attractive, simple solutions rather than devote time, resources, and effort on dealing with problems considered unimportant or not pressing. This tendency was reinforced by a misunderstanding of, or a lack of will to deal with, the *core* of this problem, the fact that Kahane's support was based on ideas that have deep roots in Israeli society, views for which Kahane was a catalyst, not a midwife.

The Kahanist phenomenon did not go the way the decision makers wanted. Kahane refused to simply fade away. He became better known to the public and his ideas received wider public attention. Kahane recognized that the seeds of acceptance of his radical ideas had been sown and had germinated. The positive reaction of the public to his ideas encouraged him to intensify the campaign against the Arab population. In an article dated 11 May 1979 entitled, "It Cannot Continue," Kahane called for attacks on Arabs in order to teach them a lesson. In this article Kahane discussed terrorist attacks on Jewish people all over Israel, complaining that although such activities earlier had led Jews "to angrily attack Arabs and demand action," the public had now "grow[n] numb" and accepted terrorist bombs as a natural thing. He angrily advocated one ultimate solution, namely the removal of the hostile Arab minority from the land of Israel.[17]

Realizing that it would take some time for this plan to be implemented, Kahane postulated an immediate program that included the death penalty for terrorists, the expulsion of a fixed number of Arabs after every terrorist incident, and *"terror against terror"* (Kahane's emphasis). He called for the establishment of an antiterror group whose job would be to retaliate after every incident. Kahane also suggested what the government's attitude should be toward this group: "The government need never acknowledge its existence or it can deal with it on the same basis as the relationship between the PLO and the Arab host governments." Recognizing that some would see this advocacy as "immoral," to "these products of gentilized culture" Kahane recommended the words of the rabbis: "He who is merciful at a time when he should be cruel, is destined to be cruel at a time when he should be merciful."[18]

These arguments did not fall on deaf ears. A few years later it was discovered that two Jewish terrorist groups had been organized to retaliate against Arabs. The "small group" was comprised of five Kach activists who set fire to cars of Arabs.[19] The "big group," which was organized in 1980, was comprised of twenty-seven people. That group took the law into its hands, setting out to kill and maim Palestinians who were considered to be instigators of terrorist activities. Its members seriously injured two of the leaders of the National Guidance Committee and launched an attack on the Islamic College in Hebron during which three Palestinians were killed and some thirty others were wounded. The group also intended to blow up the Dome of the Rock and booby-trap five Arab buses in Jerusalem, "to show the Arabs that terrorism was a two-way street."[20] The Jewish terrorists were arrested just after they sabotaged the buses and before the buses exploded.

At the time that this terror group was active (1980–84) enough signs indicated that Kahane himself was involved in organizing attacks against Arabs. The lenient policy had to be replaced with a stringent one. In May 1980 it was decided to use one of the most antidemocratic procedures that exists in Israel against Kahane and another Kach member. Kahane and Baruch Green were put in administrative detention for six months. Section 2(a) of the Detention Law provides, "Where the Minister of Defence has reasonable cause to believe that reasons of state security or public security require that a particular person be detained, he may, by order under his hand, direct that such person be detained for a period, not exceeding six months, stated in the order."[21]

This is one of the rare occasions on which the measure has been taken against Jews. Detention was implemented after evidence was found to connect Kach with a large arsenal of ammunition in the *Hacotel* Yeshiva ("the Yeshiva of the Wailing Wall"). The charge against Kahane and Green was that they had planned assaults against Arabs and the bombing of the Temple Mount mosques. Kahane appealed to the courts but this time without any success. In his affirmation of the administrative detention, Justice Itzhak Kahan said that the danger to the state's security was so severe in this case that this extreme means represented the only way of preventing it. He explained, "I do not accept the argument that the provisions of the Law can be used only against someone who wants the destruction of the State of Israel. No such restriction is contained in section 2(a) of the Law. . . . [T]hese provisions can be used also to protect state security or public security against persons who, from a belief that they are acting in the interests of the State or in the interests of public security, commit or contemplate acts likely to impair state security or public security according to the test of a reasonable person."[22]

In the early 1980s Kahane broadened the scope of his activities. In his appearances and publications he frequently urged the necessity of fighting assimilation, stressing that it was always Arab men who seduced Jewish women. Kahane also emphasized the dual effect of the split-labor market that had been created after the Six-Day War in 1967, asserting that manual workers (mainly of Sephardi origin[23]) had lost their jobs because of the entrance of cheap Arab labor into society, and that Jews were superior to Arabs. Ideas like these, which clearly entailed discrimination against Arabs, attracted wide public attention and gained a great deal of support.

After the Six-Day War managers and contractors preferred to hire cheap Arab workers who did not demand social benefits and who were willing to work at any employment for salaries that Jews rejected with contempt. Different salaries were offered to Jews and Arabs for the same work. Some characterized the situation by saying that some jobs that Jews would not be willing to take were suitable for Arabs. From a psychological perspective this affected the lower class, comprised mainly of Sephardi Jews, who found that they no longer occupied the lowest class of society. As a result, feelings of superiority developed: there was one status for Jews and another for Arabs. Kahane propagated ideas that helped to legitimize these feelings. His entire ideology emphasized the Jew's special role in the world in general and in Israel in particular; ipso facto, it defined the status of the Arabs in society.

However, Kahane still did not succeed in translating that support into electoral gain. In 1981 Kach failed to be elected to the Tenth Knesset, receiving merely 5,128 votes (0.26 percent), only a slight improvement on the 1977 elections. In that year voices were first heard to assert that Israeli democracy should resort to defensive measures against Kahane's antidemocratic and racist ideas. A petition was submitted to the supreme court prior to the elections to disqualify Kach, but it was denied (cf. chapter 11). Two years later, the Socialist Party (Mapam) urged the need to outlaw Kach on the grounds that it was a fascist movement whose ideology, propaganda, and deeds were manifestly racist, leaving no choice but the enactment of a law to prohibit its activities. That call was exceptional for its time. The prevailing doctrine was that democracy had to endure any opinion, discriminatory views included.

The case for extending latitude to Kahane's opinions in the free marketplace of ideas was based on two different grounds: on the level of principle it was argued that every citizen in a democracy should enjoy the freedom to advocate any idea, however repulsive it may be. Israel would show its society's strength by resisting Kahane's views. This argument is in line with what I have called Arguments from Democracy (see chapter 5, "Grounds for Special Status"). It was common in political and legal circles and was expressed by Attorney General Zamir, who said that in order to defend the value of free speech we should be willing to hear exceptional views that lie outside the mainstream consensus.[24]

On the pragmatic-political level the claim was that Kahane was only a peripheral phenomenon who had no real chance of becoming a major force in politics. He could therefore be given the latitude to implement his ideas. The view was that Kahane was, and always would be, a political pawn who never would be able to increase his power substantially. An additional argument, popular among some sections of the public, held that to have someone like Kahane on the scene was a good thing in order to put the Arabs in their "right" place and to remind them that their situation could become worse if they did not behave as expected.

In April 1982 Kach received considerable public attention as a result of the evacuation of Yamit, the capital of the Rafiah settlement, which was to be returned to Egypt. Kach was one of the components of the Movement against the Retreat from Sinai. Being the most radical faction within the movement, Kach dictated the most dramatic incidents in that affair. Kahane's followers fortified themselves in an underground shelter, declaring their intention to commit collective suicide as an act of protest. Kahane, who happened to be in New York City, was rushed by the Israeli government to Yamit to persuade his supporters not to commit suicide. The entire negotiation process received wide coverage by the media in Israel and abroad, and Kahane skillfully masterminded a peaceful solution to the drama.

Two months later the Lebanon War (known also as Operation Peace for Galilee) broke out. It opened a new chapter in the history of the Israeli-Palestinian conflict, deepening the hostility between Jews and Arabs. The operation was intended to end within three days (according to Prime Minister Begin) and lasted three years. The elections of 1984 were held under its influence and that was the turning point for Kahane. Kach gained the support of 25,907 voters (1.2 percent of the votes) and thereby succeeded in entering parliament.

Indeed, looking at Kahane's attempts at election, we can discern two peaks: 1973 and 1984. The explanation for his mild success in 1973 and his achievement in 1984 cannot be separated from the wars that were waged in those years. In both cases there was an atmosphere of agitation against and dissatisfaction with the establishment. In 1973 that atmosphere resulted from the oversight of the Israeli Defense Force (IDF) intelligence, and the lack of predictive preparations when faced with the surprise attack launched by the Egyptians on Yom Kippur. However, Kahane was new in the country then and had not had time to establish himself in the political arena. In 1984 he enjoyed a much more receptive atmosphere to his views, which were by then well known.

The combination of the Lebanon War, together with severe economic problems in Israel, made his clear-cut slogans attractive to the people. The war deepened the political and ideological polarization of Israeli society, and it contributed to the radicalization of political opinions among Jews and Arabs. The Lebanon War did two main things: first, it made the Palestinians realize that nobody was going to do their job for them. The PLO had to evacuate its forces to distant places, and thus the inhabitants of the occupied territories understood that the burden was now on them to do something. Second, the Palestinians realized that they did not necessarily need a large, well-equipped army to harm the "best army in the Middle East." Terrorist acts, guerilla warfare, or mass civil violence could do enough damage; the Lebanese swamp brought about a change of consciousness, a necessary condition for any uprising.

Within the Jewish population the war deepened the split between the left and the right wings. The war also drove a wedge between the leadership and wide sectors of the population. Israeli society, tired of the vague promises of its leaders, sought solutions there and then. Kahane was there to offer his decisive plans and to capitalize on them. As the war continued, and every day more names were added to the list of Israeli casualties, feelings of hostility and hatred toward Arabs were fueled. More voices were heard calling for a harder line to teach the Arabs a lesson and speak to them in a language they understood. Kahane became the voice of "everything you wanted to say but never dared to say in the open." He supplied the nation, in a state of crisis and yearning for change, with conclusive answers.[25] In his public addresses Kahane emphasized the anti-Arab message while concealing his antisecular notions and the plan to transform Israel into a *Halacha* state, meaning a state that conducts its affairs in accordance with the Laws of the Torah. The ignorance shown by many of Kahane's secular followers regarding his plans to transform Israel into a theocracy was striking. Many of those who *were* aware of his program believed that it was more important to deal with the Arabs. Afterwards, they assumed, a modus vivendi would be found between a religious state and the current situation. They assumed that the "sacred" status quo would be kept.

Kahane appealed to the feelings of deprivation and bitterness among the lower classes, stressing that Arabs were taking work from Jews, and that the government was helping them by subsidizing their big families through generous social security benefits. Kahane's anti-establishment image helped him exploit the prevailing mood of mistrust and frustration toward the leadership and its policies. In addition, Prime Minister Begin's resignation helped Kahane win the support of Likud followers who were seeking a new charismatic leader, one who might fill the vacuum created by Begin's resignation.

From the first day of his election to the parliament, the new member of the Knesset became the target of fierce attacks. He was the man who almost everyone in the establishment liked to hate. The entire Israeli democracy seems to have been recruited to fight him and to curtail the influence of his ideas. Immediately after the 1984 elections the general director of the Education Ministry, Eliezer Shmueli, instructed headmasters throughout the country to deny Kahane entrance to schools. He also encouraged meetings between Jews and Arabs in order to bridge gaps and to increase understanding between the two parties.[26] Schools were supplied with compulsory material, produced by the Van Leer Jerusalem Institute, to teach children about democracy and civil rights, with the aim of fighting Kahane's discriminatory ideas.[27] Parties, groups, and individuals refrained from meeting and debating with Kahane, thinking that any such act might help legitimize Kach. Organizations that usually did not involve themselves in politics raised their voices in denunciation of Kahanism. One day after the election, the Second Generation to the Holocaust Remembrance organization decided to raise its voice for the first time over a political matter. This voluntary organization, composed of some 2,000 people, many of them children and grandchildren of Holocaust survivors, published a press notice saying that it was appalled by the thought that quasi-fascist ideas, similar to those expressed in another place, at another time, should be represented in the Israeli Knesset. It maintained that for too long Israel had resisted the idea that such a thing as Jewish fascism could exist. Now was the time for the Israeli system to oust this phenomenon.

Special organizations were formed to fight Kahane's discriminatory ideas. Thus, a group of citizens came together "to stop the evil," calling themselves Citizens against Racism. This was the first organization to be established in reaction to Kahane's success. During that same year the Movement for Co-Existence and against Racism was formed. In 1985 the Socialist party (Mapam) established the Youth against Racism organization. The same year Maane ("Super Organization against Racism") was formed. Composed of some twenty different organizations, it guided and headed the activities against the Kahanist phenomenon in Israel.

Two national figures stepped forward in the campaign against Kahane: the president of the state, Haim Herzog, and the speaker of the Knesset, Shlomo Hillel. They both believed that the way to fight Kahanism was by excluding Kahane, treating him as a special case, and thus deny him legitimacy. President Herzog broke a long-established custom according to which, after national elections, the president meets with representatives of all the political parties to discuss the formation of a new government. All the parties of the house but Kach were welcomed to his residence. From that point on Herzog stood at the forefront of the battle against Kach and the ideas that Kahane represented. For the first time in Israeli history the president of the state, who is supposed to represent every faction of society, decided to take a stand against a political party. The speaker of the Knesset also made every effort to curtail Kahane's legitimacy. I will deal with these efforts later on when I discuss the legal issues involved in the fight against Kahane. Here I must explain how one person succeeded in unifying almost all the parties against him and in creating a consensus against his views. This is no small feat, considering the wide differences between the left and the right wings in Israel. To comprehend this, let us take a closer look at Kahane's ideology and political platform.

The Ideology of Kach

Kahane spoke of a complete change in Israeli society; not merely a political change, but a total remaking of Israel. In Kahane's view, the only authentic Jewish state is "a state of Jewish totality," where Jewish leadership is selected on the basis of knowledge of and adherence to the *halacha,* the traditional Jewish Law. He called for the creation of "a truly Jewish state in Israel rather than a Hebrew speaking gentilized one," where people would live according to the Jewish laws.[28] In the Kach magazine, *Only Kach,* Kahane asserted that the question of law and order in a Jewish state is not the same as in the United States, France, or Australia. As the Jew is different and unique, the question of law and order is different and unique. Kahane explained that in the Western democracies, the "secular-natural" view is that the people give government the right to speak in their name, that the government is the people, and that the individual therefore must not nullify the government's decisions. The people, in this view, are the ultimate authority, and since the government represents the people, government is the ultimate authority. But this has nothing to do with the Jewish people, whose origins as a nation are not natural and evolutionary and whose authority is not derived from within but is external to it. At a defined moment in time the Jewish people became a nation: "Now, therefore, if ye will hearken unto My voice indeed, and keep My covenant, then ye shall be Mine own treasure from among all peoples; for all the earth is Mine; and ye shall be unto Me a kingdom of priests, and a holy nation. . . . And all the people answered together and said: 'All that the Lord hath spoken we will do'" (Exodus 19:5–8).

This reference to the birth of the nation was reiterated just before the death of Moses: "Ye are standing this day all of you before the Lord your God . . . that thou shouldest enter into the covenant of the Lord thy God . . . that He may establish thee this day unto Himself for a people, and that He may be unto thee a God" (Deuteronomy 29:9–12).[29]

Accordingly, the ultimate authority and the right of decision regarding the destiny of the Jewish nation lie outside the nation, in the hands of God. It is not the people who decide its future, as is the case of other nations, but the external power that crystallized it. This ultimate authority is not open to second thoughts or appeals. The entire Jewish nation comes under this authority, including the earthly government. A Jew has to respect and obey government, *as long as* this government respects and obeys the law of the Bible, respects and obeys the yoke of divine government. The government loses its authority when it nullifies the divine laws.

The implications of these views are of great significance. When the ideologist of the Jewish terrorist group, Yehuda Etzion, was asked whether he respected the legitimacy of the government, his answer was that he recognized its legitimacy as the sovereign. But he did not acknowledge the legitimacy of every law: "Every law has to be analyzed separately, whether or not it coincides with the ultimate yardstick of the Law of the Torah, as we understand it."[30] Etzion and Kahane believed that the prohibition against the abandonment of lands, and the need to settle in every place in *Eretz* ("the land of") Israel, were more than ordinary commands. These acts amounted to *Kidush Hashem* ("sanctification of the Holy Name"). This was how the struggle between the settlers and the government had to be viewed. The settlers had a right derived from God himself to act against the law. Seen in this way, nullifying illegal government orders became a command of the Torah. The concept of the Jewish nation was clear in Kahane's mind: government exists to serve the nation; the nation exists to serve the people; the people exist to serve God. When government disobeys the law, it brings anarchy, for which it is to blame, for it loses any legal and moral right to demand obedience from citizens who wish to live according to the law.[31]

Kahane did not see the democratic principle of majority rule as obligatory, because when the majority acts against the laws of the Bible, it does not count as a majority. This is a majority of evil and of course must not enjoy any right to rule. Those who object to what is required by the Bible are the ones who vilify law; *they* question the law; *they* annul order; *they* bring danger and destruction on Israel. The question is not of Jews who rebel against government who nullify the law; it is a question of Jews who wish to keep the law, who disobey government whose conduct breaches the law and tries to prevent Jews from living in accordance with the law. Kahane wrote, "Those who love Israel must learn to distinguish between the state and the government. The state is inviolate but the government is not."[32]

Kahane's views on Israeli society, its laws and practices, as well as its relations with the Arabs living in the land were directly derived from his picture of Judaism, on the one hand, and his view of non-Jews, on the other. Kahane stated that as a Zionist, his main concern was the future of Israel. To be a Jew, he said, is to understand that Jewishness is different, special. The concepts of chosenness, holiness, and separation are an integral part of the Jewish ritual. A standard of excellence, holiness, and purity exists, and the mission of the Jewish people is to maintain this standard. Kahane urged, "The Chosen people. Chosen by the father of all as a particular, special child to live the kind of life that raises man to the heights of holiness, that turns him into a thing of beauty, that makes creation comprehensible."[33]

Being associated with the chosen people rules out the possibility of choice. Kahane argued that this concept of being *chosen* and *set apart* is the first understanding Jews have to grasp, for it establishes their role on the face of the earth. It also sets out well-defined obligations for the Jew. Consequently, in Kahane's view, the concept of choice, or of "live and let live," is "the most un-Jewish of all concepts," for all Jews are one. All Jews—as the one, chosen people—are judged together. They stand together; they fall together. The sins of one are visited upon all, and hence "there are no individual seats or sides in the Jewish boat. The sinners, the choosers of evil, knock holes in the boat and we all go under."[34] Since the Jewish individual has no freedom of choice, and the sinners condemn not only themselves but others by their wrongdoing, it is no wonder that Kahane saw it right to coerce others to live according to the way of life that Judaism, in his view, demands. He stated that should he—through the democratic system—gain power, it would be totally acceptable for him to pass laws, within the democratic system, that would make people conform to Judaism.

Kahane claimed a clear intellectual, ideological, and philosophical contradiction exists between Zionism and Western democracy, between Judaism and liberal values. In contrast to the liberal tradition, Judaism demands limitation, discipline, and the subordination of the ego. Judaism declares that "unto the L-rd is the earth and all that it contains." Consequently, no such thing exists as a person's ownership of anything on this earth. Kahane postulated, "We live in a world that revels in 'freedom,' in the right to do what we wish. Rights and freedom have become the watchword of our times, and they grow like some cancerous disease into license and moral anarchy. For the Jew there can be no such thing. For the Jew there can only be the yoke of the heavenly kingdom."[35]

Kahane further explained that democracy is based on the idea that we are incapable of knowing the truth, whereas Judaism is founded on the idea that we know the truth. Therefore, those who acknowledge it should enlighten others. Kahane strongly believed that democracy is an alien idea born of the gentile mind, that democracy and humanism are the values of the Hellenists.[36] These values run counter to and stand in contradiction to the basic principles of Judaism-Zionism and a Jewish people. He said that the era of false democracy in which nothing is better than anything else and in which everything and everybody is reduced to a common denominator, invariably the lowest, is not appropriate to Judaism. A Jew must choose between Judaism and Zionism on the one hand, and Western liberal culture on the other. They are different: "The one represents spiritual life and the other death, the one truth and the other falsehood and delusion, the one blessing and the other curse."[37]

Kahane regarded the Arab population in Israel at best as thieves who entered the Jewish land when the Jews had been forcibly exiled from it. On some occasions he made derogatory references to them. Kahane opened some of his public appearances with the statement "Shalom Jews, Shalom dogs." The second part of the greeting referred to Arabs attending his assemblies. This was the case in the assemblies held in the Hebrew University, at Haifa, and at Acre. The purpose was to dehumanize the Arab population, and you may recall other experts in mass communication who resorted to similar methods. Kahane wrote that the Arabs were "a time bomb," "a malignant disease," and that they "multiply like fleas." To an English newspaper Kahane said that the Arabs "multiply like rabbits," and that Jewish women who live with Arabs are "Jews who live with animals." On other occasions he explained that the Arabs were simply "our enemies," and they were to be redeemed from this status only through proselytizing. No other ways were acceptable to Kahane because he did not trust them. He always said that there were no "good" and "bad" Arabs. There were only stupid and clever ones: the stupid declared openly that they wanted to destroy Israel, whereas the clever ones hid their intentions by speaking of compromise and peace. In truth, not one of them wanted peace. A "good Arab" was one who wished to establish a country according to the laws of Islam in the place of Israel. There were no Arab moderates, and those who seemed to be moderates differed only in tactics, not in goals. Kahane wrote, "The enemies of Israel will never make peace; they will never seek less than the total elimination of the Jewish State; they do not want compromise because they look upon us as robbers and bandits."[38]

Kahane urged an end to "the insane delusion" of peace through concessions. Jews had to recognize that peace was not possible under the given circumstances, and they did not need to "weep or wail." Zionism, he declared, "from the first, was not created primarily for peace but for a Jewish State. Hopefully, it was believed, this could be accompanied by peace. But with or without peace, the primary goal was and is a Jewish State."[39] Jews had to adopt a realistic outlook regarding their place and destiny on earth. They had to establish their priorities to give precedence to these considerations rather than to universal humanist principles. The universal principles were an obstacle to the crystallization of Jewish identity. In an interview Kahane urged that this was not the right time nor the right place to apply the rule "What is hateful to you do not do unto your fellow people."[40]

Kahane warned against the threat of Arab population growth that could destroy the Jewish state from within. Evidence showed that the Arab birth rate was more than twice as high as that of the Jews; this meant that they would achieve numerical parity with the Jews before the middle of the next century.[41] Kahane posed the question, Do the Arabs have the right to become the majority in Israel, through peaceful, democratic means? and maintained that anyone who feared such a possibility should act *now* to prevent it from materializing.

The proposed solution to the demographic problem was to induce the Arabs to leave by persuasion if possible, by coercion if necessary. According to this perspective, the non-Jew had no share in the land of Israel. This land belonged to the people of Israel; it was they who controlled and defined it. It was their vessel, their territory in which to create the society of Israel, the Torah society of God. Kahane said that he did not hate Arabs; instead, he loved Jews, and because of that he would do everything to ensure that Jews survived. The expulsion of the Arabs through the process of transfer also would result in the moral regeneration of Israeli society and would prepare the way for acceptance of the laws of the Torah, the halacha, as the law of the state.[42] Kahane cited Rashi— Rabbi Shlomo Yitzchaki: "And you shall drive out the inhabitants and then you shall inherit it, you will be able to exist in it. And if you do not, you will not be able to exist in it." Kahane urged, "[T]here is only one path for us to take: *the immediate transfer of Arabs from Eretz Yisrael. . . .* For Arabs and Jews in Eretz Yisrael there is only one answer: separation, Jews in their land, Arabs in theirs. Separation. Only separation."[43]

Nevertheless, Kahane was willing to concede that up to a certain number of Arabs, limited by the security considerations of the state, may be allowed to continue living in Israel, provided that they were deprived of all political rights and accepted some basic obligations.[44] He stated that Judaism laid down legal, halachic conditions for the privilege of being a non-Jew allowed to live in the land of Israel. These conditions postulated that the non-Jew had no rights of ownership, citizenship, or destiny in the land: whoever wished to live in Israel had to accept basic obligations. Such persons could then live in Israel as alien residents but never as citizens with any proprietary interest or political say, never as people who could hold any public office that would give them dominion over a Jew or a share in the authority of the country. Kahane's image of an alien-resident was someone who was not a citizen and did not cast a vote for a representative to the Knesset; someone who had personal rights to culture, religion, economy, and society, but no political rights. This concept served Kach purposes. The concept was based on religious grounds, and it was sufficient to exclude Arabs from potential political influence, thus avoiding the hazardous result of changing the Jewish character of Israel.

Accepting these conditions and admitting that the land was not theirs, the non-Jews could live quietly in Israel, conducting their private lives separately with all religious, economic, social, and cultural rights. Kahane asserted that "one is obligated to run miles to help a decent gentile in his personal problems but not an inch in the sphere of national equality."[45]

The Political Program

Kach undertook to carry out the following steps as part of its campaign to reorder society, if it achieved the power to do so.

Democracy would be frozen in order to allow a truly strong Jewish hand. Kahane explained that Israel should learn from the measures taken by Great Britain during World War II, at which time British democracy froze the democratic political system, suspending elections and major political rights. Israel would have to transfer the power of the people to a new system of strong and forceful government "to take over the rudder of the ship that, today, drifts toward the shoals and rocks of catastrophe."[46]

In the reformed Jewish state, intermarriage and sexual relations between Jews and gentiles would be forbidden by law. From Kahane's point of view, assimilation with the Arabs was the greatest possible threat: "[T]hat is the worst of the tragedy and the most dangerous."[47] Efforts would also be made to put a stop to the process of assimilation between Jews and Christians in the United States.[48] In Israel Kahane established the Jewish Guard of Honour to fight the danger of assimilation. He claimed that there were about 7,000 to 8,000 mixed marriages with Arabs in Israel, and that this should be regarded as a crime.[49]

Arabs would be excluded from all spheres of work.

The sovereignty of the Jewish people over the whole land of Israel should be proclaimed "by virtue of the promise of the Almighty and the historical fact of tenure and unbroken hope of return based on that promise."[50] Jews were forbidden to give up any part of the land of Israel, including the areas that were liberated in 1967;[51] unlimited Jewish settlement would therefore be allowed throughout the land of Israel together with a formal announcement of integration of the liberated lands into the state of Israel.

The Camp David agreements would be rejected altogether. There was no place for granting any autonomy to Arabs in the land of Israel.

The Israeli Communist Party, Hadash, would be outlawed, for its members were fifth columnists who cooperated with Israel's deadly enemies.

The curriculum of all public schools would be thoroughly overhauled and a large percentage of the curriculum would be given over to the study of Judaism. This was designed to put an end to the disastrous ideological bankruptcy of young Israelis who had little or no knowledge of nor emotional links with Zionism, Judaism, or Jewishness.[52] Kahane postulated, "Jewish pride will be the first order of business."[53]

A new state television and radio authority with a positive attitude toward Judaism and Jewish nationalism would be established.

No stores nor restaurants could publicly sell non-kosher food or "wave leavened bread, *chametz,* about on Passover."[54]

Bookstalls and newspaper kiosks would no longer "titillate and destroy Jewish minds and souls with pornography," and movies and theaters would no longer be free "to stand on the soapbox of 'freedom of expression and art' to demolish the purity and sanctity of the Jewish soul."[55]

Abortion would be regulated by Jewish law; "no one will be allowed to murder unborn children."[56]

Missionary work in Israel would be forbidden. Kahane saw it as a crime to allow Christian missionaries into Israel to steal Jewish souls: "[M]issionaries will be allowed to proselytize in China but not in the Jewish State."[57]

The Temple Mount would be freed of its Moslem presence, which would be "taken down from there along with their mosques" to be "carefully removed" to another site.[58]

Normal and acceptable standards of dress would be demanded, and the foreign tourists who came to Israel "will be greeted at the airports with polite welcomes to the Holy Land and with instructions on how they are expected to behave and dress and conduct themselves in our Holy land."[59]

A five-day work week would be established in Israel, with work ending at 2:00 P.M. on Friday and leisure extending until Monday morning. From Saturday night onward, Jews would be free to do what they pleased in terms of sports, vacations, and leisure; but the Sabbath day would be holy:

"No one will check to see what the Jew does in the privacy of his home but the public character of the Sabbath will be respected and demanded."[60]

Finally, it is interesting to note that in the economic sphere Kahane's demand was, "Let the people breathe!" He contended that Israel was riddled with economic inefficiency caused by the socialist bureaucratic system, which strangled individuals and prevented them from striking out on their own economic path.[61] Israel had to cut taxes instead of raise them. People should be allowed to gamble with their money in business, in the hope of making a profit. Kahane held that only free enterprise that brought in foreign investment and that encouraged domestic capitalism and incentives would allow Israel to escape from its present position as "a beggar basket-case."[62]

No wonder that the Israeli system found these proposals difficult to digest and fought against them as if acting in self-defense. The Israeli establishment viewed Kahane with disgust and shame. Kahanism was conceived as a phenomenon that did not deserve legitimization, one that contradicted everything Israel stood for as a Jewish democratic state, and one that should be tackled to reduce its influence. In chapters 11 and 12 I shall evaluate the Israeli reaction to the Kahanist phenomenon. Much of that struggle took place within the legal system. After the 1984 elections, issues concerning Kahane and his party were brought before the supreme court, which repeatedly returned them to the legislature, suggesting that the decisions had to be made by the legislative body. To understand why the court resorted to this formalistic view, it is essential to reflect on the Israeli judicial system and to see the sources from which it derives its decisions. This is the business of chapter 10. I argue that the court, in formulating its decisions, was influenced by three major sources: acts of the legislature, principles that may not be explicitly expressed in any binding legal document but which were nevertheless regarded as part of the legal system, and precedents.

Chapter 10

Legal Background:
The Foundations of the Law

The Declaration of Independence
and Normative Considerations

Israel does not have a written constitution, a bill of rights, or a basic law to protect fundamental civil rights, such as freedom of speech, of association, and of the press. As things now stand, the Knesset can pass any law that may infringe upon or diminish these essential freedoms. Theoretically, a government having a majority in the Knesset may pass a law that will cancel the need for elections. Although attempts have been made to form a constitution, one has not materialized because of an inability to reach a consensus with regard to its content. The religious parties always have opposed the idea of being governed by a written document that would be secular in its essence and may contradict the halacha. A compromise had been reached to construct the constitution in chapters in such a way that each chapter would be considered a fundamental law and would eventually form a constitution.[1]

Up to now the Knesset has adopted eleven Basic Laws on various issues.[2] These laws have some characteristics that grant them a special normative status that—according to Justice Aharon Barak of the supreme court—brings them close to having a constitutional status. He argues that no judicial norms stand above the Basic Laws.[3] However, constitutional scholars argue that it is difficult to see how these laws could be molded into a constitution,[4] since some of them (Basic Law:

Israel Lands [1960]; Basic Law: Jerusalem [1980]) do not relate to constitutional principles regarding the foundations of the political system, while those dealing with constitutional matters fail to cover comprehensively the most fundamental issue of human rights. Moreover, from the technical point of view most of the Basic Laws do not differ from conventional laws and do not enjoy any sort of immunity.[5] It is possible to cancel a Basic Law by a majority in the Knesset. It is also possible to enact a conventional law that contradicts a Basic Law.[6]

A valuable source to which the courts can appeal is the Declaration of Independence which contains the fundamental principles of the Jewish state. The Declaration was written and affirmed by the Founding Assembly, which was not an elected legislature. The Declaration was not intended to be a constitution, for it was decided that a constitution would be written no later than 1 October 1948.[7] It is not even a regular law. As its name reveals, the principles it contains are viewed as possessing a declarative validity. Indeed, the purpose of the Declaration was to deliver a message to the world with regard to the intentions of the Jewish people in establishing the state of Israel. Thus the Declaration was first conceived as a political instrument to be used at the international level.[8] At a later stage the courts resorted to it as an interpretive instrument. The Declaration was invoked when they were confronted with ambiguous legislative intent; they then preferred the interpretation compatible with the Declaration.[9] However, the Declaration could not overrule the Knesset's laws: when a law was unequivocal it was given preference over the principles of the Declaration.[10]

The Declaration of Independence was acknowledged to lack constitutional force and it did not enjoy the status of a supreme norm. Nevertheless, it was conceived to articulate the "prophecy of the people, and its credo." The court stated that each and every authority had to see the principles of the Declaration as obligatory;[11] in a more recent case it maintained that the Declaration was "a judicial norm that reflects the national charter of values."[12]

The Declaration is not the only source from which we may learn about the basic values of the state. In the absence of written statutes, the supreme court relies on principles of international law as embodied in international treaties. It refers to judicial decisions and to statutory enactments of other democracies, mainly England and the United States. The court also derives constitutional standards from normative considerations that lie beneath the text. These considerations consist of basic principles concerning law and society, the judiciary and its role in society, the aspirations of the nation, and the nation's goals and traditions.[13] Different phraseology is used by the court in different cases and no coherent jurisprudential conception directs the justices' discretion in applying the standards. The court speaks of "the basic principles on which the rule of law is founded";[14] "basic principles on which the State is founded" and "the way of life of the citizens of the State";[15] and "the basic principles of equality, liberty and justice which are the property of every enlightened state."[16] The court also refers to "basic rights that are not written in a book but directly derived from the character of our State as a democracy seeking freedom"[17] and to "constitutional principles that underlie the entire Israeli legislation."[18] The court draws inspiration from "the fundamental ideas of democratic-liberal regimes as they find expression in the classic declarations of human rights, beginning with the French Declaration of the Rights of Man and of the Citizen of 1789 and ending with the Universal Declaration of Human Rights of the United Nations of 1948."[19] In addition, a law enacted in 1980, named Foundation of Law, instructs the court that when it encounters a judicial question to which no answer may be found in statute law or case law or by analogy, it should adjudicate in the light of "the principles of freedom, justice, equity and peace of Israel's heritage."[20]

Because Israel has a centralized political system, and politics invades almost every sphere of life, the supreme court often is asked to intervene in matters of dispute between citizens and governmental authorities. The supreme court is primarily a court of appeals, considering appeals of trial court judgments and appeal decisions of the district courts. In addition, it sits as the High Court of Justice, a trial court from which there is no appeal. In this capacity, the two main roles of the court are to supervise the public administration to see that actions are made in accordance with the law and to supervise the other judicial systems (military courts, religious courts, and labor courts).[21] These roles are commonly viewed as essential in securing democracy and basic human rights in Israel. Some commentators consider the court as the sole guarantor of rights in Israel and as the only body that can prevent the collapse of the rule of law.[22] Justice Barak writes, "In a way, I . . . have the sense that we are now the framers of our unwritten constitution."[23] However, the court has refrained from using judicial discretion in many instances in which political issues have been on the agenda. On many occasions the court has not resorted to the above-mentioned normative considerations, insisting instead that the legislature should address itself to seeking remedies for political questions. This attitude was taken by the court in many of the matters concerning Kahane.

Before discussing Kahane's appeals to the supreme court, we should reflect on significant precedents that have shaped Israeli jurisdiction. Through these precedents we will be able to understand better the reasoning of the court in the appeals. Three cases with great relevance to our issue are *Kol Ha'am* (1953), *Jeryis* (1964), and *Yeredor* (1965).

Precedents

KOL HA'AM

Kol Ha'am is a case of the central adjudications in Israeli law.[24] It arose as a result of Israel's identification with the United States during the days of the Cold War. On 9 March 1953, the daily newspaper *Ha'aretz* reported that Abba Eban, the ambassador to the United States, had said that in the case of war between the two superpowers, Israel would put its troops behind the United States. The Israeli Communist party dedicated the editorials of its two newspapers to this matter, publishing fierce attacks on the government. *Kol Ha'am ("The People's Voice"),* the party's newspaper in Hebrew, called for a heightening of the struggle against the antinationalist policy of the Ben-Gurion government, "which is speculating in the blood of the Israeli youth."[25] A few days later, the minister of the interior ordered suspension of publication of the two papers, basing his decision on section 19 of the Press Ordinance (1933), which empowered him to take this measure if any matter appearing in a newspaper was, in his opinion, "likely to endanger the public peace."

The newspapers appealed to the High Court of Justice, which overruled the decision. In his judgment for the court, Justice Shimon Agranat saw the crux of the matter as the interpretation of the term *likely*.[26] He argued that several possibilities were open to the court and that the decision between them had to be made in accordance with the "intention of the legislator." The intention of the legislator, in turn, could be inferred from the basic principles of the Israeli system, which was a democratic system. He said that it was a well-known axiom that jurisprudence had to be thought of in the context of the people's national life system, and that the Israeli system could not be understood in isolation from the Declaration of Independence.[27] Justice Agranat maintained that although the Declaration of Independence lacked authoritative power, it still "expresses the prophecy of the people and its credo."[28] Hence, interpretation of the state's laws should be made in accordance with the Declaration (at 884). But the terminology used in the Declaration is general. It says that the state of Israel will be based on the foundations of freedom, but it does not specifically guarantee freedom of expression.[29]

After establishing that laws were to be interpreted according to the Declaration of Independence, Justice Agranat reflected on the possible interpretations of the term *likely* that was used in the Press Ordinance. He concentrated on two extreme possibilities: one was based on the "bad tendency" test, the other on the "probable danger" test. Both were taken from American jurisprudence.[30] According to the first test, which was popular during the 1920s,[31] a publication could be suspended if it revealed any tendency—however slight or remote—toward breaching the peace; while according to the second test, the minister of the interior had to be convinced of a link between the publication and a resulting breach of the peace, which necessarily led to the inference that such a consequence was probable. Justice Agranat rejected the bad tendency approach, arguing that it might be suitable for a country that was founded on autocratic or totalitarian principles, but that it undermined the process that constituted the essence of any democratic regime, namely, the process of investigating the truth (at 884).[32]

On the other hand, he endorsed the "probable danger" test because he thought that the statutory term *likely* fitted a probable formula better than any other.[33] This test had been advocated two years earlier in the *Dennis* case[34] as a modification to the "clear and present danger" test.[35] The probable danger test enabled the court to avoid the explicit burdens of the clear and present danger test and to substitute for them the vaguer and less demanding approach of balancing interests.[36] The probable danger test and the balancing approach also rejected the absolutist approach that assigned freedom of expression its preferred position.[37] This is because the balancing technique inevitably deprives speech of any privileged status and makes it simply one of several interests to be weighed by the courts. Concurring with the Hand-Vinson formula, Justice Agranat asserted that we should consider the gravity of the evil discounted by its improbability rather than focus on the imminence of the danger. Importing the interest-balancing approach of American law, Agranat argued that the solution had to be sought through the balancing of contradictory principles, in this case the interests of state security and freedom of expression (at 881).

Justice Agranat maintained that the minister of the interior did not give sufficient consideration to the value of freedom of expression. He concluded that the role of the minister was to consider the content of the speech and to make an estimate of its results according to the circumstances of publication. Even if the minister was convinced that danger was probable, it was still desirable to consider whether the danger was serious enough to require suspension of publication, or whether enough time was available to curtail the influence of the publication through less extreme measures, such as examination, negation, and counterexplanations (at 892).

I draw attention to Justice Agranat's assertion that speech may be suppressed only when the publication in question has left the framework of the mere explanation of an idea and has taken on the form of *advocacy,* which in the given circumstances makes it likely that public peace will be endangered (at 888). Here again, the influence of *Dennis* is noticeable.[38] However, Agranat refrained from using the term *instigation,* which describes a close connection between words and deeds (see part 1, chapter 7). He said that by *probability* he did not necessarily mean proximity in time. If the minister of the interior thought that, in the light of the given circumstances, definite possibility existed that a serious danger to public peace would ensue, then nothing should stop him from using his authority (according to section 19 [2A]), even if he estimated that the danger was not imminent.

Justice Agranat preferred the term *advocacy,* which is stronger than the notion of the mere explanation of an idea but which, unlike instigation, does not emphasize the imminence of the danger. Here his view differed from American jurisprudence, which for many years maintained the distinction between *advocacy* and *instigation.* In *Gitlow v. N.Y.* both the majority and minority agreed that advocacy could not be punished, while incitement was punishable;[39] and in *Yates* a distinction was made between the advocacy of abstract political doctrine and advocacy designed to promote specific action.[40] Elsewhere the United States Supreme Court postulated, "Decisions have fashioned the principle that the constitutional guarantees of free speech and free press do not permit a State to forbid or proscribe advocacy of the use of force or of law violation except where such advocacy is directed to inciting or producing imminent lawless action and is likely to incite or produce such action."[41]

The ruling of *Kol Ha'am* is a milestone in Israeli jurisprudence for three reasons: the origins of the "balancing approach" lie in *Kol Ha'am;* the probable danger test was endorsed as the best solution when the interests of national security, on the one hand, and fundamental freedoms, on the other hand, are weighed against one another; and the court established that when it is possible to interpret a law in different ways, the court will prefer the interpretation that is in accordance with the Declaration of Independence.

Accordingly, by invoking the Declaration, the court decided that the democratic character of the state necessitated limiting the minister's power to cases where the danger to public peace was a probability and not a bare tendency. The application was accepted.

SABRI JERYIS

The High Court of Justice refused to intervene in the district commissioner's refusal to register the group called "El Ard" ("the Land" in Arabic) as an association, noting that its objectives rejected the existence of Israel. The main objective of the group, as declared in its platform, was to find "a just solution to the Palestinian problem—through its consideration as an indivisible unit—according to the will of the Palestinian people."[42] The court upheld the decision of the district commissioner despite the organizers' assertion that no attempt should be made to engage in illegal or terrorist activities, and despite the lack of evidence proving such an intent. Speaking for the court, Justice Alfred Witkon admitted that the articles of the association did not explicitly deny the sovereignty of the state of Israel, but he claimed that this aim was implicit in them (at 679); for the goal of the group denied resolutely and absolutely the existence of the state of Israel in general and its present borders in particular. He argued, "It is *natural* that those who support the association's goal disregard the existence of the State and the rights of the Jewish People in it" (at 677, emphasis mine), because the group's demand for self-determination for the Arab people in the entire land of Palestine did not leave any possibility for self-determination to the Jewish people.

Justice Witkon concluded that history had shown that fascist and total-itarian movements had taken advantage of the freedoms of expression, press, and association granted to them by the democratic regimes, with the aim of destroying these regimes: "Those who have witnessed this in the days of the Weimar Republic will never forget the lesson" (at 679).

Justice Moshe Landau, concurring, said that according to the evidence enough reason existed to suspect that El Ard would become a fifth col-umn, betraying the duty of loyalty that every citizen should grant to the state in which the citizen lived (at 681).[43]

Thus we see that despite the straightforward rejection of the bad tendency test in *Kol Ha'am,* as well as in other cases,[44] here the court referred to the two elements of the bad tendency test—constructive in-tent and indirect causation—to outlaw an Arab national association.[45] The court took a similar position one year later, in the *Yeredor* case, when members of the same group, joined by Israeli Jews, wanted to compete in the elections.[46]

YEREDOR

The Disqualification of the Socialist List

The Central Elections Committee (CEC)[47] disqualified the Socialist List "for the reason that this candidates list is an illegal organization, since its initiators deny the integrity and very existence of the State of Israel." Justice Moshe Landau, who chaired the committee, argued that a tremen-dous difference existed between a group of people aiming to undermine the very existence of the state, or, at any rate, its territorial integrity, and a party recognizing the political being of the state but wishing to change its internal regime. He asserted that we could read into the Election Law and into the Knesset Law an implied condition that an unlawful associa-tion could not be confirmed as a list. In his opinion, the Socialist List was a new version of El Ard, which had been dissolved under section 84 of the Defense (Emergency) Regulations, 1945. The political platforms of both associations were identical. Both absolutely denied the existence of Israel. Justice Landau asserted that such a list could not be confirmed, because the Knesset, which was the sovereign institution in the state expressing the will of the people, could not incorporate within it an element that propounded the destruction of the state. Democratic procedures were not to be used to undermine the democratic regime itself.

The statements of Justice Landau were straightforward. He did not make contingent assumptions regarding the actual power of the list in question to implement its political platform. The chairperson of the CEC did not say that a list may be banned when it may endanger the foundations of the state. He refrained from discussing the magnitude of the threat (the Rawlsian Principle, see part 1, chapter 4). Instead he conclusively held that some ideas do not have any place in the parliament. A list that wishes to destroy the state should not be allowed representation in the Knesset seeking to further its ideas. This is what we, following Karl Popper, call the paradox of tolerance. Tolerance should prevail but it also has to have its limits; otherwise democracy may supply its destroyers with the means to carry out their task more quickly and efficiently. Notice that Justice Landau did not say that members of the list should be denied freedom of expression altogether. He advocated what I call qualified tolerance (see chapter 2), implying that democracy may endure any opinion, but this is not to say that each and every view has to be represented. Antidemocratic opinions deserve no legitimization by democracy to help them prosper and attract more people.

The Court's Decision

Members of the Socialist List appealed to the High Court of Justice, who in a two-to-one decision confirmed the CEC's decision. The majority justices, Shimon Agranat and Yoel Sussman, agreed with the opinion of their colleague Landau, asserting that the character of the Socialist List was in direct opposition to the purpose of the elections because its essence and objectives were to bring about the annihilation of the state of Israel. A group of people whose open political objective was to undermine the very existence of the state could not a priori have any right to take part in the process of consolidating the will of the people and could not, therefore, stand as candidates in the Knesset elections. Thus, Agranat (who was by this time the president of the court) contended that the existence of the state, its continuity and perpetuity, is a fundamental principle of the legal system, and that the Jewish character of the state must be considered a basic concept underlying its juridical order. The Elections Law should be interpreted in the light of these principles, and we may expand the authority of the Elections Committee by virtue of it, allowing it to refuse the registration of a list that denies the very existence of the state and aspires to bring its annihilation (at 387).

In this case, then, President Agranat did not observe the balancing approach he so powerfully advocated in *Kol Ha'am*. He could have struck a balance between the value of the nation's existence on the one hand and the value of freedom of election on the other. However, he chose to represent the existence of the nation as a constitutional requirement that all lists had to acknowledge, a principle not to be weighed against any other consideration. Here his approach was absolutist—in the sense that no interest was comparable to the state's existence—rather than balancing.[48]

Ruth Gavison raises the question of granting legitimacy to a list by approving it. In her opinion, when democracy does not outlaw a questionable list, it legitimizes it. I have discussed this issue in the context of explicit forms of tolerance (part 1, chapter 2). Gavison reads President Agranat's decision as saying that when the problem is the combination of a threat to democracy and a conspicuously equivocal attitude irreconcilable with the values of the state, the test is not one of probability that the danger may materialize, but a test of license, of legitimacy. Such cases do not require that the danger be present or probable.[49]

Agreeing with her view, I read the majority judgment as implying that the court has the key role, in addition to its conventional ones, of granting or preventing legitimation. The court ruled that designated reasons require, as a matter of *principle,* the disqualification of lists, and that some regulations of content must be applied. The majority justices postulated that when the contradiction between the political principles of a list and the basic principles that underlie the state is clear and manifested, the issue does not touch upon the question of the imminence or the magnitude of the danger. The court did not rule against the confirmation of the list because the justices were afraid that its ideas might gain public support. Obviously, the Jewish majority would not adopt the political ideas of the list. Instead, the court implied that these ideas could not be represented in the Knesset like any other idea, that they had no place within parliament to compete in the free marketplace of ideas. And if the law did not explicitly provide grounds for the exclusion of some ideas, then the court had to use its discretion to find a solution to this apparent lacuna. Here Justice Sussman's reasoning is of interest.

Yoel Sussman, concurring, introduced the notion of supraconstitutional considerations, emanating from natural law, which were superior to any form of legislation, whether ordinary laws or Basic Laws.[50] Justice Sussman relied on a decision of the Supreme Court of West Germany from 1953, where the court spoke of the notion of "militant democracy," which aimed to protect parliamentary functions from abusive attacks by subversive groups: "The German Constitutional Court, in discussing the question of the legality of a political party, spoke of a *'militant democracy'* which does not open its doors to acts of subversion under the cover of legitimate parliamentary activity. As far as I am concerned, regarding Israel, I am satisfied with a *'self-defending democracy,'* and we have the tools to protect the existence of the State even though we do not find them expressly specified in the Elections Law" (at 390, emphases mine).

Accordingly, the state (or rather, the CEC) possesses an implied power, similar to self-defense, to fight against subversive attempts designed to destroy Israel. The holding of this ruling was that even where the existing law did not contain a provision allowing for the disqualification of a list, it was necessary to avoid the moral incoherence involved in allowing a person who aspired to the cessation of the existence of the state and its authorities to compete in the Knesset elections. In some circumstances judicial quasi-legislation beyond the written text may be permitted to fill a gap as required by existential necessity. Justice Sussman maintained, "Just as a man does not have to agree to be killed, so a state too does not have to agree to be destroyed and erased from the map. Its judges are not allowed to sit back idly and to despair from the absence of a positive rule of law when a plaintiff asks them for assistance in order to bring an end to the State. Likewise no other state authority should serve as an instrument in the hands of those whose, perhaps sole, aim is the annihilation of the State" (at 390).

You may recall that when discussing Karl Popper's paradox of tolerance, I emphasized his assertion that it is paradoxical to allow freedom to those who would use it to eliminate the very principle upon which they rely, and that we should therefore claim in the name of tolerance the right not to tolerate the intolerant. Popper urges that we should claim that any movement preaching intolerance places itself outside the law, and that we should consider incitement to intolerance and persecution as criminal,[51] in the same way as we should consider incitement to murder or to the revival of the slave trade as criminal.[52] Acts of self-defense against the intolerant may necessitate inflicting pain upon them. Sometimes this may be the only way to prevent the pain one person is willing to cause to others.[53]

Justice Sussman's reasoning coincides with these arguments. Democracy has to find answers to the catch emanating from the practice of the very principles that underlie democracy. Arguments that convey similar notions have been employed in England by those seeking to restrict the activities of the National Front. As we have seen, an analogous argument enunciating the right to self-defense against a clamor for racist hatred was relied upon by the citizens of Skokie in their efforts to ban the Nazi march. The majority of the court, like Justice Landau, said nothing about circumstance, potential power, gravity of danger, nor similar considerations. They made no reference to any criterion. Because Justices Agranat and Sussman thought that the matter in hand involved security factors together with an ideological threat to the state and its basic principles, neither of them saw it necessary to discuss the level of the danger. This view is explicit in Sussman's reasoning. For him the subject is a matter of principle rather than one that is contingent on various facts and factors. I call this reasoning *the Sussmanian Principle,* in contradiction to the Rawlsian Principle.

The main problem with the reasoning of the majority justices is the lack of lucid distinction between endangering the existence of Israel as such and endangering its Jewish character or its democratic regime. On this point differences exist between the reasoning of the two justices. Justice Sussman did not say at all that the Socialist List had to be outlawed because it endangered the Jewish character of Israel. He spoke of defending the state against attempts aiming at its destruction. However, Justice Sussman also drew an analogy with the Weimar Republic, where the Nazi party did not pose a physical threat to Germany. Furthermore, reading what Justice Sussman had to say about "self-defending democracy," it is unclear whether "acts of subversion" include acts that threaten democracy or refer only to acts that aim to annihilate the state. In chapter 11 we shall see how crucial this distinction is between endangering the state and endangering democracy. The fight against Kahanism would have taken a different route if Justice Sussman had elaborated and clarified his judgment.

As for President Agranat's judgment, a careful reading of his reasoning reveals that he refused to confirm the Socialist List not only because it denied the existence of Israel, but also because its aims were irreconcilable with the fundamental values underlying the state. Most significant of these values was the idea of Israel as a Jewish state. Thus, President Agranat referred to the Declaration of Independence (as he did in *Kol Ha'am*), saying that we can learn from it that Israel was not only a sovereign, independent country that sought freedom and was characterized by the rule of the people; it was also established as a Jewish state in the land of Israel (at 385).

President Agranat saw the Declaration of Independence as a constitutional principle. In his opinion, a judge may refer either to the Knesset legislation or to the Declaration as grounds upon which rulings can be based. His approach may be described as *creative interpretation.*[54] If we employ a graphic description we may say that this approach is situated between the approaches taken by his two colleagues, Justices Sussman and Cohn, though closer to Sussman than to Cohn. For by appealing to natural law, Justice Sussman took upon himself the endeavor of creating law, while Justice Cohn did not regard the Declaration of Independence as a judicial norm and thus resorted to strict positivism. Let us now reflect on the opinion of the minority justice.

Justice Haim Cohn disputed the three central issues that were raised by his colleagues: the authority of the CEC, the relevance of the degree of danger, and the notion of supraconstitutional considerations.

The authority of the CEC. Justice Cohn adhered to the positivist approach, which emphasizes the existing statutes, seeing them as a binding authority. Only the rule of law can place restrictions on political rights. In his dissent, Justice Cohn was of the opinion that in the absence of a statute authorizing the CEC to refuse to register a list for reasons other than those formally provided for under the law, one could not deduce that the CEC had the power to refuse the confirmation of a list on the grounds of its ideology or its political objectives.[55] This technical reasoning evolved from his reluctance to read into the law a broad authority that would contradict fundamental principles of the Israeli system regarding the citizen's essential right to express ideas through voting. Implicit in Justice Cohn's judgment is that he did not think a political body such as the CEC should be vested with further authority in coming to decide whether a list has to be disqualified.

The seriousness of the danger. Justice Cohn's judgment confronted the issue that the majority justices avoided: whether the degree of danger was such as to provide sufficient grounds for banning the list. His view was Rawlsian rather than Sussmanian. Justice Cohn said that no evidence was brought before the court to suggest any danger likely to accrue from allowing the list to participate in the elections. Justice Cohn maintained that no proof was given of probable danger (at 381). Even if there *was* a law, it is unclear that Justice Cohn would have joined his colleagues.

Supraconstitutional principles. Resorting to this notion is problematic because it attributes a wide authority to the court. Theoretically, reference to supraconstitutional considerations can refute any law. Thus Justice Cohn, in his criticism of this notion, used language similar to that of Justice Agranat in *Kol Ha'am* regarding the bad tendency test. He asserted that in some countries the attempt to safeguard values such as the security of the state or to resist revolutions had brought about an appeal to "natural laws" that were set above the existing law with the effect of having legal precedence over other legislation, be it ordinary laws or Basic Laws. Israel, however, did not adopt such methods. Instead, "its ways are the ways of the law, and the law is given by the Knesset or by him to whom the Knesset has given its expressed authorization" (at 382). Otherwise the court would take on the role of the legislature, and confusion and uncertainty would prevail.[56]

Critical Evaluation of the Court's Decision

I agree with Justice Cohn that the notion of supraconstitutional principles is problematic. The very use of the phrase *supraconstitution* implies considerations that may be placed above the law. This notion is bound to lay itself open to attack. It is unclear, however, why Justice Sussman had to resort to this terminology in the first place. He could have diluted much of the criticism simply by using a different phrasing without changing the essence of the reasoning. While my criticism of Sussman's judgment refers in the main to its terminology, something also has to be said in regard to its content. As for content I think Justice Sussman could have relied, like President Agranat, on the Declaration of Independence, and by doing that he might have spared the need to refer to natural law. As for the terminology of Sussman's judgment, instead of speaking of supraconstitutional considerations that transcend the limits of positive law, he could have spoken of considerations that should be taken into account together with the *lex scripta*. However, both Justices Sussman and Cohn were influenced by the positivist approach, which holds that only specific rules, declared by the legislature and the courts, are the law. Justice Cohn, whose approach was conservative, believed that judicial discretion could be obtained only according to and within the confines of these rules, while Justice Sussman thought that room existed for other considerations when a case posed a dilemma to which no adequate solution existed in statute. Because he believed that *Yeredor* was such a case, and that these considerations were weighty enough to decide the case, he entitled them *supra*. In other words, unlike the positivists, Justice Sussman believed that some other considerations may be taken into account to decide a case. Here he went further than President Agranat by referring to natural law. Like the positivists, he understood his argument to be for the *higher law* theory, which holds that these principles are the rules of a law above the law.

Two years later Ronald Dworkin addressed this same issue. He eloquently conveyed a similar notion in different phrasing. In his attack on positivism, Dworkin explained that positivism is a model of and for a system of *legal rules;* but when lawyers reason or dispute legal rights and obligations, they make use of standards that do not function as rules. He called these standards *legal principles,* explaining that a *principle* is a standard that is to be observed not because it will advance or secure an economic, political, or social situation deemed desirable, but because it is a requirement of justice, fairness, or some other dimension of morality.57 Positivism misses the important roles of these standards, which properly should be classified as legal standards by virtue of their having been accepted by society as binding and part of its normative way of life. Justice Sussman did recognize the role of these standards, but the positivist influence made him read them as standards that are trying to be rules.

Applying Dworkinian terms we may understand Justice Sussman's reasoning to say that in constitutional adjudication the court should consider not only rules but also normative constitutional standards, which are part and parcel of the legal system. *Lex scripta* is supplemented by contextual characteristics that formulate what we may call *the spirit of the system*. We may sum up by saying that while the majority of the court placed its confidence in the principles of the continuity and perpetuity of the state, stressing the Jewish democratic character of Israel, the minority preferred to emphasize the need for restraint when fundamental freedoms are at stake. Justice Cohn agreed with Justice Sussman that democracy had to defend itself, and that it was necessary for some body to be vested with the authority to exclude from parliament those who betrayed the state and assisted its enemies. However, this authority had to be formulated through legislation. Accordingly, we may say that the judgments of Justices Sussman and Agranat, on the one hand, and Justice Cohn, on the other, represented two different schools in jurisprudence. The first school may be entitled the *creative* school, and the second the *formalistic* school.

I am not implying that one school is better than the other. Judges of the formalistic school can be liberal judges if they safeguard liberal principles by their reluctance to make changes, while creative judges can introduce illiberal changes if they think that the changes supply better answers to specific problems or coincide with illiberal public demands for change. However, judges in states lacking a written constitution and specific laws to guarantee fundamental human rights may be required to resort to creative judgments to protect these rights. In this case, Justice Sussman rejected the formal view that would leave us, as he implied, with our hands folded, asking us to despair. He believed that the existing legislation did not supply answers to a pressing problem that, to his mind, violated the foundations of the state. He thought it within a judge's discretion to resort to supraconstitutional notions so as to fill the apparent legislative lacuna without conceiving of this as assumption of an authority beyond the powers of the court, as Justice Cohn thought.[58] In Justice Sussman's view, the role of judicial discretion is to interpret the law so as to bring it into harmony with the foundations of the constitutional regime. Justice Sussman saw himself as an interpreter of the people's national life system whose role was not only declarative, but also creative. Following Justice Sussman we may say that in one sense the judge declares the existing law. In a more profound sense the judge also gives an authentic expression of the voice of the people, a voice that evolves from the people's creed, their national existence, and from the basic foundations of the system. These considerations I include under the heading *the spirit of the democratic system.*

Dworkin, who is associated quite wrongly by some with the modern declarative approach,[59] holds that judges must make fresh judgments about the rights of the parties who come before them. He maintains that these political rights reflect rather than oppose political decisions of the past.⁶⁰ On the one side Dworkin argues that the judge does not create rights but acknowledges them. This conception is derived from a liberal outlook that recognizes natural rights. The claim is that rights are too important to be left in the hands of judges. On the other side Dworkin contends that "judges are authors as well as critics."⁶¹ Thus, his view is akin to President Agranat's judgment in this case. In effect, Dworkin's conception of law as integrity forms a synthesis between the declarative approach and the creative school, for he does not exclude nonpositivist norms from adjudication. Dworkin writes, "Law as integrity asks judges to assume, so far as this is possible, that the law is structured by a coherent set of principles about justice and fairness and procedural due process, and it asks them to enforce these in the fresh cases that come before them, so that each person's situation is fair and just according to the same standards."⁶²

Accordingly, principles of political morality are conceived as judicial norms, within what Dworkin calls "the full law."⁶³ Consideration is also given to "background rights," which are viewed as universal, as applicable to every political framework, because they are essentially derived from conceiving persons as human beings. Such are the rights for equal respect and concern.⁶⁴

Justices Agranat and Sussman did not speak of background rights but of democratic rights. They did not say that their aim was to safeguard universal principles, but democratic principles that underlie the Jewish state. Their moral-liberal outlook, similar to Dworkin's, led them to take the creative approach to safeguard democracy. They did not say that their aim was to safeguard universal principles. Instead they said that democracy had to secure some principles for its own existence, and if the law did not provide a right answer to protect them, then the role of judges was to use their discretion in a creative way to do so.

Using Dworkin's terminology we also may say that Justice Sussman (and probably President Agranat) would have regarded this as a hard case. They would agree with Dworkin that decisions in hard cases should be based on arguments of *principle*, and that principles are propositions that describe rights.⁶⁵ Justice Sussman also would concur with Dworkin that arguments of principle justify a political decision by showing that the decision respects or makes secure some individual or group right.⁶⁶

In this case it was the right of the Jewish people to defend their state against those who wished to undermine its existence. Dworkin speaks of rights against the state, whereas Sussman speaks of the right of one group against another. Justices Sussman and Agranat emphasized the right of the Jewish people to defend their state, viewing it as crucial enough to outweigh any other interest. Their reasoning implied that the bedrock function of the courts was to assist the state in protecting itself against those who sought its annihilation through collaboration with outside enemies.

The *Yeredor* precedent played a major role in the attempts to restrict Kahane's right to be elected. In the following chapter I will reflect on those attempts. The discussion begins with a brief account of the attempt in 1981, which did not receive much attention. I continue by considering in extenso the decision of the CEC to disqualify Kach in 1984, a decision that was overruled by the supreme court.

Chapter 11

Attempts to Restrict Kahane's Freedom of Election

The *Negbi* Decision of 1981

The first attempt to restrict Kahane's right to be elected to the Knesset was made in 1981. Some members of the CEC, including its chairperson, Moshe Etzioni, wanted to prevent the registration of the Kach List. Justice Etzioni said that the aims of the list offended the principles of democracy as expressed in the Declaration of Independence. He maintained that the proposals of this list were no more and no less than the Nuremberg Laws, with the only difference being that where *Aryan* had been written, *Jew* was now written, and where *Jew* had been written, *Arab* was now written. The majority of the committee, however, did not share this opinion, and they allowed Kahane to compete in the elections.

After the CEC made its decision, a citizen, Moshe Negbi, appealed to the High Court of Justice to reverse it.[1] His argument was that the aims and principles of Kach contradicted the democratic regime of Israel, for the list called for the expulsion of Arabs, the banning of sexual relations between Jews and non-Jews, and the legislation of discriminatory laws. By doing that it induced the Arabs to rebel. Negbi also argued that the decision of the CEC to register the list contradicted the notion of supra-constitutional principles postulated in the *Yeredor* ruling. In the name of these principles Negbi sought an answer from the supreme court as to whether Kach, a list that was explicitly racist in its ideas, could run candidates in elections in a Jewish democratic state or whether it should be banned. His petition was denied on the technical grounds that the Elections Law did not provide for any appeal *against* a decision authorizing the registration of a list. Only a list that the CEC had refused to register could appeal to the court. The court (per Justice Aharon Barak) said that the committee might well be wrong in its discretion but this in itself did not supply a basis for the court to interfere.

The CEC decision of 1981 was characteristic of the attitude of the Israeli political system toward Kahane at that time. Kach was not taken seriously, and its development and rise were overlooked by the decision makers. It took them another three years to realize the seriousness of the Kahanist threat to democracy. Only in June 1984, some weeks before the elections were to take place, and in the light of the recent polls that showed Kach would succeed in entering the Knesset, did the political parties decide to take an initiative by refusing to confirm Kach. From partisan political considerations, in order to keep the balance between the right and the left blocks in the Knesset and to secure wide support for the disqualification decision, the CEC also decided to ban the leftist Progressive List for Peace (PLP).

The CEC's Decisions of 1984

The refusal to confirm the Kach List was grounded on the argument that it propounds racist and antidemocratic principles that contravene the Declaration of Independence of the state of Israel; openly supports acts of terror; tries to kindle hatred and hostility between different sections of the population in Israel; intends to violate religious sentiments and values of part of the state's citizens; and negates in its objectives the basic foundation of the democratic regime in Israel.[2] The CEC also refused to confirm the PLP on the grounds that "in this list there are indeed subversive elements and tendencies, and central persons in the list act by way of identification with enemies of the state."[3] The CEC observed that the political platform of the list was no different from the El Ard list, which was disqualified in 1965. In addition, the leader of the PLP, Muchamad Miari, was the leader of the El Ard list. Both Kach and the PLP lists appealed to the supreme court, which reversed the decisions of the CEC. In the next sections I first reflect on the reasoning of the CEC; my focus is on the struggle of Israeli democracy against Kahanism. We also will see the reasons that convinced the Knesset to use self-defensive measures with regard to the PLP. This discussion will reveal serious reservations regarding the procedure that vests a political body with a quasi-judicial authority. I will begin by considering the judgment of the court for overruling the decisions.

THE DISQUALIFICATION OF KACH

In his reasoning, the committee chairperson, Justice Gabriel Bach, urged the need to outlaw Kach, saying that the list's racist and antidemocratic principles contradicted the Declaration of Independence, and that they aimed to induce hatred and hostility between different factions of the Israeli population. As evidence Bach cited a document from 15 June 1984, where Kahane declared, "I am ready to blow up the mosques on the Holy Temple." Justice Bach also quoted letters that were intercepted by the censor in 1973, sent by Kahane to his people in the United States, in which he specifically instructed them to kill a Russian diplomat and to blow up the Iraqi Embassy. There Kahane wrote, "If we can't find some Jews willing to [do these acts] then we are Jewish Pigs and deserve what we get."[4]

Speaking of the "spirit of the law," Justice Bach referred to the company law, which states that a company will not be registered if any of its aims negates the existence of the state of Israel, or its democratic character,[5] or if a reasonable basis exists to assume that the company will serve as a cover for illegal actions.[6] The chairperson noted that from a purely formal point of view the law did not apply to Kach, which existed before the law had been enacted. Nevertheless, this law was relevant because the legislator forbade the formation of any association negating the democratic character of the state.[7]

Justice Bach also referred to the International Convention on the Elimination of All Forms of Racial Discrimination that Israel signed in February 1979. Article 1 defines the term *racial discrimination* as "any distinction, exclusion, restriction or preference based on race, colour, descent, or national or ethnic origin which has the purpose or effect of nullifying or impairing the recognition, enjoyment or exercise, on an equal footing, of human rights and fundamental freedoms in the political, economic, social, cultural or any other field of public life."[8]

Two points are relevant with regard to this reference: Kahane makes a distinction that is based on *religion,* a ground that is not mentioned in the definition of racism postulated in the convention, and furthermore, this definition relates to racism in the sense of discriminatory *action,* whereas racism as embodied in the party organization and its activities relates mainly to racism in the sense of racist *instigation*. A close connection exists between instigation and action, but Justice Bach should have explained the distinction between the two and why he thought that reference to the convention was nevertheless appropriate. Instead, the chairperson concluded that enough evidence existed to consider Kach to be a racist list according to the criteria of this convention, and that the CEC had the authority to disqualify Kach for this reason. Thus, his reasoning exceeded the essence of the *Yeredor* ruling.

Other members of the committee expressed opinions in line with their political affiliations. The representative of the leftist Civil Rights Movement (Ratz), member of Knesset Shulamit Aloni, said that we are free people who live in a society that requires recognition that the limit of one person's liberty is the liberty of another. Otherwise everyone will do whatever they want; there would be no warning signs, speed limits, nor red lights. We recognize the need for red lights, and Kach is a case where such measures are needed. If we do not put up a red light, then human rights and equality will be in danger.[9] In turn, the representative of the Communist party, Hadash, reminded the committee that six members of the Jewish terror organization were also Kach members.[10] On the other hand, the representative of the National Religious party (Mafdal) could not understand how Kahane could be called a Nazi, for all he wanted was to fight assimilation and to protect Jewish girls.[11]

Kahane, who appeared before the committee, called the Declaration of Independence a "schizophrenic document." He repeated his well-known view that an ultimately insoluble contradiction existed between a Jewish state of Israel and a state in which Arabs and Jews possessed equal rights; that full equality for all and a Jewish state were a contradiction in terms. Kahane maintained that only those Arabs who would accept the status of alien residents should be allowed to live in Israel.[12] He asked the members of the committee to vote for Judaism and against the Hellenists who wished to ban him.[13] His request was denied by the majority members in an eighteen-to-ten decision. Kach was disqualified.

THE DISQUALIFICATION OF THE PLP

A pertinent issue in the dispute between those who requested the disqualification of the PLP and those who opposed it was the announcement of

Minister of Defense Moshe Arens in which he decided not to declare the PLP an illegal association. He wrote that after reviewing the information he was convinced that elements of conspiracy were within the list, and that central figures of the list acted in a way that identified them with the enemies of the state. Nevertheless, given the circumstances (the very eve of elections), he decided not to use the section of the Defense Regulations (No. 14 [1B]) that empowered him to outlaw associations.

Another important document was a declaration by General Ben-Gal, who issued orders in 1980 to have the activities of Muchamad Miari supervised. In his argument, Justice Bach reasoned that the weight of this document should not be overestimated because of the time factor (four years had passed since the general's decision) and the lack of evidence on which Ben-Gal had based his order. Justice Bach thought that the crux of the matter was whether enough evidence existed to support the demand for disqualification. He concluded that although the evidence was unequivocal in the case of Kach, in the case of the PLP it was equivocal. He said that the committee should not ignore the defense minister's announcement, but it also had to bear in mind that this announcement was quite vague: it was unknown who the subversive elements were, where they were placed in the list, and how serious the evidence was against them. Therefore he would not recommend the PLP's disqualification.[14]

We have reason to assume that Moshe Arens refrained from outlawing the PLP because he believed that not enough evidence supported such a decision. He did not supply any documents to the members of the committee as background material. Minister of Defense Arens claimed that such documents existed but they were secret, and that he would be willing to show them to Justice Bach alone. Bach refused.

Moreover, the political platform of the PLP, which members of the right-wing parties regarded as treasonable, was similar to the previous platforms of political parties that were represented in the Knesset (Haolam Haze and Shely, each of which had two representatives in the parliament), and to the political platform of Hadash, the Israeli Communist party. Hadash had advocated a similar policy for many years without ever being accused of endangering the security of the state. As a matter of fact, the PLP wanted to join Hadash, but eventually this plan did not materialize, not so much because of ideological differences, but on the grounds of the allocation of seats and the ordering of the candidates in the unified list. The PLP and Hadash called for Israel's withdrawal from the occupied territories, including Eastern Jerusalem. Both upheld the idea of establishing a Palestinian state in these territories that would exist alongside the state of Israel, enjoying mutual recognition. This was to be achieved through negotiations between the Israeli government and the PLO. The PLO was regarded by both parties as the sole, legitimate representative of the Palestinian people.

In addition, in their appearance before the committee, the representatives of the PLP expressed their objection to the Palestinian Covenant.[15] They explicitly said that they were willing to declare this objection in their political platform,[16] maintaining that their demand was for self-determination for both Palestinians and Jews. Hence, no substantial evidence, beyond speculation, could make a strong case for disqualification.[17] The voting results, however, were seventeen to twelve in favor of the disqualification.

This procedure, which allows a political body to disqualify lists on the grounds of their ideology and political aims, raises considerable doubts. It certainly opens the gates for settling accounts with political opponents and getting rid of parties who are not liked through partisan deals. Although the court still serves as an ultimate guarantor of rights to which parties can appeal, a procedure in which the prosecutors are also the judges should not exist in the first place. The votes in favor of banning Kach were cast by the representatives of the Labor and leftist parties together with the chairperson of the CEC, Justice Bach; while the votes against the decision came from the right and the religious parties. Seven representatives of the Likud decided to abstain. With regard to the decision concerning the PLP, the votes were a mirror image of the previous decision on Kach. All seventeen votes for disqualification came from representatives of the right; the twelve votes against it came from representatives of the left. Justice Bach abstained, together with three Labor members. One representative of the Labor party did not participate in the meeting.

The court drew attention to the problem of giving a political body the power of authorizing lists in 1965. It did so again in 1984, 1988, and in 1992.[18] Up to now, however, the legislature had decided to leave the procedure unchanged. I am inclined to think that such decisions should be made by a special panel of the supreme court or by a special committee comprised of justices who would decide whether the appeals put forward should be considered at all, and whether they possessed enough weight to rule in favor of disqualification. Justice Cohn in *Yeredor* and President Shamgar in *Neiman I* refer to the West German Grundgesetz which, in their opinions, provides the appropriate solution. The Constitutional Court of the Federal Republic of Germany decides through a special procedure whether to ban parties according to section 21 (2) of the Grundgesetz.[19] Since the establishment of the German Federal Republic, two parties had been banned through this procedure: the first was the neo-Nazi party, and the second was the Communist party.[20]

In the next section I consider in detail the reasoning of the court's special panel of five justices who reviewed the decisions of the CEC.[21] A unanimous court accepted the appeals of both Kach and the PLP. I will argue that the decision regarding Kach was flawed, while the decision regarding the PLP was correct.

The Court's Decision in *Neiman*

ANALYSIS OF THE JUDGMENTS

Although in *Neiman* the court was unanimous in deciding to overrule the decision of the CEC, significant differences existed between the opinions.[22] Deputy President Miriam Ben-Porat was the only one to take a formalistic view with regard to the authority of the committee. Justices Menachem Elon and Moshe Bejski may have agreed that Kahane's right to be elected had to be curtailed, but they believed that the defense against such antidemocratic threats was the responsibility of the legislature rather than the court. Unlike Justice Ben-Porat, Justices Elon and Bejski accepted the *Yeredor* precedent, whereas Justices Meir Shamgar and Aharon Barak suggested two different tests as guidelines for the CEC when it was considering restricting the practical implementation of the right to be elected.

The Judgment of Deputy President Miriam Ben-Porat

In line with the dissent of Justice Cohn in *Yeredor*, Deputy President Ben-Porat contended that the Knesset Elections Law (1969) did not grant the CEC authority to decide whether a given list deserved to take part in the elections on the grounds of its platform or objectives. In her opinion, the CEC had only one function: to examine whether the techni-

cal conditions imposed by the Basic Law: The Knesset (1958) were satisfied. When they were, the committee had no choice but to register the list.
Deputy President Ben-Porat relied on the *Negbi* decision, where it was
argued that the Elections Law did not provide for any appeal *against* a
decision authorizing the registration of a list: an appeal to the court could
be made only if the list had been refused registration. She believed that this
showed that the main concern of the legislature—evolving from a liberal
outlook—was that a list should not be disqualified unjustly. Deputy President Ben-Porat also believed that this reasoning had to be interpreted as
indicating that the committee was not competent to judge the dangerous
character of a list. For if the intention of the legislature was to assign the
CEC the role of checking the platform and objectives of lists, then it also
had to determine some sort of judicial body that would be authorized to
examine decisions regarding the *confirmation* of lists. Otherwise the result
may be that lists that endangered the state's security may be registered for
the elections. In Ben-Porat's opinion, the asymmetry in the possibility of
appealing against a decision of the CEC would lead to an absurd situation
whereby the CEC was authorized to disqualify lists in the absence of law,
by an appeal to the court; yet a list, however dangerous it might be, could
not be reconsidered once authorized by the committee.

Deputy President Ben-Porat's reasoning was formalistic.[23] It did not
address the philosophical questions that are involved in this issue at all,
which concern the confines of liberty and tolerance. We may note two
basic similarities between Justice Cohn in *Yeredor,* and Deputy President
Ben-Porat in *Neiman:* both of them recognized the need for resorting to
the measure of disqualification in order to defend democracy. They
thought that this measure should be embodied in law, and neither of
them accepted the majority opinion in *Yeredor* regarding the authority to
disqualify lists in the absence of legislation.

The other members of the court agreed with Justice Ben-Porat's conclusion but not with her reasoning. All four justices accepted the *Yeredor*
ruling regarding the authority to disqualify lists in the circumstances that
this ruling indicated.

The Judgment of President Meir Shamgar

The main issue, as formulated by President Shamgar, was whether the
CEC was authorized to impose additional restrictions on the right to

participate in the Knesset elections despite the lack of provision in the law. President Shamgar accepted Justice Sussman's reasoning that even where the existing law did not contain a provision allowing disqualification of a list, because of its aims, a situation that allowed a list aspiring to the cessation of the existence of the state to compete in the elections was to be avoided. Nevertheless, President Shamgar, together with Justices Bejski and Elon, thought that in the absence of law this ruling should not be extended. He asserted that only "an extreme situation" permitted judicial quasi-legislation beyond the written text to fill a gap which arose from the absence of statute (para. 5, at 244–45).

Accordingly, when coming to apply the *Yeredor* criterion to Kach, the conclusion was obvious. The precedent of *Yeredor* simply did not supply any grounds for restriction. Kach did not wish to endanger the existence of the state; its aim was not to bring about the destruction of Israel. Therefore, it had the right to compete in the elections.

The issue was more complicated with regard to the PLP, and President Shamgar dedicated most of his reasoning to clarifying it. He mentioned that while in the case of the Socialist list five out of the ten candidates were former members of El Ard, in the case of the PLP only one out of the 120 candidates was a former member of that group. This was Miari, the Arab leader of the PLP. Miari himself had declared that he did not regard the PLP as the successor to El Ard. He also had expressed reservations regarding the Palestinian Covenant. No evidence was brought to show that in other forums Miari postulated contradictory opinions. On the other hand, the evidence that was brought before the committee, on which it based its decision, consisted of old, second-hand documents supplied by the army, which did not contain any facts to substantiate the view that the list endangered the state's security (para. 11–12, at 258).

Therefore, the right to be elected, which was, in President Shamgar's view, among the four main political rights (along with the right to vote, the right to convene an assembly or demonstration, and the right to address a petition) should be granted to both lists: to Kach for lack of *jurisdiction,* and to the PLP for lack of *evidence.*[24]

President Shamgar was afraid of the temptation to silence unpopular opinions. He held that a person's liberty was not to be restricted except by law and was not to be denied merely on the grounds of objection, however forceful, to the *content* of an individual's statement. President Shamgar postulated that the criteria upon which answers to questions were examined should be based on expressed statutory provision, and even more important, should be activated only as a last resort when facing a *probability* of danger. If a probability existed that the exercising of a right would jeopardize public order and security in a concrete case, the authorized statutory body could limit the practical implementation of the right in the said circumstances (para. 17, at 265). Thus, President Shamgar's reasoning was in line with what I have called the Rawlsian Principle. He did not speak of defensive steps taken by democracy against threats *in principle;* instead, his reasoning was practical. He maintained, "There must always be a logical connection between the degree of danger and the means taken; and not any advocacy, even if it raises a justified indignation, may cause the denial of the entire scope of liberty. A democracy that activates restrictions without existential necessity . . . loses its spirit and force" (at 279).

President Shamgar thought that we should refrain from resorting to the easy solution of enacting specific laws as a remedy to problems. In his opinion, the actual existence of liberties ought not be influenced by transient events or temporal sentiments, and where restrictions of fundamental rights were necessary, they ought not be improvised and shaped according to momentary needs. Israeli democracy was better served by an educational struggle than a judicial disqualification. Even in the case of unpopular opinions, argument and methods of persuasion should be allowed, and prohibitions and restrictions should be used only as a last resort (at 278). This argument reminds us of the Millian defense of freedom of expression (see part 1, chapter 6). Later we shall see that a similar line of reasoning was taken by the court when coming to consider Kahane's right to express his views through the mass communication system.[25]

The argument against enacting specific laws is valid and correct. It is preferable to find solutions to specific problems by educational means and through the open exchange of ideas.[26] I also agree that legislation should serve only as a means of last resort. The constant fear exists that such an instant remedy may prove to be a two-edged sword, opening the way for the slippery-slope syndrome in which the first attempt to restrict freedom leads to further restrictions. Moreover, laws enacted in order to meet specific problems relevant to a specific period may become obsolete and may also prove to be a burden or a nuisance at some point in the future.[27] Although the prevailing rule is that a recent law cancels an earlier law, we still must enact a law to overrule the old one. For precisely these reasons, we are likely better off extending precedents than asking for legislative prescriptions.

The Judgment of Justice Aharon Barak

The most interesting opinion, in my view, was the opinion of Justice Barak. Justice Barak disputed Justice Cohn's opinion in the *Yeredor* decision and consequently did not share the view of Deputy President Ben-Porat in this case. Contrary to their methods, he did not confront the issue from merely a technical point of view. That is, Justice Barak did not hide behind the claim of lack of authority. He said that the court acted legitimately in disqualifying lists because of the dangerous content of their platforms. Concurring with the majority view in *Yeredor,* Justice Barak thought that it lay within the committee's powers to disqualify lists. He believed that no distinction should be made between a platform that denied the existence of the state and a platform that recognized the existence of the state but denied its democratic character: the same principles of interpretation that had led to the *Yeredor* ruling—with respect to a threat to the state—also had to be applied in cases of a threat to democracy. Justice Barak noted that the Declaration of Independence, "in the light of which our legislation is interpreted," referred to the principles of "liberty, justice and peace" and assured "full equality of social and political rights to all its citizens, without distinction as to religion, race or sex." In line with Justice Agranat's reasoning in *Kol Ha'am,* Justice Barak rhetorically asked Would the state of Israel without the Declaration of Independence be the same state of Israel? (at 314). The principles that underlay the Declaration assumed not only the existence of the state, but also its essence as a democracy. Israel had to safeguard them in defense of democracy. Justice Barak maintained, "Democracy is not obliged to commit suicide in order to prove its vitality" (para. 12, at 315). By this modification Justice Barak, in effect, broadened the *Yeredor* precedent.

On the other hand, Justice Barak did not completely agree with the opinion of the majority in this important precedent. While they saw the existence of the nation as overriding other considerations (such as freedom of expression and association), and therefore not to be weighed against any other principle, Justice Barak thought that the scope existed to balance the value of the nation's existence on the one hand and the value of freedom of election on the other. Thus, he added a second modification to the *Yeredor* jurisprudence that restricted it, arguing that the exercise of the committee's authority in both cases had to be on the basis of a *reasonable possibility*[28] that the threat would actually be effected (para. 1, at 305). In this respect, Justice Barak's approach was similar to President Shamgar's. As did President Shamgar, Justice Barak argued that the CEC's authority was vested in a special circumstance where a probability existed that the use of a fundamental civil right would cause damage that was intended to be prevented. However, while President Shamgar resorted to the probability test, Justice Barak thought that this test should apply in cases where freedom of expression conflicted with public peace (like *Kol Ha'am*), or to cases where freedom of demonstration contradicted public order.[29] For the matter in hand Barak found preferable the reasonable possibility standard, which provided for wider margins of security. This standard took the middle ground between the bad tendency approach on the one hand and the tests of clear and present danger and probability on the other. It required substantial proof of reasonable possibility that the anticipated danger actually would be realized; it was not satisfied merely by the possibility of a remote danger (bad tendency). Like Justice Learned Hand, Justice Barak concluded that we should weigh interests one against the other to see whether the degree of damage, mitigated by the chance that it would not actually occur, justified the violation of a civil right so as to prevent the danger.[30]

Accordingly, when coming to apply the "reasonable possibility" standard, a balance had to be struck between a fundamental right to political expression, which was not to be denied merely because of the content of the political view, and democracy's right to defend itself. Justice Barak explained, "We are concerned with a balancing that requires a judicial position as to the probability that realization of the right to vote will prejudice the interest in the state's existence" (at 310).

The procedure for disqualifying a list was, therefore, a two-stage process: first, we had to review the content of the platform and see whether grounds occurred for disqualification, namely, whether the list in question denied the existence of the state *or* its democratic character. This was a necessary but not sufficient requirement. Next, we also had to see whether a reasonable possibility existed of the list's implementing its program. This approach, like the probability test, was in line with the Rawlsian principle.

Justice Barak's approach broadened the authority of the CEC regarding the grounds on which it could refuse the confirmation of lists. He said that this approach stemmed entirely from the creative sources of the judicial process, maintaining that this process was nevertheless constrained within limits. He asserted that judges could not raise themselves above the legislature, and that the rule of law, not the rule of the judge, reigned in Israel. Justice Barak continued, "Indeed, my approach in this case is based not on 'meta-principles' standing above the law, but on principles that pervade the law and emerge from it. It is not founded on a 'supra-constitutional' 'natural law' that annuls the statutory law. It is a positivist 'intra-constitutional' approach that examines the nature of the law and interprets it according to accepted interpretative standards. The law is, in the words of President Sussman,[31] *a creature that thrives on its environment,' which includes not only the immediate legislative context but also broader circles of accepted principles, fundamental objectives and basic standards that comprise a kind of 'normative umbrella,' spreading over the entire field of legislative acts*" (at 320–21, italics mine).

If the law were "a normative umbrella," then we could apply it when the phenomenon at issue clearly contradicted the foundations of democracy. Justice Barak was willing to concede that we could resort to this notion, but he believed that a duty still existed to take the degree of the danger into consideration, so that the normative principles were applied only when a reasonable possibility arose that the danger would be realized. Even with respect to the application of metaprinciples, we should ask *when* these principles should be employed (para. 17, at 321).

In applying his method to the appeals of the two lists, Justice Barak asserted that the court found nothing in the PLP's platform to indicate a desire to bring about the annihilation of the state or to prejudice its democratic character. The evidence was clear enough, so there was not even a need to examine the existence of a reasonable possibility. In the case of Kach, scope did exist to apply the reasonable possibility standard. The CEC was right in arguing that the content of the platform was racist, and that its principles were offensive to the democratic character of the state and to "the spirit and essence of Judaism" (para. 15, at 318). Evidence even existed that the list seriously intended to realize its positions and did not rescind them. But the question was not whether the list was serious in its designs; instead, it was whether a reasonable possibility existed that its designs would be accomplished. In Barak's opinion, no such possibility existed. All that was proved was bad tendency, which reflected the content and intentions of the list, and that alone was not sufficient. As long as no proof was given that Kach created a reasonable possibility of danger to the existence of the state or its democratic character, no alternative was left but to allow its participation in the elections.

Although he thought the reasonable possibility standard the best existing solution, Justice Barak acknowledged that it was problematic. He admitted that this standard did not constitute a precise formula that could be adopted easily in every single case. On the contrary, Justice Barak said that it left broad margins of uncertainty, that the formula was difficult because it required not only evaluation of past events, but also assessment of the probability of future events, a task that amounted to prophecy in the guise of a legal decision.[32] Nevertheless, Barak argued that political bodies were accustomed to such tasks, and that legal proceedings often called for decisions based on the examination of social processes (at 316). In spite of Justice Barak's awareness that it would be an implausible as well as an impossible task to name all the relevant criteria that had to be taken into account when considering specific bodies in a specific context, he still believed that in the absence of legislative formula this standard commended itself as the most appropriate one. He preferred to rely on the logic of politicians and judges when they came to consider each and every phenomenon.

However, we should warn that the lack of clear criteria may open the way for misuse of the committee's authority and give members of the court latitude to introduce political considerations into their decisions. Moreover, when tests are phrased in abstract terms so as to generalize, the possibility of exceptions always arises, as in the case of the Millian Truth Principle (see part 1, chapter 6). This is not to say that standards and tests should be rigid and inflexible; but when a judge admits that the range of considerations with regard to future events amounts to prophecy, then we have room to raise pertinent questions and wonder whether we are not better off in formulating guidelines in more precise terms.

Two of Justice Barak's colleagues, Elon and Bejski, criticized his reasoning. Justice Elon suggested that judges should not see themselves as prophets. He disagreed with Justice Barak on his extension of the *Yeredor* ruling to antidemocratic lists as well as on the application of the reasonable possibility test. Justice Elon argued that the *Yeredor* precedent should not be extended without specified legislation. As for the reasonable possibility test, he claimed that a contradiction appeared in allowing a party to compete in the elections in order to destroy the legislature, and that this insoluble contradiction was inherent rather than dependent on reasonable possibility that the aim would materialize (para. 4, at 291). This situation could not be allowed *in principle*.

For his part, Justice Bejski asserted that any test we might adopt immediately posed a double dilemma: one related to the time in which the defensive reaction might and should come; the other concerned the dimension of the measures that might be taken: whether these should be radical, aiming to eradicate the danger tout court, or of lesser scope (para. 4, at 327). If we follow Justice Bejski's position, the question regarding the time dilemma is At which stage should the list be prohibited? It could be either when a reasonable possibility appeared of the list's gaining representation in the parliament, or when a reasonable possibility arose of its gaining enough power to become an indispensable partner in any governmental coalition.[33] Yet, again, the prohibition of the party could occur when a reasonable possibility existed of the list's gaining a parliamentary majority.

Justice Barak did not offer any solution to the first dilemma. Addressing himself to the second dilemma, he made a series of suggestions as to how Israeli society could fight Kahanism by other means, given that the court had decided that it could not disqualify Kach. Justice Barak first suggested considering whether the damage could be mitigated by methods of persuasion, explanation, and education. Then he offered another option, arguing that danger to the state and its democratic foundations often can be reduced by use of the penal system (para. 14, at 316–17). He referred to the fact that Kahane and Green were placed in administrative detention in 1980, implying that room might exist for examining questionable activities, so grounds might be found for the removal of immunity from Knesset members involved in criminal activity.

The first suggestion alluded in fact to the Millian Truth Principle. Quoting Justice Holmes's celebrated opinion in *Abrams*, Justice Barak argued that the true test of the ideas of liberty, justice, and equality and the other fundamental principles that constitute the creed of the constitutional regime lies in their inner strength and inner truth and not in their coercive power.[34] Justice Barak maintained that the weakness of racism and the false beliefs it incites are exposed precisely in the free competition of ideas (at 322). Nevertheless, this depends on the inner strength and the inner truth being strong enough to win over the threat. If they are not, then we may have to apply coercive means. Justice Barak, like Rawls, did not assume that democracy actually possessed these inner forces. He did not exclude more radical democratic methods of self-defense but only as a last resort. We should allow democracy to play its game, and let every opinion compete in the free market of ideas as long as the consequences of allowing a marketplace of opinions are not too risky. Implicitly, the assumptions that underlie this opinion are that a democracy's benefit is in witnessing the clash between democratic and antidemocratic forces, and that this confrontation fortifies the basis of democracy.[35] In Israel, however, these assumptions have been rejected up to now. Justice Barak assumed that it might be perilous to democracy to supply more grounds for imposing restrictions on its free play. Reality, however, has shown the opposite to be the case: that by not resorting to restrictions, the authorities gave the destroyers of democracy the latitude to deepen their position. It was not the forces of democracy but the antidemocratic trends that were fortified by the free competition of opinions. More people expressed their preference for a strong hand, and strong leadership. Polls revealed that the majority of the population (especially the young) thought that "too much" democracy was available in Israel, and discriminatory views against Arabs gained popularity.[36]

The Judgments of Justices Menachem Elon and Moshe Bejski

Justice Elon, an observant Jew and a distinguished expert on Jewish Law, asserted that the most serious thing about Kach's platform was that it claimed to be based on the halacha. Racism had no place in the Jewish world, the fundamental basis of which lay in the values of equality and respect for others. Justice Elon clarified that national minorities were accorded the status of alien residents in the halacha, a status which did *not* exclude entitling them to full national and civic rights. He saw the content of Kach's ideology as in striking opposition to the morality and essence of the world of Judaism. Justice Elon joined his colleagues not because of lack of evidence that the list was dangerous, but because the law did not empower either the CEC or the court to ban a list on the grounds that it might undermine democracy (para. 13, at 303). With a line similar to that of Justices Shamgar and Barak, Justice Elon contended that society should resort first to educational methods to defend itself. He agreed with President Shamgar that the CEC's competence to disqualify racist and antidemocratic lists could be granted only by the legislature. However, while President Shamgar believed that it was undesirable to extend the authority of the CEC by law, and Justice Barak expressed his fear of an unbalanced legislation, Justice Elon thought that room existed to enact a specific law so as to meet the dangers presented by Kach. He asked the legislator to provide well-defined instructions that would specify reasons for disqualification and not to be satisfied with the present situation that opened the way to varying interpretations.

Reading Justice Bejski's decision reveals basic similarities between his judgment and Justice Elon's. Both of them briefly addressed the issue of the PLP's eligibility to participate in the elections, agreeing with President Shamgar that the objectives attributed to it were not sufficiently proven. Not enough evidence was supplied to show that the list denied the existence of the state or its integrity. Both agreed that room existed to extend the *Yeredor* ruling, but that this should be done only by legislation. In both judgments we can identify a call for the Knesset to enact a law to fight Kahanism. Justice Bejski stated that the tone of Kach's propaganda was so grating, awakening memories of the recent past, that Israel had to defend itself against it. Finally, both justices rejected the reasonable possibility standard of their colleague Justice Barak.

Justice Bejski said that he did not accept this standard, but he could not understand how one who did accept it could still think that sufficient grounds lacked for banning Kach. The publications of that list were full of racist deviltry "that even the paper cannot suffer" (at 333). A reasonable possibility of danger existed because evidence was brought before the CEC that members of Kach went to Arab villages to convince them that they had no place in Israel, and that if they did not leave voluntarily with compensation, other means would be found to make them go. We note that both Justices Bejski and Barak relied only on the evidence from the time of Kahane's arrival to Israel. They did not mention Kahane's activities in the United States. Barak said that we should take into account the past conduct of the list, its members and its head, and anticipated future dangers. Kahane's operations, especially the series of explosions in Washington, D. C., and New York City, suggested that if members of Kach were given the opportunity, then more than a reasonable possibility existed that harm would be inflicted upon the Arabs.

Justice Bejski observed that the 1980 decision that justified the administrative detention of Kahane and Green indicated that the danger posed by Kach went beyond mere words and opinions. Bejski asked rhetorically What more was required and could be offered in the way of proof that had not been shown with respect to Kach? If all this was not sufficient evidence of a danger to the democratic character of the state then, he concluded, "I know not what more could be proven" (at 333).

Accordingly, if Justice Bejski had found himself in agreement with Justice Barak on the principled question regarding the committee's authority to disqualify a list on the grounds of its platform, objectives, and activity, which shared the purpose of endangering the foundations of *democracy,* then he would have ruled that the Kach list had been disqualified lawfully. Justice Bejski, however, decided to join his colleagues in admitting the appeal not because of any lack of evidence regarding the character and purposes of Kach and the danger it constituted to the foundations of democracy, but because he had found no lawful authority to disqualify Kach. He said, "It is true that subversion of the foundation of democracy constitutes to a considerable degree subversion of the foundations of the state in its existing form" (at 325). In his view, this did not imply that the *Yeredor* precedent should be extended to bodies undermining the foundations of democracy: denying the very existence of the state was not the same as damaging the foundations of democracy. Justice Bejski explained, "I cannot find it possible to extend the *Yeredor* ruling beyond the matter that served as grounds for the majority opinion, since the statute does not contain the same 'Archimedean-foothold' upon which broad interpretation can be grounded and constructed" (at 332).

Justice Bejski's reasoning was influenced in part by his reluctance to grant the CEC any additional authority. He argued that the CEC was a political party body, and if it were empowered to decide the confirmation of lists without defined and definite legislation, then lists might be disqualified on grounds of narrow party interests. He concluded by postulating an appeal to the legislator to enact a statute in defense of democracy.

CONCLUSIONS AND CRITICISM

Evaluating the court's decision raises two separate questions. One is concerned with the authority granted to the court to disqualify lists when a lacuna (or an intentional lack of specification) occurs in the statutes regarding the matter in hand; the other is concerned with the logic and reasoning of the ruling.

The Question of Authority

The question of authority is strongly related to that concerning the scope of tolerance and the restrictions on liberty. Constitutional matters in a liberal democratic society frequently turn on the decision of the courts; we must, therefore, examine the force of philosophical principles regarding societal norms and values, when the court formulates judicial decisions in the absence of specific statutes empowering it to act. This is the context in which we should consider the authority that may be accorded to the court when it contemplates which democratic methods of self-defense are to be resorted to on the basis of principles underlying the constitutional text.

On this issue we can differentiate between three points of view in *Neiman:* those of Deputy President Ben-Porat; of Justices Shamgar, Elon, and Bejski; and of Justice Barak. With regard to the first, Ben-Porat presented a purely formalistic opinion: in the absence of statute, no authority existed to disqualify lists. She also rejected the idea of supraconstitutional considerations. On the other hand, Justices Shamgar, Elon, and Bejski accepted the idea of supraconstitutional considerations as expressed in *Yeredor.* However, they held that the issue of denying a list's participation in the elections for reasons other than denying the state's existence should not be left open for judicial interpretation. In this sense, as did Justice Ben-Porat, they did not think that the court should take a creative role in extending the *Yeredor* precedent. In turn, Justice Barak said that the CEC had the authority to disqualify lists if they negated the democratic character of the state (para. 16), and clearly he would approve such a decision if he were to find a reasonable possibility of danger even in the absence of law. That is, Justice Barak believed that the court *could* resort to a creative approach in extending precedents. Nevertheless, as did his colleagues Justices Elon and Bejski, he asserted that it was desirable that the issue of denying a list's participation in elections on the grounds of the content of its platform should be regulated through legislation and not left open to judicial interpretation. In other words, it was *preferable* to have formal grounds for action. Barak added a call for caution, saying that the present situation was preferable to unbalanced legislation (para. 18, at 321).

The *Neiman* decision was criticized for lack of creativity. Since Israel has no constitution, no bill of rights, nor even a Basic Law to defend fundamental civil liberties, the court is viewed as the only safeguard of democracy. For this reason Moshe Negbi argued that the justices of the supreme court should adopt the creative approach. He urged the court not to hide behind the lack of explicit written provision when crucial questions of a constitutional nature were at issue, leaving their resolution in the hands of politicians. Negbi, a news editor in Kol Israel, the national radio network, expressed his mistrust of the Israeli political system. In his view, because parties had failed to reach a compromise over the enactment of a law to safeguard civil rights, requiring individuals and bodies to approach the court to find assistance, the court should not refrain from taking a creative approach. Negbi was startled by the court's decision to throw the ball back to the legislature, because this meant the future of democracy was then left to the arbitrary will of parliament. He could not understand how the court could have recognized democracy's right to defend itself in 1965 and been willing to disqualify a list despite a legislative lacuna, then twenty years later refused to resort to the same approach.[37] Negbi voiced his astonishment that the justices who had acknowledged democracy's right to defend itself still did not apply self-defensive measures against Kahane. Thus, Justice Barak asserted that Kach negated Israel's basic conceptions, and the general as well as the Jewish values on which Israel establishes its national home (para. 15); Justice Bejski affirmed that the opinions of Kach were so racist that even the paper on which they were written rejected them, and Justice Elon maintained that these opinions were antipathetic to the world of Judaism and to the Jewish past. Yet they allowed Kach to stand for elections.

A similar line of criticism was adopted by Claude Klein. He asked whether what was called the "Jewish character of the State of Israel" constituted a higher principle than the democratic nature of the state. For the cynical result of the *Yeredor* and the *Neiman* decisions was that a list that denied the Jewish character of the state was to be outlawed, while a nondemocratic, discriminatory list was, in the absence of a specific statute, to be allowed to compete in the elections. Klein concluded, "With due respect to the Court, we doubt the political wisdom of such a decision, and we wonder whether political reality is not such as to reinforce its erroneous nature."[38]

Klein and Negbi represent the view that the supreme court is the only authority in which citizens can put their trust. Negbi's close acquaintance with the political system has convinced him that the Knesset cannot be trusted because it is motivated by partisan considerations and by narrow political interests. Therefore, he believes that the court must take an active role in defending basic rights; otherwise deals between parties may decide the democratic nature of the state. Negbi does not analyze the court's decisions from a judicial perspective per se, but from a more global view, relating the implications of the decision to the existing reality.

Negbi's view is extreme, for he says that only in the most minimal and necessary events should the court refrain from using its authority.[39] The court has to defend basic rights, with or without relying on a written law. Negbi's views also suffer from inconsistency. Negbi was one of the first people in Israel to raise the alarm against Kahanism by appealing to the court against the CEC's decision to confirm Kach in 1981. His entire reasoning was tailored to finding a way of outlawing Kach without any recognition that his appeal for a court of justice, rather than a court of law, could undermine the entire legal framework. Negbi, so it appears, was willing to put the court above the law, while this study strongly objects to such a thought. The court derives its authority from the law, and it has to adjudicate in accordance with the law.[40] Negbi speaks generally about preserving basic rights, forgetting that this is exactly what the court did in *Neiman:* it secured Kahane's basic right to be elected.

Notwithstanding this criticism, Negbi was right to say that the formalistic decision of the court was out of place in this case because even if we adhere to the Rawlsian reasoning and do not resort to arguments of principle, the court ignored the social and political environment in which the decision was made and its likely implications. My view is that in a state that lacks a constitution, the supreme court justices are (to use Justice Barak's phraseology) the framers of an unwritten constitution.[41] Part of their job is to consider the implications of their decisions on society and more specifically on society's democratic foundations. I have mentioned the growing popularity of Kahane's ideas, reflected by different polls, such as the poll of the Van Leer Jerusalem Institute. This issue brings us back to Alf Ross's assertion that the forces of democracy are

likely to win in places where democratic values are well rooted (cf.
chapter 5, "The Absolutist School"). I agreed with this position but questioned what the attitude should be in the case of unripe democracies.
Israel seems to be such a case. If we followed Ross's prescription, the
defenders of democracy simply would have to look on how Israel, a
democracy, surrendered to antidemocratic forces. My thesis takes precisely the opposite view. Democracy has to defend itself against such
trends and ought not to stay idle in the face of growing threats. As a
young democracy that encounters a tremendous number of problems in
every sphere of life, Israel has to be more cautious than other democracies about the strength of democratic values within its culture. Israeli
culture still is in the process of formation, and silence in the face of racist
ideas may assist the creation of some form of Jewish fascism as part of its
developing culture. It is beyond the scope of this analysis to reflect on the
entire range of problems with which Israel, as a young nation, is confronted. I only say that during a period of forty-six years we have had six
wars and a Palestinian uprising[42] that have consumed a great deal of
effort and stretched resources at the expense of overcoming the internal
schisms that exist within Israeli society. These are the schisms between
Arabs and Jews; between capitalism and socialism; between orthodox
and secular Jews; between Sephardim and Ashkenazim; and between the
cities and the kibbutzim. We may assume that these tensions have made
Israeli democracy vulnerable to antidemocratic notions; notions that appeared and were discussed more frequently in the 1980s as a result of
both Kahane's activity and the reaction of the Israeli establishment to
curtail his growing popularity.

Given these tensions and notions, the role of the judge is also to set
more defined standards for action for both politicians and the courts
when they are faced with constitutional matters, especially where attacks
on the very foundations of democracy are concerned. Hence a scope
exists for taking normative constitutional principles into account. These
principles may in some hard cases convince the court to take a creative
approach. Here are two sets of considerations that inevitably play their
part when judges come to formulate a judgment. One set is related to the
moral convictions held by the judges, influenced by their personal up-
bringing and educational background, as well as by the tradition and
values of the society in which they live. The other is concerned with the
specific legal history. Precedents and other legal facts are bound to limit

the moral considerations of judges, but they should not exclude moral considerations altogether. When faced with an unprecedented situation, in which they are required to use their discretion to find a judicial solution to a hard case (such as this one), judges should decide the case by interpreting the political structure of their community so as to find the best possible justification, in principles of political morality, for the structure as a whole.43 Accordingly, if the right of people to be treated as equals and not to be harmed by others can be defended only by creative adjudication, then creativity is not only in order but necessary. This is the case so long as the judge tries to make the creative decisions in line with previous ones rather than starting a new direction as if writing on a clean slate. In my view, *Neiman* allowed room to take unwritten values of the judicial system into account, as President Shamgar did in more recent rulings.44 And if the court could not find an answer in statute law and could not draw an analogy with *Yeredor,* it could have referred to the principles of freedom, justice, equity, and peace as the law of Foundation of Law provides (see chapter 10). The court should have done so not only because of the alarming nature of the Kahanist phenomenon, but also because questions concerning the eligibility of a list to participate in the elections inevitably are connected with granting legitimacy to the list in question.

None of the five justices raises this issue of licensing. I have argued that an issue concerning the eligibility of a list to compete in the elections necessarily involves the question of legitimacy (see part 1, chapter 2). It is not merely a question of allowing opinions the right to be heard. Of course, a court could approve something with reluctance, and judges could hold that they do not have the authority to regard something as unconstitutional without giving the impression that in some broader sense that something is right. Nevertheless, the final decision of the court is bound to influence the way in which those matters are viewed; whether they are given the status of any other matter, which may be held with or without reservation but is still free to be represented in parliament, or whether they are dismissed as matters that even the courts of justice think should have no place in society.

The Logic and Reasoning of the Ruling

All five justices did not reject the idea of disqualifying lists in order to defend democracy *as such*. They said that this measure should be resorted to with caution and only in extraordinary cases. Kach and the PLP were not seen as such cases. Regarding the PLP, the unanimous judgment was straightforward: the procedure used by the CEC to disqualify the PLP was seen as incorrect, in that it referred to either unconvincing or old documents. The court was right in its judgment. The PLP's political platform did not differ significantly from those of other parties that were allowed to compete in the elections, and no evidence brought before the court established that the list constituted any danger to the state. But the decision concerning Kach is less clear. The court should have used its authority to declare that explicit antidemocratic ideas and aims cannot claim a right to be represented in the Knesset.

Justice Barak argued that a difference existed between freedom of expression and freedom to be elected. I concur with his view that democracy must allow itself wider security margins when considering the eligibility of questionable lists. It is one thing to express views and opinions, however repugnant they are, and quite another thing to use parliamentary methods to put them into effect by legislative means (see my discussion on different degrees of toleration in chapter 2). These two issues should be dealt with separately. In addressing the issue of restricting freedom of expression I have argued that four considerations should be taken into account: the harmful (or offensive) content of the speech, the speaker's manner of expression, the speaker's intentions, and the circumstances, which must be such that the target group cannot avoid being present (see chapters 7 and 8). When we come to restricting the right of a list to be elected, the focus is on the opinions and the goals of the list and on its actions to realize them. If the content of the political platform of a given list and its explicit intentions are to bring about the *physical* annihilation of the state or to undermine democracy, and members of the list are violently acting along these lines, democracy has the right to defend itself and not to allow that list representation in parliament to further its aims by legal means. To ask democracy to place the means for its own destruction in the hands of its potential destroyers is neither morally obligatory nor morally coherent. Notice my emphasis on *physical* annihilation of the state; that is, in the Israeli context, no sufficient grounds warrant disqualification of a party that wishes to change the character of the state from a Jewish state into, say, a Canaanite state, as distinguished from aiming to destroy the Israeli state as such.

From this argument follows that Justice Barak was right in saying that scope existed to broaden the *Yeredor* ruling. He was the only judge who saw some similarity between *Yeredor* and *Neiman*. According to his line of thought, endangering democracy amounted to endangering the basic foundations of the state. Hence, lists that wished to participate in the democratic rules of the game and to gain power to implement their ideas through legislation and other democratic means had first to accept democratic principles. As Justice Bejski said, "Whoever claims rights in the name of democracy must himself act in accordance with its rules" (at 326). However, Justice Barak added a restrictive qualification to the *Yeredor* ruling: the reasonable possibility standard, and therein lies my disagreement with him. On this issue my view is similar to Justices Elon and Bejski's. I do not share either Justices Shamgar's or Barak's opinions that in the face of such dangers a standard of some sort should be applied in order to evaluate the danger, and it should then be decided what defensive means to apply. In my view Justice Agranat's "creative interpretation" approach rather than the Rawlsian approach should have been resorted to (cf. chapter 10).

Justices Shamgar and Barak believed that all parties should enjoy the right to be elected, including those who threatened the existence of the state (Shamgar and Barak), or its democratic foundations (Barak), *unless* the threat they posed was severe, unless they had a reasonable chance of translating their ideas into deeds. Their reasoning was founded on balancing and evaluating probabilities, a process that in this context, as Justice Bejski articulated in his criticism of Justice Barak, raised substantial questions. But not just the process raises doubts. The essential question is Why should we wait for the stage of probable or reasonable possibility of danger to be reached while the list in question goes from strength to strength, and meanwhile its ideas and acts undermine democracy and deliberately discriminate against others? The courts acknowledged that Kach's values were not compatible with the fundamental values of democracy and that it did not reject the use of violence to further its aims. Even if we follow Justices Shamgar's and Barak's reasoning, which, like Rawls's, concentrates attention on circumstances, the increasing popularity of Kach against a background of severe economic problems, combined with societal and national crises, posed a danger to Israeli democracy. It was not as if Kach's political platform was dubious or the intentions of its members were unclear or they did not act in accordance with their declared aims. I do not therefore see why such a list should be allowed representation in parliament to help it achieve its purposes. More fundamentally, the issue of defending democracy is a matter of moral principle rather than one that is contingent on the level or the proximity of the danger. Justice Barak preferred to consider circumstantial considerations, thereby avoiding a discussion of the ethical constraints of liberty and tolerance. I argue that moral restrictions deriving from the defense of democracy necessitate the outlawing of antidemocratic lists. A similar line of reasoning guided the framers of the European Convention of Human Rights when they enacted Article 17, recognizing the necessity of preventing specific groups from exploiting the principles enunciated by the convention in their own interests. Article 17 provides, "Nothing in this Convention may be interpreted as implying for any State, group or person any right to engage in any activity or perform any act aimed at the destruction of any of the rights and freedoms set forth herein or at their limitation to a greater extent than is provided for in the Convention."

To conclude: this study accepts Justice Barak's reasoning in part, and Justices Elon and Bejski's reasoning in part to the effect of restricting the right of parties to compete in the elections if they endanger the existence of the state *or* its democratic foundations. In line with Justices Elon's and Bejski's acceptance of the majority decision in *Yeredor* and with Justice Barak's extension of the rule, I argue that violent lists that are unequivocally antidemocratic or aim to bring about the physical annihilation of the state should not—as a matter of principle—be eligible to take part in the elections so as to enable them to further their ends. To avoid the possibility of the slippery-slope syndrome, I insist that only in these two instances may a list be disqualified. A list that wishes to participate in the democratic procedures and to gain power to implement its ideas through legislation and other democratic means must first recognize the right of the state to exist and to comply with the basic principles that underlie its democratic foundations. If the political platform of a list negates the basic requirements of democracy, those of respecting others and not harming others; if the list's ideology advocates *not* accepting these principles when they are applied to a designated group, it disqualifies itself from the right to participate in the democratic process. When democratic institutions accept such a list, they assist the promotion of antidemocratic notions.45 Therefore, no evidence of a danger, near or remote, is needed when a list aims to undermine democracy or the state. The evidence that is required concerns the *content* of the political platform of the list in question, the list's *intentions,* and the fact that *acts* were undertaken to accomplish the declared aims. The evidence must be explicit and clear, and it must be substantiated, to use Barak's contention, by "qualified administrative evidence," that is, "such testimony as any reasonable person would consider to be of probative value and would have relied upon to a greater or lesser degree" (at 304).[46] The burden of providing the evidence is on whichever party argues for refusing to confirm the list.

I review in chapter 12 other decisions of the supreme court concerning Kahane and his party. In the attempt to delegitimize Kahane after his election to the Knesset, members of the house led by Speaker Shlomo Hillel resorted to varied means of restricting Kach, not all of which were justified. After each of these attempts Kahane appealed to the High Court of Justice. The court repeatedly returned issues concerning Kahane and his party to the legislative body. The justices insisted that restrictions on essential freedoms should be backed by laws, trying to divest their judgments to the utmost of political references.[47] Thus, the court upheld Kahane's right to raise no-confidence motions in the Knesset, to submit racist bills, and to express his racist views over the radio. I begin by reflecting on the restrictions imposed on Kahane's freedom of movement and expression, and then consider the five appeals submitted by Kahane against the Speaker of the Knesset.

Chapter 12

Curtailing Kahane's Freedom of Movement and Expression

Freedom of Movement

Two weeks after his election to the Knesset, Kahane initiated a series of provocative visits to Arab communities with the avowed aim of persuading the inhabitants to emigrate from Israel. The first visit, on 30 August 1984, was to the Arab town of Umm El Fahm. When Kahane and his supporters attempted to enter the town, the a priori position of the police was to allow them to carry out their intention. At some stage, however, the police realized that a situation of substantive danger to the public peace was being created.[1] So, fearing disturbances and bloodshed, the police did not allow Kahane to enter the town. They stopped the Kach group two miles from Umm El Fahm. In this incident and in others, the police were there to intervene and to prevent bloodshed; however, their efforts to maintain public peace were not always successful. Time and again violent incidents arose between Kach supporters, who caused agitation by their visits to Arab villages, and Arabs and Jews who stood against them, blocking the way and shouting "Racism won't pass!"

Kahane knew that the denial of entry to Umm El Fahm would serve as a precedent to stop him from going to any other Arab village. He sought the assistance of the court to overrule the police's decision.[2] However, Kahane himself canceled this appeal on 4 July 1985 on the grounds that it was no longer relevant. The issue ceased to be relevant because of measures taken by the Knesset to stop the visits. In December 1984 the

Knesset House Committee voted in a twelve-to-eight decision to restrict Kahane's parliamentary immunity. The provision in law secures members of the Knesset free access to any public place.[3] The restriction was intended to enable the police to prevent Kahane from entering Arab communities in which his presence might invoke a breach of the peace.

At the time of the debate concerning this issue the attorney general, Itzhak Zamir, justified the proposed restriction by saying that the Kahanist phenomenon fundamentally contradicted the values cherished by society. It distorted Judaism, exhibiting the Jewish tradition in a twisted way. Zamir asserted that Judaism was sensitive to the lives of human beings and respected people *qua* people, whoever they were, while Kahanism impugned these beliefs. The phenomenon was also incompatible with Zionism, for Zionism aimed to establish a just society in Israel, in which everyone enjoyed the same rights irrespective of their race, nationality, or religion. Zamir admitted that he had been wrong when he refrained from acting against Kahane before the elections. He said that he had misjudged the force of Kahanism and what its resulting influence might be; that he had regarded Kahanism as a "sick phenomenon," but also as a peripheral, harmless one. Meanwhile the situation had changed. Kahane had *won legitimacy* since his election to the Knesset, and Kahanism had become a danger to society for it encouraged the violation of Knesset laws and, by so doing, it weakened the societal framework. Zamir postulated that for a member of the Knesset to act in the Knesset against the Knesset was inconceivable. He therefore urged the House Committee to act against Kahane immediately.[4]

Yossi Sarid, member of Knesset (Civil Rights Movement), one of the two Knesset members who initiated this measure,[5] explained the necessity of restricting Kahane's immunity by saying that Kahanism was a psychopolitical phenomenon. Kahane incited Arabs and Jews to murder and praised the Jewish terror organization. The serious thing was that his views had gradually received legitimization and public support. Sarid warned, "Today Kahane's views are accepted with less shock than before. More people are willing to listen to him. Kahane is already part of this place and, therefore, the Knesset has to stop him here and now."[6] Haim Ramon, member of the Knesset (Labor), acknowledged the risks involved in taking this measure but nevertheless gave his support to it, maintaining, "The voting today is the beginning of Kahane's exclusion from this House and the law, outside of Israeli society. The Knesset decides today not only on a parliamentary act, but also on an educational act. The entire youth will know that this man symbolizes an illegitimate thing, an immoral thing, [that] there is Kahane and the other 119 Members of Knesset."[7]

The plenum of the Knesset approved the proposal with a simple majority (a fifty-eight-to-thirty-six decision).

Kahane appealed to the High Court of Justice on preliminary, procedural grounds.[8] He claimed that his voice had not been heard during the debates of the Knesset House Committee. The House Committee, for its part, responded that Kahane had been invited to each and every session but had chosen not to come. Kahane was quoted as saying that he would not degrade himself by appearing before the committee. On the day of the trial, Kahane had not appeared and the case was closed. Hence the court did not have to address itself to the essence of the case, whether the curtailment of Kahane's right, granted to every member of Knesset to travel freely throughout the country without being prevented by the police, was justified.

Here, freedom of movement was interwoven with freedom of expression. Restricting Kahane's free movement was intended to prevent him from preaching his views in Arab villages. Under the Offense Principle (cf. part 1, chapters 7 and 8), this measure was justified. It was designed to abridge the expression of opinions, of which the content as well as the manner were intended to cause offense in objective circumstances that were unavoidable from the unwilling witnesses' view. Such visits to Arab villages constituted deliberate and willful attempts to exacerbate the sensibilities of the Arab population. Kahane targeted specific groups among whom he wanted to propagate his ideas of "separation" and "voluntary emigration for peace"; and by going to their places he forced them to be exposed to his racist statements and diatribes. A reflection on Joel Feinberg's three standards may prove that reason existed for introducing the restriction (see chapter 7). The seriousness of the offense standard was satisfied: Kahane intended to inflict psychological offense, which was morally on a par with physical harm, upon the Arab communities. He wanted maliciously to offend and stir up the Arab inhabitants by expressing his avowedly antidemocratic views.[9] The *Volenti* standard was certainly satisfied, because the Arab inhabitants did not feel an obligation to attend the rallies simply out of curiosity. Finally, given Kahane's motives, avoiding the demonstrations would have amounted—from the Arab residents' viewpoint—to saying that Kahanism may pass. Thus, the Arab citizens were put in such a position that either way they would be offended: if they attended the demonstrations, they would have to hear Kahane's preaching against them and his verbal insults; and if they did not, this would be interpreted as Kahane's victory. Therefore, no real choice was available to the Arabs but to attend the demonstrations and to suffer the pain caused by them. The only way of stopping Kahane from continuing his campaign of hatred was to resort to legal measures and restrict his immunity.

We also can argue that grounds existed for restricting Kahane's freedom of movement and expression under the Harm Principle. Given the fact that some of Kahane's men were armed, a possibility existed that one of them might decide to take the law into his own hands and apply more persuasive methods to clarify the speech to the Arabs. The possibility existed of words being translated into physical harm.[10]

It was one thing to prevent Kahane from entering Arab communities but quite another to refuse him access to any other places. Although preventing the infliction of severe damage upon Arab citizens who could not avoid confronting Kahane in their villages was justified, to prevent him from preaching his ideas in predominantly Jewish places was not. On many occasions when Kahane wanted to hold rallies and assemblies in public places his requests were denied. In some of these cases, Kahane was allowed to hold the rallies only after appealing to the courts.[11] I do not wish to consider all of these cases, so let me take one incident as an illustration.

On 10 March 1985 Kahane wished to enter Bar-Ilan University at the city of Ramat-Gan but was denied entry by the police. The official claim was that the measure was taken to prevent incitement against Arab students.[12] This claim strikes me as peculiar. In the first place, the police could not have known what Kahane intended to say. Visiting an Arab village, Kahane was likely to address the Arab issue, which would not necessarily be the case when he went to address a Jewish orthodox university. Second, the probability of instigation, of translating words into harmful conduct, was not great. Third, the Arab students could have avoided the meeting: a difference exists between preaching racism in an Arab neighborhood and preaching racism in universities. In my opinion, restricting Kahane's right to exercise his freedom of expression at Bar-Ilan is similar to restricting a person's right to speak at Hyde Park Corner in London (cf. chapter 7). Lastly, the discrepancy between this incident and Kahane's appearance at the Hebrew University on 28 February 1985 is glaring. I find it difficult to understand how the police allowed Kahane to speak in Jerusalem, where no fewer Arab students may be found than at Bar-Ilan, yet decided to deny his right to speak at Ramat-Gan.

The media opened another front in the struggle against Kahanism. Soon after the 1984 elections the media directors decided to introduce a ban on reviewing the activities of the movement. They spoke of an obligation to fight Kach's racist ideas. Kahane was not permitted to appear on programs;[13] his statements were not reported; newspapers turned down his requests to respond to the attacks made on him; press conferences and events organized by Kach were not covered. The decision was not to supply Kahane with any means to disseminate his views. The frustrated Kahane sought the assistance of the supreme court.

The Media's Ban on Kahane

The Broadcasting Authority in Israel is a national body whose power and influence is unique. I do not know of any other body in a liberal democratic society that possesses similar authority. Until not long ago it supervised three of the main five radio networks and the sole television network.[14] Immediately after the elections to the Eleventh Knesset took place, the News Forum of the Broadcasting Authority decided that in matters that concerned Kach and Kahane, only items of "clear newslike character" were to be broadcast. This was in order to ensure that the national media did not serve as a platform for incitement against citizens and for statements that contradicted the Declaration of Independence. Kahane appealed to the court, arguing that the decision to ban him infringed on his fundamental democratic rights, and that it was an act of "private censorship," contradictory to the principles of equal opportunity and fairness. The court, per Justice Aharon Barak (Justices Gabriel Bach and Shoshana Netanyahu concurring) accepted the appeal.[15]

Justice Barak postulated that freedom of expression is the freedom of a citizen to express his or her views and to hear what others have to say. The rights derived from freedom of expression create a comprehensive system of interrelated regulations, which crystallize—through their operation—the tradition of freedom of speech. This tradition is integrated into the constitutional framework and it constitutes a cornerstone of the democratic essence of the regime (at 268). Justice Barak maintained that the right to disseminate views through the electronic media is part and parcel of the principle of free speech. He quoted Barron, who said, "In the era of mass communication, the words of the solitary speaker or the lonely writer, however brave or imaginative, have little impact unless they are broadcast through the great engines of public opinion—radio, television, and the press" (at 269).[16]

In the light of the unique nature of the electronic media, the duty of a broadcasting authority in a democratic society is to express the views of different sections of the population. Relying on a number of American decisions,[17] Justice Barak argued that the public had the right to gain access to the media as well as to receive information about unfamiliar ideas. An unlimited marketplace of ideas should exist rather than a monopolized market. Three major reasons exist for this: the search for truth; the desire to allow individuals to express themselves; and the need to sustain the democratic regime, based on tolerance and social stability. These, among other arguments, were discussed in part 1, chapter 5. Drawing on these three major reasons, freedom of expression was perceived to be a central right under Israeli constitutional law. Justice Barak asserted that this freedom also included the freedom to express dangerous, irritating, and unconventional opinions, which the public hated and detested.[18] It also included racist expressions.

Justice Barak maintained that the way to deal with such ideas was not by silencing them but through explanation and education. The remedy for overcoming false views was not to put restrictions on speech but to increase their exposure. In this context, Justice Barak repeated (as he did in *Neiman*) Justice Holmes's renowned opinion in *Abrams* that the best test of truth is the power of the thought in question to win acceptance in the competition of the market.[19] Truth would win out through the contest of ideas.

However, agreeing with Justice Shimon Agranat's reasoning in *Kol Ha'am*, Justice Barak conceded that the right to free speech is relative. A balance has to be struck between freedom of expression and other fundamental principles, such as the dignity of human beings or the public peace. The balancing process is done by the legislature; when silence occurs on its part, then the balancing becomes the work of the court. Justice Barak reiterated his reasoning in *Neiman*, saying that the appropriate test in deciding the balance between freedom of expression and other interests was the probability test rather than the bad tendency test.

Accordingly, restrictions on speech may be introduced when it is proba-ble that the expression in question will be followed by actions that sub-stantially injure social order, the public peace, or the foundations of democracy. Justice Barak explained that the probability test came to answer the question What was the causal connection between the pub-lication of speech and the harm to other values, which constituted justi-fication for restricting speech? The test did not determine what values, besides freedom of expression, should be protected (at 290). Justice Barak specified that not every probable danger to the public peace justified restrictions on speech. Instead, the injury had to be material and real, and consideration had to be given to the magnitude of the danger and to its chances of coming about (at 294).

From the general to the particular, the Broadcasting Authority could decide its priorities regarding what should be broadcast, but it could not discriminate against specific views and opinions. Justice Barak argued that the Broadcasting Authority did not weigh the effect of Kahanist expressions on the public order—this was where it had acted wrongly. In each case it should consider the probability of substantial damage resulting from the airing of such opinions (at 308). Where no such probability arose, no justi-fication occurred for allowing prior restraint on freedom of expression.

Justice Bach submitted a separate opinion in which he agreed with his colleague's conclusion but not with his reasoning. He asserted that racial or national-ethnical incitements were offensive to the feelings of the tar-get group, and their publication constituted a breach of the public order. Such publications would probably produce such a result. Thus, Justice Bach disputed Justice Barak's assertion that even when a news item con-stituted a criminal offense because of its racist content, the electronic media had to broadcast it, unless public disorder was probable. In his view, the Broadcasting Authority had the right to refrain from airing racist incitements when it believed that their publication involved crimi-nal offense, whether or not the publication was likely to cause disrup-tions of order (at 315). Nevertheless, Justice Bach concluded that the Broadcasting Authority could not ban Kahane altogether in the unprece-dented manner to which it had resorted. It should weigh all relevant considerations honestly and reasonably, in good faith and without preju-dice, when deciding on the allocation of time to different opinions. While it had no obligation to allocate equal time to each opinion, it must not single out any of them for censorship.

Justices Barak and Bach rightly concluded that the Broadcasting Authority had acted *ultra vires* in banning Kahane. In a free democratic society we have room for any idea to be expressed, unless decisive reasons exist to abridge speech. However, decisive reasons do not mean the probability that the expression will be followed by actions that substantially injure social order, the public peace, or the foundations of democracy. The probability test is too blurred to serve as a decisive criterion. Instead, the Harm Principle and the Offense Principle are offered as the only qualifications on freedom of expression. To recall, under the Harm Principle I argued that some types of speech that inflict considerable harm ought, like any other harmful action, to be subject to restriction. And the Offense Principle supplies grounds for abridging expressions when they are intended to inflict psychological offense, which is morally on a par with physical harm, provided that the circumstances are such that the target group cannot avoid being exposed to it.

At this point I must dedicate some space to a specific point made by Justice Bach in his judgment. He said that when the state media broadcasted racist ideas they did not affirm or support them but did help them gain legitimacy (at 316). The question of granting legitimacy to a list has been one of the main considerations here to argue that violent political lists that strive to bring about the annihilation of the state and violent lists with explicit antidemocratic platforms have no place in a democratic parliament. Now, you may argue that the same reasoning should persuade us to outlaw racist expressions altogether.

In my discussion on Skokie I expressed reservations regarding the view that makes racist speech a special case, distinguishing it from other forms of speech, thereby enabling it to be excluded from the entrenched protection usually granted to speech. Instead, I have formulated the Offense and the Harm Principles. I still think that in a free democratic society we have room for every opinion to be heard, racist opinions included. If we reflect on Bach's argument, we see that he did not mean an idea gains legitimacy just from the fact of its being heard. Many extraordinary, peculiar ideas exist; being given the chance to compete in the marketplace of ideas does not in itself accord them legitimacy.

You may argue that Justice Bach expressed this view because only one television network existed in Israel, controlled by the state; therefore, any opinion that appeared on the air automatically received some sort of legitimization. This is a plausible argument. The fact that a person appears in the media several times does make him or her part of the place. Indeed, this consideration played some role in the decision of the Broadcasting Authority to ban Kahane. However, a clear-cut connection does not exist between appearing on television and gaining legitimacy as a result of that exposure. Justice Bach's reasoning does not provide grounds to infer from the legitimacy argument—with regard to restricting representation in parliament—the denial of freedom of expression. For a great difference exists between appearances on television and appearances in parliament. I agree with Justices Barak and Bach that in a democracy we cannot allow the banning of ideas solely on the basis that they are associated with a certain party or a certain person. This is in spite of the fact that their very appearance on state television may grant them some legitimacy. We can hope that educational efforts to counteract the influence will prove successful. But what democracy can afford in terms of freedom of expression is not necessarily what it can allow in terms of freedom of election. Television is not a democratic instrument. In many democratic countries television networks are controlled by wealthy people who decide what their viewers will see according to diverse interests, public as well as selfish. In other democracies, such as Israel, the government exerts a strong influence on what is broadcast. In either case, the decision about what should be shown on the screen is not made in a democratic fashion. On the other hand, parliament is a democratic institution, an essential procedure without which democracy becomes an empty word. It is too much to expect democracy to allow those who aim at its destruction to enter parliament so as to further their aim by democratic means. I would hesitate to say the same about expressing antidemocratic ideas in the media. In the media we are dealing with competition in the market of ideas, while in the parliament we are dealing with the legal possibilities of translating ideas into deeds.

In addition, so far as the legitimacy factor is concerned, a difference occurs between the legitimacy that may be accorded a person or a body of persons through appearance on television and the legitimacy accorded a party through representation in parliament. In the case of a state-controlled television network, we can say that both types of legitimacy are institutionalized. The first may be called *media legitimacy,* while the second may be called *governmental legitimacy.* They are not one and the same, although one may affect the other. Those who gain media legitimacy may become celebrities, but they do not necessarily gain legitimacy as decision makers. Some of them, surely, have no claim but to be known. They may base their status in society—through the legitimacy accorded to them by the media—on merely sensational material. On the other hand, those who enjoy governmental legitimacy or wish to gain it through election to the parliament have a different claim and a different position in society. They want to dictate the future of their society. *They have authoritative claims.* They do not only shape what we will eat for breakfast or how we will dress next summer; they can determine whether we say what we think, and to what extent coercion will prevail in society.

The final section of this chapter reflects on Kahane's five appeals against the speaker of the Knesset, Shlomo Hillel. But first an observation on the military involvement in the fight against Kahanism should be recorded. The official army radio, Galei Tzahal, decided to devote one day of broadcasting in October 1985 to refuting Kahanism and to fighting against racist trends. The commander of the radio station explained that although it should not be involved in political matters, an exception had to be made in this case. Given the scale of the problem and the fact that the army was the people's army, it could not have ignored the racist ideas to which soldiers were exposed.[20] Colonel Shulamit Ligum, public relations officer for the manpower division of the IDF, wrote, "We agree with the institutions of the state and with the vast majority of society that thinks that Kahane's messages are racist and they hurt us first because they carry within them the destruction of Israeli society and threaten the existence of the State of Israel."[21]

This statement followed the publication of a special instruction sheet concerning Kahane to all officers, issued by the chief education officer in March 1985. It declared, "It is commonly accepted that at least some of Kahane's activities undermine the stability of society, and thus endanger the entire population." The instruction maintained that Kahane's views contradicted the Zionist tradition and the "spirit of democracy." This was the first time that the IDF decided to take a stand against a Knesset member and to warn against his activities.[22]

That the military decided to join the struggle against Kahanism shows the extent of antagonism and concern felt by the commanders regarding the phenomenon. They witnessed the growing popularity of Kahane's discriminatory ideas amongst soldiers and decided to fight this trend. This fact also indicates the repugnance aroused by Kahane and his views. The consensus was that Kahanism had to be excluded from society altogether, and that the importance of this issue outweighed the interest of maintaining a clear distinction between politics and the military. But we have a matter for concern when the military becomes involved in politics and democracy. This step might have had significant effect on the relationships between the parliament and the army, although no decisive conclusion can be reached at this stage regarding the further implications of that involvement.

Kahane v. Speaker of the Knesset—Five Chapters

THE RIGHT TO SUBMIT MOTIONS OF NO CONFIDENCE

In February 1985 the Speaker of the Knesset refused to accept a motion of no confidence in the government submitted by Kach. The official excuse was that one member's political factions could not introduce such a motion. Clearly the claim was tailored against Kahane, who appealed to the court.[23]

Speaking for a unanimous court (President Meir Shamgar and Justice Eliezer Goldberg concurred without explanation), Justice Aharon Barak considered two separate issues: the definition of the term *faction,* and the issue of justiciability. He opened his judgment by reflecting on the term faction as used in Section 36 (a) of the Knesset Rules of Procedure, which holds that "any faction is allowed to put on the agenda motions of nonconfidence." Justice Barak found nothing to imply that factions of one member were not included within this term. However, the appellee based his case on two decisions of the Knesset House Committee, which determined that "one-person factions are not allowed to submit no-confidence motions."[24] Justice Barak responded that this argument could not stand because the Knesset's Rules of Procedure could be read only to say that one-person factions were allowed to submit such motions, and the Knesset House Committee could not take contrary decisions (at 155). Justice Barak proceeded by analyzing the delicate question of justiciability.

As ever, when confronted by such questions, Barak's inclination was to adopt the balancing approach. He drew attention to the fact that in H.C. 652/1981, the court (per Justice Barak) tried to determine "the golden path." The court advocated the need for striking a judicial balance based on a self-restraint on the part of the judiciary, which nevertheless did not enforce an absolute restriction on itself.[25] There the decision was that the court would not interfere in the internal affairs of the

Knesset as long as no danger appeared of offending the foundations of the constitutional framework. Applying this criterion to the case in question, the danger was considerable and the court could not abstain from interfering, for a faction that was denied the power to submit motions of no confidence was parliamentarily crippled.

Moreover, the negation of this right endangered the entire framework of parliamentary life because one of the vital functions of the legislature was to supervise the actions of the executive; preventing one faction from submitting such motions reduced the parliamentary power of controlling the government. Justice Barak obviously recognized that the chance of a one-person faction's succeeding in submitting no-confidence motions was quite slim. But, in his opinion, the question here was not tactical; it was a matter of *principle*. Judgments should be formulated on the realistic assumption that parliamentary life was in a continuous state of flux, and thus the possibility that the entire opposition could be comprised of one-person factions should be considered.

This clear analytical judgment seems immune to criticism.[26] If the only ground for the decree is the size of the list in the Knesset, then this decree might lead to the slippery-slope syndrome. It might open the way for major parties initiating further restrictions against political opponents. However, the way in which Justice Barak concluded his arguments is of interest. He said, "My opinion is that the *order nisi* should be made absolute, in the sense that we declare that the Speaker of the Knesset is not entitled to prevent the petitioner from submitting to the Knesset's agenda a motion of no-confidence, *solely* on the grounds that the petitioner is a one-person faction" (at 165, emphasis mine).

This conclusion implies that if other, more substantial grounds exist, then it is possible to prevent a list from submitting motions of no confidence. I interpret Justice Barak's statement to imply that the court cannot be of assistance to the appellee in this case, in the form presented, but that if other reasons are presented, a basis for denying parties this right may exist.

THE RIGHT TO SUBMIT BILLS—THREE APPEALS

The First Appeal

The speaker of the Knesset, Shlomo Hillel, and the Knesset Presidium refused to introduce two of Kahane's proposed laws, asserting that they would not lend their signatures to the contempt of the Knesset through Nuremberg laws. The first bill (the Authority Law) suggested that only Jews could be citizens in Israel. Non-Jews would have the status of alien residents. Consequently (among other things) they would not be allowed to vote, to serve in public office, or to reside in Jerusalem. Those who refused to accept this status would have to emigrate from the country voluntarily or nonvoluntarily.

The second bill (the Separation Law) called for the abolition of all governmental programs involving meetings between Jews and non-Jews; separate beaches would be set up; a non-Jew would not be permitted to reside in a Jewish neighborhood unless the majority of the Jews in that neighborhood agreed to it; and intermarriage and sexual intercourse between Jews and non-Jews would be banned.

The Presidium of the Knesset (the speaker and the five deputy speakers) said that "a black flag of disgrace rose over these bills in a conspicuous and unequivocal way."[27] Relying on the Knesset Rules of Procedure,[28] they argued that their authority empowered them to use their discretion in refusing the introduction of bills that degraded the Knesset. Kahane, for his part, contended that nothing in the Knesset Rules of Procedure empowered the Presidium to refuse the submitting of bills because of their content.

The High Court of Justice had to decide on two separate issues; once again the question of justiciability arose as to whether the court could intervene in the workings of the Knesset, and it had to consider the amount of discretion open to the speaker of the Knesset and deputy speakers. Regarding the first question, a fair amount of precedents rendered the petition justiciable.[29] Justice Barak (Justices Shlomo Levin and Mordechai Ben-Dror concurring) said that when a decision substantially offended the constitutional framework as that one did, the court had no other choice but to intervene (at 95). As for the question of the Presidium's authority, Justice Barak argued that every member of the Knesset had the right to submit bills, and that the speaker had only to supervise the technical aspects of the procedure. The authority of the Presidium did not include the power not to confirm a bill on the grounds of objection to its political and social content. It did not have the right to refuse to register a bill even when that bill contained normative principles that violated the fundamental values of the state. Accordingly, although believing that the petitioner's two bills were an affront to basic principles of the Israeli constitutional system, arousing "horrifying memories" and serving "to damage the democratic character of the State of Israel," Justice Barak concluded that the first commitment of the court was to strict observance of the rule of law, even when this entailed giving expression to abhorrent opinions (H.C. 742/1984, at 96). Once the petitioner was elected on the basis of this platform, the Presidium was not empowered to prevent the introduction of bills whose sole purpose, in terms of their content, was to put into effect the platform of the list.

This reasoning is in line with the *Neiman* decision. If Kach was allowed to run for elections and was elected, then we might expect it to try to further its political aims through the democratic procedures that had brought it to the Knesset. Since racism and objections to democratic values were part of its political platform, then it was entitled to use democratic measures to realize them. Any other ruling would have been inconsistent with the previous ruling. The implications were that in the absence of a restrictive legislative statute, the court had to stay silent in the face of a party whose purpose was to practice discrimination and to destroy democracy. A racist list was entitled to carry its program all the way until it succeeds in implementing it, unless a statute was introduced to put a stop to it;[30] or, more likely, unless the court was convinced of a "reasonable possibility" of danger, or maybe "probability" or another such criterion to estimate the danger. No consideration was given by the court to what I have called (following Dworkin) *normative constitutional principles,* that is, requirements of justice or fairness or similar measures of morality according to which the political structure may be interpreted. Thus, the court resorted to the formalistic view, preferring to throw the issue back to the legislature rather than use its judicial discretion.

The reasons for which I argued that the *Neiman* decision was flawed suggest that this judgment was flawed as well. The role of the court is to set judicial standards in accordance with the normative principles on which the state is founded. Here the argument in favor of the anti-discrimination act, that the Arab citizens have equal rights, is an argument of principle that should be considered by the court. Hence, scope existed to decide that bills that contradicted the democratic foundations of Israel and its character as a Jewish state (as depicted in the Declaration of Independence) should not have been regarded in the same manner as other bills. These bills opposed the notion of equal concern and respect that were the focus of both conceptions: the conception of Israel as a liberal democracy and the conception of Israel as a Jewish state. Why the court decided to give judicial assistance to a list that was explicitly anti-democratic and that exploited a twisted conception of Judaism to discriminate against others is difficult to understand.

The Knesset reacted to this decision by amending (on 13 November 1985) the Rules of Procedure of the Knesset, empowering the speaker and his or her deputies to refuse to submit bills that were, in their opinion, of a racist nature or that negated the existence of the state of Israel as the state of the Jewish people.[31] The latter part of the amendment, based on section 7A of the Basic Law: The Knesset (to be discussed shortly), was included to ensure the political support required to pass the amendment. Kahane decided again to ask for the assistance of the court.

The Right to Submit Bills—Second Appeal

The appeal was based on the argument that the court ruling took place before this amendment; therefore, the refusal to submit these bills constituted contempt of the court (under Section 6 of Contempt of Court Ordinance). A unanimous court rejected the appeal in a brief decision.[32] The justices (Barak, S. Levin, and Ben-Dror) drew a distinction between operative order and normative order, asserting that in H.C. 742/1984 they did not *order* the Presidium to present the bills. They merely declared what the existing law was and what powers might be derived from it. All that the court had said was that the appellees were not allowed to refuse to introduce the bills. Thus, by adhering to their refusal, the Presidium could be said to have acted wrongly, but this act could not be seen as being in a contempt of the court (at 488).

After this ruling one might have thought that Kahane would have given up his attempts to submit bills. This, however, was not the case. He introduced five bills before the Presidium: two of them were similar to the previous ones. The additional laws prohibited advocating religious conversion, forbade the selling of land to Arabs, and placed a veto on meetings between Jewish and non-Jewish youths. The Presidium, as expected, refused to bring them to the floor for debate. Its decision was based on the recent amendment to the Rules of Procedure of the Knesset (Section 134 [C]). Kahane, for his part, stated that he had copied two of these laws, word for word, from the great Jewish law codifier, Maimonides, and the other from the Jewish National Fund.[33]

The Right to Submit Bills—Third Appeal

Kahane's last appeal to the court on this issue was based on the ground that an order that was designed to restrict the right of a Knesset member to submit bills should be founded in a specific law and not in the Rules of Procedure of the Knesset.

Speaking for a unanimous court of five justices, President Shamgar argued that the Rules of Procedure themselves created the right of a Knesset member to initiate laws, and that they established the confines of this right. Only in exceptional circumstances of a substantial defect in an order of the Rules of Procedure was there scope for judicial scrutiny (at 399–400). This was not the case here, and in any event the court did not sit as an appeal instance regarding the decisions of the Knesset's Presidium. Therefore, Kahane's petition was denied.[34]

Two of the opinions, those of Justices Barak and Levin, deserve closer examination. Two words comprised the opinion of Justice Barak: "I concur." In the other cases concerning Kahane's rights, Justice Barak had formulated elaborate judgments. Here he preferred simply to express agreement with President Shamgar's reasoning. By taking this laconic decision Barak adopted a strict judicial view as if to say that all the data relevant to this case was similar to the data in H.C. 742/1984, with the exception that the legislature had decided to act, and now the court had to formulate decisions on the basis of the amendment to the Rules of Procedure of the Knesset.

One of the criticisms that was voiced against Justice Barak held that a discrepancy arose between his opinions in the first case, which considered Kahane's right to introduce laws, and this one. Thus, David Kretzmer asserted that in H.C. 742/1984 Justice Barak had said that the Presidium could not refuse bills on the grounds of their contents, while here Barak based his decision on a Knesset amendment that made distinctions *precisely* on the basis of content.[35] However, this was only an apparent discrepancy, not a real one, because of the introduction of the amendment. Kretzmer, among others, had high expectations for the future president of the supreme court. I have to admit that I too expected Justice Barak to take a broader view of the issue, and not simply to concur with President Shamgar without commenting on the Knesset's initiative in blocking Kahane's attempt to submit his bills. Justice Barak could have said that the court had to follow the directives of the legislature while still expressing his reservations about this amendment, if he still had reservations.

The interesting decision in this case was that of Justice Dov Levin. He concurred with the president's reasoning and added that it was right to deny the petition on different grounds. Justice Levin contended that even if the Knesset Rules of Procedure did not authorize the Presidium to refuse the submitting of Kach bills, nevertheless the court should have rejected the appeal because it was based on proposals that negated the fundamental principles upon which the state of Israel as well as Judaism were founded (at 407–8). He postulated that the common denominator of these bills lay in their explicit discrimination against non-Jews, aiming to diminish their basic rights. It could not be that this court, whose role was to support justice, would aid those who wished to force the Knesset to present such racist proposals. The court should have declared Kach's petition prima facie void because Kahane wished to found his bills on the halacha, while their *content* was invalid from a universal perspective as well as from the perspective of the principles that underlie Judaism. Moreover, Justice Levin criticized the court's decision in H.C. 742/1984, saying that if he had been among the justices in that decision, he would have rejected the appeal straightaway. He said that because of the repugnant nature of the bills, there was no reason to discuss the case at all (at 406).

Thus, Justice Levin's reasoning was in essence similar to mine, and it was in line with Dworkin's concept of normative legal principles. Justice Levin implied that some matters have no place in a democratic society, and that democratic rights should not exist for the assistance of those who wanted to exploit them in order to infringe the rights of others. Justice Levin did not speak of the licensing role of the court, but his assertion that some ideas have no place in the court implies that among the duties of the court is to act against some noxious opinions when the court reaches the conclusion that they should be excluded from the social framework.

Justice Levin's reasoning served as the basis for denying Kahane's last appeal against the speaker of the Knesset, Shlomo Hillel.[36] At first glance the case seems peculiar: the adding of a sentence when a member of Knesset takes the Knesset oath. A closer look at the dispute reveals that it was of great significance because it pitted two contradictory conceptions one against the other: one democratic and the other theocratic. The main motivation of Hillel's action was not the delegitimization of Kahane, although the results of this dispute certainly contributed to that effect. Instead, Hillel seems to have thought that the Knesset should not allow anyone to make a mockery of rules, that it should not stay silent when attempts were made to lower the status of the Knesset in the constitutional framework and to introduce qualifications to the keeping of law and order.

THE RIGHT TO QUALIFY THE KNESSET OATH

The crux of the case was the Knesset oath that every member of Knesset is required to declare upon his or her election to the Knesset. The oath reads, "I declare to be faithful to the State of Israel and to fulfill, in good faith, my mission in the Knesset."[37]

When taking his Knesset oath, Kahane added a sentence from the Book of Psalms (119), saying, "I pledge to keep your [God's] laws always, forever and after." More than two years later, in January 1987, Kahane declared before a court in the United States, "I did not take the Knesset oath as prescribed." He explained that his reading from Psalms was intended to say that his first obligation was to the law of God, not to the laws of the state; that he would obey the laws of the Knesset as long as they did not disobey a higher law.[38]

After the speaker of the Knesset discovered Kahane's intention to stipulate his loyalty to the laws of the state only if they did not contradict the laws of the Torah, he asked Kahane to declare his confidence once again, without any qualifications. Hillel warned Kahane that if he would not do that, all his rights as a member of the Knesset would be removed.[39] The speaker, we can assume, regarded Kahane's stipulation as an attempt to delegitimize law and order in Israel. Kahane appealed to the court, seeking assistance to free him from fulfilling this demand.

The court unanimously rejected the appeal; following the precedent set in H.C. 669/1985, Deputy President Miriam Ben-Porat referred to the concluding part of Kahane's declaration in the American court, where he said, "My intention in taking such oath was to modify the Knesset oath to reflect that my first responsibility is to God's law" (at 734–35).

In line with Justice Levin's judgment, Deputy President Ben-Porat said that the court was designated to consider cases in which it found a need to observe that justice was done. She maintained that only honest people with clean hands could enter through the gates of this court.[40] Under these circumstances, Kahane would not have found any support in the court, for his conduct was not honest and was not suitable for a public representative (at 735). Deputy President Ben-Porat quoted Justice Moshe Zilberg, who said, "Israel is not a theocracy, for it is not religion which administers the life of the citizen, but the law."[41] Therefore, it was an insult to think a member of the Knesset could put himself beyond the laws of the Knesset and still be considered loyal to his role in parliament, and to the state as such.

Justices Menachem Elon and Eliyahu Vinoguard presented their judgments in a similar fashion. Justice Elon referred to the first part of Kahane's confession, where he admitted that he did not take the Knesset oath as prescribed. Since Kahane did not mention this comment in his appeal, then the appeal seriously lacked honesty. It had to be denied immediately, without even consideration of the claims that Kahane was making (at 741). For his part, Justice Vinoguard maintained that if the appellant wanted to safeguard his rights as a member of the Knesset, he did not need to seek the assistance of that court; all he had to do was to make the Knesset oath again, as prescribed by the legislature, and section 16 of the Basic Law: The Knesset (1958) would not be activated against him (at 743). The court had no reason to intervene in the working of the Knesset in this case.

We may read the court's decision as stating that taking an oath provides a standard against which conduct can be measured and legitimate grounds for being ousted if that standard is not met. The state does not have to permit a person to sit in parliament when that person has not, in good faith, taken the statutory oath but has said that he or she does not feel obliged to be loyal to laws.[42]

Chapter 13

Epilogue

In August 1986 the Knesset passed a law that specifies "incitement to racism" as a criminal offense.[1] Anyone who publishes anything with the purpose of inciting to racism is liable to five years' imprisonment (144B); and anyone who has racist publications in his or her possession for distribution is liable to imprisonment for one year (144D). The term *racism* is defined as "persecution, humiliation, degradation, manifestation of enmity, hostility or violence, or causing strife toward a group of people or segments of the population—because of colour or affiliation with a race or a national-ethnic origin" (144A). Three points have to be made in this connection. First, note the absence of the term *religion* from this amendment.[2] This was the result of pressure being exerted by the religious parties.[3] A specific section (144C [b]) addresses this issue, declaring that publication of a quotation from religious books or the observance of a religious ritual should not be regarded as an offense, providing that it is not carried out with the purpose of bringing about racism. In other words, a violation of the law is committed if religious sources are used to bring about racism and if evidence is provided that this was the intention in quoting such sources.

Secondly, note that the law does not consider discrimination against individual persons. It speaks only of group discrimination.

Finally, we note that the prescription speaks of *inciting* to racism.[4] Here the language of the law is different from that used in other countries, such as Sweden.[5] The implications of this amendment are that utterances falling short of incitement may not be punished. That is, if no danger appears here and now, then the advocacy of racism is permissible.

This is in accordance with my argument (*number one*) under the Harm Principle (see part 1, chapter 7). Freedom of speech may be abridged only when likelihood of harm to the target group is present.[6]

In 1987 the Knesset House Committee unanimously recommended that the plenum deprive Kahane of his franking privileges.[7] On this issue, political barriers did not prevent an agreement. The unanimous decision was reached after it was discovered that Kahane was abusing this privilege by addressing letters to Arab citizens urging them to give up their civic rights or to emigrate. Otherwise, Kahane wrote, they would have to face "the full power of the State of Israel." The House Committee chairperson, Micah Risser, member of the Knesset (Likud), postulated that franking privileges were not granted to intimidate or degrade citizens of the state, nor to stain the Knesset's name and to transform the mailing facilities into means of disseminating racist propaganda of the lowest kind.[8] In a thirty-four-to-ten decision, the Knesset affirmed the recommendation of the House Committee.

Two years earlier the Basic Law: The Knesset (1958) was amended to include section 7A under the influence of the court rulings in *Yeredor* and *Neiman*. The section reads, "A list of candidates shall not participate in Knesset elections if any of the following is expressed or implied in its purposes or deeds: (1) denial of the existence of the State of Israel as the state of the Jewish people; (2) denial of the democratic character of the State; (3) incitement to racism."[9]

Section 7A came into existence after endless discussions between the government coalition parties. All the parties involved, Likud, Labor, and the religious parties, wanted a provision that would answer at least some of their demands. The result, given the various pressures, was bound to be problematic, and it proved to be so. At first glance the amendment supplies only three specific grounds for disqualification. A closer reading, however, reveals that it opens wide the door to the slippery-slope syndrome. To begin with, why the amendment speaks of "purposes *or* deeds" is unclear. In my view, the language of the text needs to be more restrictive, speaking of "purposes *and* deeds." Indeed, a list is expected to act according to the platform upon which it was elected. But the framers of the law opened the way to the exclusion of parties solely on the grounds of their expressed intentions. In my opinion, members of a party who merely voice their desires, doing nothing to further them and bring them about, should be subjected to the same restrictions of freedom of expression postulated in this study as any other citizen. That is, they should enjoy the freedom to express their views so long as those views do not fall under the Harm and the Offense Principles. If Kahane were not involved in illegal, violent activities; if he only talked about discriminating against others and emigration for peace without actually doing something along these lines, then democracy should tolerate him the way it tolerates people who take a stool in Hyde Park praising Hitler and declaring themselves Hitler's successor. To disqualify a list, proof should be given that the list in question incites to racism, or that acts were undertaken to bring about the end of Israel either as a Jewish state or as a democracy.

The provision is also problematic because it states that a list may be disqualified if any of the three grounds is "expressed or implied." The focus is on the word *implied*. Intentions can be implied, but activities speak for themselves. It is unclear how any one of the three categories can be implied from attempts to bring it about. And if a list can be disqualified just because one of the three issues may be implied from its activities or even from its purposes, then again the scope for curtailing this fundamental right is too broad, and the slippery-slope syndrome becomes tangible. Thus, this provision brings us back to Justice Alfred Witkon's judgment in H.C. 253/1964, where he ruled that an association can be refused registration merely on its implied aims.[10]

On the other hand, what I have said about incitement to racism in my discussion on sections 144(A-E) of the Penal Law—which were formulated under the influence of 7A—is applicable here. The language of the amendment is restrictive in the sense that it does not exclude racist platforms per se. I will discuss this issue further in the analysis of President Shamgar's judgment in *Neiman II,* below.

Section 7A served as the basis for the disqualification of Kach in the 1988 elections. That year saw a boom in the number of requests to ban lists. Besides the "traditional" requests regarding Kach and the PLP, *nineteen* additional requests occurred. Applications were made to review two ultra-Orthodox lists—Degel Hatorah and Yishy—and to disqualify two other ultra-Orthodox lists: Shas and Agudat Israel. The grounds were that these parties negated the democratic character of Israel. The PLP requested the disqualification of three right-wing lists: Tchiya, Zomet, and Moledet. Kach, for its part, appealed to the CEC to disqualify twelve lists, though its representative contended that the party was against resorting to the disqualification measure in principle, and that he would therefore vote against his own proposal.[11] The rest of the committee quickly joined the same conclusion. They saw the petition as a nuisance and as a vexing attempt to settle political accounts with the parties that had voted for the disqualification of Kach. In the end, Kach was the only list to be disqualified.

In the next sections the CEC's decision regarding the PLP will be briefly considered. This reflection may be useful to complete the analysis. Then I examine the CEC's decision not to confirm Kach and the affirmation of this decision by the High Court of Justice.

The Decision of the CEC Regarding the PLP

The request to disqualify the PLP was initiated by two parties: the Likud and the Tchiya. Two main reasons were given for the request: one was a statement made by one of the PLP leaders that the necessary condition for real peace was to give up the idea of Israel as the state of the Jewish nation; the other reason was that the PLP identified with the PLO, and that de facto it represented this terrorist organization (Miari, the PLP leader, frequently appeared in PLO conferences). Thus, the PLP had to be disqualified in order to prevent the external enemies of Israel from using its internal democratic methods to destroy it. The right and duty to defend the state of Israel as the state of the Jewish nation was superior to the right to be elected.[12]

In their appearance before the committee, the PLP representatives stated that they did not identify with the PLO; instead, they called for negotiation with it. They maintained that the PLP was not against the existence of Israel as the state of the Jewish people, but it was for the idea of two nations: one for the Jews, another for the Palestinians. Mati Peled, a general in the reserves and a member of the Knesset, explained, "We negotiate with the PLO not because we reject the idea of Israel as a Jewish State. On the contrary: because we accept this value and we want to safeguard it we have an interest in promoting discussion with the Palestinian people." He further asserted that "when I speak of the State of Israel I speak of it as declared in the Declaration of Independence."[13]

The chairperson of the committee, Justice Eliezer Goldberg, postulated the obvious, saying that the burden of proving the necessity for disqualification fell on those who requested it. They had to provide the committee with conclusive evidence that the requirements for disqualification were fulfilled. Justice Goldberg maintained that a list could be banned on the grounds of paragraph 7A (1) of the Basic Law: The Knesset (1958) only if proof was given of real or probable danger to the existence of Israel as a Jewish state. This was in line with President Shamgar's test in *Neiman*. The chairperson concluded that in the light of the evidence he did not find reasons to affirm the request.

The results of the voting reflected the political affiliations of the members. Nineteen members of the right and religious parties voted for the ban, and nineteen members from Labor and the parties of the left voted against it. Justice Goldberg's vote tipped the scales in favor of allowing the PLP to participate in the elections. The Likud party decided to use the newly supplemented section (64 [1]) to the Elections Law, which suspended the basis of the *Negbi* decision, to appeal to the court to overrule the decision. This section makes possible to appeal to the court when a list is confirmed by the CEC. Such an appeal can be presented by the attorney general, the chairperson of the CEC, or a quarter of the CEC members. The Likud's appeal was denied in a three-to-two decision.[14] The minority justices, Menachem Elon and Dov Levin, asserted that to disqualify a list it was essential to prove what were the ideological ends of the list in question. A substantial evidence showed that the PLP negated the existence of the state of Israel as the state of the Jewish people, and, therefore, it had to be disqualified. Deputy President Elon maintained that we need not prove an existing possibility of the list to fulfill its ends nor a clear and present danger nor reasonable possibility that the ideas and ends of that list might be materialized.

On the other hand, the majority justices (Shamgar, S. Levin, and Bejski) were not convinced that the evidence conclusively showed the political program of the PLP was aimed at bringing the end of Israel as the state of the Jewish people. Justice Shlomo Levin wrote that, although hesitating, he had reached the decision it was not proved, to the extent of the certainty required, that the PLP "had already passed the red line" so as to recommend its disqualification (para. 6). The question was simply one of evidence. None of the three justices resorted to the balancing method to justify his decision.

The Disqualification of Kach

The committee members' reasons for disqualifying Kach were similar to those of 1984, so there is no point in repeating them. The significant

difference between this case and the 1984 case was the introduction of
section 7A into the Basic Law: The Knesset (1958). The voting results
were conclusive. Almost all the representatives of the parties were in
favor of the decision. Twenty-seven votes were cast to ban Kach on the
grounds of paragraph 7A (2), namely that the list was antidemocratic. Six
members voted against the decision, and three members abstained. Another vote was taken on whether to outlaw Kach on the grounds of 7A
(3), namely that Kach was racist. The voting there was more decisive:
twenty-eight members voted in favor of the decision on those grounds;
five were against; and three abstained.[15]

Kach appealed to the supreme court, this time unsuccessfully.[16] Speaking for the court, President Shamgar explained that section 7A should
not be viewed as a "technical" instruction, to be applied without interpretive guidelines. Instead, the essence of the case—limiting the basic
right to be elected—carried with it the criterion that the interpretation of
the section should be restrictive and narrow, and that it should be applied
only in extreme cases. Section 7A could be used only when the ideological goals in question were dominant characteristics of the list, for which
the list existed. The conduct and aims in question had to reflect the
essence of the list, and they had to be a natural result of its *identity*. In
addition, the evidence had to be clear, unequivocal, and convincing
(para. 8, at 187–88).

President Shamgar dismissed the appellant's claim of a contradiction
between paragraphs (1) and (2) of section 7A, that the democratic character of the state might be threatened by the desire for Israel to subsist as
the state of the Jewish people. He contended that the democratic character of Israel was deeply rooted in its foundations from the day of its
establishment, as the Declaration of Independence explicitly postulated.
He maintained that the existence of Israel as the state of the Jewish
people did not negate its democratic character, just as "being French in
France does not negate its democratic character" (at 189).

President Shamgar went on to refute the second claim, which held that
the term *racism* referred only to discrimination on biological grounds;
consequently it could not be employed against Kahane.[17] He argued that
this claim was unfounded, since Section 144A of the Penal Law (1977)
spoke of "racism," inter alia, as "persecution, humiliation, degradation,
manifestation of enmity, hostility or violence, or causing strife toward a
group of people" on the grounds of their ethnic-national origins. The

court also referred to the International Convention on the Elimination of All Forms of Racial Discrimination (1966), and to laws of several European countries that viewed persecution on the grounds of national affinity as a racist phenomenon.[18]

Finally, with regard to the appellant's claim that Kahane was discriminated against by the CEC, the court refrained from delving into the philosophical issue of whether an antidemocratic, racist party had the right to make such a complaint (cf. part 1, chapter 4). The court once again (as it had done in 1965 and in 1984) drew attention to the problem of giving the power of authorizing lists to a political body. Nevertheless, President Shamgar maintained that no sufficient evidence had been brought before the court to convince it that members of the committee had acted from partisan political interests and not in a *bona fides* manner (at 194).

The main problem with the court's decision lies in its interpretation of section 7A (3). Again it concerns the use of the term *incitement*. The court assumed that racist publications are made with the intention to incite. This may be true, but if the legislature's intention was to provide grounds for the disqualification of lists that propagated racist ideas, why not then simply phrase the provision to say *publication of racist utterances* instead of incitement to racism? The use of the term incitement indicates a close connection between the publication and the attempt to act in accordance with it, and *not* that racial vilification per se may serve as a basis for disqualification of a list. President Shamgar seems to have overlooked this point. He said that in formulating the basis of this section, the legislature said nothing regarding the imminence of the danger and the probability of translating the ideas into deeds (at 187). My interpretation of the law suggests that the legislature did. My understanding of the term incitement is in accordance with the Millian Harm Principle (see chapter 7) and the use of this term in American jurisprudence. Racist incitement has to be distinguished on general free speech principles from racial or racist advocacy or preaching. Here we may recall that in *Yates v. U.S.* the court reinterpreted the *Dennis* decision in a way similar to Mill's discussion of the corn dealer. The court argued, "The essential distinction is that those to whom the incitement is addressed must be urged to *do* something now or in the future, rather than to merely believe in something."[19] Going back to President Shamgar's line of reasoning, we can say that if incitement to a conduct is punishable, then it may seem reasonable to punish that same conduct. But the latter does not necessarily follow from the former. It is questionable, or at least open to interpretation, whether racist lists *as such* are to be prohibited under the current provision in law.

President Shamgar refrained from commenting on the act of legislation that he opposed in *Neiman I*. Like others, in 1984 he would probably have preferred to have his cake and eat it too; that no limitations should be put on freedom of election, and that Kach would simply not pass the barring percentage.[20] But the Israeli electors did not allow this luxury. Kahane entered the Knesset; his discriminatory ideas became widespread, and the Israeli system's attempts to curtail their influence proved unsuccessful. Although President Shamgar was reluctant to resort to legislation in order to solve specific problems, he seems to have recognized that no other effective means of stopping Kahanism existed. Conventional methods of fighting the discriminatory ideas propagated by Kahane and his followers through education, debates, and counterarguments failed to make a serious impact in the way suggested by Mill and others, that evil ideas would be defeated by "truer," "just" ones. Research surveys showed that young people supported Kahane's ideas,[21] and that the decision to close the school gates against him did not reduce his influence. I have mentioned the Van Leer Institute's research from September 1984 that showed that a third of the young people in the sample demonstrated antidemocratic attitudes (cf. chapter 11, "The Court's Decision in *Neiman*"). Other studies showed that 50 percent of students aged thirteen through eighteen were in favor of curtailing the basic rights of Arabs;[22] 10 percent of the young were ready to join Jewish terrorist organizations, and 40 percent supported their activities.[23] Another poll from April 1986 revealed that 23 percent of the adult population supported the opinions of Kach.[24]

Polls also showed that Kahane was likely to increase his power in the Knesset.[25] The Israeli establishment, which combined its resources to reduce the influence of Kach's racist ideas, faced a reality that was and remains conducive to the spreading of those ideas and their attracting more people. The Palestinians continued their terrorist attacks on individual Jews. After each such incident, Kahane made every effort to be invited to the funerals, preaching hatred toward Arabs and calling for acts of retaliation.[26] He admitted that "each and every victim builds our movement."[27] In addition, the polls conducted so frequently as a result of the obsession with Kahane became an influential factor rather than merely a source of information. People who were afraid of identifying themselves with Kahane found out, through the polls, that many members of society shared their views. Those who implicitly supported Kahanism saw that Kahanist views had established themselves as an integral part in the marketplace of ideas. As a result, more and more people were willing to admit that in their heart of hearts they thought Kahane was right, that his movement was part of society and deserved to be recognized as such, even if some people in the establishment did not like it.

The process of building Kach up was intensified in December 1987, when the Palestinian uprising broke out. The Intifada has deepened the hatred between Arabs and Jews without changing the image of the Arab in the eyes of the Jew.[28] As a result of, and as a reaction to that Intifada, feelings of animosity and discrimination against Arabs have been strengthened. At the same time, the Israeli-Jewish population's support of democracy has lessened. More people expressed disappointment with the democratic regime, seeking a "strong leadership" that would create order without being dependent on elections. About 45 percent of the population expressed this view.[29] The majority of the Israeli-Jewish population (54 percent) thought that Jews who were involved in illegal acts against Arabs should be treated more mercifully than Arabs who took the same actions against Jews.

This is to say that Kahane and his followers succeeded in spreading two of their antidemocratic ideas to the extent of convincing the majority of their "truth." These ideas are that the law of the state is not binding when it conflicts with principles such as "an eye for an eye" and the concept of revenge,[30] and that one law is for the Jew and another for the Arab. Almost half of the population (46.4 percent) thought that newspapers enjoyed too much freedom of expression, and 61.2 percent maintained that the freedom of speech enjoyed by newspapers threatened the security of the state.[31] These figures must be startling to anyone who holds dear the values of democracy.

While Kach, the only blatantly antidemocratic party ever to appear in Israel, was disqualified from presenting itself in the elections, its discriminatory ideas increasingly gained legitimacy among the Jewish population. The banning of Kach paved the way for its authentic successor, Moledet ("Homeland" in Hebrew), whose leader, Rechavam Zeevi, is a native-born, ex-general, who propounds ideas similar to those of Kahane, only without their religious facade.[32] While Kahane as a leader was an alienated figure in Israeli society, Zeevi is salt of its earth. He probably has received the support of different segments and classes of the society that in 1988 elected two members of Moledet to the Knesset.33 Nevertheless, Zeevi owes Kahane a considerable part of his success in making the idea of an Arab "transfer" from Israel not only legitimate but also quite popular.34 Here it is of importance to consider the CEC's discussions in regard to Moledet.

The Decision of the CEC Regarding Moledet

The PLP and Ratz (Civil Rights Movement) requested the disqualification of Moledet on the grounds that the idea of transfer was a racist idea. The argument was that, in essence, the ideas of Moledet were not different from those of Kahane because they annulled the right of the Arab minority to continue living in the land of their forefathers. Moledet's plan spoke of a "consented" transfer, but the consent was between states. No one was said to have asked the approval of the deported individual. Thus, the PLP's representative argued that the idea of transfer undermined basic human rights; it negated the democratic character of Israel (section 7A[2]), and in itself it constituted an incitement to racism (section 7A[3]).35 In turn, the representative of Ratz, member of the Knesset Yossi Sarid, argued that the ideas of Moledet and Kach were one and the same.

Rechavam Zeevi appeared before the committee and explained that at least three essential differences existed between his list and Kach. Firstly, Kach was for expulsion, whereas Moledet was for consented transfer, namely emigration against compensation for property, accompanied by an arrangement that would provide the Arabs with jobs and places to live in other countries.36 Moreover, Kahane wanted to expel all Arabs, whereas Moledet spoke only of a transfer of the Arabs on the West Bank and the Gaza Strip. And thirdly, Kahane wanted a state of halacha, whereas Moledet was for a democratic state. Zeevi further explained that Moledet advocated the idea of transfer because it was democratic. Without this solution, the situation would lead to some sort of apartheid that Moledet rejected and condemned. The only political solution to safeguard democracy was to take all those not loyal to the state of Israel out of the country. Only those Israeli Arabs who would be willing to assume all the duties of citizenship would be allowed to stay. They would then enjoy all the rights of citizenship and be regarded as equal. Zeevi maintained that the idea of transfer was not racist. Instead, it was a political solution whose aim was to save blood, Jewish as well as Arab, and to ensure the security of the state. General (of the reserves) Zeevi believed that the transfer was a matter of necessity because Israel could not survive without Judea and Samaria, and it could not keep these territories with their Arab population, which was a fifth column.[37]

The chairperson of the CEC, Justice Eliezer Goldberg, concluded the debate by a brief statement that he was not convinced that legal reasons existed to justify the disqualification of Moledet. The petition was denied in a twenty-two-to-six vote. Three members abstained.

The crux of the matter concerns the transfer doctrine. Surely it is not a moral idea, but this is not the issue here. Instead the issue is whether the ideas of Moledet can be regarded as antidemocratic or as inciting to racism. Let me first examine the second issue: whether Moledet incites to racism.

The International Convention on the Elimination of All Forms of Racial Discrimination (1966) speaks of discrimination against people on grounds based on race, color, descent, or national or ethnic origin. The ground of religion is missing; still, national or ethnic origins are relevant in this context. The transfer program aims at driving the Palestinians from one place to another. Moledet's program, however, concerns only the inhabitants of the occupied territories (Judea, Samaria, and the Gaza Strip). Thus it could be regarded as *qualified* racism. The subject matter of Moledet is not the entire Arab community that lives within Israeli borders but only part of the population. Being an Arab does not qualify a person for the transfer program. A person also has to live in the occupied territories. Both requirements are essential and none is regarded as sufficient.

Notwithstanding this observation, the transfer program does aim at depriving the Palestinians of a fundamental freedom and of a basic human right, the right to live in their place of origin, in the land of their forefathers. Moreover, considering once more the Penal Law (1977), which speaks of racism, inter alia, as persecution, humiliation, manifestation of enmity, hostility, or causing strife toward a group of people because of their ethnic-national origins, no doubt the idea of transfer, by its very utterance, *does* cause these outcomes. I think that a closer examination of this issue by the supreme court is required. It should address the question of whether the idea of transfer is racist under the Penal Law.

Let me now ponder the other question, whether the idea of transfer is an antidemocratic idea. Before delving into this question, two preliminary notes should be made. The reading of Zeevi's many pamphlets, statements, and articles exhibits beliefs in democracy, in the importance of the democratic framework, and in the need of abiding by the law. Unlike Kahane, he does not wish to transform Israel to another system of ruling, namely theocracy. He wishes to further an idea and to gain it adherents through democratic means. No explicit or implicit agenda exists to annul democracy.

Moreover, the differences between Kach and Moledet are not merely cosmetic. Differences in the tone as well as differences in substance are present between the two lists. Otherwise the chairperson of the CEC would have recommended the disqualification of Moledet. Kach draws attention to the demographic problem; it calls for hatred of the foreigner, and it resorts to dehumanizing terms with the intention to affirm and establish the superiority of the Jew over the Arab. Whereas the intentions of Moledet are more modest: it calls attention only to the demographic problem in Israel, arguing that it should be treated today by rigorous means. It seems that Justice Goldberg thought that however repugnant the idea of transfer was, it should have had a place in the marketplace of ideas. It was for the Israeli electorate to decide whether or not to accept this idea.

Justice Goldberg followed the liberal tradition of Milton and Mill who assumed that the public was rational enough to recognize evil expressions, thus in a free discourse of opinions the "good" were bound to triumph over the "bad": the open confrontation of ideas strengthened the self-correcting powers of society (see chapter 5). But what if Moledet were to succeed in its campaign and the Knesset were to resort to legislation and enact the law of transfer? Would then Israel still be considered a democracy? I claim that it would not. This piece of legislation would transform Israel from a democracy to a state with explicit discriminatory laws. Israel would then become the third state in the history of mankind to base its ideology on manifestations of enmity, hostility, and the creation of strife toward a group of people on racist grounds. At best, Israel could then be called "democracy, South-African style."[38]

Nevertheless, for the time being I do not recommend the disqualification of Moledet. The list has some antidemocratic features, but, unlike Kach, it is not an explicit antidemocratic list. In addition, Moledet does not resort to violence to achieve its aims. As far as I am concerned, these considerations are significant, and they confer Moledet with latitude which I would not accord to Kach. However, I wish to call upon Israeli democracy to fight against the idea of transfer by means of persuasion and education. The ideology of Moledet negates the basic requirements of democracy, respecting others and not harming others; it advocates *not* to accept these principles when they are applied to a designated group. Therefore, the democratic institutions have the responsibility to combat Moledet's ideas in the free market of ideas. It goes without saying that if Moledet would further its ideas through coercion and violence, then it should be disqualified. But in the present situation, no solid arguments exist for disqualification. I contend this while being aware of the fact that antidemocratic forces are being promoted and fortified in Israel as a result of the institutional legitimacy that is accorded to Moledet.

Moledet participated in the 1992 elections and won three seats in the Knesset, an additional seat over the 1988 elections. Thus, although Kach was excluded from the political arena, Kahane's spirit and ideas have gained deep roots in society. The two new laws that were enacted (section 7A of Basic Law: The Knesset [1958], and sections 144 [A-E] of the Penal Law) in order to suppress racist sentiments do not contain a "magic power" to uproot them.[39] These laws can help reduce their prevalence as well as their offensive effects; these laws can lessen the malignant spread of racial prejudice and reaffirm the democratic commitment of Israeli society to the value of respecting others; but they cannot eradicate racist notions. Such an endeavor requires a great deal of time, probably longer than was required to establish the notions in the first place. Racist ideas will continue to abound in Israel as long as Arabs are conceived of as hewers of wood and drawers of water. The popularity of racist ideas will effectively be reduced if Israel continues to resort to educational means at all levels and implements political solutions that change the image, as well as the status, of the Arab. The goal should be to convey the notion of equality of being and belonging. This comprehensive notion recognizes that inequality is often a fact that cannot be avoided in many aspects of society but asserts that in some sectors of life everyone should be treated the same way, so that the basic conditions of a common life are available to all. These basic conditions are legal equality, equal right of participation in political life, and equal right to those average material provisions necessary for living together in a decent way. As Ronald Dworkin contends, the government should treat all citizens as equals, that is, as entitled to equal concern and respect; and it should treat them equally in the distribution of some resource of opportunity, or at least work to secure the state of affairs in which all are equal or more nearly equal in that respect. This notion of equality of being and belonging stresses the greatest possible participation in and sharing of the common life and culture while striving to ensure that no one shall determine or define the being of any other person.⁴⁰

This is the desired situation. The present situation in Israel can be described by the distinction between *formal citizenship* and *full citizenship*. Citizenship is commonly perceived as an institutional status from within which a person can address governments and other citizens and make claims about human rights.⁴¹ All who possess the status are equal with respect to the rights and duties with which the status is endowed. Israeli-Jews can be said to enjoy full citizenship: they enjoy equal respect as individuals, and they are entitled to equal treatment by law and in its administration. The situation is different with regard to the Israeli-Palestinians, who today constitute some 18 percent of the population.⁴² Although they are formally considered to enjoy liberties equally with the Jewish community, in practice they do not share and enjoy the same rights and burdens. They are considered second-rate citizens and have to live with limitations on their freedoms, limitations the Jewish majority does not suffer.⁴³ For example, Israeli-Palestinians pay more income tax than Jews because they do not enjoy discounts given to those who serve in the army. Arabs find it more difficult than Jews to get licenses for building additions on their flats or for building new ones. They also find it difficult to buy or even to rent a flat in a Jewish neighborhood. The budgets of Arab municipalities bear no comparison to those of Jewish municipalities. There are not enough classes in Arab towns and villages. Arabs who graduate find it difficult to get jobs in government offices.⁴⁴ Being an Arab in many cases "guarantees" that a worker's salary will be lower than that of a Jew doing the same work. And there is the Palestinian population of the West Bank and the Gaza Strip who do not enjoy citizens' rights at all. Professor Yochanan Peres made the following comment about the relationships between Israelis and the population of the occupied territories: "We have a growing and developing zone which is absolutely anti-democratic, in which anti-democratic norms prevail. This zone is the occupied territories. There a person is told which books he is allowed to read and what trees are permitted to be grown in his garden. Not only that the population has no representation; no democratic characterizations exist at all. Some of us think that it is possible to live for a long time in a situation of Doctor Jekyll in Israel, and Mr. Hyde in the territories. The reality, however, is that Doctor Jekyll becomes Mr. Hyde although he does not want to."[45]

I want to close by making some personal observations. In November 1990 Kahane was murdered in New York City. I was deeply shocked and disturbed by this. No matter what we may think about the man, his ideas and his political platform, I was disgusted by the way his life came to an end. I also felt deep sorrow, sorrow about the murder and for the likely consequences that were (and still are) to follow. Since the day of Israel's independence no assassinations of political leaders have occurred in Israel, and I hope that this murder will not open a new phase in the political discourse between extremist movements and individuals. However, I am certain that the last word has not been uttered by Kahane's followers. Vengeance they promised and vengeance there was. A gunman shot an old Palestinian couple immediately after the news about Kahane's assassination was conveyed to his family and friends. The question of how much blood will satisfy them is still unanswered.

A further question yet to be answered concerns the political future of Kach. Kahane intended to change Kach's political platform in a way that would allow him to run for office. His followers still did not find a legal way of overcoming Section 7A. Thus in the 1992 elections, the CEC decided to ban both Kach and Kahane Is Alive, a faction headed by Kahane's son, Benjamin Zeev. The two extreme splinters appealed unsuccessfully to the supreme court. The justices found no substantive grounds for assuming that the proposals and political platforms of the two movements were significantly different from Kach's platform in 1988. Justice Shlomo Levin said that ample evidence suggested continuity in the activities of Kach between 1988 and 1992. For instance, the head of Kach, Baruch Marsel, declared during an interview in *Ha'aretz* that Kach worked exactly as Kahane wanted it to work. Kach's magazine, *Only Kach,* repeated the same theses of its founder and no evidence in writing was produced to show that the platform had undergone change. Justice Shlomo Levin concluded that the movement only attempted to camouflage its activities. The CEC was, therefore, right in disqualifying Kach (para. 6).[46]

With regard to the Kahane Is Alive movement, the court in a brief ruling affirmed the CEC's decision. The court refrained from dwelling on the issue of whether the list's views were in accordance with halacha. The business of the court, argued Justice Shlomo Levin, was to check that the list's aims and activities were in accordance with Section 7A (2) (3). Undoubtedly, the answer to this question was negative, asserted Justice Levin (para. 4). The appeal was rejected.[47]

For the time being, the vacuum created by Kahane's death seems to be unfillable. The division in the Kahanist camp obviously works against the political aspirations of both movements. The fact that Kahane was a lone wolf proves to be a two-edged sword. Kahane was Kach. Kach was Kahane. Kach would never have been active in the political arena without the dominant figure of Kahane. Presumably, Benjamin Zeev Kahane will not give up easily. He will try to establish himself as the sole leader and then try again to campaign for his election. At this stage it is too early to say whether he would be able to retain his father's seat in the Knesset. One thing, however, is assured: racist ideas do prevail in Israeli society. Kahane deserves much of the credit, or rather, discredit, for making them as popular and as outspoken as they are today.

Table of U.S. Cases

Table of Israeli Cases

The reference P.D. means *Piskei Din* (*Judgments,* an official publication of the judgments of the Israeli Supreme Court).

Miscellaneous Cases from Other Jurisdictions

England

Beatty v. Gillbanks (1882) 9 QBD 308.

Jordan v. Burgoyne (1963) 2 QB 744 (DC).

O'Moran v. DPP (1975) QB 864.

Parkin v. Norman (1982) 3 W.L.R. 523.

Germany

2 *BVerfGE 1 Sozialistische Reichspartei* (23 October 1952).

5 *BVerfGE 85 KPD* (17 August 1956).

European Commission on Human Rights

Glimmerveen and Hagenbeek v/the Netherlands (1980).

Notes

Part One

1. Cf. D. D. Raphael, "Toleration, Choice, and Liberty," p. 234.
2. Thomas I. Emerson, *Toward a General Theory of the First Amendment,* p. 61.
3. Preston King, *Toleration,* p. 12; and Raphael, "Toleration, Choice, and Liberty," are exceptional in arguing that the term *toleration* has a broader purpose than the term *tolerance.*

Chapter 1: Tolerance and Liberty: General Insight

1. See, for instance, Susan Mendus, *Toleration and the Limits of Liberalism,* p. 3. Mendus writes in her introduction to *On Toleration,* p. 3, that three justifications are given for toleration: that it is a requirement of prudence, that it is a requirement of rationality, and that it is a requirement of morality.
2. Cf. Raphael, "Toleration, Choice, and Liberty," p. 234.
3. Isaiah Berlin, "Two Concepts of Liberty," p. 141. Berlin maintains this by elaborating on quite an old idea of the distinction between negative and positive liberty. Negative liberty is said to be the absence of external restraints on an individual's liberty, while positive liberty is said to be the individual's ability to develop his or her potentialities as a human being. For critical discussion on the two concepts of liberty see C. B. Macpherson, *Democratic Theory,* ch. 3; and G. C. MacCallum, "Negative and Positive Freedom."
4. Berlin, *Concepts and Categories,* pp. 190–92. For an opposing view see Peter Jones and Robert Sudgen, "Evaluating Choice." I should clarify that the fact that a person who decides to marry eight times does not make him or her freer than another who decides to marry only once and does not make use of the divorce option.
5. Steven L. Ross, "A Real Defense of Tolerance," p. 127.
6. Joseph Raz, *The Morality of Freedom,* p. 375; "Autonomy, Toleration, and the Harm Principle."

7. Raz, *The Morality of Freedom,* p. 204.

8. Marxists probably will have some reservations regarding this assertion.

9. Martin Hollis, *Models of Man,* p. 125.

10. T. M. Scanlon, "A Theory of Freedom of Expression," p. 162.

11. William E. Connolly, *The Terms of Political Discourse,* p. 155.

12. Ibid.

13. The issue of the problem of free will concerning the possibility of transcending all hereditary and environmental influences is not considered here. Instead, the notion of autonomy that is conveyed assumes interchange between self and society. For discussion on the assumption that each of us, when we act, is a prime mover unmoved, see Roderick M. Chisholm, "Human Freedom and the Self." See also C. A. Campbell, *In Defence of Free Will,* pp. 35–55. Criticism of this view is presented by Harry G. Frankfurt, "Freedom of the Will and the Concept of A Person," and by Galen Strawson in his comprehensive study *Freedom and Belief,* esp. pp. 25–60.

Chapter 2: The Scope and Characterizations of Tolerance

1. Herbert Marcuse, "Repressive Tolerance," p. 99.

2. Ibid., p. 100.

3. Mary Warnock, "The Limits of Toleration," pp. 126–27 (italics mine).

4. Ibid., p. 127.

5. Ibid., p. 139.

6. Cf. the Hart-Devlin debate. Patrick Devlin, *The Enforcement of Morals;* and H. L. A. Hart, *Law, Liberty, and Morality.* I may add that in the last decade, the age of AIDS, a setback is apparent in the status of the homosexual community in society.

7. Karl R. Popper, *The Open Society and Its Enemies,* vol. 1, p. 265. See also his "Toleration and Intellectual Responsibility," in Susan Mendus and David Edwards, eds., *On Toleration,* pp. 17–34.

8. Mendus, *Toleration and the Limits of Liberalism,* p. 19.

9. Ibid., p. 20.

10. Cf. Robert K. Merton, "Manifest and Latent Functions," in Merton, *Social Theory and Social Structure,* pp. 19–84. For its criticism see Colin Campbell, "A Dubious Distinction? An Inquiry into the Value and Use of Merton's Concepts of Manifest and Latent Functions."

11. On the distinction between *formal* and *full* citizenship, see T. H. Marshall, *Citizenship and Social Class.* I say more about this subject in chapter 13.

12. I do not mean to say that people should always refrain from rising to

fight for just causes that seem to have little chance of success. Galileo Galilei confronted the church administration and led humanity to a major scientific breakthrough, but he also paid the highest possible price a person can pay. All I am saying is that when people feel that existing conditions allow only a small chance of influencing society in a certain direction, and that they may be required to pay a high price for their effort, then we may understand the motives that bring them to adopt a latent form of toleration.

13. Wiggins lucidly expresses this liberal outlook by saying that human interests and concerns are as indefinitely various and heterogeneous as are human predicaments. Even moral interests and concerns are indefinitely various and heterogeneous. Therefore, no general reason exists to expect that a common moral consciousness will issue in some rational disposition to single out just one from among all the moral or practical alternatives apparently available in any situation (cf. David Wiggins, *Needs, Values, Truth,* p. 174).

14. *Oxford Advanced Learner's Dictionary of Current English,* s.v. "compromise."

Chapter 3: Why Tolerate? The Respect for Others Argument

1. Cf. Bruce A. Ackerman, *Social Justice in the Liberal State,* pp. 11, 43, 346–48.

2. Cf. Will Kymlicka, "Liberal Individualism and Liberal Neutrality," p. 900.

3. Writings by John Stuart Mill in which he discusses the subject of freedom and its limitations include the article "Law of Libel and Liberty of the Press" (1825); his chapter on the methodology of social science in book 6 of the *System of Logic* (1842); his books *Principles of Political Economy* (1848), *Dissertations and Discussions* (1859), *Considerations on Representative Government* (1861), and *Utilitarianism* (1863); and chapter 26, on the freedom of the will, of *An Examination of Sir William Hamilton's Philosophy* (1865). The subject is analyzed in Mill's essay "The Subjection of Women" (1869) and in the most extensive way in *On Liberty* (1859).

4. Mill, *On Liberty,* pp. 114–15 (all references are to *Utilitarianism, Liberty and Representative Government,* 1948, Everyman's edition).

5. Ibid., p. 114.

6. Ibid., p. 77.

7. Ronald M. Dworkin, *Taking Rights Seriously,* pp. 266–78; "Liberalism," in *A Matter of Principle,* pp. 181–204.

8. See, for instance, Peter Nicholson, "Toleration as a Moral Ideal."

9. John Dewey, *Freedom and Culture,* p. 127.

10. Marcuse, "Repressive Tolerance," pp. 96–98.

11. John Rawls, "Liberty, Equality, and Law," sect. 3; "Justice as Fairness."

12. Dworkin, *Taking Rights Seriously,* pp. 150–83, 266–78; "Liberalism," pp. 181–204. We may note that Kant spoke only of respecting people. He wanted to divorce our attitude toward others from any compassionate feelings. Dworkin introduced the additional notion of concern for others. By *concern* is not meant anything so demanding as giving equal weight to the welfare of a stranger as a person does to the welfare of his or her children. Instead, it is giving equal weight to a person's life and autonomy. In other words, the right to equality of concern and respect is a right people possess not by virtue of their birth or merit or excellence but simply of their status as human beings with the ability to make their own plans and give justice.

13. See Ronald M. Dworkin, "Hard Cases," pp. 1069–71.

14. I am not suggesting that currently widespread agreement exists in constitutional democracies that all people should be accorded the same rights and opportunities. Unfortunately this is not the case. I think, however, that this is one of the major ideas of liberalism and that liberal democracies should strive to apply it. I add, sharing Jean Hampton's view, that we have an obligation as philosophers committed to arguing with and thus respecting our fellow human beings to persuade opponents of this idea and thus to change their minds (cf. Jean Hampton, "Should Political Philosophy Be Done without Metaphysics?" p. 813).

15. The case would be different if the sadistic community were to exist as a subculture within a liberal democracy. I will expand on this issue in chapter 4.

16. Dworkin, "Liberalism," pp. 196, 198; *Taking Rights Seriously,* pp. 272–73.

17. Dworkin's terms *concern* and *respect* signal the values of well-being and autonomy, respectively: we ought to show equal concern for each individual's good and equal respect for the individual's autonomy. Cf. Allen E. Buchanan, "Assessing the Communitarian Critique of Liberalism," p. 879.

18. Some groups of people, such as the retarded or autistic, lack the basic characteristics of rationality or the ability to communicate with others and to identify alternatives. These groups are accorded different kinds of respect and concern. Cf. R. S. Downie and Elizabeth Telfer, *Respect for Persons,* pp. 34–35.

19. Cf. Immanuel Kant, *Foundations of the Metaphysics of Morals,* section 2, esp. pp. 52–53.

20. *Babylonian Talmud,* Sabbath 31a.

21. Kant, *Critique of Practical Reason,* p. 169. Cf. Roger Scruton, *Kant,* p. 65.

22. For discussion on the use of the terms *obligation* and *duty,* see R. B. Brandt, "The Concepts of Obligation and Duty."

23. Cf. Kant, *Foundations of the Metaphysics of Morals*, pp. 54–55. Kant maintains that the "principle of humanity and of every rational creature as an end in itself is the supreme limiting condition on freedom of the actions of each man" (p. 55).

24. Cf. Ronald M. Dworkin, "What Liberalism Isn't," p. 47. In comments he made on a draft of this chapter, Dworkin acknowledges that some conceptions of a good or decent life could not be realized in a liberal state because what they enjoy would be either forbidden or economically impossible. Thus, we may respect our fellow parent A, respect A's decision to steal from B (say in order to buy his or her children food for the day), think that the act of stealing is wrong, and with all due respect find an appropriate way to punish A. This is perfectly consistent with the Respect for Others Argument.

25. Cf. Ackerman, *Social Justice in the Liberal State*, pp. 11, 43, 346–48.

26. Ibid., pp. 43, 49, 54, 348.

27. Ibid., p. 348 (italics mine).

28. *Yates v. U.S.* 354 U.S. 298 (1957), at 1075. See also *Noto v. U.S.* 367 U.S. 290 (1961), and *Brandenburg v. Ohio* 395 U.S. 444 (1969).

29. Raz, *The Morality of Freedom*, p. 108.

30. Robert Nozick, *Anarchy, State and Utopia*, pp. 33, 48–51, 271–74; Ackerman, pp. 11–12, 347–78; Ronald M. Dworkin, "Why Liberals Should Believe in Equality?" p. 32, and *A Matter of Principle*, pp. 191–94, 205; Will Kymlicka, *Liberalism, Community, and Culture*, pp. 76–85, 95–96; Peter De Marneffe, "Liberalism, Liberty, and Neutrality," p. 253.

31. We have seen that Ackerman assumes that people pursue forms of social life in accordance with their conceptions of the good. As he does, other liberals use the term *ideals* and the phrases *ways (or plans or forms) of life* and *conception of the good* interchangeably. Cf. John Rawls, *A Theory of Justice*, sect. 68; Raz, *The Morality of Freedom*, chap. 5; Kymlicka, *Liberalism, Community, and Culture*, esp. chaps. 4 and 5.

32. A well-ordered society is roughly one with just institutions and that accepts Rawls's two principles of justice. Cf. "A Well-Ordered Society," and "The Idea of an Overlapping Consensus," p. 10.

33. Rawls, *A Theory of Justice*, p. 448.

34. Raz, *The Morality of Freedom*, pp. 134–35.

35. Marxists hold that the liberal conceptions are prejudiced by bourgeois capitalist considerations (cf. C. B. Macpherson, *The Real World of Democracy* and *The Life and Times of Liberal Democracy*. See also M. Fisk, "History and Reason in Rawls' Moral Theory," especially pp. 57–67). For a feminist perspective, see Alison M. Jaggar, *Feminist Politics and Human Nature*, and Andrea Nye, *Feminist Theory and the Philosophies of Man*.

36. In 1951 Ben-Gurion wrote, "The immigration of today is mainly from

the east, the countries of Islam in Asia and in Africa, where Jews of late could draw little enlightenment from Jewish or any other culture." Cf. *Rebirth and Destiny of Israel* (London: Thomas Yoseloff, 1959), p. 409.

37. Israel regards Western tradition and culture as the "significant other," as the frame of reference to which it wants to be associated. Its leaders hold that Israel maintains "a stable democratic regime," that it guarantees a maximum degree of civic freedom, and that its "government holds no sway over that which is in a man's heart, or over aught concerning science, aesthetics and art" (cf. David Ben-Gurion in "Towards a New World," in *Israel: Years of Challenge* [London: Anthony Blond, 1964], p. 233; "Laws or a Constitution," in *Rebirth and Destiny of Israel* [London: Thomas Yoseloff, 1959], pp. 363–80, 280. See also the Education Law [1953] that speaks of striving to establish Israeli society on "liberty, equality, tolerance, mutual assistance and love of mankind").

38. For further discussion see my paper "Neutrality, Culture, and the Nation-Building Ideology," The Rich Seminar, Yarnton, Oxon. (1991).

39. Cf. Robert Nozick, *Philosophical Explanations*, p. 448. I am aware that some people would object to this supposition. Joseph Raz, for example, told me that people he knows would not agree with it.

40. John Rawls, "The Priority of Right and Ideas of the Good," p. 263; Peter De Marneffe, "Liberalism, Liberty, and Neutrality," p. 253.

41. Cf. De Marneffe.

42. Rawls, "The Priority of Right," p. 262.

43. Raz, *The Morality of Freedom*, p. 110.

44. Ibid., pp. 110–11, 134–36. Raz uses the terms *doctrine* and *principle* interchangeably.

45. Rawls, "The Priority of Right," p. 263.

46. Cf. Rawls, *A Theory of Justice* and "Justice as Fairness"; Dworkin, *A Matter of Principle*; Ackerman, *Social Justice in the Liberal State*; Charles Larmore, *Patterns of Moral Complexity*.

47. Cf. Ronald M. Dworkin, "What Is Equality? Part 2: Equality of Resources."

48. Dworkin, "Can a Liberal State Support Art?" in *A Matter of Principle*, pp. 229, 233.

49. This view is implied by the Kantian approach. Vinit Haksar, *Equality, Liberty, and Perfectionism*, p. 179, postulates a second version that does not carry this implication. According to this version, we can respect others by respecting their way of life and conception of the good without necessarily respecting their autonomy.

50. Ronald M. Dworkin, "In Defence of Equality," p. 26. This statement, among others, proves Raz wrong in saying that "anti-perfectionism is based on

restraint, on not doing as much good as one can" (*The Morality of Freedom*, p. 111).

51. Dworkin, "In Defence of Equality," p. 27 (Dworkin's italics).

52. In "What Liberalism Isn't," p. 47, Dworkin writes, "Whatever we may think privately, it cannot count, as a justification for some rule of law or some political institution, that a life that includes reading pornography or homosexual relationships is either better or worse than the life of someone with more orthodox tastes in reading or sex. Or that a life suffused with religion is better or worse than a wholly secular life." See also his "Liberalism" and "Can a Liberal State Support Art?" in *A Matter of Principle*. Rawls, in *A Theory of Justice,* sect. 50, argues that from the point of view of the parties in the original position, no form of life is *intrinsically* better or worse than another form of life. Cf. Ackerman, *Social Justice in the Liberal State,* p. 6; and Kymlicka, *Liberalism, Community, and Culture,* pp. 33–36.

53. Cf. Michael Sandel's distinction between the *minimalist* or pragmatic view and the *voluntarist* view in "Moral Argument and Liberal Toleration: Abortion and Homosexuality."

54. Dworkin, "Do We Have a Right to Pornography?" in *A Matter of Principle,* p. 352.

55. Raz, *The Morality of Freedom,* p. 401.

56. Ibid., p. 417.

57. In comments made on a draft of this chapter, Dworkin distinguishes between abstract autonomy as a general condition, within which a conformist life can be chosen and led, and autonomy as a substantive kind of life to lead, which emphasizes self-creation and the other virtues of originality. Dworkin argues that a liberal state is committed to abstract autonomy. The question remains whether reasons exist for a liberal state to actively promote substantive autonomy.

58. Raz, *The Morality of Freedom,* p. 417. See also Vinit Haksar, "Autonomy, Justice and Contractarianism," and *Liberty, Equality, and Perfectionism,* passim.

59. Haksar argues in *Equality, Liberty, and Perfectionism,* p. 205, that autonomous people sometimes find autonomy such a burden and cause of despair that they might be willing to opt for a nonautonomous life. Raz made a similar argument during a private discussion with me.

60. In *A Theory of Justice,* Rawls, like Dworkin (who speaks of *universal* background rights to equal respect and concern), aspired to formulate a theory that would be applicable to any time and place. Rawls contended that his theory was neither produced by specific historical and social circumstances nor intended to defend any existing order. The theory was constructed with regard to the human situation "not only from all social but also from all temporal

points of view" (p. 587). However, in the Dewey Lectures and subsequently, Rawls abandons this effort. Political philosophy, he now asserts, is always addressed to a specific "public culture," and, therefore, "we are not trying to find a conception of justice suitable for all societies regardless of their particular social or historical circumstances. We want to settle a fundamental disagreement over the just form of basic institutions within a democratic society under modern conditions." See "Rational and Full Autonomy," p. 518. See also "Justice as Fairness: Political not Metaphysical," p. 225. On the changes in Rawls's thinking during the 1980s, see Richard J. Arneson, "Introduction"; William A. Galston, "Pluralism and Social Unity"; and Gerald Doppelt, "Is Rawls's Kantian Liberalism Coherent and Defensible?" All three articles appear in *Ethics* 99 (1989).

61. Rawls, *A Theory of Justice*, p. 331.

62. Alan Montefiore, ed., *Neutrality and Impartiality*, pp. 224–25. See also Mill, *Utilitarianism*, p. 42, where Mill explains that to be partial is inconsistent with justice, while impartiality does not seem to be a duty in itself but is instrumental to some other duty.

63. I am not speaking of all groups within society, but only of those which accept the Respect for Others Argument. Groups of terrorists, murderers, rapists, etc., are subject to partial treatment by government.

64. The analogy between games and politics focuses on the need for safeguarding some basic rules. A game could hardly exist if some footballers would decide to wear spurs on their shoes during the match. We would regard this as a clear violation of the rules and as defeating the notion of a *game* altogether.

65. Dworkin, "In Defence of Equality," p. 26.

Chapter 4: The Respect for Others Argument and Cultural Norms

1. Rawls acknowledges that a disputed question is whether and in what sense conceptions of the good are incommensurable. He states that incommensurability is to be understood as a political fact, an aspect of pluralism; namely, that political understanding is not available as to how to commensurate these conceptions for settling questions of political justice (cf. "The Idea of an Overlapping Consensus," p. 4).

2. Rawls, "Justice as Fairness," pp. 225–30.

3. Rawls speaks only of "just constitutional regimes." He admits that the questions of whether the corresponding form of life would be viable under other historic conditions, and whether its passing is to be regretted, are still left open. Cf. "The Priority of Right and Ideas of the Good," p. 266.

4. Ibid., pp. 265–66. See also Rawls, "Fairness to Goodness," sect. VI; and

"Representation of Freedom and Equality," sect. II. A similar view is enunciated by Berlin, who holds that we cannot conceive of a situation that would
enable a joint realization of all values in one society. It is impossible to suppose that all goods and ideals can be united into a harmonious whole without
loss: logical, psychological, and sociological limits exist to what range of
values one society can respect in the lives of some of its citizens (cf. Bernard
Williams's introduction to Berlin's *Concepts and Categories,* pp. xi–xviii).

5. Cf. Rawls, *A Theory of Justice,* sects. 33–35; "Fairness to Goodness,"
sect. VI; "Representation of Freedom and Equality," sect. II; "Justice as Fairness," sect. VI; "The Priority of Right and Ideas of the Good," sect. VII.

6. Critics have argued plausibly that conceptions of the good exist in our
society that fail to exhibit a consensus concerning primary goods and the political values inherent in Rawlsian justice as fairness (such as the good as com-
petitive economic achievement or the good as worker-controlled, unalienated
labor). Cf. Gerald Doppelt, "Is Rawls's Kantian Liberalism Coherent and Defensible?" p. 848.

7. "Primary goods" are "things that every rational man is presumed to
want." These are rights and liberties, opportunities and powers, income and
wealth. Cf. Rawls, *A Theory of Justice,* pp. 62, 92. In May 1993 Rawls participated in a conference at Tel-Aviv University, launching his new book, *Political
Liberalism,* in which he reconsiders some of the issues dealt with in *A Theory
of Justice.* I asked whether he now thinks that culture is a primary good, and
his answer was, "I did not think about it."

8. Cf. Will Kymlicka, *Liberalism, Community, and Culture,* pp. 166–68.

9. Ibid., p. 172.

10. For example, cultural minorities may need veto power over certain decisions regarding language and culture and may need to limit the mobility of
migrants or immigrants into their homelands. Such rights are held by French
Canadians and by aboriginal peoples in Canada, the United States, and Australia. Cf. Will Kymlicka, "The Rights of Minority Cultures, Reply to
Kukathas," p. 140.

11. Here I acknowledge Will Kymlicka's contribution, made in his comments
on a draft of this chapter.

12. Kymlicka, *Liberalism, Community, and Culture,* p. 176.

13. "Disrespecting" others may amount in this context to denying a person
the right to live as a free, autonomous human being.

14. Kymlicka makes this argument in his comments on a draft of this chapter. He now explains that the question of whether to interfere in the business
of minority cultures in order to promote our liberal conception depends on
many factors, including the severity of violations of rights within the community; the extent of division within the community on the issue of restricting in-

dividual rights; the existence of any treaty obligations (e.g., historical promises made to immigrant groups); the nature of the proposed interference; and so forth.

15. In his comments on a draft of this chapter, Kymlicka agrees that we should indeed interfere with practices such as widow-burning, because they constitute very severe violations of human rights. I am not sure what his stance is on female circumcision.

16. Nozick, *Philosophical Explanations,* pp. 505–6.

17. Rawls, *A Theory of Justice,* p. 219.

18. Ibid.

19. Ibid., p. 220.

20. Cf. Thomas Scanlon, "A Theory of Freedom of Expression." I reflect on Scanlon's theory in chapter 5.

21. We may distinguish between treating all conceptions of the good with equal concern and respect and treating individuals with equal concern and respect. In this as well as in many other instances, however, one necessarily determines the other. Rawls concedes that we may rule decisively against some conceptions without feeling guilty for failing to show the holders equal concern and respect.

22. X acknowledges that democracies do not always open their borders to immigrants. Democracies can and do set quotas on immigration and may decide that for some reasons they are not willing to admit immigrants to their territory. X refers here to the right of democracies to limit immigration on the grounds of immigrants' beliefs. Only in special cases should this serve as grounds for restricting immigration.

23. We may recall Rawls's assertion that we should allow pluralism of religious beliefs, however strong the convictions, but we should not tolerate attempts to transform society into a theocratic society. Cf. chapter 4, "The Dilemma."

24. Cf. Colin Sparks, *Never Again,* esp. pp. 12–42. See also Marvin Glass, "Anti-Racism and Unlimited Freedom of Speech."

25. The example speaks of England but it can refer to any other liberal democratic state. However, it should be noted that in the case of England, under the Race Relations Act of 1976, it is a crime for a person with the intent to stir up hatred against any section of the public distinguished by color, race, nationality, or ethnic or national origins to publish or distribute threatening, abusive, or insulting matter, or to use in any public place insulting words, if the matter or words are likely to stir up hatred against that section on grounds mentioned above (cf. part 1 of the Race Relations Act). On the laws of other countries concerning racist speech see Lee C. Bollinger, *The Tolerant Society,* pp. 253–56.

26. F. A. Hayek, "Individual and Collective Aims," p. 47.

27. Glenn Tinder, "Freedom of Expression, the Strange Imperative," p. 168.

28. Rawls, *A Theory of Justice,* p. 218.

29. Anthony Skillen, "Freedom of Speech," p. 140.

30. Ibid., p. 142.

31. Ibid., p. 148.

32. Similar reasoning is employed by Norman Dorsen, who argues that we should not suppress speech because of the fear of an underground movement (cf. "Is There A Right to Stop Offensive Speech? The Case of the Nazis at Skokie").

33. Scanlon, in his defense of *political* speech, reaches the same conclusion. See chapter 5.

34. As Bollinger argues in *The Tolerant Society,* pp. 197–200.

35. Skillen, Dorsen, and Bollinger, among others, may fit into what may be called the consequentialist school, as distinguished from the absolutist school, which I shall consider in chapter 5.

36. Skillen, "Freedom of Speech," p. 145.

37. Ibid., p. 145.

38. In *Chaplinsky v. New Hampshire* 315 U.S. 568 (1942), the court ruled that a "fighting words" speech is in itself hurtful by its very utterance, inflicting injury or tending to incite immediate breach of the peace. In Britain, the fighting words doctrine came into expression in Lord Parker's phraseology, that a speaker must insult the audience in the sense of hitting them with words for an offense to be committed (*Jordan v. Burgoyne* 2 Q.B. 744, 1963).

39. Cf. *Rosenfeld v. New Jersey* 408 U.S. 901 (1972).

40. Alexander Meiklejohn and Alf Ross also share this view (cf. chap. 5).

41. Thomas I. Emerson, *Toward a General Theory of the First Amendment,* pp. 60–61; *The System of Freedom of Expression,* p. 9. For criticism of the "action"-"expression" approach see John P. Yacavone, "Emerson's Distinction," and Lillian R. BeVier, "The First Amendment and Political Speech," esp. pp. 319–22. Emerson provides some counterarguments in "First Amendment Doctrine and the Burger Court," esp. pp. 477–81.

Chapter 5: Freedom of Expression

1. Peter P. Nicholson, "Toleration as a Moral Ideal."

2. Ibid., pp. 169, 170.

3. On the self-realization and self-fulfillment arguments see Frederick Schauer, "Must Speech Be Special?" See also Kent Greenawalt, *Speech, Crime, and the Uses of Language,* pp. 26–27, 31–33.

4. Scanlon, "A Theory of Freedom of Expression," pp. 155–62. See also,

Emerson, *Toward a General Theory of the First Amendment*, pp. 5–6; and Simon Lee, *The Cost of Free Speech*, pp. 63–69, 130.

5. Franklin S. Haiman, *Speech and Law in a Free Society*, p. 181.

6. Mill, *On Liberty*, p. 112.

7. Cf. Frederick Schauer, *Free Speech*, chaps. 4, 5; and David A. J. Richards, *Toleration and the Constitution*, chap. 6. For criticism of these arguments, see Owen M. Fiss, "Free Speech and Social Structure," esp. sect. 1. Fiss speaks of autonomy and rich public debate, arguing that autonomy may be insufficient to ensure a rich public debate and may even become destructive of that goal.

8. Cf. Joseph Raz, "Free Expression and Personal Identification," pp. 311–12, 324.

9. David A. J. Richards, "Free Speech and Obscenity Law," p. 45.

10. Cf. Mill's *Utilitarianism* (pp. 28–29): "[M]oral associations which are wholly of artificial creation, when intellectual culture goes on, yield by degrees to the dissolving force of analysis."

11. A line of thinking connects many of the arguments expressed here. Mill, for instance, had in his mind a pyramidical view in which rationality is set at the base as a precondition for exchanging ideas and communicating with others. Free speech is conducive to the promotion of autonomy and self-government, which, in turn, are conducive to human progress and truth and thus happiness (cf. Mill, *Principles of Political Economy*, p. 458).

12. Cf. Mill, *On Liberty*, pp. 79–84. This issue is discussed by John Skorupski in *John Stuart Mill*, pp. 376–83.

13. *Abrams v. United States*, 250 U.S. 616, 630 (1919). See Mill, *On Liberty*, p. 111, and Justice Black in *Martin v. Struthers* 319 U.S. 141 (1943). For criticism of the marketplace of ideas approach, see C. Edwin Baker, *Human Liberty and Freedom of Speech*, pp. 6–24.

14. Aryeh Neier, *Defending My Enemy*, is an ardent advocate of this view. See, for example, pp. 4, 110–11, 135, 146–47.

15. Cf. Mill, *On Liberty*, p. 112.

16. Skillen, "Freedom of Speech," p. 150.

17. Cf. Dorsen, "Is There A Right to Stop Offensive Speech?" p. 133.

18. Cf. Cass R. Sunstein, "Free Speech Now," p. 259.

19. Bollinger, *The Tolerant Society*, pp. 198–200.

20. Emerson, "First Amendment Doctrine and the Burger Court," pp. 426–28.

21. Cf. Raz, "Free Expression and Personal Identification," pp. 311–12.

22. Emerson, "First Amendment Doctrine and the Burger Court," p. 428; *Toward a General Theory of the First Amendment*, pp. 11–15; *The System of Freedom of Expression*, p. 7; and Greenawalt, *Speech, Crime, and the Uses of Language*, pp. 24–25.

23. Greenawalt, *Speech, Crime, and the Uses of Language,* pp. 25–26.

24. Franklin S. Haiman, *Speech and Law in a Free Society,* p. 94 (italics mine).

25. Ibid., p. 426 (italics mine).

26. In the United States the absolutists believe that the command of the First Amendment is absolute in the sense that no law that restricts freedom of speech is constitutionally valid. Justice Black was the leading advocate of the absolutist approach. Cf., e.g., *Martin v. City of Struthers* 319 U.S. 141 (1943); *Barenblatt v. United States* 360 U.S. 109 (1959) (Justice Black dissenting); *Konigsberg v. State Bar of California* 366 U.S. 36 (1961) (Justice Black dissenting).

27. Cf. Alexander Meiklejohn, *Political Freedom,* pp. 8–28, 101–24. See also Hugo L. Black, "The Bill of Rights."

28. This is not to say that the First Amendment is not subject to regulations at all. Meiklejohn explains that its purpose is to make people self-educated, to make self-government a reality, asserting that the First Amendment does not protect speech. Instead, it protects political freedom in speech or whenever else it may be threatened. It protects the freedom of those activities of thought and communication by which we govern. See Meiklejohn, "What Does the First Amendment Mean?" p. 471; "The First Amendment Is an Absolute," p. 255.

29. Cf. *Garrison v. Louisiana,* 379 U.S. 64 (1964), where the Court ruled, "speech concerning public affairs is more than self-expression; it is the essence of self-government."

30. Cf. Meiklejohn, "The First Amendment Is an Absolute," pp. 260–61; "The Balancing of Self-Preservation Against Political Freedom" and "Freedom of Speech." See also William O. Douglas, *The Right of the People,* esp. pp. 35–66; and Michael J. Perry's defense of free speech, aiming to secure it an overwhelming immunity, "Freedom of Expression."

31. Schauer, *Free Speech,* p. 41. Justice Frankfurter, in his *Dennis* opinion, 341 U.S. 494 (1951) at 519, 525, referred to Meiklejohn's book and described the absolutist school as "a sonorous formula which is in fact only a euphemistic disguise for an unresolved conflict." He further characterized the absolute statements as "dogmas too inflexible for the non-Euclidean problems to be solved."

32. Meiklejohn, "The First Amendment Is an Absolute," p. 261.

33. *Schenck v. U.S.* 249 U.S. 47 (1919).

34. Other criticisms are concerned with the distinction that Meiklejohn tries to draw between public and private speech and with the immunity he wishes to grant to political speech. Cf. Zechariah Chafee's book review of Meiklejohn's *Political Freedom,* pp. 899–901; and Robert H. Bork, "Neutral Principles and Some First Amendment Problems," esp. p. 31.

35. Alf Ross, *Why Democracy?* p. 237.

36. *Gitlow v. N.Y.* 268 U.S. 652, 673 (1925).

37. Cf. Alf Ross, *Why Democracy?* p. 238.

38. Ibid., p. 241. In a similar manner, R. M. MacIver, in *The Web of Government,* p. 200; and *The Modern State,* p. 153, maintained that the democratic principle requires that all opinions be allowed free and full expression, and that opinion can be fought only by opinion because only thus is it possible for truth to be revealed.

39. Ross's stand is unclear with regard to cases of libel, defamation, and slander. His theory excludes protection from propaganda that makes use of "inadmissible means," or which aims at using violence (*Why Democracy?* p. 237). Ross, however, does not explain the meaning of "inadmissible means." Ross asserts that we cannot doubt that freedom of speech as a democratic idea cannot mean that any verbal statement should be legal, and that several kinds of verbal or written utterances are forbidden without this having anything to do with a limitation of the democratic freedom of speech (ibid., p. 234).

40. Ibid., p. 116.

41. These speech-acts include expressions that can bring about injury or damage as direct physical consequence; assaults; defamation and interference with the right to a fair trial; Holmes's assertion that we would not protect a person who falsely shouts Fire! in a crowded theater; expressions which cause a severe harmful act by someone else; and expressions which might cause a drastic decrease in the general level of personal safety (cf. Scanlon, "A Theory of Freedom of Expression," pp. 158–59).

42. Geoffrey Marshall pointed out to me the case of Thorpe, member of Parliament in Britain, who was blackmailed with regard to his secret homosexuality. Thorpe approached a friend and explained to him why it was important to kill the blackmailer, saying that otherwise Thorpe's party might be defeated in the elections. Thorpe could have argued that he only persuaded to murder, and that he did not incite to murder.

43. Scanlon, "A Theory of Freedom of Expression," p. 161.

44. Ibid., p. 167.

45. Cf. R. M. Dworkin's introduction to *The Philosophy of Law,* p. 15. Further criticism is made by C. Edwin Baker, *Human Liberty and Freedom of Speech,* pp. 51–52.

46. T. M. Scanlon, "Freedom of Expression and Categories of Expression," p. 521.

47. Ibid., p. 535.

48. Ibid., p. 534.

49. I refer to the residents of Skokie, who are the direct audience. Of course, one may argue that in reality the audience would be much wider through the work of the media.

50. After the National Socialist Party of America announced its intention to hold a march in Skokie, the Board of Trustees of the Village of Skokie passed three ordinances designed to prevent the NSPA from marching—a permit requirement, a prohibition of incitement to racial hatred, and a ban on the wearing of military-style uniforms. I shall elaborate on the Skokie affair in chapter 8.

51. Scanlon, "A Theory of Freedom of Expression," p. 170.

52. For detailed discussions see, inter alia, John C. Rees, "A Re-reading of Mill on Liberty"; C. L. Ten, *Mill on Liberty*; John Gray, *Mill on Liberty: A Defence*; John Skorupski, *John Stuart Mill*.

53. J. S. Mill, *System of Logic*, book 6, 9:2, p. 586.

54. Mill, *On Liberty*, p. 136.

55. Ibid., p. 137.

Chapter 6: Why Tolerate? The Millian Truth Principle

1. Cf. Justice Holmes in *Abrams v. U.S.* 250 U.S. 616 (1919); Justice Brandeis in *Whitney v. California* 274 U.S. 357 (1927); and Justice Frankfurter in *Kovacs v. Cooper* 336 U.S. 77 (1949).

2. Cf. John Milton, who published his *Areopagitica* in 1644, advocating that because truth is a perpetual progression, every idea should be tolerated.

3. Mill, *On Liberty*, p. 79.

4. Mill, "Appendix," in *Dissertations and Discussions*, 1:474; reprinted under the title "Democracy and Government" in G. L. Williams, ed., *John Stuart Mill on Politics and Society*, p. 184.

5. Mill, *On Liberty*, p. 83.

6. Ibid., p. 95. Bearing these arguments in mind, I find it quite puzzling to reflect on Mill's reaction when he was asked to join a society he did not appreciate. Mill declined the invitation of the Neophyte Writers Society, commenting that he was not interested in aiding the diffusion of opinions contrary to his own but only in promoting those he considered "true and just" (23 April 1854). Cf. Francis E. Mineka and Dwight N. Lindley, eds., *The Later Letters of J. S. Mill, 1849–1873*, p. 205.

7. Mill, *On Liberty*, p. 89.

8. Mill, *Utilitarianism*, p. 21. Note Mill's caution in phrasing this exception to one of his most "sacred" ideas, appealing to "all moralists" in support.

9. Ibid., p. 41.

10. Mill, "Law of Libel," in Geraint L. Williams, ed., *John Stuart Mill on Politics and Society*, pp. 160–61.

11. Mill, *On Liberty*, p. 138.

12. I thought that possibly the term *annoyance* had a stronger sense in the

nineteenth century than the one prevailing today. The first edition of the *Oxford English Dictionary,* however, did not supply grounds to validate this suspicion.

13. You may argue that Mill was talking not about public figures but private people. He, however, refrained from qualifying his assertion and did not make this assumption explicit.

14. In specific categories of cases, prior restraint by injunction is thought legitimate (as it is sometimes in cases of libel, privacy, security, contempt of court, and copyrights).

15. Mill, "Law of Libel," p. 160.

16. Mill, *On Liberty,* p. 112. The United States Supreme Court accepted this reasoning in *New York Times v. Sullivan* 376 U.S. 254 (1964).

17. Mill, *On Liberty,* p. 78. In a letter to Sterling (20–22 October 1831), Mill wrote, "In the present age of transition, everything must be subordinated to freedom of inquiry." See Francis E. Mineka, ed., *The Earlier Letters of J. S. Mill, 1812–1848,* p. 77.

18. Mill, *On Liberty,* p. 90.

19. Eric Barendt, in *Freedom of Speech,* pp. 10–13, notes that it is facile to argue that in all circumstances the best remedy against evil speech will be more or better speech, and that it is facile to argue that it would be wrong to prohibit even false speech. Barendt admits that if opinions are not contested, their vitality will decline. Nevertheless, Barendt thinks that a government worried that inflammatory speech may provoke disorder is surely entitled to elevate immediate public order considerations over the long-term intellectual development.

20. Rawls, *A Theory of Justice,* p. 3.

21. John Rawls, "Construction and Objectivity," p. 564.

22. Rawls, "Rational and Full Autonomy," p. 519.

23. Rawls, *A Theory of Justice,* p. 219. The relevant virtue of Rawls's constructivist theory consists in its justice rather than its truth. Instead of evaluating different claims to truth by reference to how true they really are, it abstains from any such judgment and tries only to deal with them fairly. The moral force of his theory lies not in its claim to some ontological status that can be described as "true," but in its reasonable dealing with different conceptions of the true. That is why justice as fairness is a political, not a metaphysical doctrine.

24. The Respect for Others Argument and the Truth Principle both supply grounds for liberty of expression. While the Respect for Others Argument (as formulated above) may be applied both to action and expression, the Truth Principle refers to the category of expression alone.

25. Haiman, *Speech and Law in a Free Society,* p. 73.

26. Cf. Baker, *Human Liberty and Freedom of Speech,* pp. 194–224.

27. Notice in this connection Mill's recommendation to label a drug with some word expressive of its dangerous character so as to inform the buyer that the thing he or she possesses has poisonous qualities (cf. *On Liberty,* p. 152).

28. Consideration of how the research is published is crucial. It is one thing to release the same study under the same circumstance in a violent pamphlet and quite another thing to publish it in a scientific journal. Although I am inclined to think that we should prohibit the first type of publication, I would not urge prohibition of the second.

29. A radical argument may hold that the decisive question here is not whether the racist claim of the distinction between noble and inferior races is true or false. Even if the research contains grains of truth, the issue is not that our truth contradicts the other's. Instead, that very truth and its resultant conclusions with regard to the destiny of the races, namely that the superior, ipso facto, should rule the world, and the inferior be doomed to perish, is harmful and destructive. It, therefore, does not deserve to be tolerated and contested in the marketplace of ideas. Tolerance is not the guiding formula in such a case, for tolerance means respect for people, and it ought not to be granted to those who base their views on degrading others. This view, however, may introduce excessive restrictions on freedom of expression. I discuss this issue further in chapter 8.

30. Cf. Mill's corn dealer example, *On Liberty,* p. 114. In chapter 7 I shall consider in detail the distinction between advocacy and instigation.

31. Another possibility of infection that is hypothesized is by way of saliva. HIV is present in saliva and it could be transferred from a HIV carrier to another through saliva if the other has a cut in his or her mouth.

32. Scanlon, "Freedom of Expression and Categories of Expression," pp. 519–50.

33. W. H. Masters, Virginia E. Johnson, and Robert C. Kolodny, *Crisis: Heterosexual Behavior in the Age of AIDS,* pp. 83–92.

34. I discussed this matter with two specialists at Oxford. Dr. Anne Edwards of the Radcliffe Infirmary asserts that theoretically a very slim chance exists for becoming infected with HIV by contact with contaminated toilet seats or from mosquito bites. She adds that it is immoral to publish such hypotheses without substantiated evidence. Dr. Tim Pito of the John Radcliffe Hospital agrees. He thinks that the toilet seat hypothesis is "rubbish" and that the mosquito bite theory is quite implausible. Dr. Pito argues that Masters and Johnson know nothing about AIDS and that they probably wanted "a bit of a fun." He adds that it is almost impossible to refute hypotheses that suggest a very low risk.

35. Hannah Arendt, "Truth and Politics," p. 104. Arendt makes a further point which I dispute. She assumes that truthfulness has little to contribute to the change of world and circumstances, which is among the most legitimate activities (p. 123). I do not see why the mere telling of facts leads to no action whatsoever, as Arendt claims. The very selection of the facts *in itself* is frequently *intended* to bring about some action (or inaction).

36. Scanlon, "A Theory of Freedom of Expression," pp. 161–62.

37. Richards, *Toleration and the Constitution,* pp. 240–42.

38. When people speak of the content of the speech, they may refer to its *truthfulness,* or to its *consequences,* or to both. Here I refer not to the truthfulness of the speech, but to the consequences that it is intended to bring.

Chapter 7: Boundaries of Freedom of Expression

1. Mill, *On Liberty,* p. 75.

2. We have seen in the previous chapter that the qualifications presented in "Law of Libel and Liberty of the Press" are quite problematic.

3. Mill, *On Liberty,* p. 78.

4. Ibid., p. 114.

5. Mill acknowledged the importance of intentions in other places. For instance, speaking of employing military commanders by ministers, Mill said that as long as a minister trusts his military commander he does not send him instructions on how to fight. The minister holds him responsible only for intentions and results (cf. "Appendix," *Dissertations and Discussions,* 1:471–72).

6. *Gitlow v. N.Y.* 268 U.S. 652, 673 (1925).

7. *Schenck v. U.S.* 249 U.S. 47 (1919).

8. In this instance it does not matter whether the intention of the agent was only to do this specific act and not to bring about harmful consequences. The agent may say that he or she wanted only to break the silence or to attract public attention, and that he or she did not think of creating panic. Still the agent will be held accountable for the action. The same reasoning guides us in prosecuting those who pull emergency switches in trains just because they could not resist the temptation of touching those "beautiful red buttons."

9. Zechariah Chafee, *Free Speech in the United States,* p. 397.

10. Mill, *On Liberty,* p. 153.

11. John Skorupski, *John Stuart Mill,* pp. 347–59, speaks of the concept of moral freedom that is conceived by Mill as rational autonomy. The autonomy we value as an independent part of our own good is the freedom to lead our own life. But this is not just freedom to do as one likes, either. Autonomy is sovereignty over our life, not sovereignty over anyone else's life.

12. Mill, "Bentham," in *Dissertations and Discussions,* 1:386.

13. In *Utilitarianism* (p. 45), Mill explained, "We do not call anything wrong, unless we mean to imply that a person ought to be punished in some way or other for doing it; if not by law, by the opinion of his fellow-creatures; if not by opinion, by the reproaches of his own conscience. This seems the real turning point of the distinction between morality and simple expediency. It is a part of the notion of Duty in every one of its forms, that a person may rightfully be compelled to fulfil it."

14. Situations exist where the offense made by the defamatory remarks is immediate and irreparable and when no time is available for a reply. An example would be the publication of false accusations against a rival candidate on the eve of an election, claiming that he or she listens in on the discussions held in the offices of the other candidates.

15. Joel Feinberg, *Offense to Others*, pp. 1–2.

16. Ibid., p. 26.

17. Scanlon, "Freedom of Expression and Categories of Expression," p. 527.

18. Cf. David Kretzmer, "Freedom of Speech and Racism."

19. On this point I concur with Ronald Dworkin, who expressed this same view in comments on one of my papers.

20. Accordingly, pornography may be dealt with under the confines of the Offense Principle. This issue, however, calls for separate analysis.

Chapter 8: Applying the Offense Principle: The Skokie Controversy

1. Skokie has the highest number of survivors of the Holocaust of any city in the United States, outside New York City.

2. In *Brandenburg v. Ohio* 395 U.S. 444 (1969), the court ruled that the expression of a particular idea may not be suppressed unless it is both directed to and likely to incite or produce imminent unlawful conduct (at 447). See also *Hess v. Indiana* 414 U.S. 105 (1973).

3. *Village of Skokie v. NSPA* 373 N.E. 2d 21 (1978). Chief Justice Vinson wrote in *Dennis v. U.S.* 341 U.S. 494 (1951) that the basis of the First Amendment is the hypothesis that speech can rebut speech, propaganda will answer propaganda, free debate of ideas will result in the widest governmental policies. Justice Powell argued in *Gertz v. Robert Welch* 418 U.S. 323 (1974) that under this amendment there is no such thing as a false idea.

4. Under constitutional precedents, the threat of violence could not serve as an argument to prevent assemblies, rallies, and the like. Cf. *Terminiello v. Chicago* 337 U.S. 1 (1949); *Feiner v. New York* 340 U.S. 315 (1951); *Edwards v. South Carolina* 372 U.S. 229 (1963); *Tinker v. Des Moines* 393 U.S. 503 (1969); *Street v. New York* 394 U.S. 576 (1969); and *Bachellar v. Maryland* 397 U.S. 564 (1970). In England the most notable case is *Beatty v. Gillbanks* 9

QBD 308 (1882). The reasoning of the British courts on this issue is similar to that of the American courts, holding that the hostile audience problem should not serve as grounds for suppression of demonstrations.

5. *Chaplinsky v. New Hampshire* 315 U.S. 568 (1942). See also *Cohen v. California* 403 U.S. 15 (1971). In Britain the *fighting words* doctrine came into expression in Lord Parker's "hitting them with words" phraseology for an offense to be committed. Cf. *Jordan v. Burgoyne* 2 QB 744 (1963).

6. *Skokie v. NSPA* (1978), at 24; *Village of Skokie v. NSPA* 366 N.E. 2d 347 (1977), at 357. See also *Collin v. Smith* 447 F. Supp. 676 (1978).

7. Feinberg, *Offense to Others*, pp. 86–93. For an incisive criticism of this view see Robert Amdur, "Harm, Offense, and the Limits of Liberty." Note that the Supreme Court ruled, in *Stromberg v. California* 283 U.S. 359 (1931), that the display of a symbol may communicate ideas no less than the articulation of words.

8. For a different viewpoint that regards racialist speech as political, see Scanlon, "Freedom of Expression and Categories of Expression," p. 538.

9. Feinberg, *Offense to Others,* pp. 87–88. I find Feinberg's arguments confusing, for he also writes that the feelings of a Jewish survivor of a Nazi death camp as a small band of American Nazis struts down the main street of his town "cannot be wholly escaped merely by withdrawing one's attention, by locking one's door, pulling the window blinds, and putting plugs in one's ears." Feinberg maintains that the offended state of mind is at least to some degree independent of what is directly perceived (p. 52).

10. For a similar line of argumentation see Bollinger, *The Tolerant Society,* p. 60. Bollinger further argues that we should grant a wide latitude to freedom of expression, although the speech in question may be harmful, because of the societal benefits derived from the lessons learned through toleration (p. 198). The contesting argument holds that to tolerate speech abusing racial groups is to lend respectability to racist attitudes, which in their turn may foster an eventual breakdown of public order (cf. Barendt, *Freedom of Speech,* p. 161).

11. Quite surprisingly, and without much explanation, Feinberg does not justify the decision that allowed the march. He states that we can have sympathy for the American Civil Liberties Union (ACLU) decision to back the Nazis but that he disagrees with this stand. (Cf. *Offense to Others*, p. 93.) In a private discussion with me he admitted that he did not make his position explicit enough and expressed regret for not fully clarifying his reasoning.

12. Those who hold the fighting words doctrine (or the hitting with words doctrine) as valid may argue that some types of speech *as such* should be restricted no matter where they are pronounced. I do not endorse this view.

13. Cf. Feinberg, *Offense to Others*, p. 87.

14. The court did recognize it three years after *Brandenburg*. In *Rosenfeld v. New Jersey* (408 U.S. 901, 1972), Justice Powell asserted that "the shock and sense of affront, and sometimes the injury to mind and spirit, can be as great from words as from some physical attacks."

15. Cf. Feinberg, *Offense to Others*, p. 2.

16. Haiman, *Speech and Law in a Free Society*, p. 425.

17. Ibid., pp. 425–26 (Haiman's italics).

18. Ibid., p. 97.

19. Ibid., p. 154.

20. Bollinger, *The Tolerant Society*, pp. 197–200. See also Dr. William Niederland's letter, *New York Times* (7 February 1978); Donald Alexander Downs, *Nazis in Skokie*, chaps. 1, 8; and the statement of Sol Goldstein, a survivor of a concentration camp whose mother was killed by the Nazis, in Neier, *Defending My Enemy*, p. 46.

21. Scanlon, in "A Theory of Freedom of Expression," contemplates that an assault is committed when one person intentionally places another in apprehension of imminent bodily harm. He maintains that instances of assault necessarily involve expressions since an element of successful communication must be present (p. 158).

22. On several occasions the United States Supreme Court considered whether some types of speech are of only "low" First Amendment value. Among them are the fighting words doctrine (*Chaplinsky v. New Hampshire* 315 U.S. 568, 1942); incitement (*Dennis v. U.S.* 341 U.S. 494, 1951); obscenity (*Miller v. California* 413 U.S. 15, 1973); and false statements of fact (*Gertz v. Robert Welch* 418 U.S. 323, 1974). Cf. Geoffrey R. Stone, "Content Regulation and the First Amendment."

23. *Village of Skokie v. NSPA* 366 N.E. 2d 347 (1977).

24. Donald Vandeveer, "Coercive Restraint of Offensive Actions," p. 177.

25. On the laws of other countries concerning racist speech see Bollinger, *The Tolerant Society*, pp. 253–56.

26. In addition, under the Race Relations Act of 1976 speakers can theoretically be prosecuted if they use threatening, abusive, or insulting words in public. Section 70 of this act inserted a new section (5A) into the Public Order Act of 1936. The section made it an offense for any person to publish or distribute written matter or to use in any public place or at any public meeting words that were threatening, abusive, or insulting in a case where hatred was likely to be stirred up against any racial group. This law altered the previous law in that it was no longer necessary, as it had been under section 6 of the Race Relations Act (1965), to prove that the accused intended to stir up racial hatred. It did not, however, confer any powers to ban demonstrations or meet-

ings by racialist organizations. Prosecutions for incitement to racial hatred require the consent of the attorney general.

27. Several speakers in Parliament justified the legislation prohibiting racist expressions on the ground of the fear, alarm, and distress caused to members of minority groups. Cf. W. J. Wolffe, "Values in Conflict," p. 94.

28. Cf. *Parkin v. Norman* (1982) 3 W.L.R. 523.

29. Cf. part III, "Racial Hatred." According to the attorney general, fifteen prosecutions for incitement to racial hatred have been brought between March 1986 and November 1990 under part 3 of the 1986 act, or under section 5A of the 1936 Act (180 *Parliamentary Debates* [1990–91], p. 88W).

30. Fifth Report of the Home Affairs Committee of the House of Commons 1979–80, HC 756, para. 51. Cf. Barendt, *Freedom of Speech,* p. 198.

31. In 1948 the home secretary invoked the Public Order Act to ban all political marches in London for three months after the Fascists marched through Jewish areas of London. The same reaction recurred in the 1970s after the National Front decided to march through immigrant areas.

32. International treaties speak of "the right to freedom of *peaceful* assembly" (italics mine). Cf. Article 2 of the European Convention of Human Rights; Article 20 of the Universal Declaration of Human Rights; and Article 21 of the United Nations International Covenant on Civil and Political Rights.

33. Home Office, *Review of Public Order Law,* Cmmd. 9510 (White Paper) (May 1985), pp. 23–24.

34. Part II of the Public Order Act 1986 speaks of the imposing of conditions on public processions, holding that if a senior police officer reasonably believes that the procession in question "may result in serious public disorder, serious damage to property or *serious disruption to the life of the community* . . . he may give directions imposing on the persons organising or taking part in the procession such conditions as appear to him necessary to prevent such disorder, damage, disruption or intimidation" (sect. 12, italics mine). The courts, it seems, interpret the above as being in line with the breach of the peace reasoning.

35. Home Office, *Review of Public Order Act 1936* (Green Paper) (April 1980), pp. 11–12.

36. Home Office, *Review of Public Order Law* (White Paper) (May 1985), p. 23.

37. Bollinger, *The Tolerant Society,* p. 34. In a similar vein, Neier rightly contends that speakers characteristically carry their messages to places where their views are anathema. However, he fails to distinguish incidents of protest from demonstrations aiming to offend a specific target group who cannot avoid being exposed to it (*Defending My Enemy,* p. 142).

38. *Discrimination* means "any distinction, exclusion, restriction or prefer-

ence based on race, colour, descent, or national or ethnic origin which has the purpose or effect of nullifying or impairing the recognition, enjoyment or exercise, on an equal footing, of human rights and fundamental freedoms in the political, economic, social, cultural or any other field of public life" (Cf. International Convention on the Elimination of All Forms of Racial Discrimination, Article 1 [1]).

39. Samuel Krislov, in his reference to the Ku Klux Klansmen in robes, asserts that we forbid such paramilitary uniforms precisely because they symbolize and, therefore, threaten and intimidate. The manner of expression constitutes clear content. In a similar fashion, those who object to the burning of flags in public argue that they do not object to the message, but to the action. They would apparently agree with those who see flag desecration as a legitimate form of expression so that in such cases the content of the expression, and its manner, are inseparable (*The Supreme Court and Political Freedom,* p. 151).

40. In *Tinker v. Des Moines School District* 393 U.S. 503 (1969), the court ruled that the wearing of black armbands in school to protest the Vietnam War is closely akin to pure speech. In Britain a divisional court upheld the conviction of the defendants who were wearing black berets and dark glasses at the funeral of an IRA member, arguing that berets were generally recognized as the uniform of those associated with militant Republican purposes (cf. *O'Moran v. DPP* [1975] QB 864).

41. In Britain, section 1 of the Public Order Act (1936) places a general prohibition on the wearing of political uniforms in any public place or at any public meeting. The feeling is that this measure is necessary to suppress any attempt on the part of a political group to parade as a uniformed force. In Germany it is prohibited to wear in public or in assemblies uniforms, parts of uniforms, or similar mode of clothing as an expression of political convictions (cf. VersG [Law of Assembly], section 3[1]). In addition, the Nazi trauma convinced the legislators to include in the Penal Law specific prohibition (sect. 86a[1]) of the use of Nazi symbols in public or during assemblies.

42. Cf. Scanlon, "Freedom of Expression and Categories of Expression," p. 521.

43. I refer to the residents of Skokie, who are the direct audience. But you may argue that in reality the audience would be much wider through the offices of the media.

44. For stimulating discussions on the Rushdie affair, see Simon Lee, *The Cost of Free Speech,* pp. 73–105, and Joseph Raz, "Free Expression and Personal Identification," pp. 319–23.

45. Cf. Herbert McClosky and Alida Brill, *Dimensions of Tolerance,* p. 24. See also Feinberg, *Offense to Others,* p. 52.

46. A similar line of reasoning guided the framers of the European Convention of Human Rights when they enacted articles 9, 10, and 17. Note the language of Article 17: "Nothing in this Convention may be interpreted as implying for any State, group or person any right to engage in any activity or perform any act aimed at the destruction of any of the rights and freedoms set forth herein or at their limitation to a greater extent than is provided for in the Convention." A case in point concerning the right to freedom of expression in general and freedom of expression in the context of elections in particular is *Glimmerveen and Hagenbeek v/the Netherlands* (1980) 18 *Decisions and Reports.* European Commission on Human Rights, pp. 187–208.

Chapter 9: The Kahanist Phenomenon

1. I sought to interview Kahane during my research and to ask his opinion about the contents of this chapter. Kahane, however, refused to speak or to comment.

2. Kahane wrote, in *The Story of the Jewish Defense League,* that as long as anyone attempted to repeat the Holocaust, "never again there be that same lack of reaction, that same indifference, that same fear" (p. 5).

3. Cf. Shlomo M. Russ, "The 'Zionist Hooligans,'" pp. 170, 310–57; and Janet Dolgin, *Jewish Identity and the JDL,* chap. 1.

4. Robert I. Friedman, *The False Prophet,* p. 5.

5. Five notable incidents occurred between October 1970 and April 1971: on 6 October 1970 an explosion ripped through the PLO's New York City offices; on 23 November 1970 a pipe bomb blasted the glass of the Intourist and Aeroflot offices; on 8 January 1971 a bomb exploded outside the Soviet cultural building in Washington, D. C. The same month three cars of Soviet diplomats were destroyed by firebombs. On 30 March a pipe bomb exploded outside the Communist Party national offices in Washington, D. C.; and on 22 April 1971 a bomb went off at the Soviet freight office. The same week a heavy explosion rocked the Soviet trade delegation office in Amsterdam. Each of these explosions was followed by a telephone caller declaring, "Never Again."

6. On 21 March 1971 more than a *thousand* league members and supporters were arrested when they blocked traffic near the Soviet Mission in Washington, D. C.

7. Kahane and eleven of his men were charged with this conspiracy. The government was willing to dismiss indictments against nine of the defendants if three would plead guilty. Those three (Kahane, Bieber, and Cohen) were convicted under title I of the act, which is concerned with the transportation of firearms across state lines, and under title II, which deals with legal pro-

cedures regarding the making of firearms (cf. Russ, "The 'Zionist Hooligans,'" pp. 487–535; Friedman, *The False Prophet,* p. 122.

8. A few years later Judge Weinstein explained his decision not to put Kahane behind bars by saying that the fact that Kahane appeared to be motivated by consideration of the welfare of others rather than himself, and the recommendations of authorities that probation be utilized in such circumstances were among the reasons that persuaded the court to decide on probation (cf. *United States v. Kahane* 396 F. Supp. 687 [1975]).

9. In January 1972, explosions at two offices of impresarios for Soviet performers killed one person and injured over a dozen people. Insufficient evidence was found to connect Kahane directly to these incidents.

10. *United States v. Kahane* 527 F. 2d 491 (1975).

11. As late as 1979, a superior court judge in Los Angeles dismissed a felony complaint against Irving Rubin, a leader of the JDL, who had been charged with soliciting the murder of American Nazis. At a press conference Rubin said, "[W]e are offering $500, that I have in my hand, to any member of the community . . . who kills, maims, or seriously injures a member of the American Nazi Party." The judge accepted the argument of the attorneys from the American Civil Liberties Union (ACLU) that these utterances were political hyperbole intended to promote national media exposure and evidencing a lack of serious intent to solicit the commission of crime. Thus, they were protected by the First Amendment. A state appellate court, however, in a two-to-one vote, overruled the lower court's ruling (cf. *People of the State of California v. Rubin* 96 Cal. App. 3d 968 [1980], *cert. denied,* 101 S.Ct. 80 [1980]).

12. Cf. Yair Kotler, *Heil Kahane,* pp. 153–54 (Hebrew). In 1973 the British Criminal Code Ordinance of 1936 was still in force. It was replaced in 1977 by the Penal Law. Seditious intention was defined, inter alia, as either raising discontent or disaffection amongst inhabitants of the state or promoting feelings of ill will and hostility between different sections of the population. Cf. Part II, ch. viii, section 60 (1). Compare to Section 136 (3) and (4) of Article One of the Penal Law, in *Laws of the State of Israel,* Special Volume: Penal Law.

13. The roles of the attorney general in Israel (the title in Hebrew is legal advisor to the government) are broader than those of the attorney general in England. The attorney general is the main legal figure in Israel but is not a political figure.

14. Quoted in Kotler, *Heil Kahane,* p. 290.

15. Kahane wrote, "Where are the Jews who strike now immediately at a Soviet diplomat, causing Brezhnev to cancel his trip to the United States that stops the *d'étente* that will decimate Soviet Jewry" (Cf. *Protocol No. 14 of the Central Elections Committee* [17 June 1984], p. 11 [Hebrew]).

16. Cr.A. 167/1973, the Jerusalem District Court. Cf. Friedman, *The False Prophet,* p. 158. The case was not published.

17. "It Cannot Continue," 11 May 1979, published in English by Kach International, Brooklyn, New York.

18. Ibid.

19. Cf. Noami Gal-Or, *The Jewish Underground,* pp. 32–34 (Hebrew). According to Friedman, this group, which called itself TNT (Terror against Terror) committed hundreds of terrorist bombings and beatings, as well as several murders (*The False Prophet,* p. 239).

20. Cf. Haggai Segal, *Dear Brothers,* p. 181.

21. Emergency Powers (Detention) Law, 5739–1979. This law, in fact, replaced a less liberal procedure enacted by the British mandate authorities as Emergency Regulations.

22. *Kahane and Green v. Minister of Defence.* Appeal on Administrative Detention. No. 1/1980, at 261. The view then was that the court's only business was to check the formal requirements of the ordinance. The prevailing opinion was that if the Defense Ministry decided to take such a measure, there was bound to be sufficient reason to believe that this act was necessary to protect public safety. Nowadays the court does consider the discretion of the defense minister. The court is willing to scrutinize this discretion, and sometimes questions are raised with regard to the need for such an extreme measure.

23. Commonly three segments are distinguished in Israeli Jewish society: *Sephardim, Ashkenazim,* and *Sabras.* Roughly speaking, Sephardim are Jews whose origins are from Asia and Africa, whereas Ashkenazim are Jews from Europe and America. Those who are born in Israel are called Sabras.

24. Itzhak Zamir on 30 June 1983. Cf. Moshe Negbi, *Paper Tiger,* 120 (Hebrew).

25. The American Council for Foreign Relations conducted a research project on Israeli society in 1984 through 1985. It concluded that the people were emotional and indecisive and deeply split in regard to their political, material, and spiritual preferences. It also asserted that the gaps within the Jewish population, not to mention the gap between Jews and Arabs, had deepened. In addition, the research warned of the danger of fundamentalist Jews disobeying the law, *Yedioth Ahronoth,* 10 May 1985.

26. While the general director advised the mainstream of the education system to encourage meetings between Jews and Arabs, the religious section of the ministry—which is in charge of the orthodox schools in Israel, and as such enjoys the autonomy to decide its policy separately from the instructions of the general director and the minister—directed its schools not to allow such meetings. It also published a new educational series, entitled "On the Good Earth," which emphasized the sole right of the Jewish people to Eretz (the land

of) Israel, asserting that the Arabs had no roots in the land and that the idea of Arabs sitting together with Jews under the same tree was a utopia. Only a few religious leaders publicly denounced Kahane and his programs. When the Ashkenazi chief rabbi of Israel was asked to publish an address denouncing Kahane, he refused.

27. Every year one topic is selected by the Ministry of Education to be thoroughly discussed in schools. The year 1986 was dedicated to the study of democracy. In 1987 the Israeli Declaration of Independence was selected to be the focus.

28. A Kach flyer, undated, entitled, "A Message to the Jewish Community from Rabbi Meir Kahane" (English).

29. "Only Kach," no. 2 (1986), p. 36.

30. Aviva Shabi, "In Tel-Mond I established the redemption movement," *Yedioth Ahronoth*, 6 January 1989.

31. On 25 August 1989, in the *Jewish Press*, Kahane openly called for revolution in Israel because the government "is incapable or unwilling to protect to the utmost, and in every way possible, the lives of its citizens." Since, in Kahane's view, the only way to suppress the Palestinian Intifada was to expel each and every Arab, something that the government was not willing to do, Kahane contended the government "loses every legal and moral right to rule." Cf. Friedman, *The False Prophet*, p. 269.

32. Kahane, *The Story of the Jewish Defense League*, p. 323.

33. Meir Kahane, *Listen World, Listen Jew*, p. 15.

34. Meir Kahane, *Uncomfortable Questions for Comfortable Jews*, pp. 262–63.

35. Kahane, *Listen World, Listen Jew*, p. 19. In *Uncomfortable Questions for Comfortable Jews*, Kahane wrote that Judaism defines freedom as follows: "'For no man is free but he who occupies himself in the study of *Torah*' (*Avot* 6:2). The only freedom recognized by Judaism is that which is within the bounds, the framework of *halacha*" (p. 129).

36. *Hellenism* was one of Kahane's favored terms. In Hebrew this term conveys, in addition to the cultural notion, a notion of betrayal. Jews who conformed to Greek culture and religion were considered traitors. Some of them were executed as such by the Maccabees.

37. Kahane, *Uncomfortable Questions for Comfortable Jews*, p. 179.

38. Kahane, *Listen World, Listen Jew*, p. 139.

39. Kahane, *Uncomfortable Questions for Comfortable Jews*, p. 271.

40. Raphael Mergui and Philippe Simonnot, *Israel's Ayatollahs*, p. 87.

41. This assumption did not forecast the mass *aliya* from the Soviet Union, which started in 1989. In an article in English (without date or place of publication) prior to the immigration movement, entitled "For Israel: A Govern-

ment of National Emergency," Kahane in his picturesque language contended, "The demon of demography roars with satanic laughter as the huge Arab birthrate and the pitiful Jewish one . . . combine to threaten the continued existence of Israel as a Jewish State." He maintained that "the blunt contradiction between Zionism-Judaism and western democracy is glaring as Israel faces a clear threat to its existence either through Arab bullets or babies."

42. Kahane wrote, in *They Must Go,* "The Arabs of Israel represent *Hillul Hashem* (defamation of God) in its starkest form. . . . Their transfer from the Land of Israel thus becomes more than a political issue. *It is a religious issue, a religious obligation, a commandment to erase Hillul Hashem.* . . . Let us remove the Arabs from Israel and bring the redemption. *THEY MUST GO"* (pp. 275–76, Kahane's italics and emphasis).

43. Ibid., p. 7 (italics mine).

44. Ibid., p. 252.

45. Kahane, *Uncomfortable Questions for Comfortable Jews,* p. 173.

46. From "For Israel: A Government of National Emergency." This article was written under the influence of the Palestinian Intifada.

47. Kahane, *Uncomfortable Questions for Comfortable Jews,* p. 206.

48. Kahane, *Listen World, Listen Jew,* p. iv. An undated Kach flyer (in English) entitled "Don't Date Gentiles" states: "Intermarriage is the spiritual Auschwitz of the Jewish People." The message to the "Young Jew" clearly postulates that "Life is not ours to do with as we see fit. Only the sick, selfish animalist babbles about his 'right' to do with his life whatever he wishes without any restraint or obligation. It is *not* 'my' life or 'my' business or 'my' right. We are not islands unto ourselves." This is because "You are a link to a glorious past and the initiator of a glorious future," and "*You have no right"* to throw away that Judaism which "your grandparents so struggled for and *died for.* . . . You have no right to rob *your children and theirs and all the generations who will come from you* . . ." (emphases are within the text).

49. Cf. interview with Kahane in Mergui and Simonnot, *Israel's Ayatollahs,* p. 80.

50. Kahane, *Listen World, Listen Jew,* p. 137.

51. Notice the nuance: the parties of the right in Israel refer to the West Bank and the Gaza Strip as "the liberated territories," whereas parties of the left refer to them as "the occupied territories."

52. Kahane, "For Israel: A Government of National Emergency," published in English by Kach.

53. Kahane, *Uncomfortable Questions for Comfortable Jews,* p. 268.

54. Ibid., p. 271.

55. Ibid.

56. Ibid., p. 272; and Kahane, *Listen World, Listen Jew,* p. 20.

57. Kahane, *Uncomfortable Questions for Comfortable Jews,* p. 272; see also *The Story of the Jewish Defense League,* p. 310.

58. Kahane, *Uncomfortable Questions for Comfortable Jews,* pp. 272–73.

59. Ibid., p. 272.

60. Ibid. (italics mine).

61. Ibid., pp. 273–74.

62. Ibid., p. 274.

Chapter 10: Legal Background: The Foundations of the Law

1. The "Harari Resolution" of 13 June 1950 (5 Knesset Proceedings). References in brackets are page numbers of the supreme court's judgments.

2. Basic Law: The Knesset (1958); Basic Law: Israel Lands (1960); Basic Law: The President of the State (1964); Basic Law: The Government (1968); Basic Law: The State Economy (1975); Basic Law: The Army (1976); Basic Law: Jerusalem (1980); Basic Law: Judicature (1984); Basic Law: State Comptroller (1988); Basic Law: Freedom of Occupation (1992); Basic Law: The Individual's Dignity and Liberty (1992).

3. Aharon Barak, *Judicial Discretion,* p. 319 (Hebrew). A translation of the book into English (albeit in a shorter version) was published by Yale University Press in 1987.

4. Cf. Amnon Rubinstein, *Constitutional Law of Israel,* pp. 280–81; Moshe Negbi, *Above the Law,* pp. 32–35 (both in Hebrew); and Ruth Gavison, "The Controversy over Israel's Bill of Rights," p. 119.

5. Some of the laws are entrenched, in the sense that an absolute majority is required to change them. For example, Basic Law: The Knesset (1958) provides that the election method can be amended or canceled only by the consent of at least sixty-one Knesset members and that emergency regulations may not affect the law absent a two-thirds majority (sects. 4, 44, 45). Basic Law: The President of the State (1964) is entrenched so as to ensure that it could not be altered by emergency regulations (sect. 25). Basic Law: The Government (1968) requires an absolute majority in order to be altered by Emergency Regulations (sect. 42). See also sections 4 and 5 of Basic Law: Freedom of Occupation (1992) and section 12 of Basic Law: The Individual's Dignity and Liberty (1992).

6. A contesting view (expressed by Eli Salzberger in a private discussion) is that these Basic Laws can be molded into a constitution, provided that two additional Basic Laws will be enacted—Basic Law: Human Rights, and Basic Law: Legislation. The last named will regulate the legal framework and provide answers to the above-mentioned problems. I must say that in the current political affairs in Israel, the passage of a comprehensive Human Rights Law appears impossible.

7. An English translation of the Declaration of Independence can be found in Henry Baker, *The Legal System of Israel,* pp. 8–10. Many argue that the date mentioned in the Declaration refers to the establishment of the assembly, not to the writing of a constitution.

8. Cf. High Court (henceforward H.C.) 10/1948. *Ziv v. Gubernik.* The court referred to the first part of the Declaration as having a normative status. This part is concerned with the establishment of Israel as a sovereign state.

9. Cf H.C. 73/1953; 87/1953. *Kol-Ha'am v. Minister of the Interior;* and Election Appeal (E. A.) 1/1965. *Yeredor v. Chairman of the Central Committee for the Elections to the Sixth Knesset,* to be discussed in the next section. See also H.C. 262/1962. *Perez v. Kfar Shmaryahu Local Council,* where the court ruled that a municipality must rent community halls to non-Orthodox Jews for religious services. The same year, on the question Who is a Jew? the court invoked the Declaration as an instrument for the interpretation of the Law of Return (see the judgments of Justices Haim Cohn and Moshe Landau in H.C. 72/1962. *Rufeisen v. Minister of the Interior*).

10. Cf. Civil Appeal (C.A.) 450/1970. *Rogozinsky and Others v. the State of Israel,* where the court held that when the will of the Knesset, in light of the laws it enacted, is clear beyond doubt, then this will should be respected even if it cannot be reconciled with the principles of the Declaration.

11. Justice Yoel Sussman's opinion in H.C. 262/1962 *Perez v. Kfar Shmaryahu.*

12. H.C. 953/1987. *Poraz v. The Mayor of Tel-Aviv.*

13. Cf. Aharon Barak, *Judicial Discretion,* p. 97; and his "Freedom of Speech in Israel: The Impact of the American Constitution," p. 241.

14. H.C. 163/1957. *Lubin v. Tel-Aviv Municipality.*

15. H.C. 262/1962. *Perez v. Kfar Shmaryahu Local Council.*

16. Justice Haim Cohn in H.C. 301/1963. *Striet v. the Chief Rabbi of Israel.*

17. H.C. 243/1962. *Filming Studios v. Geri.*

18. Justice Haim Cohn in H.C. 175/1971. *Abu-Gush Music Festival v. Minister of Education.*

19. Per Deputy President Moshe Landau in H.C. 112/1977. *Fogel v. Broadcasting Authority.*

20. Foundation of Law, 5740–1980, in *Laws of the State of Israel* 34 (1979–80).

21. For further discussion see Asher Maoz, "The System of Government in Israel."

22. Cf. Negbi, *Above the Law,* p. 84 (Hebrew).

23. Aharon Barak, "Freedom of Speech in Israel," p. 248.

24. H.C. 73/1953; 87/1953. *Kol-Ha'am v. Minister of the Interior.* A translation of the case can be found in *Selected Judgments of the Supreme Court of*

Israel, Vol. I, (1948–53), pp. 90–124. For thorough discussions of this case see Pnina Lahav, "American Influence on Israel's Jurisprudence of Free Speech," and A. E. Shapiro, "Self-Restraint of the Supreme Court and the Preservation of Civil Liberties" (Hebrew, with summary in English).

25. A similar article was published in the party's Arabic newspaper *Al-Ittihad.*

26. The two other members of the court, Justices Yoel Sussman and Moshe Landau, did not submit separate written opinions.

27. The Declaration of Independence states, "The State of Israel . . . will be based on the foundations of freedom, justice and peace as envisaged by the prophets of Israel; it will uphold complete equality of social and political rights to all its citizens irrespective of religion, race or sex; it will guarantee freedom of religion, conscience, language, education and culture; it will safe-guard the Holy Places of all religions."

28. Cf. President Moshe Smoira in H.C 10/1948. *Ziv v. Gubernik.*

29. Prime Minister David Ben-Gurion rejected the demand of the Commu-nist party to include this right in the Declaration. He said, "This is not a con-stitution; in the matter of constitution we will have . . . a separate meeting" (*Protocols of the State Provisional Council,* Vol. I [14 May 1948], pp. 11–23).

30. Justice Shimon Agranat was very much under the influence of the Amer-ican legal system. He transplanted many of its principles to Israeli jurispru-dence. Cf. Lahav, "American Influence on Israel's Jurisprudence of Free Speech," passim.

31. Cf. *Pierce v. United States* 252 U.S. 239 (1920); *Schaefer v. United States* 251 U.S. 466 (1920); *Gitlow v. N.Y.* 268 U.S. 652 (1925).

32. Compare to Z. Chafee's fierce attack on the bad tendency test in his *Free Speech in the United States,* chaps. 1, 2.

33. Justice Agranat looked at the *Shorter Oxford Dictionary,* where the term *likely* is defined as "seeming as if it would happen . . . probable . . . giving promise of success . . . come near to do or be"; and the term *probable* is "that may reasonably be expected to happen."

34. Judge Learned Hand was the originator of this formula in *United States v. Dennis* 183 F. 2d 201 (1950). Chief Justice Vinson adopted it in *Dennis v. United States* 341 U.S. 494 (1951).

35. The clear and present danger test was formulated by Justice Holmes in *Schenck* (1919), stating, "The question in every case is whether the words are used in such circumstances and are of such a nature as to create a clear and present danger that they will bring about the substantive evils that Congress has a right to prevent" (at 52). It was further developed by Justice Brandeis in *Whitney v. California* 274 U.S. 357 (1927).

36. The balancing approach weighs societal and individual interests against

each other. It first appeared in majority opinions of the American Supreme Court in the late 1930s and early 1940s. During the 1950s this approach was established as a rival to the clear and present danger test. See *American Communication Association v. Douds* 339 U.S. 382 (1950). Nowadays balancing analysis is quite ingrained in all areas of constitutional law. For further discussion, see T. Alexander Aleinikoff, "Constitutional Law in the Age of Balancing," esp. pp. 943–45.

37. The preferred position doctrine held that freedom of speech is a vital medium through which the public interest is pursued and hence is entitled to exceptionally rigorous judicial protection. The doctrine was enunciated by Justice Stone in *United States v. Carolene Products Co.* 304 U.S. 144 (1938), fn. 4. See also *Jones v. Opelika* 316 U.S. 584 (1942); *Murdock v. Pennsylvania* 319 U.S. 105 (1943); and *Thomas v. Collins* 323 U.S. 516 (1945).

38. Cf. 341 U.S. at 544, where Justice Frankfurter said, "[T]here is underlying validity in the distinction between advocacy and the interchange of ideas." He acknowledged that such a distinction could be used unreasonably by those in power against hostile or unorthodox views.

39. *Gitlow v. New York* 268 U.S. 652 (1925).

40. *Yates v. United States* 354 U.S. 298 (1957).

41. *Brandenburg v. Ohio* 395 U.S. 444, 447 (1969). See also *Kingsley Int. Pictures Co. v. Regents of the University of New York,* where the court ruled, "Advocacy of conduct proscribed by law is not . . . a justification for denying free speech where the advocacy falls short of incitement and there is nothing to indicate that the advocacy would be immediately acted on" (360 U.S. 684, 1959, at 689).

42. H.C. 253/1964. *Sabri Jeryis v. Haifa District Commissioner* (at 675).

43. Justice Zvi Berenson concurred, saying that he had nothing to add to his colleagues' judgments.

44. H.C. 241/1960. *Kardosh v. Registrar of Companies;* Further Hearing (F.H.) 16/1961. *Registrar of Companies v. Kardosh;* Criminal Appeal (Cr.A.) 126/1962. *Dissenchik and Others v. Attorney General;* H.C. 243/1962. *Film Studios v. Geri.*

45. Cf. Lahav, "American Influence on Israel's Jurisprudence of Free Speech," pp. 66–67.

46. Election Appeal (E. A.) 1/1965. *Yeredor v. Chairperson of the Central Committee for the Elections to the Sixth Knesset.*

47. The Knesset Elections Law (Consolidated Version) 5729–1969 empowers the CEC to supervise the elections process. This committee is a political body comprising all parties represented in the Knesset in proportion to their power. It is chaired by a judge of the supreme court.

48. Justice Aharon Barak criticizes President Agranat for taking this approach. See his "President Agranat," esp. p. 142 (Hebrew).

49. Ruth Gavison, "Twenty Years to Yeredor Ruling," pp. 146, 170 (Hebrew).

50. This notion is discussed by Shlomo Guberman in "Israel's Supra-Constitution," pp. 455–60.

51. Popper fails to distinguish between *preaching* and *inciting,* as the Millian theory and American jurisprudence do. I return to this issue in the epilogue (chap. 13).

52. Popper, *The Open Society and Its Enemies,* 1:265. Cf. part I, chap. 2 *supra.*

53. Onora O'Neill, in "Lifeboat Earth," in *International Ethics,* explains in a similar fashion, "The right of self-defence which is a corollary of the right not to be killed is a right to take action to prevent killings. If I have a right not to be killed then I have a right to prevent others from endangering my life, though I may endanger their lives in so doing only if that is the only available way to prevent the danger to my own life. Similarly, if another has the right not to be killed then I should, if possible, do something to prevent others from endangering his life, but I may endanger their lives in so doing only if that is the only available way to prevent the danger to his life. This duty to defend others is *not* a general duty of beneficence but a very restricted duty to enforce others' rights not to be killed" (p. 263, italics O'Neill's).

54. Positivists would be inclined to call this approach the judicial legislation approach.

55. The law grants formal powers to the committee; section 6 of the Basic Law: The Knesset (1958) sets out only two prerequisites for candidacy to the Knesset—Israeli citizenship and an age of at least twenty-one. All Israeli candidates who are twenty-one years of age or over enjoy the right to be elected unless a court has deprived them of that right by virtue of some law. The Knesset Elections Law (Consolidated Version) 5729–1969 provides some additional technical requirements, like a specified number of signatures, a deposit of a sum of money, etc.

56. However, Justice Haim Cohn in his article "Faithful Interpretation in Three Senses" defends the duty of the judge to interpret the law on occasion in a way that is contradictory to its phrasing. This is in order to advance the "spirit of justice." He even asserts, referring to the majority decision in *Yeredor,* that the judge owes loyalty to the principles on which the democratic regime is founded (p. 6).

57. Ronald M. Dworkin, "The Model of Rules." Later, in "Law's Ambitions for Itself," Dworkin makes a distinction between the positive law and "the full law," urging judges to reject positivism and instead adopt "the interpretive model."

58. Arguably Justice Cohn did not think that a legislative lacuna occurred at

all. The legislature intended to provide *only* formal grounds for disqualification, and so it did.

59. Cf. Barak, *Judicial Discretion,* pp. 165, 307; and "Judicial Legislation," p. 36. Dworkin does accept some of the components of the declarative model (known also as the "phonograph theory"), as formulated by Montesquieu, *The Spirit of Laws* (1823) and William Blackstone, *Commentaries on the Law of England* (1979). Dworkin's theory, however, especially as it comes into expression in *Law's Empire,* better fits the creative interpretation approach.

60. Dworkin, "Hard Cases," p. 1063.

61. Dworkin, *Law's Empire,* p. 229.

62. Ibid., p. 243; see also pp. 87–113, 400–413. In a more recent essay ("Unenumerated Rights: Whether and How *Roe* Should be Overruled?") Dworkin clarifies that integrity in law insists that judicial decision be a matter of principle, not compromise nor strategy or political accommodation. He maintains that integrity holds "vertically and horizontally." By "vertically," Dworkin means that a judge who claims a particular right of liberty as fundamental must show that his or her claim is consistent with the bulk of precedent, and with the main structures of the constitution. By "horizontally," Dworkin means that a judge who adopts a principle must give full weight to that principle in other cases he or she endorses (pp. 393–94).

63. Ronald M. Dworkin, "Law's Ambitions for Itself," p. 176.

64. Dworkin, "Hard Cases," pp. 1069–70; "Liberalism," in *A Matter of Principle,* pp. 181–204. Cf. part 1, chapter 3 of this book.

65. Dworkin, "Hard Cases," pp. 1057, 1067; see also "Political Judges and the Rule of Law," in *A Matter of Principle,* pp. 9–32.

66. Cf. Dworkin, "Hard Cases," p. 1059.

Chapter 11: Attempts to Restrict Kahane's Freedom of Election

1. H.C. 344/1981. *Negbi v. Central Committee for the Elections to the 10th Knesset.*

2. Cf. *Protocol Number 14 of the CEC,* 17 June 1984, pp. 48–49. See also E. A. 2/1984. *Neiman and Avneri v. Chairman of the Central Committee for the Elections to the 11th Knesset.* P.D. 39 (ii), 238.

3. *Neiman,* at 238.

4. *Protocol Number 14 of the CEC,* p. 11.

5. The language of the law is general. Therefore the term *negates* may cover expressions advocating these ideas and not only those inciting them.

6. In Germany another argument served as grounds for disqualifying the Socialist Reich Party. There it was argued that if a party's internal organization did not correspond to democratic principles, it could be concluded that the

party sought to impose upon the state the structural principles that it had implemented within its own organization. Article 21 provides the grounds for avoiding any repetition of the one-party state that molded the Third Reich. Cf. BVerfGE 2, 1.

7. *Protocol Number 14 of the CEC*, p. 13.

8. International Convention on the Elimination of All Forms of Racial Discrimination, Article 1 (1).

9. *Protocol Number 14 of the CEC*, p. 16.

10. Ibid., p. 26.

11. Ibid., pp. 34–35.

12. Cf. Kahane, *Listen World, Listen Jew*, p. 7; *Uncomfortable Questions for Comfortable Jews*, p. 48.

13. *Protocol Number 14 of the CEC*, p. 39.

14. *Protocol Number 15 of the CEC*, 18 June 1984, pp. 138–40.

15. Section 21 of the covenant declares that the aim of the PLO is to free the *entire* land of Palestine.

16. *Protocol Number 15 of the CEC*, p. 76.

17. The dean of the Tel Aviv law faculty, Amos Shapira, said that the political platform of the PLP did not make any claim against the existence of the state of Israel, and it did not incite people to use violence and terror. The advocacy for establishing a Palestinian state on the West Bank and the Gaza Strip did not supply sufficient grounds for disqualifying it. Cf. Moshe Ronen, "There Is No Place to Disqualify the PLP," *Yedioth Ahronoth* (3 June 1984), p. 3.

18. The *Neiman I* decision of 1984 will be discussed in the next section. The *Neiman II* decision of 1988 and E. A. 2805/1992. *Kach v. Chairperson of the Central Committee for the Elections to the Thirteenth Knesset* will be considered in the epilogue (chap. 13).

19. Section 21 (2) reads, "Parties which, by reason of their aims or the behavior of their adherents, seek to impair or abolish the free democratic basic order or endanger the existence of the Federal Republic of Germany, shall be unconstitutional. The Federal Constitutional Court shall decide on the question of unconstitutionality." Cf. Donald P. Kommers, *The Constitutional Jurisprudence of the Federal Republic of Germany*, p. 222.

20. BVerfGE 2, 1 Sozialistische Reichspartei (23 October 1952); and BVerfGE 5, 85 KPD (17 August 1956).

21. Such a review is rare and occurs only "if the Supreme Court's decision contradicts a previous ruling of the Supreme Court or is a matter of importance, difficulty, or first impression and there is, in their opinion, need for additional review" (sect. 30 [b] of Courts Law. Consolidated Version, 1984). Usually the panel of the court consists of three justices.

22. E. A. 2/1984. *Neiman and Avneri v. Chairperson of the Central Committee for the Elections to the Eleventh Knesset.*

23. However, in December 1989 a mock trial was conducted involving issues of freedom of expression in an imaginary state known as Protonia. Miriam Ben-Porat, who was one of the five justices deciding the case, concurred with the majority who declared that all civil liberties flow from the *universal principles protecting the dignity of persons and their equality,* and that accordingly freedom of speech does not include any right to promote malicious racial incitement.

24. Cf. Claude Klein, "The Defence of the State of Israel and the Democratic Regime in the Supreme Court," p. 404.

25. H.C. 399/1985. *Kahane v. Board of Directors of the Broadcasting Authority.*

26. Studies indicate a positive correlation between education and tolerance. Cf. Samuel Stouffer, *Community, Conformity, and Civil Liberties;* James W. Prothro and Charles M. Grigg, "Fundamental Principles of Democracy"; David G. Lawrence, "Procedural Norms and Tolerance"; John L. Sullivan, James E. Piereson, and George E. Marcus, "A Reconceptualization of Political Tolerance"; and John L. Sullivan, James E. Piereson, George E. Marcus, and Stanley Feldman, "The Sources of Political Tolerance."

27. In England, for example, two statutes from 1797 still exist today: the Incitement to Mutiny Act and the Unlawful Oaths Act, which were enacted out of the fears and anxieties regarding revolutionary activity in the 1790s.

28. This criterion was used by the court in Cr.A. 126/1962. *Dissenchik and others v. Attorney General* (per Justice Sussman); and in Cr.A. 696/1981. *Azulai v. State of Israel.*

29. Cf. H.C. 153/1983. *Levi and Amit v. Southern District Police Commander* (per Justice Barak); and H.C. 292/1983. *Temple Mount Loyalists v. Police Commander of District of Jerusalem* (per Justice Barak).

30. Compare to Learned Hand in *United States v. Dennis* 183 F. 2d 201, 212, C.A. 2d (1950): "In each case [the courts] must ask whether the gravity of the 'evil,' discounted by its improbability, justifies such invasion of free speech as is necessary to avoid the danger." This is also Frederick Schauer's opinion (*Free Speech,* p. 199).

31. Cf. H.C. 58/1968. *Shalit v. the Interior Minister.* Justice Sussman became the president of the court in 1977.

32. Reference was given to Justice Jackson in *Dennis* (at 570).

33. In the current political situation in Israel, three seats can make the difference between a Labor coalition and a Likud coalition. After Kahane's election to the Knesset, polls at some stages showed that if elections were to have been held then, Kahane would have gained eleven seats in the Knesset. Shortly

before the 1988 election, the forecast was that Kach would have three or four mandates.

34. Justice Holmes said, "The ultimate good desired is better reached by free trade in ideas—that the best test of truth is the power of the thought to get itself accepted in the competition of the market, and that truth is the only ground upon which their wishes can be carried out." *Abrams v. United States* 250 U.S. 616 (1919).

35. These arguments are in line with Lee Bollinger's reasoning (cf. part 1, chap. 5, "Grounds for Special Status").

36. A research project conducted by the Van Leer Jerusalem Institute in September 1984 showed that one-third of the youth in the sample held anti-democratic attitudes. Twenty-eight and four-tenths percent said that a strong regime with leaders who were not dependent on parties should be established. Sixty percent thought that the Israeli Arabs should not enjoy full equality of rights, and 42 percent supported the limitation of democracy so as to enable curtailing the civil rights of Arabs. A similar percentage was in favor of the opinions of Kach. Cf. Ehud Sprinzak, *Every Man Whatsoever Is Right in His Own Eyes*, pp. 167–68 (Hebrew). One girl was quoted as saying, "The Jews had a Holocaust in Europe . . . so now there will be holocaust to the Arabs. There is no other possibility. This is what we have" *Yedioth Ahronoth*, 28 June 1985.

37. Negbi, *Above the Law*, pp. 86–95 (Hebrew).

38. Klein, "The Defence of the State of Israel and the Democratic Regime in the Supreme Court," p. 414. The contesting view was that on such an issue concerning the fundamental right to be elected, the court should not use its discretion and resort to the creative approach. Zeev Segal justified the decision, arguing that the court's ruling was right since the court wanted to defend the basic principle of the rule of law. Segal does not address normative considerations, asking what the preferable answer is to the issue at hand. He does not consider the implications of the decision for Israeli society, nor does he ask what the law should be. His concern is with what the court should do in order to safeguard the rule of law. In his opinion, the role of the court is neither to create nor to curtail rights. Its role is only to secure respect for existing rights. Since the only exception in this case, postulated in *Yeredor*, is not relevant, no grounds to extend this ruling exist. Cf. *Israeli Democracy*, p. 83 (Hebrew).

39. Negbi relies on Justice Zvi Berenson in H.C. 287/1969. *Meiron v. The Labour Minister.*

40. It is worth quoting the opinion of President Itzhak Ulshan in H.C. 29/1962. *Shalom Cohen v. Minister of Defence:* "Sometimes the feeling of justice and the desire to make justice tempt [the court to enlarge its authority]. But if the 'rule of law' principle is not vain talk there is a must to overcome

this temptation . . . (at 1029). There is an authority to give assistance for justice when the law provides some basis. Authority cannot be based merely on the reflections of the judge, however noble they might be."

41. Barak, "Freedom of Speech in Israel," p. 248.

42. At the time of the Gulf War (January–February 1991), Israel was once again in a state of war, living under continuous missile attacks, although it was said not to be involved in the war.

43. Ronald M. Dworkin calls this theory of adjudication "a naturalist approach" (cf. "'Natural' Law Revisited," pp. 165–88).

44. H.C. 483/1986. *Aloni Member of Knesset and Others v. Minister of Justice;* and M.A. (Miscellaneous Application) 298/1986. *Citrin and Nvo v. Disciplinary Court.*

45. Cf. *Glimmerveen and Hagenbeek v/the Netherlands* (1980). *Decisions and Reports* 18 European Community H.R., pp. 187–208.

46. References were given to H.C. 442/1971. *Lanski v. Minister of the Interior;* and to H.C. 297/1982. *Berger v. Minister of the Interior.*

47. Judges in countries that lack a written constitution are apparently more careful when facing political matters than their colleagues in countries with a written constitution. More similarities occur between Israeli and British judges than between Israeli and American judges. Israeli and British judges try to leave political decisions in the hands of the legislature, whereas American judges see law as a positive instrument of national policy and thus have less hesitation in dealing with political matters. On this issue see H. Street, *Freedom, the Individual, and the Law,* esp. pp. 290–95.

Chapter 12: Curtailing Kahane's Freedom of Movement and Expression

1. Testimony by Commander Karty. 100 *Divrei Haknesset* (Knesset Proceedings), 11 Knesset. 36th meeting. (25 December 1984), p. 885.

2. H.C. 587/1984. *Kahane v. Minister of Police and the Inspector General.* The case was never published. I was able to trace it thanks to Commander Hana Hirsch of the Israeli police.

3. Knesset Members (Immunity, Rights, and Duties) Law, 5711–1951. Section 9 (a) states, "A direction prohibiting or restricting access to any place within the State other than private property shall not apply to a member of the Knesset unless the prohibition or restriction is motivated by considerations of State security or military secrecy."

4. *Al-Hamishmar,* 20 November 1984. See also Yair Kotler, *Heil Kahane,* pp. 287–92 (Hebrew).

5. The other member of Knesset was Edna Soloder from the Labor Party. Kahane called them S.S. (Sarid-Soloder).

6. I have reservations regarding this statement. Kahane's ideas, rather than Kahane himself, were established in Israel. Kahane the person remained, until the last day of his life, quite an alienated figure.

7. 100 *Divrei Haknesset,* 11 Knesset. 36th meeting. (25 December 1984), pp. 885–905.

8. H.C. 43/1985. *Kahane v. Knesset House Committee* (from 1 April 1985). The case was not published. Here I acknowledge gratitude to Mr. Zvi Inbari, the Knesset.

9. In an interview done a few years later, Kahane was asked why he was engaged in activities such as visiting Taibe and Umm El-Fahm. He answered that his aim was to scare the inhabitants and to make them realize that time was not on their side, that they had to leave immediately. See Mergui and Simonnot, *Israel's Ayatollahs,* p. 50.

10. Under the Harm Principle (*argument number one*) any speech that incites the causing of physical harm to designated individuals or groups ought to be curtailed (cf. chap. 7, "The Millian Arguments").

11. On 24 September 1984 Kahane appealed to the court against the Israeli police because they refused to give Kach a license for holding an assembly in one of the parks in Jerusalem. Finally the license was granted, and Kach withdrew its appeal. Kahane appealed again on the same grounds in November 1985, after his request to hold an assembly in a public place in the city of Beer-Sheba was denied. The appeal was withdrawn after the permission was granted.

12. Section 6 of the Police Ordinance permits the police to refuse a license to hold a demonstration if, among other things, a reasonable basis exists to suspect that it will involve criminal offenses such as rioting (in contravention of sect. 152 of the Penal Law), incitement to rebellion (in contravention of sect. 133 of the same law), or incitement to any other offense (in contravention of sect. 34 of the same law).

13. In Britain a similar ban is placed on members of the IRA.

14. Not long ago Channel 2 was also established under the supervision of the Broadcasting Authority. Nowadays, a cable system is run by private initiators.

15. H.C. 399/1985. *Kahane v. Board of Directors of the Broadcasting Authority.* A summary of the case appears in *Israel Law Review* 23 (1989), pp. 515–17.

16. J. A. Barron, *Freedom of the Press For Whom?* p. xiii.

17. *Whitney v. California* 274 U.S. 357 (1927); *Red Lion Broadcasting Co. v. FCC* 395 U.S. 367 (1969); *Columbia Broadcasting v. Democratic Comm.* 412 U.S. 84 (1973).

18. Cf. Cr.A. 255/1968. *State of Israel v. Ben-Moshe;* H.C. 153/1983. *Levi and Amit v. Southern District Police Commander;* H.C. 14/1986. *Laor v. Censure Council of Films and Plays.*

19. *Abrams v. United States* 250 U.S. 616 (1919), at 630.

20. One of the items presented in the broadcast was the result of research showing that 3 percent of the population wanted Kahane to become prime minister and 26 percent demanded that he should take part in the leadership in accordance with his power in the Knesset. Still, 51 percent asserted that "the man and his movement should not take part in anything" (cf. *Ha'aretz*, 15 October 1985).

21. Quoted by Kahane in complaint about the persecution he suffered. See *Uncomfortable Questions for Comfortable Jews*, p. 290.

22. Cf. Reuven Pedhatzur, "It Is Agreed Upon that Some of Rabbi Kahane's Activities Endanger the Citizens of the State," *Ha'aretz*, 5 March 1985.

23. H.C. 73/1985. *Kach v. Speaker of the Knesset*.

24. Resolutions from 20 March 1967 and from 30 July 1979.

25. H.C. 652/1981. *Yossi Sarid v. Speaker of the Knesset, Savidor*, at 203.

26. For further discussion of this case, see Menachem Kanafi, "A Digest of Selected Judgments of the Supreme Court of Israel," pp. 219–24.

27. H.C. 742/1984. *Kahane v. the Presidium of the Knesset* (at 89).

28. Article 134 (b) reads, "A member wishing to exercise his right to initiate a bill shall present it to the Speaker of the Knesset and the Speaker of the Knesset and the deputies, *after they certify the bill*, will lay it on the table of the Knesset" (italics mine).

29. H.C. 652/1981. *Yossi Sarid Member of Knesset v. Speaker of the Knesset, Savidor*; Application for Leave to Appeal (A.L.A.) 166/1984. *Tomchey Tmimim Mercasit Yeshiva v. State of Israel*; H.C. 73/1985. *Kach v. Speaker of the Knesset*.

30. Klein, in "The Defence of the State of Israel and the Democratic Regime in the Supreme Court," p. 417, questions the logic of this decision and asks whether it means that the Presidium would be able to reject the same bills if they were tabled by a list that did not originally present a policy containing racist and antidemocratic principles and thus did not have any difficulty in being registered. He concludes, "Such a distinction would not make sense; nevertheless, it is the logical result of the [court's] reasoning."

31. Section 134 (C) of the House Rules.

32. H.C. 306/1985. *Kahane v. the Presidium of the Knesset*.

33. Those claims were rejected by distinguished scholars who argued that the laws included partial quotations that did not truly reflect Maimonides' views and that, in any event, were not applicable to current reality.

34. H.C. 669/1985; 24/1986; 131/1986. *Kahane v. the Presidium of the Knesset*.

35. David Kretzmer, "Judicial Review of Knesset Decisions," p. 137.

36. H.C. 400/1987. *Kahane v. Speaker of the Knesset*.

37. Section 14 of Basic Law: The Knesset.

38. As a matter of fact, Kahane had made the same statement already in August 1984, in a telephone interview with *The New York Times*.

39. In accordance with section 16 of Basic Law: The Knesset, which provides that so long as the representative will not make the oath as required, the representative will not enjoy the rights of member of the Knesset.

40. Cf. President Moshe Smoira in H.C. 29/1952. *St. Vincent de Paul Monastery v. Tel-Aviv City Council*.

41. H.C. 202/1957. *Seedis v. the President and Members of the Rabbinical High Court*.

42. Compare to *Albertson v. Millard*, 106 F. Supp. 635 (1952), where an American court ruled that the state had no duty to permit Albertson to run for Congress on a communist ticket when he could not, in good faith, take the statutory oath "to protect and defend the Constitution of the United States" (at 644). Accordingly, we may think that room existed for another application for judicial review, that of the Speaker of the Knesset against Kahane, who clearly sought ways of bypassing the rules of the Knesset. A complaint against Kahane for deception could have been made if legal grounds were to be found. However, Basic Law: The Knesset (1958) does not include a section that provides grounds for contempt of the Knesset. This precedent shows that the Knesset should try to resolve this issue through legislation, as it did with regard to the issue of the submitting of bills.

Chapter 13: Epilogue

1. Sections 144 (A-E) of Penal Law, Amendment No. 20 (1986).

2. Compare to, for example, France, Canada, and Sweden, where specific laws speak of discrimination on religious grounds. Cf. Law (No. 72-546 of 1972) on Combating Racism in France; section 15(1) of the Canadian Charter of Rights and Freedoms (1982); and Chap. 16, section 8 of the Swedish Criminal Code (1982). See also the International Covenant on Civil and Political Rights of 1966, which provides in Article 20(2) that "any advocacy of national, racial, or religious hatred that constitutes incitement to discrimination, hostility, or violence shall be prohibited by law."

3. The enactment was approved in a fifty-seven-to-twenty-two decision, and among its supporters was Kahane, against whom the law was aimed. Cf. *Divrei* (Proceedings of) *Haknesset*, 11th Knesset, Vol. 105 (5 August 1986), at 4029.

4. Compare, for example, to the French Law on Combating Racism, which speaks of inciting to racism, but which also speaks of discrimination against individuals.

5. Chap. 16, section 8 of the Swedish Criminal Code (amended in 1982)

reads, "Anyone who publicly or otherwise in a declaration or other statement which is disseminated to the public threatens or expresses contempt for an ethnic group or some similar group of persons, with allusion to race, color, national or ethnic origin or religious creed, shall be sentenced for agitation against ethnic groups by imprisonment of up to two years or, if the crime is petty, to a fine."

6. For further discussion of this amendment see Eliezer Lederman and Mala Tabory, "Criminalization of Racial Incitement in Israel," pp. 55–84. The authors express three main concerns with regard to it: first, they argue, the criminal law may not be the proper means for regulating racist behavior. Second, limiting freedom of expression causes uneasiness, especially where the regulation takes the form of criminal sanctions. Third, some religious groups voiced reservations that the criminalization of racial incitement "might cast shadows on certain religious writings and prayers."

7. Section 11 (d) of the Knesset Members Law, 5711–1951 states, "Any letter sent by Member of the Knesset from the Knesset building to anywhere in the country is free of charge."

8. 107 *Divrei Haknesset* (1987), pp. 1920–25.

9. Basic Law: The Knesset. Amendment No. 9. 1155 *Sefer Hachukim* (1985).

10. H.C. 253/1964. *Sabri Jeryis v. Haifa District Commissioner* (at 679). Cf. chap. 10, *supra*.

11. *Protocol no. 19 of the CEC* (7 October 1988), pp. 8–10.

12. *Protocol no. 18 of the CEC* (6 October 1988), pp. 2–13.

13. Ibid., pp. 38–39.

14. E.A. 2/1988. *Ben-Shalom and Others v. the Central Committee for the Elections to the 12th Knesset.*

15. After Kach had been banned by the CEC and was awaiting the decision of the High Court of Justice, Kahane was asked whether he would like to have one hour of public legitimacy. His answer was that he did have legitimacy, that he did not seek love but truth. On the question of whether he would accept any decision of the court, whatever this might be, he answered positively, saying that he kept the law, "at least in order to get to a position of power. The leftists cannot use the claim of breaching the law against me." Cf. Ronit Vardi, "Kahane Is Waiting in the Corner," *Yedioth Ahronoth,* 14 October 1988.

16. E.A. 1/1988. *Neiman and Kach v. Chairperson of the Central Committee for the Elections to the 12th Knesset.*

17. Kahane repeatedly said that it was impossible to accuse him of racism or to compare him with the "monster of Germany" since he recognized the absolute right of any Arab, through proper Jewish conversion, to become as good a Jew as anyone so born; he agreed to the right of any non-Jew, including an Arab, who accepted a status of "alien resident," to remain in the land with full

personal rights; and since he never even remotely called for the deliberate, premeditated killing of Arabs.

18. Penal Laws of Austria (Sections 283 and 302); Bulgaria (Section 196); Denmark (Section 266B); Finland (Chapter 13[5]); France (Section 72–545).

19. *Yates v. United States* 354 U.S. 298 (1957). See also *Gitlow v. New York* (1925).

20. Cf. Gavison, "Twenty Years to Yeredor Ruling," p. 188.

21. The period after the election of Kahane to the Knesset was quite good for the research institutes. The media, in its anxiety over Kahanism, closely followed the development of the phenomenon, with the effect that almost every month at least one newspaper ordered a poll on the society's reaction to Kahane, his ideas and activities.

22. The study was conducted by Dr. Binyamini from the Hebrew University (cf. *Yedioth Ahronoth,* 20 March 1985). A later study from June 1985 showed that 40 percent of the youth supported Kahane or opinions that Kahane advocated (cf. *Ha'aretz,* 6 June 1985, p. 1).

23. *Ha'aretz,* 12 June 1987, p. 3. The research was conducted by "Dahaf."

24. *Davar,* 14 April 1986.

25. Polls that were held between January and June 1985 showed that if elections were to be held, Kach would receive five seats. From August through September 1985, the forecast was eleven (!) mandates to Kach. In March 1986 the forecast went down to three mandates, and it was steady until September 1988, just before the elections to the Twelfth Knesset took place, when the forecast indicated at least three seats to Kach.

26. The months between July and October 1985 were saturated with terrorist incidents in Israel and abroad. In July, two teachers were murdered and another citizen killed in Nablus. In August, a citizen was murdered in Tul-Karem. In September, three Israelis were assassinated in Cyprus. In October, seven Israeli tourists were killed by an Egyptian soldier in Sinai. Two days later there was the Achilla-Lauro incident (7 October 1985). Another day passed and a soldier opened fire on Jewish prayers in Tunis; and on 9 October, two Israeli sailors were assassinated in Barcelona.

27. *Yedioth Ahronoth,* 2 September 1985.

28. On the impact of the Intifada on Israel and the Palestinian population see my article, "The Intifada: Causes, Consequences, and Future Trends."

29. In the last decade, a poll has been conducted every year to reflect on the extent to which democratic values are rooted in Israeli society. The results have repeatedly showed that some 30 percent of the Jewish population hold antidemocratic views. The Intifada led to a significant change, with the effect that in January 1990, 45 percent expressed willingness to have "strong leadership that will not be dependent on elections."

30. Some people from the left explicitly advocate disobeying the law on conscientious grounds in response to the demand to serve in the occupied territories or in Lebanon. Members of this group, *Yesh Gvul* ("There Is a Limit"), do not resort to violence and certainly do not advocate discrimination. But, like rightist extremists, they argue that some values stand beyond the law. By adhering to this claim, they help to undermine the rule of law and order in Israel. Cf. Itzhak Zamir, "Boundaries of Obedience to Law," (Hebrew).

31. Dov Goldstein, "Democracy Goes Bankrupt," *Maariv,* 25 January 1990; and Itzhak Ben-Horin, "Democracy Goes Down," *Maariv,* 10 February 1990.

32. Interestingly enough, *zeev* in Hebrew means "wolf," but his popular nickname is Gandhi.

33. Kahane gained the support of the poor and deprived classes of society, while we can assume that the votes for Gandhi came from people of the middle class. Cf. Gershon Shafir and Yoav Peled, "'Thorns in Your Eyes . . .'" pp. 115–29 (Hebrew).

34. A study conducted by the newspaper *Maariv* (13 January 1986) revealed that 42 percent of the population thought that the Arabs should be induced to leave Israel. Another piece of research from June 1988 showed that 41 percent of Jewish citizens supported the idea of transfer. The research also indicated that 27 percent of high school pupils declared their intention to emigrate; and 45 percent thought that Israel was *too* democratic (cf. Amos Keinan, "41%, 45%, 27%," *Yedioth Ahronoth,* 10 June 1988). But much depends on the phrasing of the question. *Yedioth Ahronoth* reported on 16 November 1990 that 20 percent supported the transfer.

35. *Protocol No. 20 of the CEC.* (9 October 1988), pp. 23–27.

36. There is a hidden agenda as well, revealed in discussions with political activists of Moledet. In private communications they emphasize the need to get rid of the Arabs, to transfer them by whatever means. The idea of consent is not prominent and it seems that they view it as necessary for reasons of propaganda and pragmatism in phrasing.

37. *Protocol Number 20 of the CEC,* pp. 33–53.

38. As these lines are written, President De Klerk is still facing problems in his efforts to lead his country from the darkness of apartheid to a liberal form of democracy.

39. The Penal Law deals with punishing individuals for deeds they have done, whereas section 7A deals with defending democracy by preventing future damage that the list in question might cause to the framework of Israel.

40. Ronald Dworkin, "What Rights Do We Have?" in *Taking Rights Seriously,* pp. 272–73; and "Liberalism," in *A Matter of Principle,* p. 190. See also John H. Schaar, "Equality of Opportunity and Beyond," pp. 151–52.

41. Cf. Herman R. Van Gunsteren, "Admission to Citizenship." See also Marshall's classic essay, *Citizenship and Social Class* (1950).

42. The vast majority of Arabs in Israel define themselves as Palestinians.

43. A research project in July 1987 showed that 50 percent of the Jewish population were unwilling to regard the Israeli-Arabs as equal citizens (Eli Tavor, "Israel is too democratic," *Yedioth Ahronoth*, 20 March 1988). Another piece of research from June 1989 revealed that 45 percent of the Israeli-Arabs did not feel "at home" in Israel; 69 percent said that discrimination against Arabs occurred frequently. Only 35 percent of the Israeli-Jews thought the same.

44. Cf. Zeev Sheef and Ehud Yaari, *Intifada*, pp. 215–17 (Hebrew).

45. Itzhak Ben-Horin, "Democracy Goes Down," *Maariv*, 10 February 1990.

46. Cf. E.A. 2805/1992. *Kach v. Chairperson of the Central Committee for the Elections to the 13th Knesset.* President Shamgar, concurring, stressed again that the decision of whether lists ought to be disqualified should be made by a judicial instance, remote from partisan political considerations. The other three justices, Netanyahu, Or, and Matza, concurred without submitting separate opinions.

47. Cf. E.A. 2858/1992. *Movshovitz and Kahane Is Alive Movement v. Chairperson of the Central Committee for the Elections to the 13th Knesset.* The other four justices, D. Levin, Netanyahu, Or, and Matza, joined with their colleague without submitting separate opinions.

Selected Bibliography

Sources in English

Ackerman, Bruce A. 1980. *Social Justice in the Liberal State*. New Haven and London: Yale University Press.

Aleinikoff, T. Alexander. 1987. "Constitutional Law in the Age of Balancing." *Yale Law Journal* 96, no. 5:943–1005.

Amdur, Robert. 1985. "Harm, Offense, and the Limits of Liberty." *Harvard Law Review* 98, no. 8:1946–59.

Arendt, Hannah. 1969. "Truth and Politics." In P. Laslett and W. G. Runciman, eds., *Philosophy, Politics, and Society*, pp. 104–33. Oxford: Blackwell.

Arneson, Richard J. 1989. "Introduction." *Ethics*, 99, no. 4:695–710.

Baker, C. Edwin. 1989. *Human Liberty and Freedom of Speech*. New York: Oxford University Press.

Baker, Henry E. 1961. *The Legal System of Israel*. Tel Aviv: Steimatzky's Agency.

Barak, Aharon. 1987. *Judicial Discretion*. New Haven and London: Yale University Press.

———. 1988. "Freedom of Speech in Israel: The Impact of the American Constitution." *Tel Aviv University Studies in Law*. 8:241–48.

Barendt, Eric. 1987. *Freedom of Speech*. Oxford: Clarendon Press.

Barron, J. A. 1973. *Freedom of the Press for Whom: The Right of Access to Mass Media*. Bloomington: Indiana University Press.

Benn, Stanley I. 1988. *A Theory of Freedom*. Cambridge, England: Cambridge University Press.

Bentham, Jeremy. 1970. *An Introduction to the Principles of Morals and Legislation*. London: Athlone Press and University of London.

Berlin, Isaiah. 1967. "Two Concepts of Liberty." In Anthony Quinton, ed., *Political Philosophy*, pp. 141–52. Oxford: Oxford University Press.

———. 1980. *Concepts and Categories*. Oxford: Oxford University Press.

BeVier, Lillian R. 1978. "The First Amendment and Political Speech: An Inquiry into the Substance and Limits of Principle." *Stanford Law Review* 30, no. 2:299–358.

Black, Hugo L. 1960. "The Bill of Rights." *New York University Law Review.* 35:865–81.

Blackstone, William. 1979. *Commentaries on the Law of England.* 4 vols. Chicago and London: The University of Chicago Press.

Bollinger, Lee C. 1986. *The Tolerant Society.* Oxford: Clarendon Press.

Bork, Robert H. 1971. "Neutral Principles and Some First Amendment Problems." *Indiana Law Journal.* 47, no. 1:1–35.

Brandt, R. B. 1964. "The Concepts of Obligation and Duty." *Mind* 73:374–93.

Buchanan, Allen E. 1989. "Assessing the Communitarian Critique of Liberalism." *Ethics* 99, no. 4:852–82.

Campbell, C. A. 1967. *In Defence of Free Will.* London: Allen & Unwin.

Campbell, Colin. 1982. "A Dubious Distinction? An Inquiry into the Value and Use of Merton's Concepts of Manifest and Latent Functions." *American Sociology Review* 47, no. 1:29–44.

Chafee, Zechariah. 1946. *Free Speech in the United States.* Cambridge, Mass.: Harvard University Press.

———. 1949. "Meiklejohn: Free Speech and Its Relation to Self-Government." *Harvard Law Review* 62:891–901.

Chisholm, Roderick M. 1982. "Human Freedom and the Self." In Gary Watson, ed., *Free Will,* pp. 24–35. Oxford: Oxford University Press.

Cohen-Almagor, Raphael. 1991. "The Intifada: Causes, Consequences and Future Trends." *Small Wars and Insurgencies* 2, no. 1:12–40.

Connolly, William E. 1983. *The Terms of Political Discourse.* Oxford: Martin Robertson.

De Marneffe, Peter. 1990. "Liberalism, Liberty, and Neutrality." *Philosophy and Public Affairs* 19, no. 3:253–74.

Devlin, Patrick. 1965. *The Enforcement of Morals.* Oxford: Oxford University Press.

Dewey, John. 1939. *Freedom and Culture.* New York: G. P. Putnam's Sons.

Directives of the Attorney General on the Matter of Administrative Detention. 1983. *Israel Law Review* 18, no. 1:150–59.

Directives of the Attorney General on the Matter of the Freedom to Demonstrate. 1983. *Israel Law Review* 18, nos. 3–4:511–24.

Dolgin, Janet L. 1977. *Jewish Identity and the JDL.* Princeton, N.J.: Princeton University Press.

Doppelt, Gerald. 1989. "Is Rawls's Kantian Liberalism Coherent and Defensible?" *Ethics* 99, no. 4:815–51.

Dorsen, Norman. 1988. "Is There a Right to Stop Offensive Speech? The Case of the Nazis at Skokie." In Larry Gostin, ed., *Civil Liberties in Conflict,* 122–35. London and New York: Routledge.

Douglas, William O. 1958. *The Right of the People.* New York: Doubleday.

Downie, R. S., and Elizabeth Telfer. 1969. *Respect for Persons*. London: George Allen and Unwin.

Downs, Donald Alexander. 1985. *Nazis in Skokie*. Notre Dame, Ind.: University of Notre Dame Press.

Dworkin, Gerald. 1988. *The Theory and Practice of Autonomy*. Cambridge, England: Cambridge University Press.

Dworkin, Ronald M. 1967. "The Model of Rules." *University of Chicago Law Review* 35, no. 14:14–46.

———. 1975. "Hard Cases." *Harvard Law Review* 88, no. 6:1057–1109.

———. 1977. *Taking Rights Seriously*. London: Duckworth.

———. 1978. "No Right Answer?" *New York University Law Review* 53, no. 1:1–32.

———. 1981. "What Is Equality? Part 2: Equality of Resources." *Philosophy and Public Affairs* 10:283–345.

———. 1982. "'Natural' Law Revisited." *University of Florida Law Review* 35, no. 2:165–88.

———. 1983a. "In Defence of Equality." *Social Philosophy and Policy* 1:24–40.

———. 1983b. "What Liberalism Isn't." *The New York Review of Books* 29, nos. 21–22:47–50.

———. 1983c. "Why Liberals Should Believe in Equality?" *The New York Review of Books* 30, no. 1:32–34.

———. 1985a. *A Matter of Principle*. Oxford: Clarendon Press.

———. 1985b. "Law's Ambitions for Itself." *Virginia Law Review* 71, no. 2:173–87.

———. 1986. *Law's Empire*. Cambridge, Mass.: Harvard University Press.

———. 1992. "Unenumerated Rights: Whether and How *Roe* Should be Overruled?" *The University of Chicago Law Review* 59, no. 1:381–432.

———, ed. 1977. *The Philosophy of Law*. Oxford: Oxford University Press.

Emerson, Thomas I. 1966. *Toward a General Theory of the First Amendment*. New York: Random House.

———. 1970. *The System of Freedom of Expression*. New York: Random House.

———. 1980. "First Amendment Doctrine and the Burger Court." *California Law Review* 68, no. 3:422–81.

Feinberg, Joel. 1984. *Harm to Others*. New York: Oxford University Press.

———. 1985. *Offense to Others*. New York: Oxford University Press.

Fisk, Milton. 1975. "History and Reason in Rawls' Moral Theory." In Norman Daniels, ed., *Reading Rawls*, pp. 53–80. Oxford: Blackwell.

Fiss, Owen M. 1986. "Free Speech and Social Structure." *Iowa Law Review* 71:1405–25.

Frankfurt, Harry G. 1982. "Freedom of the Will and the Concept of a Person." In Gary Watson, ed., *Free Will*, pp. 81–95. Oxford: Oxford University Press.

Friedman, Robert I. 1990. *The False Prophet.* London: Faber and Faber.

Galston, William A. 1989. "Pluralism and Social Unity." *Ethics* 99, no. 4:711–26.

Gavison, Ruth. 1985. "The Controversy over Israel's Bill of Rights." *Israel Yearbook of Human Rights* 15:113–54.

Gibson, James L., and Richard D. Bingham. 1985. *Civil Liberties and Nazis.* New York: Praeger.

Glass, Marvin. 1978. "Anti-Racism and Unlimited Freedom of Speech: An Untenable Dualism." *Canadian Journal of Philosophy* 8, no. 3:559–75.

Gray, John. 1983. *Mill on Liberty: A Defence.* London: Routledge & Kegan Paul.

Greenawalt, Kent. 1989. *Speech, Crime and the Uses of Language.* New York: Oxford University Press.

Guberman, Shlomo. 1967. "Israel's Supra-Constitution." *Israel Law Review* 2, no. 4:455–60.

Haiman, Franklin S. 1981. *Speech and Law in a Free Society.* Chicago and London: University of Chicago Press.

Haksar, Vinit. 1973. "Autonomy, Justice and Contractarianism." *British Journal of Political Science* 3:487–509.

———. 1979. *Equality, Liberty, and Perfectionism.* Oxford: Oxford University Press.

Hampton, Jean. 1989. "Should Political Philosophy Be Done without Metaphysics?" *Ethics* 99, no. 4:791–814.

Hart, H. L. A. 1963. *Law, Liberty, and Morality.* London: Oxford University Press.

Hayek, F. A. 1951. *J. S. Mill and Harriet Taylor.* London: Routledge and Kegan Paul.

———. 1987. "Individual and Collective Aims." In Susan Mendus and David Edwards, eds., *On Toleration,* pp. 35–47. Oxford: Clarendon Press.

Hillel, Naomi. 1989. "A Digest of Selected Judgments of the Supreme Court of Israel." *Israel Law Review* 23, no. 4:506–56.

Hollis, Martin. 1977. *Models of Man.* Cambridge, England: Cambridge University Press.

Holmes, O. W. 1887. *The Common Law.* London: Macmillan.

———. 1897. "The Path of the Law." *Harvard Law Review* 10, no. 8:457–78.

Home Office [of Great Britain]. 1980. *Review of Public Order Act 1936* (Green Paper).

———. 1985. *Review of Public Order Law.* Cmmd. 9510 (White Paper).

Horton, John, and Susan Mendus, eds. 1985. *Aspects of Toleration.* New York: Methuen.

International Convention on the Elimination of All Forms of Racial Discrimination, in *United Kingdom Treaty Series.* 1969. Vol. 36–87, pp. 2–13.

Jaggar, Alison M. 1983. *Feminist Politics and Human Nature.* Totowa, N.J.: Rowman & Allanheld.

Jones, Peter, and Robert Sudgen. 1982. "Evaluating Choice." *International Review of Law and Economics* 2:47–65.

Kahane, Meir. 1975. *The Story of the Jewish Defense League.* Radnor, Pa.: Chilton Book Co.

———. 1981. *They Must Go.* New York: The Institute of the Jewish Idea.

———. 1983. *Listen World, Listen Jew.* New York: The Institute of the Jewish Idea.

———. 1987. *Uncomfortable Questions for Comfortable Jews.* Secaucus, N.J.: Lyle Stuart.

Kanafi, Menachem. 1987. "A Digest of Selected Judgments of the Supreme Court of Israel." *Israel Law Review* 22, no. 2:219–24.

Kant, Immanuel. 1969. *Foundations of the Metaphysics of Morals.* Trans. Lewis White Beck, with critical essays. Indianapolis, Ind.: Bobbs-Merrill Educational Publishers.

King, Preston. 1971. "The Problem of Tolerance." *Government and Opposition* 6, no. 2:172–207.

———. 1976. *Toleration.* London: G. Allen & Unwin.

Klein, Claude. 1985. "The Defence of the State of Israel and the Democratic Regime in the Supreme Court." *Israel Law Review* 20, nos. 2–3:397–417.

Knott, David G. 1989. "Liberalism and the Justice of Neutral Political Concern." D. Phil. thesis. Oxford University.

Kommers, Donald P. 1989. *The Constitutional Jurisprudence of the Federal Republic of Germany.* Durham, N.C.: Duke University Press.

Kretzmer, David. 1987. "Freedom of Speech and Racism." *Cardozo Law Review* 8:445–513.

———. 1988. "Judicial Review of Knesset Decisions." *Tel Aviv University Studies in Law* 8:95–155.

Krislov, Samuel. 1968. *The Supreme Court and Political Freedom.* New York: The Free Press.

Kymlicka, Will. 1989a. *Liberalism, Community, and Culture.* Oxford: Clarendon Press.

———. 1989b. "Liberal Individualism and Liberal Neutrality." *Ethics* 99, no. 4:883–905.

———. 1992. "The Rights of Minority Cultures, Reply to Kukathas." *Political Theory* 20, no. 1:140–46.

Lahav, Pnina. 1981. "American Influence on Israel's Jurisprudence of Free Speech." *Hastings Constitutional Law Quarterly* 9, no. 2:23–108.

Larmore, Charles. 1987. *Patterns of Moral Complexity.* Cambridge, England: Cambridge University Press.

Lawrence, David G. 1976. "Procedural Norms and Tolerance: A Reassessment." *APSR* 70, no. 1:80–100.

Lederman, Eliezer, and Mala Tabory. 1987–88. "Criminalization of Racial Incitement in Israel." *Stanford Journal of International Law* 24:55–84.

Lee, Simon. 1990. *The Cost of Free Speech*. London: Faber and Faber.

Levin, Michael. 1985. "Negative Liberty." In Ellen Frankel Paul, F. D. Miller, and J. Paul, eds., *Liberty and Equality*, pp. 84–100. Oxford: Blackwell.

Linde, Hans A. 1970. "'Clear and Present Danger' Reexamined: Dissonance in the Brandenburg Concerto." *Stanford Law Review* 22, no. 6:1163–86.

Lowy, Marina O. 1989. "Restructuring a Democracy: An Analysis of the New Proposed Constitution for Israel." *Cornell International Law Journal* 22, no. 1:115–46.

MacCallum, G. C. 1970. "Negative and Positive Freedom." In A. de Crespigny and Alan Wertheimer, eds., *Contemporary Political Theory*, pp. 106–26. London: Thomas Nelson. Reprinted from *Philosophical Review* (1967).

McClosky, Herbert, and Alida Brill. 1983. *Dimensions of Tolerance: What Americans Believe about Civil Liberties*. New York: Russell Sage Foundation.

MacIver, R. M. 1926. *The Modern State*. Oxford: Clarendon Press.

———. 1959. *The Web of Government*. New York: Macmillan.

Macpherson, C. B. 1972. *The Real World of Democracy*. Oxford: Clarendon Press.

———. 1973. *Democratic Theory: Essays in Retrieval*. Oxford: Clarendon Press.

———. 1977. *The Life and Times of Liberal Democracy*. Oxford: Oxford University Press.

Maoz, Asher. 1988. "The System of Government in Israel." *Tel Aviv University Studies in Law* 8:9–57.

Marcuse, Herbert. 1969. "Repressive Tolerance." In R. P. Wolff, *A Critique of Pure Tolerance*, pp. 95–137. London: Jonathan Cape.

Marshall, T. H. 1950. *Citizenship and Social Class*. Cambridge, England: Cambridge University Press.

Masters, William H., Virginia E. Johnson, and Robert C. Kolodny. 1988. *Crisis: Heterosexual Behaviour in the Age of AIDS*. London: Grafton Books.

Meiklejohn, Alexander. 1953. "What Does the First Amendment Mean?" *The University of Chicago Law Review* 20, no. 2:461–79.

———. 1961a. "The First Amendment Is an Absolute." *Supreme Court Review*, pp. 245–66.

———. 1961b. "The Balancing of Self-Preservation against Political Freedom." *California Law Review* 49, no. 1:5–14.

———. 1965. *Political Freedom*. New York: Oxford University Press.

———. 1966. "Freedom of Speech." In Peter Radcliff, ed., *Limits of Liberty*, pp. 19–26. Belmont, Calif.: Wadsworth.

Mendus, Susan. 1989. *Toleration and the Limits of Liberalism*. London: Macmillan.

———, ed. 1988. *Justifying Toleration*. Cambridge, England: Cambridge University Press.

Mendus, Susan, and David Edwards, eds. 1987. *On Toleration*. Oxford: Clarendon Press.

Mergui, Raphael, and Philippe Simonnot. 1987. *Israel's Ayatollahs*. London: Saqi Books.

Merton, Robert K. 1967. *Social Theory and Social Structure*. New York: Free Press.

Mill, J. S. 1869. *Principles of Political Economy*. London: Longmans, Green, Reader and Dyer.

———. 1948. *Utilitarianism, Liberty, and Representative Government*. Everyman's Edition. London: J. M. Dent.

———. 1961. *System of Logic*. London: Longmans, Green.

———. 1971. *Autobiography*. Oxford: Oxford University Press.

———. 1973. *Dissertations and Discussions*. Vols. 1–2. New York: Haskell House Publishers.

———. 1975. "The Subjection of Women." In *Three Essays*, pp. 427–548. Oxford: Oxford University Press.

———. 1976. "Law of Libel and Liberty of the Press." In Geraint L. Williams, ed., *John Stuart Mill on Politics and Society*, pp. 143–69. Glasgow: Fontana.

———. 1979. *An Examination of Sir William Hamilton's Philosophy*. In J. M. Robson, ed., *Collected Works*, vol. 9. Toronto: University of Toronto Press.

Milton, John. 1875. *Areopagitica: A Speech for the Liberty of Unlicensed Printing*. London: Oxford University Press.

Mineka, Francis E., ed. 1963. *The Earlier Letters of J. S. Mill, 1812–1848*. Vol. 12 of *Collected Works*. Toronto: University of Toronto Press.

Mineka, Francis E., and Dwight N. Lindley, eds. 1972. *The Later Letters of J. S. Mill, 1849–1873*. Vol. 14 of *Collected Works*. Toronto: University of Toronto Press.

Montefiore, Alan, ed. 1975. *Neutrality and Impartiality*. Cambridge, England: Cambridge University Press.

Montesquieu. 1823. *The Spirit of Laws*. London. Translated by Thomas Nugent.

Neier, Aryeh. 1979. *Defending My Enemy*. New York: E. P. Dutton.

Nicholson, Peter. 1985. "Toleration as a Moral Ideal." In John Horton and Susan Mendus, eds., *Aspects of Toleration*, pp. 158–73. New York: Methuen.

Nimmer, Melville B. 1968. "The Right to Speak from Times to Time: First

Amendment Theory Applied to Libel and Misapplied to Privacy." *California Law Review* 56, no. 4:935–67.

Nozick, Robert. 1974. *Anarchy, State, and Utopia.* New York: Basic Books.

———. 1984. *Philosophical Explanations.* Oxford: Clarendon Press.

Nye, Andrea. 1988. *Feminist Theory and the Philosophies of Man.* London: Croom Helm.

O'Neill, Onora. 1985. "Lifeboat Earth." In Charles R. Beitz, M. Cohen, T. Scanlon, and A. J. Simmons, eds., *International Ethics,* pp. 262–81. Princeton, N.J.: Princeton University Press.

Pennock, J. Roland, and John W. Chapman, eds. 1983. *Liberal Democracy.* New York: New York University Press.

Perry, Michael J. 1983. "Freedom of Expression: An Essay on Theory and Doctrine." *Northwestern University Law Review* 78, no. 5:1137–1211.

Popper, Karl R. 1962. *The Open Society and Its Enemies.* Vols. 1 and 2. London: Routledge and Kegan Paul.

———. 1987. "Toleration and Intellectual Responsibility." In S. Mendus and D. Edwards, eds., *On Toleration,* pp. 17–34. Oxford: Clarendon Press.

Prothro, James W., and Charles M. Grigg. 1960. "Fundamental Principles of Democracy: Bases of Agreement and Disagreement." *Journal of Politics* 22, no. 2: 275–94.

Raphael, D. D. 1970. *Problems of Political Philosophy.* London: Pall Mall Press.

———. 1971. "Toleration, Choice and Liberty." *Government and Opposition* 6, no. 2:229–34

———. 1980. *Justice and Liberty.* London: Athlone Press.

Rawls, John. 1963. "The Sense of Justice." *Philosophical Review* 72: 281–305.

———. 1967. "Distributive Justice." In Peter Laslett and W.G. Runciman, eds., *Philosophy, Politics, and Society,* pp. 58–82. 3d ser. Oxford: Blackwell.

———. 1971. *A Theory of Justice.* Oxford: Oxford University Press.

———. 1974. "Two Concepts of Rules." In Philippa Foot, ed., *Theories of Ethics.* Oxford: Oxford University Press. Reprinted from *Philosophical Review* 64 (1955), 3–32.

———. 1975. "Fairness to Goodness." *Philosophical Review* 84: 536–54.

———. 1979. "A Well-Ordered Society." In P. Laslett and J. Fishkin, eds., *Philosophy, Politics, and Society,* pp. 6–20. 5th ser. Oxford: Basil Blackwell.

———. 1980a. "Rational and Full Autonomy." *The Journal of Philosophy* 77, no. 9:515–35.

———. 1980b. "Representation of Freedom and Equality." *The Journal of Philosophy* 77, no. 9:535–54.

———. 1980c. "Construction and Objectivity." *The Journal of Philosophy* 77, no. 9:554–72.

———. 1982. "Social Unity and Primary Goods." In A. Sen and B. Williams, eds., *Utilitarianism and Beyond*. Cambridge, England: Cambridge University Press.

———. 1985. "Justice as Fairness: Political not Metaphysical." *Philosophy and Public Affairs* 14, no. 3:223–51.

———. 1987a. "Liberty, Equality, and Law." In Sterling M. McMurrin, ed., *The Tanner Lectures on Human Values*, pp. 1–87. Cambridge, England: Cambridge University Press.

———. 1987b. "The Idea of an Overlapping Consensus." *Oxford Journal of Legal Studies* 7, no. 1:1–25.

———. 1988. "The Priority of Right and Ideas of the Good." *Philosophy and Public Affairs* 17, no. 4:251–76.

Raz, Joseph. 1986. *The Morality of Freedom*. Oxford: Clarendon Press.

———. 1988. "Autonomy, Toleration, and the Harm Principle." In Susan Mendus, ed., *Justifying Toleration*, pp. 155–75. Cambridge, England: Cambridge University Press.

———. 1991. "Free Expression and Personal Identification." *Oxford Journal of Legal Studies* 11, no. 3:303–24.

Rees, John C. 1960. "A Re-reading of Mill on Liberty." *Political Studies* 8, no. 2:113–29.

———. 1985. *John Stuart Mill's "On Liberty."* Oxford: Clarendon Press.

Richards, David A. J. 1974. "Free Speech and Obscenity Law: Toward a Moral Theory of the First Amendment." *University of Pennsylvania Law Review* 123, no. 1:45–91.

———. 1986. *Toleration and the Constitution*. New York: Oxford University Press.

———. 1988. "Toleration and Free Speech." *Philosophy and Public Affairs* 17, no. 4:323–36.

Ross, Alf. 1952. *Why Democracy?* Cambridge, Mass.: Harvard University Press.

Ross, Steven L. 1988. "A Real Defense of Tolerance." *The Journal of Value Inquiry* 22:127–45.

Russ, Shlomo Mordechai. 1981. "The 'Zionist Hooligans': The Jewish Defense League." Ph.D. diss., City University of New York.

Ryan, Alan. 1970. *The Philosophy of John Stuart Mill*. London: Macmillan.

Sandel, Michael. 1989. "Moral Argument and Liberal Toleration: Abortion and Homosexuality." *California Law Review* 77:521–38.

Scanlon, Thomas M. 1977. "A Theory of Freedom of Expression." In R. M. Dworkin, ed., *The Philosophy of Law*, pp. 153–71. Reprinted from *Philosophy and Public Affairs* 1, no. 2 (Winter 1972):204–26.

———. 1979. "Freedom of Expression and Categories of Expression." *University of Pittsburgh Law Review* 40, no. 3:519–50.

Schaar, John H. 1970. "Equality of Opportunity and Beyond." In A. de
    Crespigny and Alan Wertheimer, eds., *Contemporary Political Theory,*
    pp. 135–53. London: Thomas Nelson.
Schauer, Frederick. 1979. "Speech and 'Speech'—Obscenity and 'Obscenity':
    An Exercise in the Interpretation of Constitutional Language." *Georgetown
    Law Journal* 67, no. 4:899–933.
———. 1982. *Free Speech: A Philosophical Enquiry.* New York: Cambridge
    University Press.
———. 1983. "Must Speech Be Special?" *Northwestern University Law Re-
    view* 78, no. 5:1284–1306.
Schwartz, Adina. 1973. "Moral Neutrality and Primary Goods." *Ethics*
    83:294–307.
Scruton, Roger. 1982. *Kant.* Oxford: Oxford University Press.
Segal, Haggai. 1988. *Dear Brothers.* New York: Beit-Shamai Publications.
Shamir, Michal. 1987. *Kach and the Limits to Political Tolerance in Israel.* Tel
    Aviv: Golda Meir Institute.
Shapira, Amos. 1987. "Confronting Racism By Law in Israel—Promises and
    Pitfalls." *Cardozo Law Review* 8:595–608.
Skillen, Anthony. 1982. "Freedom of Speech." In Keith Graham, ed., *Contem-
    porary Political Philosophy,* pp. 139–59. Cambridge, England: Cambridge
    University Press.
Skorupski, John. 1989. *John Stuart Mill.* London and New York: Routledge.
Sparks, Colin. 1980. *Never Again.* London: Bookmarks.
Stone, Geoffrey R. 1983. "Content Regulation and the First Amendment." *Wil-
    liam and Mary Law Review* 25, no. 2:189–252.
Stouffer, Samuel. 1955. *Community, Conformity, and Civil Liberties.* New
    York: Doubleday.
Strawson, Galen. 1986. *Freedom and Belief.* Oxford: Clarendon Press.
Street, H. 1972. *Freedom, the Individual, and the Law.* Harmondsworth, En-
    gland: Penguin.
Sullivan, John L., James E. Piereson, and George E. Marcus. 1978. "Ideologi-
    cal Constraint in the Mass Public: A Methodological Critique of Some New
    Findings." *American Journal of Political Science* 22:233–49.
———. 1979. "A Reconceptualization of Political Tolerance: Illusory Increases
    1950's–1970's." *APSR* 73, no. 3:781–94.
———. 1982. *Political Tolerance and American Democracy.* Chicago: Univer-
    sity of Chicago Press.
Sullivan, John L., James E. Piereson, George E. Marcus, and Stanley Feldman.
    1978–79. "The Development of Political Tolerance: The Impact of Social
    Class, Personality, and Cognition." *International Journal of Political Educa-
    tion* 2:115–39.

———. 1981. "The Sources of Political Tolerance: A Multivariate Analysis." *APSR* 75, no. 1:92–106.

Sunstein, Cass R. 1992. "Free Speech Now." *The University of Chicago Law Review* 59, no. 1:255–316.

Ten, C. L. 1980. *Mill on Liberty.* Oxford: Clarendon Press.

Tinder, Glenn. 1979. "Freedom of Expression, the Strange Imperative." *The Yale Review* 69, no. 2:161–76.

Traynor, Roger J. 1978. "The Limits of Judicial Creativity." *Hastings Law Journal* 29, no. 5:1025–40.

Vandeveer, Donald. 1979. "Coercive Restraint of Offensive Actions." *Philosophy and Public Affairs* 8, no. 2:175–93.

Van Gunsteren, Herman R. 1988. "Admission to Citizenship." *Ethics* 98, no. 4:731–41.

Warnock, Mary. 1987. "The Limits of Toleration." In S. Mendus and D. Edwards, eds., *On Toleration,* pp. 123–39. Oxford: Clarendon Press.

Wedgwood, Ruth. 1988. "Freedom of Expression and Racial Speech." *Tel Aviv University Studies in Law* 8:325–37.

Wiggins, David. 1987. *Needs, Values, Truth.* Oxford: Blackwell.

Williams, Bernard. 1980. "Introduction." In Isaiah Berlin, *Concepts and Categories,* pp. xi–xviii. Oxford: Oxford University Press.

Williams, Geraint L., ed. 1976. *John Stuart Mill on Politics and Society,* pp. 143–69. Glasgow: Fontana.

Wolffe, W. J. 1987. "Values in Conflict: Incitement to Racial Hatred and the Public Order Act 1986." *Public Law,* pp. 85–95.

Wollheim, R. 1973. "J. S. Mill and the Limits of State Action." *Social Research* 40, no. 1:1–30.

Yacavone, John P. 1973. "Emerson's Distinction." *Connecticut Law Review* 6, no. 1:49–64.

Sources in Hebrew

Barak, Aharon. 1982. "On the Judge as Interpreter." *Mishpatim* 12:248–56.

———. 1983. "Judicial Legislation." *Mishpatim* 13:25–80.

———. 1986. "President Agranat: 'Kol Ha'am'—The Voice of the People." In A. Barak, ed., *Essays in Honour of Shimon Agranat,* pp. 129–44. Jerusalem.

———. 1987. *Judicial Discretion.* Tel Aviv: Papyrus.

Barak, Avner. 1989. "The Probability Test in Constitutional Law." *Iyunei Mishpat* 14, no. 2:371–407.

Berenson, Zvi. 1973. "Freedom of Religion and Conscience in the State of Israel." *Iyunei Mishpat* 3:405–13.

Central Elections Committee [State of Israel]. 17 June 1984. Protocol No. 14.

————. 18 June 1984. Protocol No. 15.

————. 5 October 1988. Protocol No. 17.

————. 6 October 1988. Protocol No. 18.

————. 7 October 1988. Protocol No. 19.

————. 9 October 1988. Protocol No. 20.

————. 28 May 1992. Protocol No. 17.

————. 3 June 1992. Protocol No. 18.

Cohn, Haim. 1976. "Faithful Interpretation in Three Senses." *Mishpatim* 7:5–14.

Gal-Or, Noami. 1990. *The Jewish Underground: Our Terrorism.* Tel Aviv: Hakibbutz Hameuchad.

Gavison, Ruth. 1986. "Twenty Years to Yeredor Ruling—The Right to Be Elected and the Lessons of History." In A. Barak, ed., *Essays in Honour of Shimon Agranat,* pp. 145–213. Jerusalem.

Kahane, Meir. 1973. *The Challenge—The Chosen Land.* Jerusalem: Center for Jewish Consciousness.

————. 1978. *Forty Years.* Jerusalem.

Kotler, Yair. 1985. *Heil Kahane.* Tel Aviv: Modan.

Lahav, Pnina. 1976. "On the Freedom of Expression in the Supreme Court's Rulings." *Mishpatim* 7:375–422.

Menuchin, Ishai, and Dina Menuchin, eds. 1985. *The Limits of Obedience.* Tel Aviv: The Yesh Gvul Movement.

Negbi, Moshe. 1981. *Justice under Occupation.* Jerusalem: Cana.

————. 1985. *Paper Tiger: The Struggle for a Press Freedom in Israel.* Tel Aviv: Sifriat Poalim.

————. 1987. *Above the Law.* Tel Aviv: Am Oved.

Ravizki, Aviezer. 1986. *Kahanism as a Phenomenon of Awareness and of Political Life.* Jerusalem: Shazar Books.

Rubinstein, Amnon. 1980. *Constitutional Law of Israel.* Jerusalem: Schocken.

Segal, Zeev. 1988. *Israeli Democracy.* Tel Aviv: Ministry of Defence.

Shafir, Gershon, and Yoav Peled. 1986. "'Thorns in Your Eyes . . .': Socio-Economic Characterizations of the Voting Sources for Rabbi Kahane." *State, Government, and International Relations* 25:115–29.

Shapiro, A. E. 1973. "Self-Restraint of the Supreme Court and the Preservation of Civil Liberties." *Iyunei Mishpat* 3, no. 2:640–50.

Sheef, Zeev, and Ehud Yaari. 1990. *Intifada.* Tel Aviv: Schocken.

Sprinzak, Ehud. 1986. *Every Man Whatsoever Is Right in His Own Eyes.* Tel Aviv: Sifriat Poalim.

Zamir, Itzhak. 1986. "Boundaries of Obedience to Law." In A. Barak, ed., *Essays in Honour of Shimon Agranat,* pp. 119–27. Jerusalem.

General Index

Index of Cases

Note: principal references are in bold.

U.S. Cases

Israeli Cases

The reference P.D. means *Piskei Din* ("Judgments," an official publication of the judgments of the Israeli Supreme Court).

Miscellaneous Cases from Other Jurisdictions

ENGLAND

GERMANY

EUROPEAN COMMISSION ON HUMAN RIGHTS